The New Realism

The New Realism

Writings From China after the Cultural Revolution

Edited by Lee Yee

HIPPOCRENE
BOOKS, INC.

Library of Congress Cataloging in Publication Data
Main entry under title:

The New realism.

Translations from Chinese works chiefly selected
from literary magazines published in China.
Contents: A reflection of reality / Lee Yee — Sons
and successors / Ru Zhijuan — Li Shunda builds a house /
Gao Xiaosheng — (etc.)
1. Chinese literature—20th century—Translations
into English. 2. English literature—Translations from
Chinese. 3. Realism in literature. 4. Chinese literature
—20th century—History and criticism. I. Yee, Lee.
PL2658.E1N48   1983   895.1'5'08   83-4337
ISBN 0-88254-794-1
ISBN 0-88254-810-7 (pbk.)

Contents

The New Realism

Introduction

A REFLECTION OF REALITY

LEE YEE

An Entirely New View of Chinese Society

In early spring 1979 a body of literature emerged in China which differed radically from that of the past. Creative works, literary criticism and theory reflected unique perceptions, characterizations and purposes. In this very short period in China's history, the genre of New Realism established itself as a viable and profound force in society. New Realism produced literary works which revealed aspects of the reality of the Chinese experience previously suppressed in literature: an economic system at a virtual halt, decreasing productivity in poorly managed factories, extreme poverty for those in the villages, administrative organizations riddled with corruption and materialism and a bureaucracy unreceptive to the needs of its people.

The disclosure of some of the less pleasant aspects of reality is achieved through vivid images and character portraits. The emphasis in this new literature focuses on the frustrations and restraints imposed upon the people by the cadres whose abuse of status and power and prestige releases unrelenting oppression, and by a social system which perpetuates social and economic disparities. The Chinese people depicted in the literature of this period are low spirited, perplexed, and oppressed. Yet, in the midst of difficult and complex situations, the Chinese people are applauded by the writers of this period as being simple, diligent and hard working.

For those living in the People's Republic of China the suffering is not merely literary. It is not simply spiritual. The devastation is

3

physical as well. It is easier for us abroad to endure the pain of their experience and to face the injustices and the failures, but to the people of China the reality of failure is manifested in the intolerable conditions that define their lives.

With the fall of The Gang of Four, Communist Party newspapers and magazines began to reveal some of the failures and contradictions within Chinese society. Reactions from leftists abroad were at first skeptical, a refusal to accept the notion that the new society was, in fact, drastically flawed. The writings of New Realism continued, however, and slowly began to have an effect on the deeply-rooted feelings socialists had for the Chinese Communist Party.

To a conscientious writer in China, the need to accurately describe the realities of the Chinese experience is compelled by a sense of mission for the people, and complicated by the knowledge that past literary efforts to reflect the actual state of society were repressed. As a result of the surge of New Realism, many impressive literary works were produced on both the mainland and Taiwan. Since the People's Republic of China has a far greater population, the quantity of literature produced on the mainland during this period exceeds that of Taiwan. Longer novels such as *Red Flag Score* and *Li Zicheng* have been written in the People's Republic. The quality of the literary accomplishments of Taiwan, however, surpasses that of the mainland. The literature of Taiwan clearly and vividly exposes the social contradictions in China and more accurately reflects the extent of their influence upon society.

The Literary Background of New Realism

Prior to 1978 the literature of China revealed and preserved images of a flawless, idealistic society created and nourished by the Cultural Revolution. Conceptions of the party's ideological consistency, vitality and viability were exported abroad through various Chinese news media and literary works. Many aspects of the reality of life in China were not exposed or expressed. Repression and government control dominated literary efforts. Leftist docrine had cast a shadow over Chinese literature, distorting the images of reality which it delineated. In an article published in the *Shanghai Literary Review*, Liu Binyan stated, "There is this awkward phenomenon: Literature and life are riding on two mutually irrelevant rails. What is written is one thing, actual life is another. They are two totally different worlds. For a long period of time the literary works of China were not accurately reflecting reality,

but were functioning to reinforce the images which top level officials wanted to perpetuate."

The literary trends in China, like those of other counries, follow a distinct developmental pattern. A literary nadir accompa-
nies periods of great prosperity, while there is a surge when periods of repressive, despotic rule are about to end and the pro-
spects of increased freedom seem more plausible. During the
Tang dynasty, poetry flourished under the corrupt government of
Emperor Tang Xuan Zhong and waned in the prosperous period
of the Zhen-Guang Reform. Tang poetry reached its apex while
the country was experiencing social and political deterioration.
Similarly, the decline of a powerful family in *Dream of the Red
Chamber* symbolized the decline of the Qing Dynasty. After the
May Fourth Movement, the dawn of liberalism brought twenty to
thirty years of literary prosperity to China.

In 1942 Mao Zedong published his "Talks on Art and Literature." This statement, long regarded as the classic guide-
line for literature in China, clearly defines standards and literary
imperatives for writers. Literature must emphasize the positive
revolutionary character and commitment of workers, peasants
and soldiers. Literature must serve the political ends defined by
the party.

The Russian proletarian literary model became the standard
for Chinese writing, employing the ethic and ideology of socialism to educate the people. Following the so-called "war of liberation" and the founding of the People's Republic of China, the
combined influences of Mao's literary imperatives, Stalin's "socialist realism" and the Russian proletarian literary model produced a body of literature in China which was strictly doctrinal.
This type of literature evaded contradictory social issues and denied political inconsistencies. Early post-1949 literature presented images of a society of peace, harmony and prosperity.

From 1956-1957, during the period of the Hundred Flowers, a
group of writers began to reexamine and subsequently challenge
accepted literary doctrine. Writers such as Qin Zhaoyang, Zhou
Bo, Zhong Dianfei, Chen Yong and Liu Shaotang viewed literature as a means to reflect the discord and contradictions which
existed in the reality which they perceived. Using the pen name
"He Zhi," Qin Zhaoyang wrote an article entitled, "Realism — A
Broad Path," in which he distinctly expressed dissatisfaction
with the established Russian literary model.

The literary movement of 1956-1957 marks the birth of the
genre of New Realism. In its aversion to affirming the validity of
conventional literary doctrine and practice, it produced works

which differed dramatically from those of the past. Following the Anti-Rightist Movement of 1957, these new concepts were repressed. Once again Chinese literature was reduced to a state of social silence.

After the fall of The Gang of Four in 1976, many senior cadres were reinstated to old positions; others were promoted as a result of the deaths of superiors. Almost immediately, a philosophical contradiction became operative within the party because cadres did not simply resume old positions, but old perceptions and behavior as well. Almost as compensation for their own suffering during the period of the Cultural Revolution, many senior cadres now took advantage of the power which their new positions offered.

A creative literature, which sought to accurately reflect reality, again began to emerge. The cliches perpetuated by dogmatism appeared less frequently in literary works.

In November 1977 the publication of Liu Xinwu's short story "The Class Teacher" marked the beginning of the period of the "literature of the wounded." The writing during this period focuses on and graphically depicts the tragedies occasioned by the Cultural Revolution and its aftermath.

During the Third Plenary Session of the Central Committee of the Communist Party in late 1978, the objectives of liberation of thought and promotion of democracy were put forth. As a result, a significant number of literary works seeking to reflect social and political realities emerged from May 1979 through the spring of 1980. This is the period of the New Realism.

The literature of New Realism focused on disclosing a comprehensive image of reality rather than exploring the historical tragedy that had been exposed by the literature of the wounded. Works such as "Manager Qiao Assumes Office," "General, You Must Not Do This!" and "Between Man and Demon" probe the social and political complexities of bribery, selfishness, exercise of personal prerogatives and lavish abuse of power among officials. The indictment in "Manager Qiao Assumes Office," as well as in other literary works of this period, is against the bureaucratic priority of political survival in a system which appears to have forsaken certain moral possibilities and permitted abuse. The literary works of New Realism reveal the existence of a widespread philosophy in which power and profit have become goals, corrupting and distorting the aspirations of the socialist ideal.

This new literary surge created a tremendous controversy in Chinese society. When "Manager Qiao Assumes Office" was published, the *Tianjin Daily News* printed critical reviews denouncing the story for four consecutive days. After the publication of "General, You Must Not Do This!" the poet was continually harassed by officials. "Between Man and Demon" was publically condemned as being a "disgrace to the Communist Party" and an "attack on the Four Items of Persistence!"

After a short period of time, however, editors of Communist Party newspapers and literary magazines became less harsh in their criticism of this new literature. Subsequently, the New Realism enjoyed greater acceptance and wider publication and readership. This in itself served as an incentive for other Chinese writers. "Manager Qiao Assumes Office" received first prize for The Outstanding Short Story of 1979.

In March 1979 Liu Binyan's treatise, "Concerning the Disclosure of Darkness and Reflection of Life," was published in the *Shanghai Literary Review*. Liu Binyan urged literary workers to intervene in China's social and political crises by exposing bureaucratism and self-proclaimed communists — really imposters — who had joined the party, and by defining mistakes made by the proletarians themselves. Two months later, in May 1979, People's Literature Publishing House of Shanghai compiled and published a collection of works written during the Hundred Flowers period (1956-1957). The selections included in this anthology, entitled *Fresh Flowers Blooming Once Again* had previously been condemned as "poisonous weeds." Its publication was a signal that the direction of Chinese literature was indeed changing.

In the September 1979 issue of *Shanghai Literary Review*, an article entitled, "The Important Mission of Socialist Literature: Oppose Bureaucratism," openly challenged the accepted literary model. The article clearly defines bureaucratism as a system of prerogatives, special favors and bribery, and as "a hindrance to the Four Modernizations." The authors, Peng Yunqing and Yang Zhijie, challenge Chinese writers to a new consciousness and sense of purpose: "We, as revolutionary literary workers must never whitewash reality, but bravely fight against bureaucracy with our pens! This is the major mission of Socialist Literature."

Until the latter part of 1979 New Realism as a genre was only hazily defined. The surge of new literary works produced around this time solidified the definition and purpose of literature, reaffirming a philosophical commitment which had begun almost twenty years earlier. The emergence and mission of the new, revolutionary literature had become an undeniable reality and a profound force in China.

At the Fourth Literary Symposium in 1979, Bai Hua, Liu Binyan, Lin Shaotang and other writers implored all of China's literary workers to accept their social responsibilities and political obligations. Writers must expose social contradictions, bureaucratism and political inequity and injustice. These writers stressed the importance of reflecting the voices and conditions of the people through literary works.

New Realism defies the restriction of doctrinal confinement. It is not created to blindly praise the society, but to expose the totality of reality. It does not exist to whitewash and subdue, but to define clearly mistakes and contradictions. New Realism is a profound and insightful literary movement, committed to the resolution of problems through the disclosure of their existence. From this perspective, the contributions of New Realism benefit both party officials as well as the people. Through an accurate reflection of social, political and economic realities, the nation can be led to implement workable solutions to its problems and can ultimately achieve a viable political future. Literary works such as "Manager Qiao Assumes Office," "General, You Must Not Do This!" and "Between Man and Demon" have been instramental in moving in this direction.

In the Villages and Factories

Prior to the emergence of New Realism, the serious economic and agricultural problems which confronted the people were virtually unexplored. Earlier literary works depict a viable agricultural policy and a government striving to improve the democratic rights of the peasants working within a flawless ideological system. In "A Place Forgotten by Love," Zhang Xian describes the twenty-odd-year process of deterioration in the quality of rural life in China. The disregard for the livelihood and welfare of the people is a theme supported by another major work of this period. In "Li Shunda Builds a House," the struggle for achieving an adequate standard of living is explored. The story follows the progress of a man's effort to save money to move his family in turn from a mat on a boat to a thatched shack, a hog house, and a simple three-room home. Li Shunda eventually saves enough money and buys the materials needed to build his home. Due to The Big Steel and Iron Smelting Movement of 1958, however, these materials are confiscated by the commune to be used for the construction of furnaces and bulldozers.

The story further explores the nature of the suppression of the individual's needs to the arbitrary will of authorities through the description of the situation that the parents of Li Shunda's daughter-in-law must face. When one official wishes to "rearrange the mountain and the river" to construct a canal, their home and all the others in the way of the future riverbed are destroyed.

In another case presented in this story, a brigade destroys a large number of well built homes, relocating residents to a "New Village" where poorly constructed homes are provided.

The reality of Chinese rural life for the past 20-odd years, as depicted in the New Realism, portrays a leadership which is insensitive to the needs of the people, unconcerned with their personal struggles and aspirations and obsessed with prestige and power. A character in "Li Shunda Builds a House" prophetically proclaims, "Nobody has any regard for the livelihood of the common people!"

Factory life is vividly reflected in "Manager Qiao Assumes Office." The author describes a large electrical machinery plant after the Cultural Revolution. Manager Qiao works diligently to increase productivity in a factory which has become overstaffed and inefficient. His efforts result in the reorganization of personnel, meeting of production deadlines and a savings to the plant of nearly six hundred thousand *yuan*.

The sequel to this theme in "Manager Qiao Assumes Office, Part Two" clearly defines Qiao's struggle with the absolute authority of the bureaucracy, its dictates and its interference with his effective administration. This short story goes beyond the realm of philosophical statement to explore the problems created by lack of competition in industry and China's difficulty in promptly delivering goods for export.

Corruption and the Bureaucracy

A central concern expressed in the works of New Realism is the corruption, degeneration and abuses by what Mao Zedong called "the bureaucratic class." The special privileges and prerogatives exercised by cadres are depicted in the works of this period as oppressive to all aspects of Chinese society. The poem "General, You Must Not Do This!" openly criticises a high level government official who orders the demolition of a kindergarten in order to build an elaborate, modern home valued at several hundred thousand *yuan*. The absolute and unchallenged exercise of personal prerogatives at the financial, spiritual and physical expense of the people is a recurring theme in New Realism. The play "If I Were For Real" provides another example of the exploration of this sense of moral degradation in society.

Abuse of military prestige is revealed in the screenplay "In

The Archives of Society." In this work a senior military cadre, a member of the Lin Biao clique, rapes and humiliates a young girl, Li Lifang. The drama spans the period from the beginning of the Cultural Revolution to 1971, revealing the ever present and continuing moral degradation which has characterized military control.

The image of personal corruption in the bureaucracy is not all pervasive in recent Chinese literature. Works such as "Middle Age" and "Sons and Successors" portray the cadre protagonists as individuals truly devoted to the proletarian struggle yet hampered by a way of life which has a devastating effect on their ability to make moral choices. Thus, the emphasis in these works shifts from one of individual degradation to an exploration of Chinese society and history which have inhibited the realization of the socialist ideal.

An insightful portrait of philosophical contradictions is skillfully drawn in the character of Qin Bo in "Middle Age." "An old lady of Marxism-Leninism," Qin Bo is politically astute and fluent in socialist terminology. As a character, Qin Bo represents the duplicity inherent in the political reality of China. On one hand her allegiance to the party surpasses even her emotional commitments. When her husband is in need of an eye operation, Qin Bo reminds hospital personnel "to be responsible to the Revolution and the party." Yet Qin Bo is also depicted as frequently using revolutionary rhetoric to exercise her own prerogatives for her personal interest. This profound ideological contradiction is a tragic commentary on social reality in China.

In "Sons and Successors" the contradiction of personal and party interests is vividly portrayed in the relationship between a mid-level cadre and her son: "Children! When did they first appear in our lives? And when was it that they managed to capture the commanding heights of the Revolution?... It's as if from the very moment they were born they began to occupy a dominant position. I don't know about other people, but Tian Jing had once said that her only worry was about setting up things for her children..."

Works such as "Sons and Successors" are not quite as shocking in their portrayal of immorality and abuse as is "In The Archives of Society." This work approaches the character and consequences of a complex bureaucracy on a more sophisticated and philosophical level. Yet in both of these literary approaches the underlying problems, the real conflicts and their political and social consequences, remain vividly unresolved.

Emphasis on the People

Prior to the New Realism, literature existed primarily as a glorification of the character of party member-cadres and soldiers. After the formation of The People's Republic of China, despite Mao Zedong's philosophical emphasis on the heroism of the people, literary works continued to express praise, regard and respect only for party officials. The image of the people and their struggle with moral and philosophical issues was clouded by the image of their absolute dependence upon cadres for leadership and resolution of problems. In literary works in which a civilian *was* positively portrayed, the apsect of his or her character which was emphasized was the close connection with and dependence upon party officials.

Thus, a positive image of the real commoner in China was repeatedly absent in the literary works of the past. At the expense of the people, party members were virtually deified in literary works which preceded New Realism.

By contrast, the New Realism exposes this false image by focusing attention on the abuses and moral degradation of the "bureaucratic class." When a cadre is depicted as possessing a genuine moral commitment, it is generally juxtaposed to the contradictory realities of his or her position. Qiao Guangpu and Shi Gan in "Manager Qiao Assumes Office" and Shang Qi in "In the Archives of Society" provide explicit examples.

Qiao Guangpu, despite his tough efficient exterior, needed the comfort of his wife during difficult periods. Shang Qi was arrested for investigating and exposing a senior official's crime of rape.

The portrayal of party members as less than infallible human beings immersed in states of moral and philosophical contradiction and confusion is characteristic of the genre of New Realism. China's people have achieved new stature and respect through this form.

Li Shunda in "Li Shunda Builds a House" is ordinary. He is not a party member. He possesses an integrity and moral commitment which clearly overcomes the unjustified oppression which he suffers as a result of the personal prerogatives of party members.

The real heroes of New Realism are the oppressed. True empathy is evoked in the conflicts and moral introspection of such characters. The unique strength, courage and high moral aspirations of China's people are reflected in the New Realism.

A New Social Structure

The obliteration of class differences and the liberation of the people to become "real" and "free" is the professed ideal state of both socialism and communism. The socialist ideal, which was conceived as a means to eliminate differences among people, is presented in the literature of New Realism as a system which has simply created new divisions. The differences between those who once owned productive property and those who did not have been eliminated. The cadre system, however, has created new divisions within society. These divisions are not based upon material attributes, as in the past, but rather upon the distribution of power. Power from the central government to the local districts flows through a complex, bureaucratic organization of cadres. The chasm which this system has created in Chinese society and its impact upon the people is critically explored in the works of New Realism. In "Sons and Successors," a mother with a revolutionary past expects her son, "to become a dragon" some day. Her son complains, "I can't go on like this...I can't become a dragon and I know that I am not made for it either. I am no dragon, nor do I want to be one. I just want to live my own life." His love for a girl also preoccupied with the more mundane rather than the political aspects of life sharpens his conflicts with his mother, who rebukes the girl as a "vixen." "What is the point of living in the world," replies the girl, "if it isn't for some good food and nice clothing? I have not done anything bad."

The generation gap in Chinese culture is reflected in the writers themselves as well as in the literature which they have produced. Among middle-aged writers of this period, criticism toward party members and cadres is less harsh than that expressed by younger authors. There is an empathy which apparently emerges from having experienced the political and cultural upheaval which has been responsible for the current malady. Among younger writers, the criticism of the corruption is both severe and unrelenting. To these younger writers, the glorious past of the Communist Party is merely history. Their collective reality is defined by the conditions that characterized the period following the Cultural Revolution, a time in which members of the party's privileged stratum exercised individual prerogatives to achieve personal power. The working conditions and environment in which these young writers have developed and grown have brought them into close contact with the struggles of the lower strata of society.

Authority Strikes Back

The literary works of New Realism differ radically from those of the past. The image of reality as reflected by the writers of this new genre depicts diligent workers, peasants and intellectuals barely surviving in an ideological system riddled by the abuse of personal power and status by cadres at all levels. Without exception, the most significant literary achievements of this period present images of a complex bureaucracy of cadres who exercise personal prerogatives at the expense of socialist ideology. The immoral and degenerate image of the bureaucratic class depicted in the New Realism was attacked by party newspapers and magazines.

From January 23, 1979 to February 13, 1980 the Creative Plays Symposium was held in Beijing. Representative samples of the literature of New Realism were examined. The comrades at the symposium concluded, "that the mentality of prerogatives, special favors and privileges among a certain number of leading cadres does exist," and that, "revealing and criticizing this phenomenon through literature is absolutely necessary." However, they collectively asserted the belief that "it is a mistake to state that there is a privileged class. It is also a mistake to abandon political goals by singling out and further exaggerating the extent of bureaucratic malfeasance and cadres' use of special prerogatives to describe social contradictions... Writers must take into account and express the positive social forces that are attempting to conquer negative phenomena in society.... "The comrades agreed that the "overly melancholy tone" which characterizes the literature of New Realism "prevents the people from seeing hope, from feeling that good will eventually prevail over evil and from strengthening the people's faith in the worth of their struggle to attain their ideals."

On January 16, 1980 Deng Xiaoping wrote a report entitled, "Today's Conditions and Responsibilities" in which he stated: "We must call for peace and unity...The activities of counter-revolutionaries and other adversaries should be dealt with seriously...Our party's newspapers and magazines should become the ideological center of peace and unity for the entire country. Magazines, newspapers, broadcasting and television should consider the promotion of peace and unity and the raising of young people's socialistic awareness to be their basic responsibility...It is impossible for literature to be independent of politics. Any progressive and revolutionary worker cannot but think of his works' social influence and must consider, therefore, the interests of the nation and the party...We sincerely wish that all comrades in the Republic can regularly and automatically defend the public interest by continually working to enhance a socialistic consciousness...The party 'wishes,' without compulsion, that literary workers first consider the public interests."

In a report on the Creative Plays Symposium, *The People's Daily* concluded that, "literary works should be beneficial to the construction of modernization, to peace, unity and to the enlightenment of the people's social awareness." The principle of the writer's ethical responsibility implies the description of an overall conception of reality and implores writers not to simply dwell on negatives and failures but to present a more comprehensive and sympathetic picture of reality to their readers.

Although no actual restrictions were placed upon writing or publication, accessibility and recognition for the works of New Realism became difficult to attain. "If I Were For Real" was only performed before limited audiences in a few major Chinese cities. The play, a sardonic comedy, was deemed unworthy and criticized for its inaccurate characterizations. Official criticism of both "If I Were For Real" and "In The Archives of Society" was focused on the belief that many characters in these works displayed "petty bourgeois ideas, qualities and actions." The genuine sympathy expressed by the authors for the struggles in which these characters are engaged was viewed by the government as an allegiance to the ideology of the bourgeoise.

Conclusion

The emphasis in governmental policy since early 1980 has been on the social and political responsibility of the writer. The government implores authors to use literature as a means to enhance peace and unity within the society. This appeal forces writers to make an ideological determination as to the means by which these ends are best achieved. Attempting to determine whether peace and unity are effected through honest reflections of the totality of reality or achieved only through the silencing of social, political and economic discord is a decision with profound implications and repercussions.

Faced with the overwhelming evidence of problems and abuse, a conscientious Chinese writer is compelled to appeal to the public. The ethic of "reflecting reality" requires writers to abandon personal interests and to unite in a common perception of the responsibility of literature to reflect that which is unreasonable and inconsistent in reality. Committed to defining art in functional terms, New Realism writers take up themes that were unexplored in previous literary efforts.

Ye Wenfu, author of the poem, "General, You Must Not Do This!" makes this perception explicit in his explanation of his decision to publish his poem: "One day, I happened to pass by the nearby street of Bo Hui Jie. Clouds of dust flew as heavy loading trucks passed by. Standing by the roadside, I saw a hoist busily working beyond the high walls. Rows of modern apartment houses were taking the place of the Rear Palace where the Empress Dowager used to live. My vision was suddenly blurred. Although I had heard that they had spent millions on a large scale construction project, this was the first time I had seen such a concrete realization of its implications. I was standing right in front of this glamorous modernization!...Now I finally understood why certain cadres in various levels dared to squander people's blood and sweat. I was reminded of Qin Ershi and Yang Guang at that instant...Due to various historical restrictions, I wonder if our spectacular proletariat class revolution can be exempt from the same fate as that of the corrupt feudal system." People familiar with the geography of Beijing are all aware that the poet Ye Wenfu was writing about Zhung Nan Hai, a residential area for the highest level government officials.

Literary achievements of the 1930's, such as *The Family* by Ba Jin and "New Years Blessing" by Lu Xun, urged the reformation of society. Through their explicit characterizations, portraits and images of reality, these works have aroused grief and concern which may subsequently become a motivation for change.

Literature and the social order are intimately related. Historically, periods of social chaos have been concomitant with the development of literary trends which reflect unrealistic and embellished images of society. Literary works which attempt to expose a discordant reality and its social and political contradictions generally precede and often initiate periods of unified, harmonious social order. Democracy is the foundation of peace; autocracy, the root of chaos.

The literary works which the government currently receives favorably, publicizes and promotes are those which "raise new blood of socialism." The pretext that the internal peace, social harmony and political unity of China can be preserved through a body of literature which misrepresents images of reality is simply an excuse for preventing writers from exposing the total reality of the Communist Chinese experience nationally and internationally.

In the January 1980 issue of *Report of the Times*, several works of New Realism, especially "In The Archives of Society," although unmistakably significant in their reflection of social realities, were criticized by the majority of comrades at the Creative Plays Symposium as "having serious drawbacks that lead to an incorrect direction and are artistically unreal." These plays were not allowed on either stage or screen.

As a result of the government's condemnation, the surge of New Realism began to wane by mid-1980. On July 9, 1980 a reporter from *The People's Daily* attempted to spark renewed support for New Realism in his article, "Concluding Historical Experience by Insisting on the 'Double Hundred' Policy." Wen Yi Bao, in an outspoken commentary on the 1980 symposium, echoed this sentiment: "Let us not dismiss them (the works of New Realism) as anti-party and anti-socialist poisonous weeds or else the revolutionary, realistic literary movement will come to a premature end, turning literature, once again, into mere sweet lies."

The images which New Realism evokes are shocking, frightening and often painful. Yet the harsh reality which is exposed can become a stimulus to re-evaluation, re-direction and re-dedication. Had the growth and development of New Realism been unrestricted, it might have continued to explore and expose reality on a deeper, more all-encompassing level. Nevertheless, New Realism has created a new awareness and has become a powerful and profound influence upon Chinese thought. Literary historians will surely praise the significance of the output of this period.

Ten of the selections in this book have been selected from literary magazines published in China. "If I Were For Real" has not been publicly released. Many other appropriate articles have been omitted. Among the many works produced during this brief period, it is difficult to choose only eleven for evaluation and study. Many worthwhile literary works have not been included. In addition, for reasons of space, a number of stories have been abridged. The editor takes full responsibility for this choice of those selected for this volume.

Sons and Successors

RU ZHIJUAN

(Translated by Ellen Klempner)

I'd been standing watch at Tian Jing's bedside for more than an hour. It was only a few days into autumn, not quite six in the evening and the sky was just beginning to dim. I sat in a single room of the intensive care ward helplessly witnessing my friend's death. Her life was slipping away; she was ebbing breath by breath, thread by thread...dissolving into the light of early evening. Despite my ability to think objectively about Tian Jing and my cool attitude toward this inexorable fact, I found this process hard to take. And after running into her son Kuai Chi a moment ago on the stairs, I'd become even more pensive.

I was the one who had recruited Tian Jing into the Party. My husband had died fairly young, as had hers, leaving me with no children or household burdens, and we soon became close friends. A very capable person, she could do men's work as well as women's. Even though she had become a middle-echelon cadre, she would still do chores at home like fixing lamps and putting mop-heads together. She was constantly on the run, usually sloppily dressed with her hair in disarray, but yet she kept that two-room apartment of hers bright and clean. Needless to say Kuai Chi was always immaculate. The teachers at her school often said, "Our party secretary Tian is like a janitor when she's at school and a regular laborer at home." The way I see it, that was both good and bad — her expectations for her family played much too important a role in her life.

Yet now she was lying there so quietly, no struggle, no groaning, as if she felt no pain at all. But I knew just how much she suffered as she somberly and silently waited for the last moment. The lines at the corners of her mouth now looked as if they had been chiseled into place, carved out by her pig-headed tenacity.

From time to time she would open her eyes and look at me or at the high, dark ceiling and ask weakly, "What time is it?"

"Six o'clock."

"What about him?" The "him" in question was Kuai Chi. I could only answer according to our prior arrangement. "He went to take a nap."

Her murky gaze stopped at a fixed point in space. "That's fine — if that's what really happened," she said slowly and clearly.

"Don't worry." I knew she was beginning to worry again, and so in an attempt to divert her attention and make her last moments happier, I told her how her favorite student, Jia Minghua, had skipped a grade and passed the university entrance exams. He would be going to college very soon.

"Jia Minghau...what Jia Minghua?" She was a bit out of it now.

"The student who made you a cabinet last summer. You said his father had died and his mother remarried and that he'd been learning carpentry every since he was small."

She fixed her gaze again, but you couldn't tell if she remembered him or not, so I continued: "I bumped into him a few days ago in front of your house. He had come to visit you."

"Humph!" she let out. "That phony!" she muttered. "Sleeps in his new shirts, I suppose. Couldn't fool anyone but a corpse...and I'm not one yet!"

She was still thinking about Kuai Chi. I could only keep my mouth shut.

I'd been coming to see Tian Jing constantly ever since she had taken a turn for the worse. Today, as I came puffing up the stairs to the second floor ward, I saw a young woman sitting on a bench by a window near the stairwell. Her long, long curly hair was coiled up on top of her head, and the bangs on her forehead had been meticulously arranged to give a casual appearance. Her eyes, already flawless, had been made to look even larger and brighter by the eye shadow applied around the lids. Under the perfectly straight nose was a full, lightly lipsticked mouth. Beneath the form fitting bell bottoms of her grey western-style suit was a pair of matching grey leather shoes. The only thing to break up the monochrome was the small, blood-red Georgette scarf around her neck. She sat there, meeting all the glances thrown her way without a trace of timidity. I thought to myself this must be her—Wang Jiali.

"Vixen!" That was how Tian Jing referred to Wang Jiali. And sure enough, under her influence, Tian Jing's son had begun to grow sideburns, his hair had gotten longer and he'd started to wear checkered shirts. The problem was Kuai Chi had been very docile up till now, and Tian Jing had become used to it. He had never gone against his mother's will, nor had he ever wanted to because everything had been arranged so well for him, so comfortably. Well, maybe it hadn't been the best possible arrangement, but it wasn't the worst either. But now he faced the problem of choosing a wife, and all the pains his mother had taken collapsed like a house of cards, making her seem like a fussy old nag. As a result Tian Jing was brokenhearted, and her son wasn't too happy either.

Three months ago Kuai Chi had ignored Tian Jing's opposition and brought Wang Jiali home for the purpose of, as he put it, making his mother "widen her knowledge" and get used to Wang Jiali. However, he really underestimated his mother's strength. The hitherto mild mannered Tian Jing had gone so far as to point at Wang Jiali and say, "No one like you has ever lived in my house, and no one ever will, unless it's over my dead body!" Wang Jiali turned around and walked out without a word. The next day. Kuai Chi left home and moved into the factory. Tian Jing came to see me, glowering inflexibly. "I won't compromise! I won't compromise!" she repeated. I tried to convince her that it wouldn't hurt to make an effort to understand just what it was that young people really wanted nowadays, but she just shook her head, saying, "Vixen! Vixen!" and walked out. Later on, I tried to talk to her one more time, but to no avail.

The deadlock between mother and son didn't end until it was discovered that Tian Jing's lung cancer had spread and she was admitted to the hospital. Kuai Chi moved back home then, and their relationship improved somewhat, but Wang Jiali was still on their minds even though mother and son wisely avoided all mention of her. And now the person sitting right there by the stairwell was very possibly Wang Jiali herself.

In all fairness, she was really quite pretty. I was just about to take another look at her when she stood up all wreathed in smiles. "You must be Auntie Liu?"* she asked. Then continuing in the soft Shanghai dialect that flowed effortlessly: "I saw your picture in Kuai Chi's photo album. He talks about you a lot!"

"Oh!" I didn't know what to say and just stood there thinking how intelligent she seemed. Fortunately, Kuai Chi came rushing out of Tian Jing's hospital room just at that moment, stripping off his work clothes as he walked revealing a snow white shirt and a pair of western-style pants. He seemed stunned for a moment when he saw me standing together with Wang Jaili, but still he

*Younger people in China often address older people as aunt or uncle to express respect and affection. There is no real relationship here.

managed to introduce us. "Aunti Liu, this is Wang Jaili." He spoke with a despondent expression, as if to tell me, "See? There's nothing wrong with her."

Immediately understanding Kuai Chi's unspoken message, Wang Jiali's smile disappeared and she turned her head away, pretending to have a great interest in a patient who was walking by.

"How's your mother?" I asked Kuai Chi. Actually, I was just trying to change the subject.

"The doctor said she'll be all right for the time being."

"Oh...Have you gone in to see her?" I asked Wang Jiali, trying to be casual.

She lowered her head and shook it slightly.

I didn't care to delay any longer. "I'm going in to see her for a short while," I said. I hadn't taken more than a few steps when Kuai Chi called me to a halt.

"Auntie Liu!" He thought for a while, biting his dry lips, then spoke: "Could you stay with her until ten o'clock?"

"What for? I thought you were staying."

"Well, to be honest..." He only managed to get half a sentence out when I noticed Wang Jiali shoot him a look, stopping him dead.

"Go ahead and speak. Auntie Liu isn't an outsider," the girl said, throwing me a compliment and a hint to Kuai Chi at the same time. Obviously, she was much more sophisticated than he was.

"Wang Jiali and I are going to attend her older brother's wedding." He removed the rest of his work clothes while talking and then drew out a striped maroon tie from Wang Jiali's bag and proceeded to tie it at a lightning pace. Still working on the tie he went on, "Of course, Little* Wang's parents will be there. Plus they'll bring the son of a high cadre with them to introduce to Little Wang. We're going to be checking them out and they'll be checking us out. So what can we do? I have to go! I realize how sick mom is, but I...." He paused for a minute and carelessly rolled up his work clothes, stuffing them into the bag and continued, "I still have my life to live...." He pulled a brand new jacket out of the bag.

I saw no reason to make my position known, so I just stood there, staring blankly. Then Wang Jiali spoke: "We borrowed these clothes, you know. And this is not the sort of thing we can

---

*It is a common Chinese habit to address people with either the word "Xiao" (little or young), or "Lao" (old), before the surname (such as Wang, Li, Zhang etc.), depending on the age and status of the person addressed.

let anyone know, not even my own mother. No one else will know except us. If we say anything at all at this party, it'll just be about how great Kuai Chi's apartment is." Wang Jiali's eyes were brimming with tears at this point.

What could I say to them? I was ignorant about their values and their human relationships. I thought I knew Kuai Chi until now. But to these two young people, under these circumstances, I just didn't know what to say. I could only stand there, stupefied, watching Kuai Chi put on that...jacket as if he were pulling a rabbit out of a hat. His whole appearance suddenly changed. He became...became...well, impressive. That head of long hair went well with the new clothes and no longer seemed so offensively conspicuous. He was standing on one leg now, changing into leather shoes as he spoke: "I told Mom I was sleepy and wanted to go home and take a nap. If she asks about me, just tell her that." He finished putting on the shoes and stood there. "Lying to a sick person is a virtue," he said. He had avoided looking at me the whole time he was talking, but now he looked at me and said, "Don't blame me, Auntie Liu!"

Wang Jiali, who had been standing to one side without uttering a word, added, "There's nothing I can do either!"

"All right. You...you go ahead," I said, nodding in agreement. I really didn't know what else to say.

At this the two of them took their things, and casting a smile in my direction, took off down the stairs.

Fortunately, Tian Jing didn't bring up the subject of her son again. I noticed that she was breathing with difficulty, her chest rising and falling rapidly. I called in a nurse who hooked her up to an oxygen tank. Her condition became a bit more stable after that and she just lay there, silently looking at me, her eyes gradually misting over with a layer of tears. I knew she had to be thinking of her son, whom she both loved and hated. I hurried to turn on the overhead lamp, but its dim, yellowish light only served to increase the cheerless atmosphere. I could only force a smile and sit down beside her, trying to think of some of the happiest, most glorious moments of her life to talk about. Ever since she joined the army thirty-two years ago at the age of twenty, we had been working in the same city, and I had never lost contact with her. Which memories would console her? There must be some high points in the long struggle of a Communist Party member. But what were hers?

She had been party secretary in a high school these two years since the downfall of the Gang of Four. Actually, it was in name only because she was in poor health. Her most prominent worry for the past two years had been Kuai Chi's job—it was not ideal. He was working in a textile factory, oiling the machinery, alternating day and night shifts. It was a tough job and held little possibility for future advancement. So Tian Jing went through a lot of trouble, looking up old senior cadres she had served under and old comrades, telling everyone, "I don't have any requests for myself. I'm too old for that. My only worry is setting things up right for my son." I don't know how often I heard her say this. Finally, she managed to get him transferred into the factory's propaganda department, but that had its shortcomings too because there still wasn't a bright future for a person without special skills. However, now that she was working in a school, Tian Jing was in an opportune position to find a good teacher to coach her son in math and science. But because Wang Jiali had made her appearance in Kuai Chi's life, I really wouldn't care to guess how much effect the coaching had on him.

Like the vast majority of cadres at the time, Tian Jing had to "stand aside" during the Cultural Revolution. All she got each month was a little money for living expenses, so things were extremely hard for her. In addition to making her own clothes, which she already knew how to do, she had to learn how to cook. This she learned quite well and anything that came out of her kitchen was tasty, even green vegetables and turnips. In the midst of all this adversity she still managed to save seven *yuan** a month to pay for a mediocre violin tutor for Kuai Chi. I remember one winter she borrowed forty *yuan* from the cadre school to buy him a practice violin. Violins were a scarce commodity then. She had to run around to all the second hand shops in Shanghai to find a suitable instrument. This wasn't easy because either the price wasn't right or the violin wasn't to her liking. Finally, after dashing about all day, she found one with a decent tone for forty-two *yuan*. She was so happy the evening she found it. The whole thing was very moving, but also a little pathetic. Two years later, when Kuai Chi was assigned work in a state-run textile factory, Tian Jing prepared a banquet and even handed out candy in celebration. Naturally that was the end of the violin lessons.

I held her thin, bony hand in mine. It was so cold! I was just about to put it back under the covers when it suddenly squeezed my own hand. Tian Jing was looking at me through half-open eyes. "What are you thinking?" she asked.

"I...I was thinking of how you escorted those prisoners of war in the war of liberation." In my quandary I had hit upon the cli-

*One yuan is approximately equivalent to $0.67 (U.S.).

max of her life. What fiery days those were! What a flaming youth! And sure enough, the corners of her mouth moved a bit. It had made her feel better!

Kuai Chi's voice suddenly flashed through my mind: "All I ever hear about is 'The Past'! Will there ever be an end to it?"

"No! It'll never end! Besides you, all your mother has IS the past!" I answered silently. Ai! That had sounded so crude in tone and so weak in content. When had it happened anyway? Damn! I was feeling a bit demoralized now...Oh yes! It was in the spring of 1947, not long after Tian Jing had joined the army. The Battle of Laiwu had just started and Jing and I had been sent to the front lines from the cultural troupe to do prisoner of war work. We had to escort one hundred twenty POW's out of a forward position to a camp forty miles away. The combat company that had captured them could only afford to send four soldiers to help. No sooner had we left the forward position than we realized that the territory we were covering was a battlefield that hadn't been cleared yet. The Kuomintang army had tried to hold fast to their position here, and the whole place was strewn with corpses, documents, papers, and more importantly, guns and ammunition. If only a few of the prisoners picked up some hand grenades, the situation could reverse itself and the six of us, with our four guns, would be helpless! I was extremely anxious but had no way of raising the problem to the other comrades since I was bringing up the rear. Our four soldiers were marching at the sides of the contingent, and Jing was leading. The battlefield seemed to stretch out endlessly and there was no sign of human life. I was sweating and feeling tense when, all of a sudden, I heard a crisp, sharp voice up front issuing a command: "Everyone, hands up and run!"

What a girl, Jing! Growing up in the middle of the "anti-mopping up operation" really paid off with some valuable experience! I thanked her in my mind as I ran, huffing to catch my breath. As our contingent turned onto a path between the fields, I could see her small, thin figure running as fast as a little deer. In a half hour we covered several miles, safely passing the danger zone.

Later, she worked in the P.O.W. camp for a period of time. I heard once that she and two of our men were escorting a group of P.O.W.'s to another location, when they encountered an air attack. The KMT prisoners-of-war had never had the experience of being bombed before, and they panicked, scattering every which way, looking for a safe place to hide. Somehow, Jing managed to gather them all up and lock them into a small one-room house together with our two soliders and herself. Those P.O.W.'s finally calmed down when they saw the cool expression on her face and realized that she was prepared to perish together with them if need be. After the whole battle was over, three members of our cultural troupe had won second class merit citations, and Tian Jing was one of them.

Tian Jing's ashen face was now wearing an expression of rapt attention. Perhaps she was re-living in her mind that period of time; that life, long since past, full of combat and the vitality of Youth, of suffering and joy. Sighing with emotion, I said, "There were three people who won second class citations then. One was you, one was Ji Zheng, who later got killed after being made Company Vice Political Officer... Who was the other one?"

"Little You. You Mei. She's the wife of a military district department chief now. Spends half the time staying in hotels."

"Ah, yes! Her! Now I remember." Tian Jing had once taken her two bottles of "Ten Ingredient Special Tonic" when she was trying to get Kuai Chi into the P.L.A. I heard that You Mei had given her a big lecture, full of condescending hems and haws. But in fact, she had already set her own kids up quite nicely. One had become a cadre in the army, and the other had made it into the party somwhere. Tian Jing came back swearing she'd never go to see her again. Actually, I don't think you can judge a person by just one instance like this. Little You had a milk-white complexion — she was from Jiaodong in eastern Shangdong Province. I remember she had been working in a front-line hospital back then. Actually, it was just a bunch of reed mats patched together. Then one day enemy airplanes discovered their location and made them the target of a wave-bombing attack, three planes attacking in turns. Little You kept cool and safely moved the wounded soldiers in the reed-mat tent under her charge out of the way. During the savage strafing, she had lain on top of a severely wounded soldier, protecting him with her own body. Afterwards, it was the wounded comrades who requested that she be given a citation. I met her once by the elevator of the Yanan Hotel a few years ago as she was coming out of the dining room, toothpick in hand. The snow was swirling about outside, but she was just wearing a woolen shirt and a pair of soft-soled felt shoes. She said she was in Shanghai for medical treatment. Actually, when you stop to figure it, she must have been about fifty years old, too, but her skin was still soft and clear. I wonder what disease she could have had?

I squeezed Tian Jing's thin hand and straightened out her straw-like hair. "...then, once our troupe was having a victory celebration when a guest came running up just to give you a small pistol and three bullets. You remember, don't you?" I said, forcing a smile.

"Old Kuai!" Tian Jing's eyes opened wide and an excited expression came over her face. "I'd met him in the P.O.W. camp. He was a brigade commander."

"We all could sense what was up then. Everybody was saying you were probably in love."

A smile danced in Tian Jing's eyes as she spoke: "I didn't know about anything in those days. No one really paid much attention to me either, but for some reason he'd noticed my name. He asked me why I was named Jing, 'the well,' and I said there were always droughts where I cam from. So then he asked wouldn't it be better to call me Hai, 'the sea.' I said, 'No, seawater is useless for farming.' He said, 'Well then, a pond is still better than a well.' I said, 'After Liberation we'll have everything, but right now just call me 'the well.' " She spoke very quickly and clearly, but her excited state didn't seem good to me, so I didn't dare encourage her. But oh, Jing! Jing of those days! I was still calling to her in my mind, searching....

She paused for a second, then continued, "Later, when I first knew I was pregnant, I decided right away what to name the baby—Chi, 'the pond'..." Then she fell silent. After a while her lips started to tremble violently and a choking, gagging noise came from her throat. There seemed to be a half-estinguished fire in her eyes still burning faintly with resentment, indignation and grief. Then she exploded. "Old Kuai!" she shouted hoarsely, "I haven't let the family down!...I never had even one day of ease and comfort. I...." Suddenly she threw off my hand and began pulling at her sweater, trying to undo the buttons. Before I had a chance to help her, she had already torn it open and had pulled out a stack of deposit slips from her undershirt pocket, frantically searching among receipts with face values of thirty *yuan*, fifty *yuan*, and even one hundred *yuan*. Ah! What a hard life she'd had! She even borrowed money from me during those days when everyone had to stand aside and try to survive on a living allowance. At last she found what she was looking for—a slip for five thousand *yuan*.

"What has been the purpose of my life? Hasn't it been precisely for...?" she said, clutching the slip in her hand. I grabbed her hand again: "You lived for the Revolution, Jing; for maintaining the revolutionary way of hard struggle and plain living. You're the daughter of a poor peasant and can bear any hardship. Isn't that right?" I lied. I could hear Kuai Chi's voice again: "Lying to a sick person is a virtue." Yes, just like opium and morphine.

Tian Jing nodded her head. As I expected, what I had said enabled her to get hold of herself, but in a short while she started up again.

"This is mine and this family is mine! I'm not giving this to anyone, and certainly not to that vixen!" she said in a stern voice, somehow managing to prop herself up as she spoke. Then she went on looking at me with widening eyes: "I'm a member of the Communist Party. I don't have any inheritance to pass on. Give, ...give this to the party as dues!" Finishing her speech, she collapsed back onto the pillow soaked with sweat as if she had spent every last drop of strength. She was still holding the deposit slips tightly. I understood her and was a bit annoyed at her falseness, but I still attempted to reassure her.

"If you want to hand in dues, you can do it yourself. Why don't you just let me put these things away for you," I said as I lifted up her shirt pocket and carefully put the slips back one by one. She relaxed a little. Then I noticed her sweat was rather sticky and gave her a tranquilizer to let her sleep awhile. I straightened up and leaned back on the chair.

Children! When did they first appear in our lives? And when was it that they managed to capture the commanding heights of the Revolution?...It's as if from the very moment they were born they began to occupy a dominant position. I don't know about others, but Tian Jing had once said that her only worry was about setting up things for her children. And the Revolution? Her answer was: "The Revolution is safe and secure in China now."

The hospital room was peaceful and quiet. The ceiling seemed especially high. Maybe it was because the room was so narrow. The wattage of the overhead light was very low. It's dull glow veiled a lot of the ominous signs on Tian Jing's face and at the same time added to the lonely atmosphere.

A pair of bright, sparkling eyes came nearer and nearer. Then I saw the eye shadow around lids and a blood-red scarf. It was Wang Jiali! I could see her clearly now, moving about that bright, gleaming two-room apartment as if she owned the place. The rooms were a little messier now but seemed somewhat warmer. Wang Jiali was speaking to me with a little smile on her face, but the voice I heard was Kuai Chi's: "...*I know what mom's dream is — she wants me to become a great man and do great deeds, but her position just isn't high enough for me to become a great man and do great deeds. First, she wants me to learn how to play the violin, then she wants me to study math and science. It's like her main talent lies in torturing me. But it's no good anymore. I'm twenty-eight years old. I'll never become a great man or do great deeds. Nor do I have the ability to become a great man and do great deeds. And I'm certainly not going to pretend to be something I'm not. I just want to have a good life. For this I do have to thank mom—she gave me a little capital to live on...Little Wang's working in a little street association factory. Is that her fault? But mom won't even look at her. So she likes to dress up. Does that get in the way of the Four Modernizations? But mom looks down on that too. She criticizes every little thing about Little Wang. What does she want? I'm not a great man and can't do great deeds. I just want to have a good life. Get it? A good life!"* The voice got louder and louder and more unfamliar.

No, I don't get it. I don't understand. I was seized with terror. Really! I didn't recognize that voice at all. And I didn't know what he meant by "a good life."

Wang Jiali giggled and sat down on the sofa, looking even more satisfied. *"Isn't that the purpose of living in this world — to eat, to dress? It's not like I'm going out and doing anything bad."*

"Complete philistine! Bourgeois thinkers. And you, you Vixen!" Tian Jing suddenly appeared, the oxygen tube still attached to her nose, but her voice sounded just the way it had when she'd been healthy.

"What do you mean bourgeois? We don't steal. We don't rob. We don't exploit anyone or have any ambitious designs. How can you call us bourgeois?" Kuai Chi was speaking now, his head turned around sharply.

"And you're the proletariat, I suppose? I think feudal might be a better world for your thinking. You say I'm bourgeois? Hoping for a better life is bourgeois? Then why don't you just not pass on anything at all?" Wang Jiali was still smiling as she spoke. *"But there's no way you can get away with that! Sooner or later this world is going to belong to us, and when it does, we're going to seek the truth from facts. We know how to look at things!"*

Proletariat, bourgeoisie, plus an illegitimately nurtured feudalism—all living together at the same time under one roof. What a mixed up age! Shaking my head I woke up from my half-asleep state. It was a bit chilly. Tian Jing was still sleeping. I put her hand back under the covers. It was icy, cold, as were the blankets. Then I suddenly realized what a frightening thing Tian Jing was facing. She wanted to pass on her world. It was imperative for her. But to whom could she pass it on? To a useless son and his vixen? Could she offer her entire world to them.

"What time is it?" Tian Jing opened her eyes and looked at me. She was waiting for her son.

I looked at my watch. It was a quarter to nine. "Eight o'clock."

I deliberately made it seem earlier so she would think that her son had returned quickly when he came back later. She cocked her head to one side and murmured. "I want to go home." A teardrop trickled down from the corner of her eye.

"All right," I said, putting my arm around her shoulders. "I'll take you home as soon as it gets light."

She nodded and closed her eyes again, but her breathing was quite rapid. She was waiting for dawn. I stood up, wiped the tears from my eyes, and started walking around the room. Could she make it until dawn? I would've taken her home right then and there if it had been possible. That sparkling clean home was hers. It was what she was familiar with and she wouldn't have too many chances to see it again.

The only window in the room had a northern exposure and it faced out onto the hospital wall. At the foot of the wall was a cricket, chirping miserably in the cold. And in another room a baby was crying. Somewhere in a far off place a festive banquet was reaching a climax. I wondered how much assurance the tenth-degree cadre's son had of victory. Next to me a human life was dying, but life itself had not come to a halt, continuing forward in the quiet of the night. "Life goes on, but where is it going?" I brooded to myself. Then the two made-up eyes appeared in front of me again, and little white ears pierced out from under the soft, coiled up hair. I don't know why, but for some reason I imagined a pair of blood-red earrings dangling from them *"What's the right direction, you ask? From the 70's to the 80's!"* she said, eyes sparkling. *"Every proletarian hopes to have a better life for the future."*

"Maybe you're right. I don't know..." I answered pensively.

The door behind me opened and Wang Jiali's beautiful face disappeared. I looked at my watch—nine-thirty. Kuai Chi had actually come back a half hour early. Not bad! But then I heard the door being closed very lightly and carefully. It wasn't Kuai Chi after all. Turning around, I only saw Jia Minghua, his head soaked with sweat, standing by the door with some wooden object over his shoulder, staring dumbly at Tian Jing with eyes wide open.

"Jia Minghua! You're here!" Who knows why, but as soon as I saw him, I felt an inexpressible joy, as if I were meeting with an old friend.

"I told the nurse I'd only come in for a few minutes. I had no idea Teacher Tian was as sick as...this!"

"Weren't you going to Beijing? How come you haven't gone yet?"

"I'm going tomorrow. I had some things to do so I put it off for a few days. I had no idea that Teacher Tian was so sick. Otherwise I would have come to see her earlier." He remained standing by the door as he spoke as if one extra step would have had a bad effect on the patient.

"Sit down!" I said, moving the only chair in his direction. "How did you think of coming here?"

"I've already paid visits to all of our school's teachers. If it weren't for this," he said, pointing to the object on his shoulder, "I'd have come here ages ago."

"What is it?"

"I made Teacher Tian a backrest for her bed." He let the object on his shoulders drop lightly to the floor and opened it up. All you had to do was press a button under the two armrests and you could automatically adjust the angle of the backrest. However, what I was paying attention to during this demonstration was not so much the backrest, although it was undeniably ingenious, but rather that sweaty head of hair of his and his enthusiasm and warmth. Jia Minghua had a rather scrawny build and wasn't very tall. His face was rather ordinary, except for those two bright, black eyes, but there was something terribly honest and simple about that ordinary face of his. Then, probably noticing that I wasn't reacting to his demonstration, he was abashed, and began to put away the backrest, saying, "It isn't anything much, really. I just wanted Teacher Tian to have something to lean on."

"You've done a nice job, and it's even nicer that you came." I went over and patted his hand. "But I'm afraid Teacher Tian may not need that thing," I said very softly.

He opened his eyes wide and looked at me, then at Tian Jing, totally stunned. "Does she need blood? Mine's good—type O!" he said, looking at me again.

I shook my head, but before I had time to speak. I noticed something wrong with Tian Jing's breathing. She was struggling. "My boy's coming soon," she said.

"Tian Jing, what's the matter?" She didn't make a sound but only clutched the clothing about her chest. After a while she spoke up: "The money, give it to him, to my son." You could hear the phlegm in her throat as she talked.

I felt my own heart thud to a stop for a second, but then it quickly resumed beating. The moment of parting had come. But Jing! Wait awhile!

"Doctor!" I could only wave my hand at Jia Minghua, but he caught the meaning of my gesture and the empty hallway immediately resounded with the sound of his footsteps. I straightened up and took a look at my watch. It was exactly ten o'clock. Kuai

Chi should be back any minute. Perhaps Tian Jing could hold on until then and pour out her last hopes and instructions.

A dear friend was about to become a part of the past, taking with her things very familiar to me. I knew that I wouldn't be around much longer either. The future belonged to Jia Minghua, to Kuai Chi and Wang Jiali, and, of course, to the high cadre's son too. They would have high points in their lives, some exceeding ours, some perhaps not. But, whatever happened. I hoped their high points wouldn't be subjected to compromises, expediency or antagonism.

Just them I heard Minghua running back with the doctor.

Li Shunda Builds A House

GAO XIAOSHENG

(Translated by Ellen Klempner)

I

The older generation of peasants always used to say: "Eat rice gruel for three years and you can buy yourself a cow." That sounds simple enough, but in reality it's not quite so easy. Think about it for a minute — if you have to cut down on rice that much for three years, just imagine how much you'll have to cut back on everything else! Besides, that little maxim is meaningless. How can you save anything if you can't afford to eat rice in the first place?

That pretty much is what Li Shunda's situation had been before Liberation, so he had never dreamt about buying a cow. But after Land Reform he made a resolution — he was going to build himself a three-room house based on just that spirit of eating nothing but gruel for three years.

Li Shunda wasn't too sure as to just how many of those three years of gruel would be needed to build a three-room house, but in any case, things were different now after Liberation — you could save up a little surplus with strict budgeting and careful spending. Therefore Li Shunda was quite confident.

Li Shunda was 28 years old then, with a head of coarse black hair framing his dark, ruddy face. He was of medium height, but with those broad shoulders and wide chest he was like a little iron tower — the very picture of strength. There were three able-bodied people in his family of four (himself, his wife, a sister and a son), so when they were assigned 6.8 *mu*[1] of good land, he felt

[1]One mu is roughly equivalent to one-sixth of an acre.

31

full of energy, almost as if he could hoe a trench right through the center of the earth! So what was there to worry about in building a three-room house? One could see the firm resolve in his dull eyes and in the straight, broad nose that seemed to press down heavily on his wide lips. It was a resolve so strong that not even a water buffalo could have budged it!

Nothing could have shaken his determination. His mother, father and one-year-old brother had all died just because they lacked a house. They had been a family of boat people and had spent their days wandering up and down the Yangtze River, living on what fish they could catch. They had been at it so long they weren't even sure where their ancestors had come from originally. The boat was a wreck by the time it had been passed down to Li Shunda's father. The nails were rusted and the boat itself was full of holes, with an especially big one in the reed-mat awning. It wasn't good for fishing anymore and certainly couldn't weather a storm, so the whole family had to change its profession. They did a little bit of everything: collecting scraps, gathering snails, and some of them even went into the business of trading home-refined sugar for rags. And all this just for a few mouthfuls of rice gruel! Then on one cold winter's day during the twelfth lunar month of the year 1942 they docked their old boat by Chen Village. A gusty wind was blowing and the sky looked ominous as Li Shunda, only nineteen years old, lead his fourteen-year-old sister to shore to trade for rags and gather scraps. By early evening they had already walked ten miles before they decided to turn back, but by that time the wind had stopped and the snow was falling thick and heavy from the leaden sky. They soon lost their way. Fortunately, the two of them wandered into an old deserted temple and made it their refuge for the night. When they rushed back to Chen Village early the next morning, they found their boat under a heavy mound of snow and their mother, father and little brother lying frozen stiff on the doorstep of a peasant's house. Apparently the boat had been about to collapse and the family went to the village seeking help. But who would dare to open his door to them in those chaotic days of war and destruction? The residents of Chen Village all had mistaken them for bandits as the three cried for aid outside their homes, and they were left to freeze to death in the snow. Oh God, have you no eyes? Earth, have you no conscience? Who can understand the plight of the poor...!

Li Shunda and his sister wept by the bodies of their parents. There wasn't a single resident of the impoverished village who didn't feel grieved at the sight. Later the residents dragged the sunken boat up onto the shore and cut it in two. They used half to make coffins for the dead. They turned the remaining half of the boat on end to make a little shanty for Li Shunda and his sister to live in, putting it next to the graves. And that is how Li Shunda came to make his home in Chen Village.

After the War of Resistance against the Japanese, civil war came and the KMT government again starting drafting recruits. No one was willing to go, but the *baozhang*[2] had already taken the government's draft fee and Li Shunda, an outsider with no kith or kin, was the most likely candidate. So the *baozhang* forced him to sell himself into service for the price of one hundred fifty kilograms of grain. Before his departure Li Shunda took a last look at their doorless shed. Afraid that his sister would be raped while he was gone, he decided to use what he had earned in selling himself to build a four-foot wide straw hut. Not until he had accomplished this task was he ready to wipe the tears from his eyes and go off, rifle cradled in his arms.

However, dying for the KMT was about the last thing Li Shunda was willing to do, and he deserted after three months, just after reaching the front. But then in the following year the *baozhang* sold him off again. Altogether Li Shunda sold himself into the army three times. The second time he used the entire sum to buy the land his straw hut occupied; the third time he spent the money on the plot which held his parents' graves. But damn it all! Even if he had sold himself another three times, the money still would've ended up in someone else's hands!

Thanks to that four-foot wide hut he at least managed to get himself a wife. His sister had brought home an orphaned beggar girl to keep her company while he was away in the army. The girl later became his wife and gave birth to a chubby little baby boy.

Li Shunda and his family received land in the land reform, but didn't get a house since Chen Village had only one landlord who lived in a nearby city, and you couldn't exactly move his house back to the countryside. So Li Shunda had to think of something else. He figured that he and his sister would need two rooms (his sister's room would go to his son after she married), but the stove and a place for sitting and sleeping would occupy half a room, so they'd need another room to keep pigs and sheep and store firewood. It looked like at least three rooms would be necessary for a family. And that became the goal of Li Shunda's struggle after his own liberation.

²A local official in charge of 100 families under the KMT.

II

Maybe it doesn't show much vision or ambition for a liberated person to uphold building a three-room house as an ultimate goal, but the way Li Shunda saw it, building a three-room house was a lofty aspiration which he would surely realize under the Communist Party and the People's Government. He was sincerely willing to follow the Communist Party all the way, as his actions have proved — even to this day.

To Li Shunda, building socialism meant to build "an upstairs and a downstairs with electric lights and a telephone." However, the way he viewed the matter, a house of two floors wasn't as practical as a one-story home. He himself would rather have the downstairs and do without the upstairs, but he didn't know for sure if building a one-story house was socialism or not. As for electricity he was in favor of it, but the telephone he could do without. It wasn't like he had a lot of friends and relatives so what was the use of a phone? If the child broke it he would have to spend money to fix it; that might mean going to the pawn shop. Who needs to bring that type of ruin upon the family! He had expressed all these opinions quite openly at the time and no one had thought anything of it.

None of the other peasants looked down on Li Shunda's goal. On the contrary, they felt he had set his sights too high. Someone once gave him a piece of advice which started off with a local saying: "Ten *mu* of land and a three-room house are hard to get anywhere in this world, even more so here!" Another said, "If you want to build that house, you're going to have to put up with hardship for the rest of your life." Then someone else said, "Things are easier now after Liberation, but I expect it'll still take you over ten years."

And their advice was pretty accurate too. For example, some land on either side of the Shanghai-Ningpo railroad was occupied by the town of Benniu. The setup and structure of people's houses on either side was drastically different: Eighty percent of the houses in the western half were made of only dried mud and straw, while in the eastern half they were mostly brick and tile houses. In comparison, Chen Village, located over one hundred miles east of Benniu, didn't have one single straw house except for the one belonging to Li Shunda. So, despite his poverty, he had come to take fine houses for granted. Still, building a three-room house was easier said than done, and this time around poor Li Shunda had really bitten off more than he could chew.

Li Shunda would always react to everyone's comments with a

smile and say, "It couldn't be any harder than it was for the Foolish Old Man who moved the mountain." His thick lips seemed to pull on his ponderous nose when he talked, making the act of speech very strenuous for him. So his simple words gave the impression of carrying a lot of weight.

From that day on Li Shunda and his family started their epic battle. It was an exceedingly difficult one. Every grain of rice was acquired using the simplest tools and the most arduous labor; every cent was saved through the most primitive techniques. They understood how great accomplishments are often created by the accumulation of very small acts and so showed an amazing, carefree yet enduring spirit of industry and thrift. There were times when the labor of Li Shunda and his entire family couldn't even cover their normal living expenses. On days like that they would resolve to go hungry, each family member reducing his or her gruel allotment by a half bowl at each meal, saving the remaining six bowls as surplus. Then there were days when no one could go out and work due to heavy rain or snow. They would take advantage of this "unemployment" by spending the whole day in bed, thus reducing their food intake even more. The grain they managed to save by combining three meals into two would be entered into the family "Income" column.

To give another example, they stopped adding oil when they cooked vegetable congee and would throw in a few soybeans instead—after all, oil is pressed from soybeans, isn't it? Using the same logic, when they cooked snails they would add a spoonful of broth from the rice pot instead of liquor. The reason? Liquor comes from grain, of course, and grain should be saved whenever possible. For years they raised chickens without eating eggs and would wait until the Dragon Boat Festival before they would touch the one piece of meat they had left on their parents' graves for the Festival of the Dead.

Whenever he had any free time, Li Shunda would take up the old family business again, wandering through the streets and lanes carrying sugar over his shoulder to trade for scraps. When he got home he would sort out the various rags, old newspapers, cotton wadding and torn shoes to sell to the purchasing station. Sometimes he could made a tidy little profit that way, plus he could cut down on a lot of living expenses since there would always be something like trousers or rubbers that, with just a little repair, he could salvage for himself out of the pile of junk. When these recycled waste products that he had acquired for his own use were beyond repair, he would simply channel them back into the scrap heap to be resold. The costs of this business were quite low because he would process the sugar that he sold at home from maltose he could purchase cheaply. Yet his own son had no idea what sugar was, or whether it was sweet or salty until he was eight years old, when he tasted a piece at the instigation of a little friend. Unfortunately, he was caught in the act by his mother who made him swear to turn over a new leaf. She gave him such a hard spanking that he squealed like a stuck pig while she went on and on about how he was going to be the ruin of the whole family by gobbling up their three-room dream, and how he could only blame himself if he should fail to get a wife!

But the thing that won people's admiration most was what happened to Li Shunda's sister, Shunzhen. Shunzhen was already twenty-three at the time of land reform in 1951. This was before the government had begun to call for late marriages. So, according to the custom prevalent then, she had reached the perfect marriageable age. A capable, hard-working girl, Shunzhen was also extraordinarily pretty. If you took a closer look at her, she looked exactly like her brother except for her nose which was a little smaller and her lips which were a little thinner. But it was just this little bit that made all the difference and allowed nature to show off its greatness.

Shunzhen was a tall, slender girl with a fine oval face. The combination made her appear very delicate, so there were more than just a handful of men from neighboring villages who were pleading for her hand in marriage. But she rejected every one of the prospective suitors, no matter how wealthy or worthy his character, saying that she was still too young to think about marriage. Shunzhen's brother had taken care of her since she was a small child and she was determined to pay him back. She knew that it would be very difficult for him to reach his goal without her help. If she got married it would mean the loss of a strong, reliable helper, and she would take with her the 1.7 *mu* of land listed under her name. It would have been a great reduction of manpower and would have severely undermined the Li family's economic base. Therefore she was more than willing to dedicate the best years of her youth to her brother and his cause.

So it wasn't until the end of 1957 that Li Shunda could buy all the materials needed to build a three-room brick and tile house and that Shunzhen at the advanced age of twenty-nine could finally marry a thirty-year-old bachelor from a nearby village. The groom had had to support his elderly parents and a crippled sister. The family was utterly destitute, which was why he had remained single for so long. Thus more hardship and deprivation were all Shunzhen had to look forward to. That didn't particularly bother her, though, because she had long since become used to that kind of life.

III

The following year Li Shunda was short of just one thing — money to hire carpenters and to pay for the food to feed them, but he figured that problem could be solved within a year's time. Besides, land became publicly owned after the commune had been set up and Li Shunda could choose any piece of land he pleased to build his new house. What could be more ideal than that?

However, Li Shunda was, after all, not a revolutionary but a follower. He would always do what Chairman Mao said and stick steadfastly with the party to the very end. Anything that any party member said was a direct order as far as Li Shunda was concerned and he would carry it out all the way. So when he heard one night that an earthly paradise of perfect harmony was about to be realized in which everyone would share everything, it was a great awakening for him. Things had improved somewhat since Liberation eight years earlier. For example, didn't Li Shunda now have enough construction materials to build a three-room house? So why not put everybody's things together and construct socialism even faster? Besides, Li Shunda thought to himself, our construction is for everybody so everybody ought to pitch in. No one's individual plans were necessary anymore; everyone would be able to lead wonderful lives in the future ideal society. So what's the big deal about such a pathetically tiny piece of personal property when it would be so much more glorious to contribute it to the *cause*? There's no reason for misgivings! Everything will be public property — and nobody will be cheated.

So Li Shunda thought and thought, and when he finally came to this conclusion (one can't deny it was a selfless one) it came as an illumination, making him feel revitalized and full of energy. True, he shed a few bitter tears when his bricks were taken away to build an iron-smelting furnace; and yes, it was quite painful for him when his lumber was used to construct handcarts. Even his few remaining tiles went to make the roof of the collective pig shed. But when he thought of his family's future happiness, he felt consoled and exceedingly pleased. In addition, recent events had caused him to change his mind about houses of two stories — he now felt they were definitely superior to one-story houses because grain stored on the second floor wouldn't mold and people could avoid skin diseases like eczema. The way he looked at it, he'd be better off waiting until he was assigned a nice two-story house rather than giving himself the unnecessary burden of building a three-room house.

And so Li Shunda's thinking became totally emancipated. He was happy to contribute anything to the collective, no matter what. Even if their old, broken-down bed was needed he wouldn't hesitate a bit about giving it up because, after all, hadn't he and his wife both grown up without ever having slept on a bed? To tell the truth Li Shunda's wife, the ex-beggar girl, had a few more misgivings (or was it common sense?) than he, but the severe typhoon, the "communist wind," had blown everything and everyone out of control by this time; too much common sense could only bring grief, so she chose to keep silent. Still, she did manage to hide away one iron pot, saving it from being melted down in the smelting furnace, so they didn't have to wait in line to buy a new one after the collective dining hall closed down.

Later, people came to their senses and started to build socialism all over again, although this didn't happen until all the money had run out and no one could play games anymore. Generally speaking, everyone agreed that it was too unpleasant to belabor thsi disaster they had wrought, but Li Shunda couldn't help feeling bad about it. He had paid quite a number of tearful visits to the "battlefield" before it was cleared up, just standing there on the deserted beach staring at the tumbled furnaces and the discarded hand-driven bulldozers, thinking of the six years of blood and sweat, of all the grain saved by tightening his belt, of the sugar he had grabbed from his son's hand, of his sister's wasted youth...

IV

The government's policy on compensation was, needless to say, very popular, but it was the collective that had used up Li Shunda's building materials, not the state. The collective would also have to implement the compensation policy, of course, but with what? There weren't enough materials left over to be returned to anyone, and it would have been extremely difficult to compensate people with cash now that the collective's money reserves had reached rock bottom. The only thing the cadres could do was to try their best to raise Li Shunda's political consciousness so that he would be willing to make sacrifices and accept the lowest possible price in compensation for his losses.

Li Shunda's losses weren't small, either, but his political awareness really did get raised because this was the first time that anyone had put so much painstaking effort into his ideological education. The secretary of the district's party committee, Comrade Liu Qing, a man of integrity held in high esteem by the people, had made a special visit to Chen Village just to see Li Shunda. In the heart-to-heart talk that ensued, Secretary Liu explained, it wasn't that his things had been lost due to corruption or graft, nor was it that someone had had it out for him and deliberately took his belongings. The intentions of the party and government had been good — everything had been purely for the purpose of speeding up the pace of socialist construction so that everyone could enjoy a life of happiness and well being a bit earlier. The state and the collectives had invested so much more than Li Shunda in the attempt to achieve this goal and had accordingly lost a lot more. Still, despite the government's incalculable losses, the party had decided to compensate people for their personal losses. Who, other than the Communist Party, would ever do something like that? When had something like this ever happened before? Only the Communist Party had ever been that concerned about the peasants' welfare. Comrade Liu went on to say that he hoped Li Shunda would understand the party's difficulties and take on a part of the losses himself for the sake of the collective. He pointed out how the party had learned important lessons from the experience of the past few years, so future development should be faster. As soon as the economy, nationally and in the collective, took a turn for the better, things would improve for the individual too. Turning the subject to Li Shunda's case, Secretary Liu told him that there would be too many difficulties involved in building a three-room house now, but that he shouldn't lose hope because once they got over this hump things would go a lot easier. Finally, he said that he'd make sure that the supply and marketing cooperative provided Li Shunda with as much maltose as possible for his sugar and rag trade no matter what the circumstances.

Li Shunda had always been an emotional person, and now that he was getting personal guidance and concrete aid from Comrade Liu Qing, it didn't take long before the tears started streaming down his face. Needless to say, he agreed to everything without the slightest objection.

There were also twenty thousand tiles that could conceivably have been returned, but, they had been used to build the roof of the brigade's seven-room pig shed which was still standing intact.

But if they took them down, they still wouldn't be able to get hold of new tiles right away, and the pigs would have had to be raised in the open. Besides, tiles are fairly fragile objects, and if you keep pulling them apart and taking them down, you stand to lose quite a few. Finally, after some discussion, Li Shunda and the brigade agreed that each party involved should take into consideration the difficulties of the other. So the final decision was that it would be best not to take them down. The brigade, however, agreed to lend two rooms of the pig shed to Li Shunda as temporary living accommodations. Actually, living in the pig shed was better than living in their old straw hut, because each of the rooms was a roomy ten paces wide and the ceiling was nearly four meters high. The only problem was that the roof sloped down a bit, so the back end was rather low (lower than Li Shunda's height, in fact); but then the new occupant didn't exactly have to go swaggering about with his chest thrown out either, so generally speaking there wouldn't be too much of a problem. Besides, Li Shunda had grown up crouching under the awning of a boat, so naturally he didn't have any objections.

That's how the compensation problem was solved. But despite how sincerely he tried to understand the cadres' attempts to straighten out his thinking, Li Shunda learned an important lesson. Before, in the old society, he'd always thought that having cash on had was risky because of inflation. Therefore, whenever he had a little extra money, he'd buy things and store them away. But this experience in the new society taught him that storing up goods wasn't secure and that the safest thing would be to save up money and stash it under his pillow. Unfortunately, these were exactly the "anti-party" sentiments easily detected by the particularly sharp nose of the "left" wing.

From 1961 to 1965, Li Shunda was again able to accumulate just enough money to build a three-room house thanks to the "Sixty Articles on Agriculture" and the help of Comrade Liu Qing in securing him maltose. But this time he didn't buy a single thing. He had come to a definite decision: Either he would wait until he had enough to buy everything all at once and build his house immediately, or he wouldn't build it at all. The way he saw it, this way he could minimize unforeseen liabilities and avoid repeating past mistakes.

However, because of this backward-looking peasant cleverness of his, just when he felt sure that he wouldn't fall into the same old trap again, he tripped on the road ahead of him. (To tell the truth, trying to lead people like him is damn tiring!)

Goods and materials were really plentiful back then, with just about everything in unlimited supply. But would Li Shunda buy anything? No! And a few years later when the market got tight and you had to know the ropes in order to buy anything, he was still saving to buy everything all at once. What a dummy! But then again, it isn't really fair to blame him. After all, how many geniuses are there in the world?

V

Under normal circumstances Li Shunda had felt that he made a rather successful follower — he was sincere and his emotions were never forced. But after the start of the Cultural Revolution he just couldn't keep up anymore. Besides, he didn't know who to follow now even if he had wanted to what with people running around all over the place, each of them yelling, "Only I am right!" Li Shunda's mind was in a state of utter confusion as to who was right and who was wrong, what was real and what was false. The only thing he could do was to hunker down, as it were, and keep a low profile without following anyone. People often say: "Everyone knows the difference between right and wrong." This little proverb may sound impressive, but that's only because it hadn't gone through the Cultural Revolution! In reality it was much too naive. It's not enough to listen to someone's on-stage speeches, you have to observe his actions off-stage as well. Perhaps the expression, "Everyone knows the difference between good and evil" might be more appropriate. But in any case, Li Shunda was very unhappy and his unhappiness was intimately related to his desire to build a house. As he watched the violent, blustering tumult of the Cultural Revolution, he realized that this time it was not the same as in 1958. Back then it was just a matter of a few things getting ruined, but now it was human beings that were being destroyed — you could lose your life at the drop of a hat. It was clear that he couldn't build his house now; but worse, the future was so indefinite. Who knew what tomorrow would bring? To tell the truth, Li Shunda was feeling a bit disgusted with it all. But on the other hand he felt joy in the fact that he had moved into the pig shed, because he would have run a very definite risk of being robbed of the house money stashed under the pillow if he were still living in the isolated straw hut by the riverside.

Actually, Li Shunda's thinking was too backwards — civilized people living in civilized eras have no need of such barbaric measures. One day a local "little red book" -toting rebel leader paid a visit to Li Shunda's home together with the production team head, fully armed in broad daylight. This person evidently had become the new director of the commune's brick and tile factory, and was quite an upholder of justice. As it turned out, he had heard that Li Shunda was having trouble finding bricks for his new house and had come by to help him solve that problem. He roundly cursed the capitalist-roader Liu Qing for not working for the interests of the poor and lower-middle peasants. It appeared that it was now his turn to be savior. All Li Shunda had to do was give him two hundred and seventeen *yuan*, and he would take care of buying ten thousand bricks for him which he could pick up next month. It all sounded much too perfect and therefore quite suspicious. But the way Li Shunda figured it, they were in the same production brigade, and although they weren't too close, they did see each other almost every day, and he'd never heard of the man doing anything bad. Also, he would probably want to do some good deeds now that he was out there making revolution, and it wasn't likely that he would go and cheat people right off the bat. Besides, he had the production team leader with him plus a gun and the precious little red book. As far as friendship or power or convictions went, he had it all. This was the first time Li Shunda had encountered such a combination of hard and soft tactics. So despite the fact that he had had what it took to be a three-time deserter, he immediately fell victim to the new director's intimidating carrot-and-stick techniques and tremblingly turned out the grand sum of two hundred and seventeen *yuan*.

Li Shunda probably could have picked up the goods the next month, but unfortunately he ran into the most unexpected foul luck — he was invited by the security forces to come down and explain a few matters, namely: his place of origin, family background, and where his rifle was (he'd joined the reactionary army three times before, remember?). He was also expected to account for his reactionary statements and actions. (For example, saying things like "houses of two floors aren't as good as one-story houses," and "you can't afford to fix a telephone if it breaks" were vicious attacks on socialism.)

It's not necessary to go into what happened later since everyone knows what occurred during the Cultural Revolution and Li Shunda didn't talk much about it either after he got out. Two things, however, were terribly interesting. One was that just when he couldn't take it any more and was crying for help, who should come to his rescue but the new director of the tile and brick factory. After it was all over the two of them came to a private agreement never to mention the two hundred and seventeen *yuan* again. The second thing was that the house in which Li

Shunda had been locked up was quite solidly built, which enabled him to have an extremely clear outline in his mind of how he
would build his future home.

Later, when he limped home following his release, supported
by his son (now aged nineteen), Li Shunda was met by his tearful
wife and sister, who asked him what it had all been for and if he
had suffered. His hoarse answer was short but rather enigmatic:
"They're evil! My house!"

He couldn't work for over a year after that because of the pain
in his lower back, and on cloudy days or between seasons his entire body would ache down to the very bones. True, he'd never
been treated this way before, but he had had a hard life since the
day he was born, full of bumps and bruises. So why was he so
soft and fragile now? That was the strange thing. Could it be that
he had turned revisionist? He found the thought rather frightening. He could turn into a cow or a horse, but never a revisionist!
Being a revisionist was like having an albatross around the neck
— you couldn't eat it; it just hung there like a bizarre decoration,
a lifeless thing that wouldn't die, but would pass itself down for
generation after generation like a family heirloom. If his son, already nineteen years old, were to carry on the tradition, where
would he ever get a wife? Moreover, he hadn't yet built the house
which was such a basic requirement in finding a daughter-in-law.

All this terrified Li Shunda and made him superstitious. Since
boyhood he'd heard quite a number of stories, and among them
were tales about people who changed into all sorts of different
things. They'd always contain the line, "And at the break of day
he changed into an X X X X." Before the metamorphis began, of
course, inevitably there were a variety of bizarre physical sensa-
tions such as aches and pains in the entire body, feverishness, ir-
ritability, etc. Now that Li Shunda was feeling rather poorly he
developed a real aversion to the darkness and would struggle
every night to keep his eyes open so as to avoid changing unwit-
tingly into something in his sleep. His vigilance has been excellent. To this very day he hasn't changed into anything.

Li Shunda tried to think of some amusing recreational activities that would help him ignore the pain during those nights of
self-enforced sleeplessness, but he didn't have a radio and reading was out because he could only recognize a few characters.
(Besides, it would have been a waste of lamp oil.) So the only
thing left was to recall all the old stories, opera lyrics and children's songs he had heard in his youth. Later on, when he was
feeling a little better he went out again, carrying-pole on shoulder, to engage in the sugar and scrap trade. He would constantly

be singing one particular tuneless little ditty to tease the children. According to him, the lyrics had all come back to him during those sleepless nights. But whatever the case may be, it was quite clear from the song exactly what had been on his mind then. It went something like this:

How strange, how strange, how very strange
Grandpa's sleeping in the cradle

How strange, how strange, how very strange
An eight-man table in a pocket

How strange, how strange, how very strange
The rat has bitten the cat's belly

How strange, how strange, how very strange
The dog sent the weasel to guard the chickens⅚

How strange, how strange, how very strange
The toad's got a piece of swan meat⁵

How strange, how strange, how very strange
A big ship's overturned in the sewer

How strange, how strange, how very strange
A tall man's become a short man's ladder

Ai yaya, watermelon rind on a scabby head
The clams are full of piss and
The balloon's got a belly full of hot air
Long-robed god of evil, nothing but mud
How strange, how strange, how very strange
A snake's crawled into a statue of Buddha
Smelling the incense, putting on airs

It was generally acknowledged that this old children's song was supposed to be packed full of strange events. However, different people have different things on their minds and usually like to throw in the strangest things they can think of. But if you had tried to trace the origins of Li Shunda's version, he would have completely denied that he had added anything to his own. He was no writer and wasn't going to put anything down on paper,

⅚Adapted from the Chinese expression, "The weasel goes to pay his respects to the hen." Implies bad intentions.

⁵From the Chinese expression, "A toad lusting after a swan's flesh." In other words, aspiring after something one is not worthy of.

in black and white — that would have been tantamount to exposing a vulnerable point. Dumb though he may have been, he had been through too much not to realize that if that bunch—those rebelling against the authorities and the authorities among the rebels—wanted to get you, it wouldn't matter what you had done. What mattered was what they wanted out of you—for example, his two hundred and seventeen *yuan*.

One day when he was visiting a neighboring village, singing his little song and pursuing his sugar trade, Li Shunda ran into the old district party secretary, now capitalist roader, Liu Qing, who had been sent there to be reformed by labor. Overwhelmed with mixed feelings of joy and grief, the two couldn't bear to part. When Liu Qing finally begged him to sing his "How Very Strange" song again, Li Shunda didn't show the slightest hesitation. His heavy voice, full of misery and indignation, shook the air as he sang and the two men wept.

VI

Li Shunda began to feel a little disheartened as another year dragged past without a full recovery from his aches and pains. He often wondered to himself how many years he had left and why he should even bother to build a house. Even the proverbial Foolish Old Man had to rely on his descendants to finish moving the mountain, so why was it so terribly necessary for him to complete the house himself? Besides, he had accumulated a little money and had made a few contributions of his own, so you couldn't call him a total flop. But alas! The mundane minds of mortal men! Li Shunda still could not free himself from this one earthly desire. His son was already twenty! How could he get a wife without a house? And who would be willing to move into a pig shed? Also, there was no way he could find his son a beggar girl as he had done in the past. Fine opportunities like that no longer existed. This was serious! How could he have grandsons without a daughter-in-law? And without grandsons, how could he have great-grandsons? Would China enter into communism without a descendant of Li Shunda there to enjoy it? How could that be? So it looked like the house just had to be built, and as soon as possible. Still, his son would probably have to postpone any wedding plans until he was well past the government's stipulated age for getting married.

So, after a bit of wavering, Li Shunda pulled himself together and went into action. Picking up the old, half-rotten basket that he used to gather scraps, he set off, swaying as he went, walking slowly from town to town in search of materials. However, despite having gone through all the streets and alleys, even those of the county seat, he couldn't find a thing for sale. It wasn't until he made inquiries at a store that he found out that he would have to have written permission from three official levels before he could buy just one brick. Li Shunda realized it would be futile to keep running around like this. He would just have to apply to the team, brigade and commune. Fortunately he had brought his basket with him and had earned over ten *yuan* selling the scraps he had picked up along the way, so even though he hadn't found any building materials, the day hadn't been a complete waste.

The next step, obviously, was to try to get the team and brigade cadres to give him a certificate of permission. But they just laughed and said, "What's the use of a certificate? Sometimes there may be a few things available. Sometimes there's simply nothing at all. You won't find anything even if we give you a certificate." Li Shunda refused to believe it and thought they were just trying to place obstacles in his path, but he didn't dare argue back. Instead, he decided to hang around patiently all day — sort of a sit-in. But it was to no avail. The man totally ignored him. When it came time to go home for dinner and he discovered Li Shunda still sitting there, he just said, "Go on home. I'm locking the door." So there was no choice but to go back home. However, he came back and sat there all day the very next day. This went on for three days all together until the man finally lost his patience: "You think pestering me is going to help, don't you! You just won't listen to good advice!" he said. "All right. If you think it's going to do you any good, I'll give you a certificate!" And sure enough, he gave it to him. Ecstatic with joy, Li Shunda went off to the supply and marketing cooperative, only to have the clerk there laugh in the same way the team and brigade cadres had. "Forget it," he said, looking at the certificate. "There's nothing available."

"When will there be something?"

"Don't know. You'll just have to keep coming back when you have time."

From then on Li Shunda would come to the supply and marketing cooperative to ask about materials six days out of seven — just like a student going to school. This went on for half a year and he still hadn't bought one brick. Even though he often sighed at Li Shunda's stupidity, the salesclerk had a good heart and was finally moved by the petitioner's spirit. He told him quietly one day, "Save your energy. Don't keep coming here. These last few years of revolution have really made a mess of everything. Even if occasionally a little bit of something comes by, there's not even enough to go around to cadres, let alone to you. If you run across anything at all, it'll just be a lot of old leftovers that everyone else has rejected and you'll have to pay top price for them too. It just isn't worth it. You really ought to think of some other way."

Li Shunda was greatly disappointed upon hearing this bit of sincere advice, but also extremely grateful. He couldn't help but ask for counsel: "What other way is there?"

Unable to make up his mind at first, the clerk hesitated, then said, "Would you have any good friends or close relatives who are cadres?"

"No," answered Li Shunda heavily. "I don't have any relatives other than my brother-in-law, and he's a peasant."

"Then there's no way out for you," the clerk said sympathetically. "Nowadays it's knowing people that counts, not getting official certificates. If you don't know the right people, the only alternative is buying materials on the black market."

Li Shunda took this advice very seriously and from then on thought of nothing but how to buy materials on the black market. Unfortunately, it turned out that the clerk really didn't have any experience in that sort of business and had no understanding of the complexities of black market trade. Evidently ten thousand bricks would normally go for two hundred and seventeen *yuan* on the black market, and you had to pay first and then wait nearly a year before you could pick up the goods. Then, more often than not, there was the problem of swindles. Li Shunda had already been taken in once and wasn't all that eager to part with his money again. As a result he spent another three years running around — who knows how many miles he covered. He talked to hundreds upon hundreds of people without getting hold of anything.

Finally, it was the clerk who was willing to help him out again — this time he managed to buy him one ton of lime at the official price. The lime had originally been allotted for use in the silkworm house, but they had been consistently converting dry fields into rice paddies for the past year. The few remaining mulberry trees still left standing were not nearly enough to provide for even a few silkworms. So the clerk had simply taken advantage of the situation and bought up the unused lime at what was a bargain price in those days. Li Shunda was very grateful for this and wanted to buy the clerk a pack of good quality cigarettes to express his thanks. But again, he couldn't get hold of any. Then one day he happened to run into the former director of the brick and tile factory (he had since been promoted to the post of chairman of the factory revolutionary committee). Li Shunda recalled that he was always smoking good cigarettes. Surely he would be willing to sell a pack! After all, he had once treated him rather badly. So Li Shunda went off to visit the new chairman, hoping that an unabashed attempt to cotton up to him would work. It did. The chairman very readily accepted Li Shunda's fifty cents and produced an unopened pack of *Daqianmens* from his pocket. But just as he was going to hand them to Li Shunda, he opened up the pack, removed one cigarette and proceeded to light it, saying, "I've only got this one pack. I wouldn't do this favor for anyone else but you, you know."

Li Shunda took the pack, now containing only nineteen cigarettes, and presented it to the clerk, but the clerk absolutely refused to take it. Finally he smoked one, which made Li Shunda feel a little better, but insisted that he take the remaining eighteen back with him.

On the way back home, Li Shunda thought of how he had done something improper that day, something he had never done before — he had actually given cigarettes to both his enemy and his benefactor! By dinnertime he was really furious and cursed his son, calling him a good-for-nothing. It was all his fault! Twenty-five years old and still mooching off his parents!

VII

This nonsense went on for quite a few years and Li Shunda's house still hadn't been built. But he certainly had made a reputation for himself. Finally, not only was the co-op clerk moved by his tenacity and determination, but God as well. "God" in this case was none other than his future daughter-in-law, Xinlai. A girl from a neighboring village, she had long since established a relationship with Li Shunda's good-for-nothing son, Xiao Kang, and didn't care if the house hadn't been built yet. Anyway, she was already in love with him, so it could wait until after they were married. Her father, however, was adamantly opposed. No matter what anyone said to him, there was no way he was going to allow his daughter to move into a pig shed. He tried to convince Xinlai with his own exemplary behavior. After all, he had managed to build a two-room house despite his poverty. And he hadn't acquired his first daughter-in-law until he had finished it either. He cursed Li Shunda, calling him an idiot and an incompetent weakling.

But, as they say, pride goeth before a fall. Heaven just loves to play jokes. Before a year was out everything had changed. That bunch who had overthrown the capitalist roaders in the commune, now themselves the faction in power, had discovered (much to their annoyance) that a river now under their jurisdiction was as bent as an old man's back. So for the purpose of "reordering the face of the land," they insisted on mobilizing thousands of workers and using even more workdays to make it into a ramrod-straight model river. It was going to be so perfect that even those advanced life forms on Mars would praise the greatness of the planet Earth when they saw it! Unfortunately, Xinlai's family home was right smack in the riverbed of this future model river (other houses were there as well), so they had to take the house down and move. The commune gave them a moving subsidy of one hundred and fifty *yuan* per room, but still they had to borrow another three hundred *yuan* to cover all the costs involved in taking the house apart and putting it up again elsewhere, and that was only enough to re-build one room and a half. Xinlai's father lost a lot of weight in the process and his hair turned almost totally white. He had the added humiliation of having to receive an education at the hands of his own daughter, who was now recommending that he learn from Uncle Li Shunda. He was so astute, he never acted rashly and all his money was still safely stored beneath his pillow, not one penny less than when he had first put it there. Really, one has to have a good understanding of the whole situation before going out to do something like building a house! Having run out of arguments, her father had to admit defeat and allow his daughter to make her own decisions.

Li Shunda was quite pleased. In addition to having a daughter-in-law, he was aware that she had given complete theoretical affirmation of his actions. Needless to say, he was overjoyed. On his son's wedding night he had quite a few drinks. Suddenly inspired, he soon began to speak in rather mysterious ways: "A jack's better than a king nowadays, and a deuce can beat an ace. You were in too much of a hurry to build your house. We've had the biggest earthquake of the century, and people would rather live in cow sheds, so what do you still want to build a house for? My ten thousand bricks were gobbled up by the kiln demon and I still have less worries than you!" He would've continued, too, but his wife was extremely vigilant and came to his rescue immediately giving him a lecture in front of the new in-laws: "You'll say anything when you're drunk, won't you! Have you forgotten those days when your very bones ached?" she said, thus ending her husband's monologue and changing the subject, much to everyone's relief.

From that day on Li Shunda stopped thinking up vain schemes of how he would buy construction materials, contenting himself instead with wandering about here and there, carrying-pole on shoulder, collecting waste products for the state and earning a little money for living expenses. But strange as it may have seemed, there were still quite a few people out there building houses! Li Shunda couldn't help feeling terribly envious and would go to investigate almost every time he heard of a house going up, asking who had built it, where the materials had come from and so on. You could've filled a book with all the different answers he got. But actually, it wasn't all that interesting — High officials have things sent to the doorstep, minor officials go through the back door, but the common people can only beg, nothing more than that. As a result, his poor neighbors actually began to admire Li Shunda and praise him for his cleverness in having avoided many aggravations and for his remarkable understanding of the times. Finally a friend of his violated the taboo: "There isn't one brick, one tile of mine that I didn't get through the black market," he said angrily. "And it cost me the price of four rooms to build these two rooms. Then on the day I put up the roof beam, that brigade head, the one who got where he is by being a rebel, came over and invited himself to dinner. He had the nerve to say I never would've been able to build the house if it hadn't been for the Cultural Revolution! That bastard! Does he think I built my house the way he got that feudal office where he works, by fighting for it!?"

Li Shunda's knowledge of architecture had by this time already reached a high level. But who can fathom the infinite depths of the universe and nature's boundless creation? The wonders of this world are as numerous and as ceaseless as the waves in the sea — volumes could be written about them. How could anyone bear to turn away and not look? We won't deal with the petty details at great length, if you don't mind, dear reader, but it would be a real shame if we let those wonders go by without recording them for posterity. For example, there was one particular production brigade in which all the residents had to tear down their houses so that they could be rebuilt somewhere else into a "New Village," as it was to be called, consisting of neat rows of two-story buildings. All the materials that came from the old houses were sold to the commune on a depreciated basis, and if you wanted to move into one of the new houses, you had to pay out good money and buy it. Li Shunda was very excited when he heard about it because he thought that the goal of "an upstairs and a downstairs" would soon be realized. So, foregoing the scrap trade for the day, he dashed off for an on-the-spot investigation.

Li Shunda had passed through this area before, but now everything had completely changed. In every lane of every village people were tearing down their houses and moving the materials to a big field by the roadside where the first row of new buildings was going up. Everyone was discussing the issue passionately, if not fiercely, agreeing unanimously that this was the first time something like this had happened since the beginning of the world. Some people were even shedding tears. The tiles that had been stripped down from some of the roofs were still stained with ash from the kiln — it was obvious they had never been touched by rain, and now they were going to be "emancipated" again. Watching all this, Li Shunda began to feel that his failure to build his house for the past twenty years had in fact been a blessing. Still, he couldn't help feeling envious when he thought of the past efforts of the people now dismantling their houses (at least they had lived in houses!). Sighing with regret, he began to make his way home, head bowed, when suddenly he heard someone shout, "Hey! Sugar peddler!"

Lifting his head he saw an old man with a little girl standing by the roadside, watching the construction. He looked terribly familiar, but Li Shunda just couldn't remember who he was. Then the old man said with a laugh, "You mean you don't recognize me anymore?"

"Secretary Liu!" said Li Shunda, suddenly realizing who the old man was. "It's you! Are you still doing labor reform?" Who would have thought that the old secretary would've aged so fast. You could hardly recognize him! He obviously had suffered a great deal over the past few years. Li Shunda suddenly felt a wave of grief.

"I'm still laboring, all right, but I haven't reformed," answered the old secretary, still smiling. "And what about you? You here to collect some more material for your "How Very Strange" song?

"Don't make fun of me now, Secretary Liu!" said Li Shunda, feeling very embarrassed. "This is the making of a 'New Village,' that we're seeing here — you know, 'an upstairs and a downstairs'. I didn't realize until today that the difference between old and new was in these buildings, not in whether we collectivize or not."

The old secretary uttered a little sigh. "Ai! If you've got something to say, just say it," he said.

"Of course it doesn't matter if I tell you," said Li Shunda with a laugh. "But I can't deliberately break the law either. Some time ago I was criticized for expressing reactionary opinions when I said two-story buildings weren't as good as one-story buildings. But after seeing all this today I still don't like it. Such fine houses! And some of them were new, too. But they're all being torn down to be rebuilt somewhere else. And for what purpose? Why not just use all that effort and do a good job planting the fields? But not even the ghosts in hell would dare say anything like this!"

Not only did the old secretary not offer any arguments against these reactionary opinions of Li Shunda's, he nodded his head in agreement. "For what purpose? That's a good question," he answered seriously. "Let me tell you...There are some people who want to use this as their ladder to success. I think you're very well aware that the foundation of our new countryside is collectivization. But some people want to bring back the old days and they've found that the organizational form of the commune can be used to suit their goals. You've got to keep opening your eyes wider. I mean, just look at what we have here: The poor and lower-middle peasants worked so bitterly hard for twenty years to build what little housing they have, and now someone shouts, 'tear them down!' and they've got to tear them down. You think they give a damn if the masses live or die? But yet the commune is still called a commune!"

Although this was something of an awakening for Li Shunda, he still couldn't totally comprehend what Secretary Liu had said, and just stood there silently, with his mouth and eyes wide open, looking respectfully at the old man.

Secretary Liu ended his speech with an indignant snort. Then, lowering his head, he took a look at the little girl and pointed to Li Shunda. "Say 'hello grandpa'," he said.

The little girl responded affectionately, which greatly moved Li Shunda. He stuffed a piece of sugar into her little hand and called her the sweetest little doll in the world. This was the first time that fifty-four year old Li Shunda had ever been called grandpa. As an outsider who had come to Chen Village picking rags, he found it extremely heartening and was so touched by the experience that all other thoughts were dispelled from his mind.

VIII

Li Shunda didn't find out until the Spring Festival of 1977, when he went to Secretary Liu's home to take him some sugar, that the old man had assumed office again and was back working for the district. Li Shunda was overjoyed at the news, and so, after giving the little girl some sugar and eating a few of her mother's pastries, he ran off excitedly in the direction of the district office, thinking to himself that he just had to be able to get his hands on building materials now that he had a district party secretary for a friend.

The meeting between those old friends was highly affectionate, as might be expected, but as soon as Li Shunda mentioned the matter of building materials the old secretary fell silent, an expression of hesitation and disapproval coming over his face. Li Shunda's heart was a-flutter. Something had gone wrong! Then the old secretary began to speak: "I understand your difficulties, old friend," he said slowly. "I really appreciated the 'How Very Strange' song you used to sing, but you and I can't allow ourselves to do 'strange' things now, can we?"

"Secretary Liu," Li Shunda answered, "I won't if no one else does, but that sort of thing is still standard practice. Don't you think it's pretty unfair to me if I'm the only one to lose out because I don't?"

"It's a hard thing to try to change accumulated habits after ten years of general disorder. The time has come for us to set things right, and if we don't, all our plans to build China will end up nothing more than empty words. We just cannot do certain things simply because others do. As far as the district cadres go, the first step is to start with myself; as far as the masses are concerned, wouldn't it make sense to begin with the singer of the 'How Very Strange' song?"

Li Shunda was confused. He had mixed emotions about this. On the one hand, he couldn't help feeling proud that the old secretary was asking him to join in taking the lead in rectifying things; on the other hand, he couldn't help feeling disappointed that his high official friend wouldn't be of any use to him after all. Li Shunda had become rather shrewd during the Cultural Revolution and wasn't willing to lose out on that end again. After thinking about it for a bit, he began to form his answer. "Secretary Liu, I'll go along with anything you say," he said clearly and affirmatively. "But first of all, there's something I've got to say: If you don't want me to do 'strange' things, I can comply, but don't you waiver! Don't open the back door to people who are closer to you or have more prestige than me, and don't make people laugh at me and say I made friends with you for nothing. 'Cause if you do, you're going to find me rebelling against you!"

The old secretary roared with laughter. Then picking up a pen, he quickly wrote down everything Li Shunda had just said and told him, "Let me read this back to you." Then, having found that their two versions matched perfectly, he said, "Take this and have someone write it up into a big character poster and stick it up in my office."

Li Shunda was astonished: "No I won't! That would be making a fool out of you!"

"Not at all," replied the old secretary. "On the contrary, it would be of great help to me. What I'm really scared of is some of those high-prestige people coming by with their disgusting requests! If you put up the poster for me, you can help me avoid doing something that might be embarrassing."

Li Shunda cheerfully went off and followed his instructions.

Then in the winter of 1977, Li Shunda became very busy all of a sudden. The old secretary, Comrade Liu Qing, had done a little work on the director of the brick and tile factory (the old Cultural Revolution chairman) and had made him pay compensation to Li Shunda in the form of ten thousand bricks. The commune revolutionary committee had granted approval of his request to purchase eighteen concrete horizontal beams. Then that man of good will, the clerk at the supply and marketing cooperative, informed Li Shunda that rafters were now available in unlimited supply. This time around Li Shunda's house was going to get built for sure! There was no way he and his family of four could move all that stuff back by themselves, however, so he had to ask his sister and all the various in-laws to help. And come they did, rowing boats and pushing wheelbarrows — a really big production. Even Xinlai's father joined in and worked up a merry sweat!

Unfortunately, there was one little fly in the ointment, and it had a bit of a dampening effect on everyone's spirits. When it came time to transport the ten thousand bricks, events took an unexpected turn: The man at the factory refused to give them the goods even though Li Shunda had a big boat docked near the factory gates, ready to go. Putting on a false smile, he said, "You haven't bought the horizontal beams yet. If you take the bricks now they'll just sit there without being used. Why don't you wait a little longer." Li Shunda argued with the man till he was red in the face and told him the horizontal beams had already been secured. But this character understood Li Shunda better than Li Shunda did and flatly asserted that he knew he didn't have the beams yet. Fortunately, Xinlai's father ran over at this moment and quietly told Li Shunda what "horizontal beams" really meant, based on his own experience in buying bricks. This was a great revelation to Li Shunda, and he immediately went to the co-op to buy the man two cartons of the very best cigarettes. Soon afterwards, they were finally able to load up the boat with the bricks, much to everyone's delight. Later on, when it came time to pick up the concrete horizontal beams, Li Shunda didn't have to be told what to do and immediately handed a carton of cigarettes to the person in charge. (That way he could avoid having to be told that he had not bought rafters yet!)

Li Shunda felt terribly ashamed that he had done something to corrupt another person and didn't dare tell the old secretary. He could get no peace of mind afterwards either and frequently woke up in the middle of the night thinking about what he had done, scolding himself, "Damn! I really ought to change for the better!"

Manager Qiao Assumes Office

JIANG ZILONG

I

There was an awkward silence at the enlarged Party committee meeting, something which rarely occurred at the Electrical Equipment Bureau, especially when Huo Dadao was sitting in the chairman's seat. Only this time it wasn't one of those dull, depressing silences; it was more like the deadly lull that precedes fill its quota even though the Gang of Four had been out of power for two and a half years. The situation was intolerable. A capable man had to be sent there to put things right. The problem was *who* to send. Quite a number of cadres in the bureau had the free time but few were qualified and fewer still were willing to be appointed. People were anxious to be promoted, not vice versa; and who wanted to take over such a mess?

Huo remained calm as usual, his eyes sweeping about the room as he studied each face in its turn. Finally, his gaze focused on a darkly-tanned face, tough and fleshy, with bushy eyebrows, deep-set intense eyes and high cheek-bones—the very image of strength, Qiao Guangpu, director of the Electrical Appliance Company. Qiao was fidgeting with a cigarette he had taken out of Deputy Head Xu Jingang's pack. Though he had given up smoking ten years earlier during a period of illegal detention, he often fidgeted with other people's cigarettes whenever he was agitated or concentrating on something. Staring at the cigarette, he clenched his teeth and the muscle of his left cheek twitched. Huo smiled imperceptibly; he was certain now who would break the ice and what would be the solution.

56

Qiao crushed the expensive Tulip cigarette. As he reached out for another Xu stopped his hand and said, "Listen, Qiao, if you don't smoke, don't waste them like this. No wonder the smokers all steer clear of you at meetings."

The room roared with laughter.

Without raising his eyes, Qiao began to speak in a steady voice, "I'd like to work in Heavy Electrical Machinery Plant #1. I hope the committee will consider my request."

It was a bombshell. Surprised, Xu offered him a cigarette and queried, "You must be kidding, Qiao?"

It was indeed the surprise to end all surprises that Qiao should volunteer to work in a factory. He was already a company director, an important yet easy job. He had the help of the head of the bureau plus the factory managers to do all the donkey work. If things went well he'd be promoted. If the reverse, he could shift the blame to his superiors or his subordinates. All he had to do was pass on instructions and issue orders. A director had a lot of freedom and power — an easy job with good pay, an ideal one in the eyes of many old cadres. Yet Qiao wanted to leave such a post to be plant manager. What had got into his head?

Qiao's eyes scanned the meeting room and finally met Huo's. For an instant they exchanged glances.

"I'm fifty-six and pretty fit. My blood pressure's a bit high, but that doesn't matter. If I fail and the plant doesn't fulfill the quota set by the state, I'll pack up and go back to cadre school to raise chickens and ducks."

His determination left him no room for second thoughts. Huo raised his eyes and looked at him with deep appreciation. Here was a man of action, a dependable man.

"Is there anything else?"

"Yes. I'd like to have Shi Gan with me to be the party secretary. I'll be the manager. We were old partners."

This caused another stir. Everybody knew that Shi Gan was no longer the man he used to be. A modest man, what he needed was a peaceful life. Would he be willing to take the job?

For a moment Qiao was silent. His cheek began to twitch again.

"That's what you think," someone said. "But how can you be sure Shi will want to be your partner this time?"

"I've sent a car to the cadre school to fetch him. He'll have to accept whether he wants to or not. Besides..." Qiao turned to Huo and continued, "if the party committee agrees, I'm certain he'll go with me. By the way, I'd like to say a few words about job transfer. A party member must obey the party's decision. Of course, one's opinion must be considered, but it is the party which has the final say and which assigns posts to its members regardless of rank."

As Qiao was glancing at his watch, Shi entered, almost as if on cue. At first glance, he simply looked like an old peasant, but one could tell by the composure with which he made his entrance that he was in fact, an old experienced cadre who had frequented the room quite often. Shi was small and slow-moving, but his appearance concealed an underlying shrewdness. Though he had just turned sixty, his face, creased with deep lines, made him appear much older. He nodded like a stranger in response to the warm greetings of his ex-colleagues, keeping his mouth shut, not uttering a sound. He refused the seat Huo offered him and remained standing, ready to leave any minute as if not knowing why he had been summoned.

Qiao rose to his feet and said, "I shall first talk it over with Shi."

Then he took Shi's arm and walked him out of the room. After they sat themselves down in armchairs in Huo's office, Qiao looked at Shi, distressed to see that he seemed a different man.

In 1958, after completing his studies in the Soviet Union, Qiao was appointed the manager of Heavy Electrical Machinery Plant #1 and Shi Gan was made the party secretary. As a result of their efforts the plant soon became a model. Shi was a witty, humorous fellow and a good talker. During the Cultural Revolution much of what he had said was criticized. During his illegal detention Shi often remarked to Qiao, "All my troubles were caused by my tongue. It spills out whatever's in my mind." He got particularly irritated when being interrogated by the so-called rebels at criticism meetings. If he kept silent they accused him of being uncooperative; if he answered them it only added more fuel to the fire. Qiao, who was also criticized at the same time had a way of dealing with his interrogators. He called it "tuning out." At first, like Shi, he listened attentively to those criticisms, but the more he listened the angrier he became. He would perspire profusely and afterwards was completely exhausted. Then gradually he got used to it. Qiao was fond of Beijing opera, so in meetings he'd tune out and silently sing an aria to himself. Quite pleased with himself, he told Shi about his method. Unfortunately, Beijing opera was not Shi's cup of tea and it didn't work for him.

Once, in the autumn of 1967, during a struggle meeting, Shi was ordered to stand on a makeshift platform set on two trucks. Getting down at the end of the meeting, he slipped and fell, biting off the tip of his tongue. Saying nothing, he swallowed the blood in pain. Since then the two friends had separated. Shi never again spoke in public. When his injury had healed he was sent to do physical labor in the bureau's cadre school. Later, when he was offered work in the city, he refused, saying he couldn't talk. When the news of the Gang's arrest was announced, Shi went to the city and drank wine in celebration. But he returned to the cadre school that same night because he could not leave his "three armies." He was responsible for hundreds of chickens, dozens of ducks and a flock of sheep and so was nicknamed the "Commander of Three Armies." He had resolved to live in the countryside for the rest of his life. But early that morning Qiao had sent a friend to fetch him on the pretext that there would be an important meeting.

Having told Shi what was on his mind, Qiao waited hopefully for his support.

Under Shi's strange, inquiring gaze Qiao became rather uneasy. There seemed to be a disturbing remoteness and distrust between old friends. At last Shi spoke in a low, indistinct voice. "Why on earth pick me? I won't take the job!"

"Listen, Shi!" Qiao's voice was anxious. "Do you really want to hide away like a hermit in the country? Are you as scared of struggle as others say?"

Shi nodded. But Qiao jumped to his feet, denying it. "No! You're not like that! You can fool others but not me!"

"I've only got half a tongue...I'd bite off the rest if I could!"

"Nonsense! You've got two tongues. One to help me and one to convince people. You often encouraged me in crises. No one can replace you. You're the best party secretary I've ever met. You must come and work with me now."

Shi sighed. For an instant there was agony in his eyes. "I'm a disabled man," he said. "I can't give you any help. I may even disappoint you."

"Pull yourself together, Shi! You're more than a gifted speaker and you've got a good head on your shoulders. You've lots of experience and guts. On top of all that we've worked well together for years. All I'm asking is that you give me advice at crucial moments."

Still shaking his head, Shi replied, "I'm way out of date and I've no energy left."

"What crap!" Qiao was about to lose his temper. "You're as fit as a fiddle. How can you talk like that? OK, you lost part of your tongue, but that doesn't mean you lost your whole head!"

"I mean I just don't give a damn any more!"

"What?" Qiao yanked Shi to his feet and looked straight into his eyes, then snapped, "Just say that again! Where's your confidence in the party? Your courage? Your sense of responsibility?"

Shi tried to avoid Qiao's eyes. He felt ashamed for being such a coward. But he would never admit it publicly.

In a mocking tone Qiao said as if to himself, "It's ironic really. The Central Party Committee's determined to modernize our country, and now that the main obstacles have been removed all we need is good leaders. Yet look at our cadres. No confidence, no guts! If you ask them to do something they try to pass the buck or simply refuse with all kinds of excuses. Don't they feel any responsibility as party members? I'm like a soldier. Ask me to do something and I'll try my best. There's nothing strange in that, but some people these days take it as seeking the limelight. Perhaps others call me a fool behind my back!"

Shi was hurt again; his shoulders shook. Qiao added earnestly, "Shi, you must come with me, even if I have to drag you there."

"Listen, Giant..." Shi began after a sigh. The familiar nickname immediately warmed Qiao's heart. But Shi resumed his distant tone again, "So long as you won't regret it, I don't mind. If you think I'm no good, just tell me so. I can go back to the cadre school."

When the two returned to the meeting room the members had already reached a decision.

"Qiao will take up his new post tomorrow,' Huo told Shi, "and you can go there in a couple of days. Have a rest first. If you don't feel quite fit, go to the hospital for a thorough check-up."

Shi Gan nodded and left.

Huo turned to Qiao and said, "Someone's anxious to take your place!" He then eyed the others and asked, "Any other recommendations? Better put your cards on the table now and let us see them."

There was a deathly silence. They all knew Huo's rule: Speak up at a meeting or forget it.

Xu, Huo's deputy, broke the silence by saying, "Ji Shen of the same plant Qiao is going to hopes to be transferred to work in the electrical appliance company under the bureau because he's not in good health." After him some other members made their recommendations.

His eyes gleaming, Huo said angrily, "Recommending oneself isn't something new. After all, Qiao recommended himself. But your recommendations are completely different. If we accepted them all we'd have fifteen deputies in the bureau. The six companies under the bureau would have ten or fifteen directors each. I doubt if they'd accept that. If you aren't fit enough to work in the factories, how can you be fit to work in the company? It isn't a rest home. Do you think the work here isn't important? All those who need to recuperate can take sick leave. Go and register in the organization department. But we won't accept just anyone. We'd rather leave places vacant than appoint parasites at the expense of the country. I like Qiao's style of work. From now on, those who do well will be rewarded and promoted, while those who make serious errors will be penalized and demoted! Some cadres pester their friends to find them new posts when they fail at their own jobs. This only encourages officials to hold on to one job while seeking a better one. No wonder the workers say that their managers aren't really interested in their work. How can a cadre run a factory well with this mentality?"

Xu spoke up again. "Ji Shen is the manager of the electrical machinery plant. Now that we've decided to send Qiao and Shi there, what should he do?"

"He can be the deputy manager," Huo said firmly. "If he does well he'll be promoted. If he doesn't he'll be demoted until he finds a job he can do. Of course, this is my opinion. We can discuss it."

Xu whispered to Qiao, "Things will be worse when you get there."

Qiao shrugged, "I never expected it to be easy."

II

It was late in the evening when Qiao got home. The air in his room was rather stale, so he opened the door and windows. He was thirsty for a cup of tea, but since there was no hot water in the thermos, he had to make do with cold water. Then sitting at his desk he selected a book entitled *Metallurgy* from beneath a stack of books. He drew out a photo, the background of which was Lenin's tomb in Moscow's Red Square. In the foreground stood Qiao and a girl. In his light western suit Qiao looked young and very handsome but faintly ill at ease. The attractive girl was smiling at him sweetly. Qiao closed his eyes and buried his head in his hands. The photo slipped from his fingers to the desk....

In 1957 Qiao, already in his final year of study in the Soviet Union, had gone to gain practical experience in the Leningrad Power Plant as an assistant manager. Tong Zhen, the girl in the photo, was a college student working on her graduation thesis. She was soon attracted to Qiao, a man who was intolerant of fear, suspicion and flattery. Tong fell in love with him despite the fact that he was ten years her senior and married. Qiao, too, was very happy to meet another Chinese in this foreign land and treated her like a younger sister, protecting her as if she were still a child. But that was not what she wanted. Sometimes she felt jealous, seeing him brooding, missing his wife.

Qiao returned home first and was appointed the manager of Electrical Machinery Plant #1, a new enterprise which badly needed technicians. Tong, after graduation in 1958, returned to work under Qiao. Tong's nephew, Xi Wangbei, was an apprentice in the same plant. By chance he discovered that his aunt was in love with Qiao. Being headstrong and suspicious, Xi began to hate Qiao, believing he was trifling with his aunt. Though ten years younger, he appointed himself his aunt's guardian and kept an eye on her. He went out of his way to prevent her from meeting Qiao. Quite a few young men wanted to court her but Tong sent them away, saying she would never marry. This made Xi even more irritated and he put all the blame on Qiao. In his eyes, Qiao was a playboy who was ruining his aunt's life.

Seven years later the Cultural Revolution started. Xi became the leader of a faction and Qiao was the main target of his attack. Apart from labeling Qiao as a capitalist roader, Xi called him a womanizer. To protect his aunt he never went into details. Some of his men, however, were interested in the romantic angle and magnified the whole affair by making up stories about Tong and Qiao. Tong was greatly hurt. In her eyes people like Qiao, who were able to run a modern factory, were rare. He had enjoyed high prestige before, but now his reputation was ruined. People did not really hate those who had not followed the party line, but those who were immoral were always despised. How could she clarify the situation? She blamed herself for making Qiao suffer more than other so-called capitalist roaders. She wrote to tell him that she had decided to commit suicide. But Xi, ever cautious, caught her in time. Since then Qiao had felt indebted to the two women in his life.

Qiao's wife had been the head of the propaganda department in a university. In spite of the gossip about her husband, she had never doubted him. She died mysteriously when being illegally detained for investigation in early 1968. With bitter regrets Qiao confessed before the portrait of his late wife that he had once wavered before Tong's passionate words and that he had sometimes felt drawn to her. He made a vow never to speak to Tong again. When his youngest son started college Qiao was left alone, leading the life of a monk, as if deliberately torturing himself to show his faithfulness to his late wife and children.

He didn't know what prompted him to ring Tong up and ask her to come over. "What do I want?" he asked himself in surprise. If he had not volunteered to return to the plant, the affair would have been finished forever. How could they work together again after all that trouble? Only ten years ago they were cruelly slandered. Now Qiao realized that Tong was still important to him despite his efforts to forget her. His feelings were so complicated, he could not work them out. "Better get a grip on yourself," he told himself. "There's a lot to do tomorrow." All of a sudden he sensed someone at his shoulder. He looked up. His heart missed a beat when he saw Tong standing beside him. He jumped to his feet and gripped her hands, whispering, "Tong Zhen! Tong!..."

Tong shuddered and withdrew her hands from his hold. Then she turned around, wiped away her tears and made an effort to control herself. Her appearance had changed so much that Qiao was quite shocked. Though she was only a little over forty, Tong's hair was streaked with grey. Her soft black eyes conveyed a deep bitterness. There was no sign of their former warmth and courage. Qiao's heart ached. This promising and talented woman engineer could have done much. Now there was no sign of the idealistic, energetic girl she had once been. Was it only time which had made her age so quickly?

Both of them felt rather awkward. Though Qiao searched for warm yet suitable words to break the silence, in the end he blurted out, "Tong, why didn't you get married?" He hadn't intended to ask this. Even his voice didn't sound right.

"What do you mean?" she retorted.

He waved his hand as if brushing away all duplicity. Suddenly he came closer to her and said, "Why should I pretend? Tong, let's get married. Tomorrow or the day after tomorrow? Agreed?"

Though she had waited for this moment for twenty years, Tong was almost thrown off balance by his proposal.

"Isn't it a bit sudden?" she said softly. "Why the rush?"

Now that the ice was broken, Qiao replied with his usual enthusiasm and strength. "Look, our hair is already grey. How can you talk about rushing it? We don't need to prepare anything for the wedding. We can just throw a party and announce our marriage, that's all."

Her face, glowing with happiness, looked younger. "You know how I feel," she murmured. "You decide."

"So it's settled," he said joyfully, holding her hand again. "When I go back to work at the plant tomorrow, I'll tell our friends and relatives that our wedding will take place the day after tomorrow."

"Go back to the plant to work?" Tong was startled.

"Yes. The bureau's party committee decided this morning that Shi Gan and I should go back to the plant. You know we're old partners."

"Oh no! No!" Tong protested. She wanted to be transferred after their wedding to a new factory where no one would know anything about their past and where they could live in peace. But how would people at the plant react to Qiao's return and their marriage? She shuddered at the thought of the gossip and slander. Moreover, Xi, who had been Qiao's most vicious persecutor, was now a deputy manager. How could they work together?

"You're doing very well in the company," she said unhappily. "Why do you want to come back?"

"The work in the company doesn't really suit me," he replied. "I don't like office work."

"Our plant's a mess. Do you think you can sort things out?"

"Well, if we let all the big factories like ours remain in chaos, modernization will remain a dream. Getting the plant into shape will be like commanding a battle in a war. I don't like playing just a minor role. I'm not too old. I want to accomplish something before it's too late."

Tong's feelings were a mixture of happy surprise and uneasiness. It had been his sense of responsibility to his work, his ability and his masculinity that had made her love him. Now many years later, though he was still the same man, she was asking him to give up his career. She murmured, "I've never seen a man his age with such drive."

"Drive, like youthfulness, is independent of age. It doesn't only belong to the young, nor does it vanish with age." He saw how she had aged not only in her appearance but also in her ideas. People were fed up with politics; their psychological wounds were difficult to heal. He suddenly felt that a big responsibility had been placed on him. Hugging her like a young man, Qiao said warmly, "I say, engineer, where are all the plans you kept whispering to me about? Don't you remember you wanted to make 600,000, 1,000,000 or 1,500,000 kilowatt generators? We even hoped to build the first nuclear power station in our country with a capacity of a million kilowatts. Have you forgotten all that?"

Her engineer's heart began to thaw.

Qiao continued, "We must get the latest information from abroad. In the fifties and early sixties we could keep up to date. But now I know nothing about new developments. By the way, after our marriage will you teach me English for an hour a day?"

Tong nodded warmly, looking into his eyes. She felt secure beside him, more determined and confident. "Funny, you haven't changed in the least. After all you've been through you're still so idealistic," she said with a grin.

"How can we alter our nature?" he chuckled. Not wishing to change the subject, he continued to encourage her, his eyes fixed on the slender woman. "I was put through the mill—so what? You know the old saying, 'Stone whets a sword; hardships strengthen will power.'"

He asked her to show him around the plant. She was reluctant and he teased her. "What was the word you cursed me with? I remember, it was 'coarse,' wasn't it? Funny, how this 'coarse' man can talk about love? Listen, love is a strong passion. You've longed for it. Now it's here. You don't have to fear it, let alone hide your feelings and suffer for it. I'm only worried that your passion is drying up like your interest in politics."

"Nonsense!" Tong denied, blushing. "A woman's love never dries up." Overwhelmed by emotion, she kissed him passionately.

On their way to the plant she persuaded him not to marry her right away on the pretext that, for her, her wedding day was of vital importance and that she had paid a lot more for it than other women. She wanted ample time to prepare. Qiao agreed.

III

The two of them first entered Workshop Eight which was nearest the entrance. The familiar look of the shop floor made every bone in Qiao's body cry out for work. His hands were itching to touch the lathes. Then he thought of the twelve advanced workers whom he had trained, each in charge of a processing section.

"All your advanced workers are in other jobs now," Tong told him. "They have become foremen, warehouse keepers, janitors, inspectors and so on. Don't you remember how four of them condemned you at the criticism meeting, saying you had corrupted them with material incentives? Don't you feel any grudges against them?

"No," Qiao said firmly. "At those meetings, everybody raised their fists and shouted slogans against me. If I begrudged that, I wouldn't be back here. If those twelve men are no longer pacesetters, then I'll have to train new ones. We must have the most skillful workers and best products."

While talking to Tong, Qiao walked from lathe to lathe. Nothing pleased him more than feasting his eyes on purring machines turning out top quality products.

Qiao halted before a young man who was casually throwing turbine blades onto a pile on the ground while humming a foreign pop song. Qiao picked up some of the blades to examine them and found that most were defective. Staring at the young worker, he snapped, "Stop singing!"

Not knowing who Qiao was, the youngster winked at Tong and sang louder:

> O mother!
> Please keep your cool.
> Young people are just fools!

"Stop it!" Qiao shouted. His authoritative voice and furious eyes startled the turner. "Are you a lathe operator or a rag-picker?" he continued, "I bet you don't know anything about the operating rules!"

Obviously Qiao was an official, and his air of authority silenced the youth. Taking a white handkerchief from Tong, Qiao wiped the lathe. The handkerchief turned black.

"So is this the way you look after your lathe?" Qiao demanded, his eyes fixed on the young man. "Keep this handkerchief hanging on your lathe until you've cleaned it. If I can't pick up any dirt with it the next inspection, you can have a white towel."

Many workers had gathered around them.

"Comrades," Qiao said to them, "I'll ask the equipment section to hang a white towel on each of your lathes tomorrow. Let the towel tell us in the future whether or not you look after your machines well."

Some of the old workers recognized Qiao and quietly withdrew. Red in the face, the young lathe operator was too embarrassed to say anything. He nervously hung the blackened handkerchief on a lever which he apparently had never touched. This brought him more trouble.

Qiao, having noticed the dirty, greasy lever, asked, "What's that lever for?"

"I don't know."

"But there's a notice explaining how to use it, isn't there?"

"It's in a foreign language. I don't understand it."

"How long have you been working at this lathe?"

"Six years."

"And for six years you've never touched that lever?"

The young man nodded. His face contorted in anger, Qiao turned to the others. "Who can tell him how this works?"

No one replied. Some certainly did not know, while others did not want to further embarrass their young comrade.

"Engineer, will you tell him?" Qiao asked Tong.

Tong, to ease the tension, explained what it was for and how it worked.

"What's your name?" Qiao asked.

"Du Bing."

"Du Bing, eh? Well, Du Bing, you hum while you work; you don't grease your lathe in six years. I won't forget your name, you can be sure of that!" Then changing his tone from sarcastic to severe, Qiao continued: "Tell your foreman that this lathe needs overhauling at once. I'm the new manager."

When Qiao and Tong turned to leave, they heard someone whisper, "Just your luck, Du Bing. He's our former manager!"

Another said, "An expert like him, he knows at a glance what's wrong."

"With bums like him around," Qiao said angrily, "even the best equipment we import will be damaged."

"Do you think he's one of the worst?" Tong asked.

"Well, I find it shocking that not a single person bothered to look into such matters for six years. The cadres are so careless, so irresponsible. As a chief engineer, I must say you've done pretty well!" Qiao added, tongue in cheek.

"But if the manager is so negligent, how can you blame people like us? Tong retorted indignantly.

As they entered Workshop Seven they saw a young German testing a boring machine. Qiao was impressed when he was informed that the young foreigner had been working day and night since his arrival in China. Tong told him that he had been sent by the German firm, Siemens, to iron out the snags in the electrical part assembly operation. His name was Therl and he was only twenty-three years old. This was his first visit to the Orient, and he had come via Japan which was why he was seven days late. Afraid that this might be reported to his firm, he had worked extremely hard and had solved the problem within three days instead of the scheduled seven or ten. Though he was an expert and a hard worker, he liked to tell jokes and have a good time.

"He's so young, yet he's able to do the job independently abroad," Qiao said in admiration. Then he sent Tong to get the foreman in charge of work that day. Before the man could greet him, Qiao said, "Ask all those under thirty to come here and watch how Therl works. And ask Therl to say something about himself and how he learned his skill. I'm thinking of inviting him to give a talk to all our young workers before he leaves."

The man did not question Qiao's identity and complied with a smile.

Qiao heard some people murmuring behind him and turned around. They were workers from Workshop Eight, who had rushed to see him when they had learned that Qiao was the man who had severely criticized Du Bing.

"You won't learn anything by staring at me," Qiao told them. "Go and watch that young German over there." He sent a man to gather all the young workers in his workshop together, especially Du Bing.

Just as he finished speaking an old worker pulled him aside and whispered. "Do you want a foreigner to set an example?"

Qiao was startled to see that the man was Shi Gan! In his overalls and old blue cap he looked like a worker. Qiao was glad to see that Shi still had some fighting spirit left.

Shi seemed a little sullen, regretting his decision. Earlier that afternoon he took a look around and talked to a few workers whom he did not know. Because of his injury, he spoke indistinctly, and people thought something must be wrong with him. In this way he learned a lot that Qiao could not. The workers in this plant were rather confused ideologically. The idol many had worshipped was gone. They had lost their national pride and faith in socialism. After years of being deceived, manipulated and criticized, they had become demoralized. In addition, there were three groups of cadres in the plant: those who had been cadres before the Cultural Revolution; those who had risen to power during it; and the group Ji Shen had brought with him. The older people still hurt, while the young felt resentful. Shi worried that one day the contradictions would flare up and the three groups would clash head on, causing renewed conflict within the party. Not only chaos awaited Qiao and him, but also bitter political rivalries. They were up against a very difficult situation.

Shi was furious with himself for getting involved in such a mess. Political struggles had taught him a great deal. Now he seldom became excited in public and avoided pretentiousness of any kind. With his feelings thus hidden, he believed he could resist any temptation. So how on earth did Qiao persuade him that very morning? He was quite certain that this return would do both of them no good. Qiao could never be a politician. He had begun working even before the announcement of his appointment. That was no way for a manager to behave. He did not want to talk to Qiao right now, but, surprised to see Tong beside Qiao, could not help warning him, "You musn't get married for at least six months."

"What do you mean?" Qiao was perplexed.

Shi told him briefly that the news of the management reshuffle had leaked out and that some were gossiping that Qiao had only come back to marry Tong Zhen.

"All right," Qiao said shortly, "I might as well be hanged for a sheep as for a lamb. We'll hold the wedding ceremony in the auditorium tomorrow evening. You'll be our witness."

Shi tried to leave but Qiao caught him. Then Shi complained, "Didn't you ask me to give you advice? But when I do you don't listen!"

After a while Qiao muttered, "OK. I'll listen to you. After all, it's a personal thing. But tell me, the decision to reshuffle was made only this morning. How on earth did people learn about it this afternoon?"

"That's nothing unusual. These days news travels faster over the grapevine than through official channels. Rumors are proved by documents. Right now the plant's party committee is having an urgent meeting. My instinct tells me it has something to do with our return." But instantly Shi regretted telling him what he had guessed. He must keep a hold on his emotions. Once again, he felt himself sinking in a swamp with Qiao.

On an impulse Qiao dragged Shi and Tong to the plant building. The meeting room on the first floor was brightly lit, with cigarette smoke filtering out of its wide open windows. Someone was making a speech in a loud voice, talking about the next day's production campaign. This worried Qiao. He immediately went to make a phone call to Huo Dadao. Then the three of them entered the room.

IV

People were surprised at the sudden appearance of the three gate crashers. Ji Shen fixed his eyes on Tong, who immediately looked away, wishing to escape since she wasn't on the party committee.

"What's brought you here?" Ji asked, as though he knew nothing about the reshuffle.

"Just taking a look," Qiao said in a loud voice. "We heard that you were having a discussion on production. We'd like to know what you think."

"Fine! Fine!"

Ji looked haggard. He had fine yet inscrutable features. "There are two items on today's agenda," he explained. "One, the suspension of Xi Wangbei at the request of the people. Two, tomorrow's production campaign. In the past I spent too much time and energy on political movements and not enough on production. But all the members of the committee are confident. Once the campaign gets going, things will improve. Comrades, we can be more specific. Qiao and Shi are the former leaders of our plant. Perhaps they can give us some good advice."

He was an experienced man, composed and steady. He was hoping to impress Qiao with how he conducted a meeting. That very afternoon he had learned of the bureau's decision by telephone and he bitterly regretted ever having joined the bureau.

It was true that he had been persecuted by the Gang of Four for ten years. But he did not suffer much because he was working as a deputy principal of a municipal cadre school in the countryside. At that time, when the cadre school was still regarded as a good socialist development, Ji realized that hiding with so many other unfortunate prominent people would be his safest bet. Being a deputy-principal, he had the opportunity to become acquainted with former high-ranking officials with whom it would have been very difficult to get in contact had it not been for the school. As Ji's subordinates, they had come to feel grateful to him for making life a little easier for them in terms of accommodations, food, work and holidays. Besides, he found it easy to get along with people, and they, in turn, found him very agreeable. Now, since most of them had been restored to their former posts, Ji had friends in many high places and had become a man of influence himself.

Two years ago he had started working in the Electrical Equipment Bureau, fully aware of the importance of this industry for China's modernization. He had experience only in personnel work and knew nothing about production. In order to get some practical experience he had asked to work in this electrical machinery plant for a couple of years. He knew that it was very useful to be a manager of a big factory because now construction and the economy were being stressed. It would pave the way for him to climb higher. He dreamed of becoming an important cadre in the bureau where he might have a chance to visit other countries. If you had been abroad, your future would be even brighter. Ji worked hard, but being only a bureaucrat and too cautious politically, he did things according to the way the wind blew. Naturally he was slow to act. When a difficult problem came up he tried to avoid it. Sophisticated yet crafty, he put his individual interests above everything else. But with these inclinations, how could he run a factory where the problems were practical and specific? In another place he might have muddled along, but certainly not here under the eyes of Huo Dadao. Ji knew that success was not merely a stroke of luck and that it depended on ability and struggle. That was why he was banking everything on a new production campaign. If that raised production, he could leave the plant a hero. Moreover, by dismissing Xi from his post, he would leave a thorny problem for Qiao which would certainly unseat him in time. The heat would be off Ji and there would be no one to judge his inadequacy. Shi, however, was not fooled, and Qiao also saw through Ji's trick.

Everybody at the meeting wondered what Qiao and Shi were up to, appearing so late at night. They were not really interested in this campaign business. Noticing the group's mood, Ji hurried to close the meeting, thinking he could thus achieve his ends. Just as he was clearing his throat to speak, Huo Dado entered. His arrival caused more commotion.

After asking what they were discussing, Huo, without any pre-ambles, announced the bureau party committee's decision to reshuffle. And finally he added, "Due to the chief engineer's long absence because of ill health, the bureau has decided to promote Tong Zhen to be the assistant chief engineer."

Tong was taken by surprise and felt very nervous. She could not understand why Qiao had not even hinted about it.

These announcements came like a lightning blow to Ji Shen. He was almost speechless for once. Checking his anger with great effort, he forced a smile and said, "Of course I accept the decisions. Both Qiao and Shi are old hands here, and I'm sure they'll do a better job than I." Then he continued, turning to Qiao and Shi, "Tomorrow I'll talk things over with you. Do you have anything to add?"

Instead of speaking, Shi closed his eyes halfway.

"I hadn't the faintest idea about the suspension of Comrade Xi," Qiao said without formality. He could not help eyeing Xi, who was sitting in a corner. By chance he caught Xi's angry glare. He averted his gaze at once and continued, "I'm not for the campaign either. Well, Comrade Ji, you're suffering from coronary thrombosis, aren't you? Can you run at top speed five times from the ground floor to the seventh floor of this office building?"

Not knowing what Qiao was driving at, Ji smiled blankly.

Qiao continued, "Well, our plant is like you, a man with coronary thrombosis. To make it leap forward will only mean suicide. To fulfill our quota by campaigns every month is no way to run a plant."

His words struck the right chord, inasmuch as the committee members had also been wondering why Ji wanted to launch a campaign to coincide with the change of leadership. With a sneer

Ji struck a match and lit a cigarette.

Noticing Ji's expression, Qiao, who had planned to say just a few words to show his attitude toward the decisions, shifted to another subject. "I haven't seen a good play for years," he said sharply, "so I can't tell if there are any good new stage directors around. But in industry I know there are a number of political directors. Whenever there's a political movement or a problem in work, they call mass meetings, give pep talks and organize parades. They shout slogans, hold criticism meetings and launch campaigns.... Factories are their stages, the workers their actors and actresses. They direct them as they wish. They're no more than cheap propagandists. They can never make good managers for a modern socialist country. Maybe it's easier to run a factory that way, but the consequences will be endless. Modernization can never be achieved by a few so-called 'campaigns.'"

Sensing something, Qiao turned to Shi who was gesturing to him to shut up. Qiao then said, "Perhaps I've gone a bit too far. By the way, I want to tell you that Tong and I got married two hours ago. Shi was our witness. We didn't want to make a fuss since neither of us is young anymore. We'll invite you for a drink later."

Surprised and delighted at this news, people began to congratulate Qiao and Tong as soon as the meeting was dismissed.

Only Tong, Shi and Xi, for their own reasons, were greatly annoyed by Qiao's announcement. Tong, in a huff, was the first to walk out of the meeting room. Without saying goodbye to Qiao she went straight to the entrance of the plant.

Huo, noticing this, nudged Qiao and urged him to chase after Tong. After Qiao had gone, Huo stopped the others who wanted to tease the bride by saying, "He's a smart one, isn't he? I've never heard of marriage first and drinks later. What about going to his home for a few drinks?"

Qiao had caught up with Tong. Her voice shaking she said, "Have you gone mad? Don't you know how people will talk tomorrow?"

"That's just what I want," Qiao explained. "Now it's out in the open, you'll have no more worries and you can concentrate on your work. Otherwise you'll be nagging at me and tormenting yourself all the time. Even an innocent walk with me would worry you to death. The more suspiciously you acted, the more trouble you'd get into. Then we would be the victims of rumor and gossip again. I'm the manager now. You're the assistant chief engineer. Hou could we cooperate under those circumstances? Now that we've made it clear that we're husband and wife, let those who wish to talk about us talk. They'll soon get bored with it. I made up my mind to announce it right on the spot. There wasn't time to consult you."

Tong's eyes glittered under the lamplight, her anger diminished. This was a day of great meaning for her, as both a woman and an engineer. A deep emotion stirred within her, as if a fire, long since dead, had been rekindled.

Huo and Shi caught up with them. Huo gripped Tong's hand congratulating her on the good news. A deep emotion stirred Tong.

Huo then told two women committee members to use his car to drive the bride to her room. "Dress her up," he said, "Then escort her to her new home. We'll be waiting there."

Tong said to Huo, "Don't bother. We'll go and register first."

"Will there be a big celebration?" one of the women asked.

"Maybe. Anyway, at least there will be some wedding sweets." Everybody laughed.

Qiao and Tong looked at Huo with gratitude.

V

It had been a fortnight since Qiao assumed office, but nothing happened; no instructions, no meetings. He was not even in his office. Where was he?

He was with the workers all day long. When you wanted him, he was nowhere to be found, yet he'd pop right up in front of you when you least expected him. No one knew what he was up to. He seemed to have relinquished his authority and let the departments, offices and workshops go to pot. Without a leader the workers did whatever they liked. The result was anarchy, and production dropped rapidly.

The bureau's operations center felt the situation was intolerable. They asked Huo several times to go there and do something about it. Huo refused to raise a finger. When pressed too hard he said tartly, "Don't you worry! Before the tiger springs, it crouches back a little. Don't you know that?"

Shi was anxious and puzzled too. He asked Qiao, "What are you waiting for? Do you have a plan?"

"Oh, yes!" Qiao replied readily. "Our plant is just like a sick man suffering from several ailments. We must find the right remedies to cure them. Before we start we must make sure our diagnosis is correct."

Shi darted a glance at Qiao who looked determined and self-confident.

"I've found out something important during the last two weeks," Qiao continued cheerfully. "Our workers and cadres aren't as apathetic as you imagined. Quite a number of them are really concerned about state affairs and our future. They make suggestions to me, argue with me, and even criticize me, saying I've let them down. It's not a bad thing to have a short period of confusion. This helps us to separate the lambs from the goats. I've already picked out a few people in my mind who will play an important role in my plan." He narrowed his eyes as he thought about the plant's future.

"Isn't today your birthday?" Shi asked all of a sudden.

"Birthday? What birthday?" Qiao was puzzled. Leafing through the calendar, he suddenly realized it was. "Well, well! My birthday today. Thanks for remembering!"

"Someone asked me if you were going to accept presents and throw a party."

"Hell no! But if you'd like to come, I'll offer you a drink."

Shi shook his head.

When Qiao got home, dinner was ready. On the table were food and wine. A woman has a good memory for such matters. Though just married, Tong remembered Qiao's birthday. Happily Qiao sat down to eat. But Tong stopped him and said with a smile, "I've invited Xi to come. Shall we wait for him?"

"Did you invite anybody else?"

'No."

Obviously she wanted the two to bury the hatchet. Qiao understood his wife's intention, but in fact he couldn't have cared less that Xi had once attacked him.

Instead of Xi, they were surprised by the arrival of a group of older cadres from the plant who had been middle-level officials before the Cultural Revolution. While some were still the heads of certain departments, offices or workshops, others were no longer cadres.

"We've come to celebrate your birthday, Old Qiao," They all greeted him jubilantly.

"Forget it," Qiao said. "If you want some wine, there's plenty. But forget about the birthday business. Who told you that?"

One bald headed man, a former head of administration, said sincerely, "Old Qiao, you may have forgotten us, but we haven't forgotten you!"

"Come now! Who says I've forgotten you?"

"Well, haven't you? You've been back for half a month. All of us have been expecting something to happen. You've really disappointed us. You know Liu, the manager of the boiler plant, don't you? The day he returned to his office he threw a dinner party that evening and invited all his old cadres. What a feast! Of course, it wasn't the food or drink that mattered, but it gave them a chance to air their grievances. The following day all of them went back to their former posts. Good old Liu! He didn't let his old comrades down!"

This got Qiao angry, but he made an effort to control himself. After all, this was his new home, not the place for a showdown.

"In the two years since the Gang fell, you still haven't let off steam?"

"The Gang's followers are still around! Xi will soon be reinstated after only a month's suspension...."

Talk of the devil! Xi suddenly entered and obviously caught the last sentence. Feigning indifference, he nodded to Qiao and sat down facing them. In fact he was ready for a fight. Sensing fireworks, Tong cleverly changed the subject and led Xi to another room on some pretext.

The guests looked at each other and rose to leave. Their bald headed leader said sarcastically, "Oh, I see. The feast isn't for us. No wonder the whiz kid will be back to his job so soon. You've made up. Fair enough, you're relatives after all."

Qiao did not insist on their staying but said coldly, "Wang, to put it bluntly, all you want is to go back to your old job or, better still, be promoted, right? Don't worry. Our trouble isn't that we have too many cadres in this plant. We need a lot more. Of course, I mean capable people who know how to do their jobs. There'll be an examination tomorrow. I don't think it matters if I tell you now. We've all been in this plant a long time and should know about such things as balanced production, standardization, systematization and detailed specifications."

The men were flabbergasted. They'd never heard such terms. What shocked them most was that even the cadres had to take the exam.

Someone grumbled, "This is very new, isn't it?"

"What's new about it?" Qiao retorted. "From now on, no one will be allowed to muddle along whether he is a worker or a cadre. To be frank, I'm most unhappy about the plant and have a lot more to complain about than you. It's time we got down to work."

Seeing the visitors off with an abrupt wave of the hand, Qiao returned to the table, scowling furiously. In an attempt to fill up the uncomfortable silence that ensued, Xi nervously sought to draw Qiao into a discussion on a number of neutral subjects as they ate, but with no success. Finally as Tong re-filled their bowls with rice, Qiao broke his silence: "You know pretty well, Xi, the decision to suspend you was not made by the new party committee. Shi must have told you that your case has been cleared. Why do you still refuse to work?"

"I want the party committee to make it clear to all the workers and staff members in the plant why I was suspended from my work. Now the investigation is over. It's been proved that, first, I never raided anybody's home or office; and second, I had no personal connection with the Gang of Four. Why did you pick on me? Just because I was the head of a faction, or because I'm a so-called new cadre? How could you make a decision based on rumor like that?

Seeing him wave his chopsticks with indignation, Qiao thought, "So now you know what it's like! You slandered others, didn't you?"

As if guessing what was in his mind, Xi changed the subject, "I request to work on the shop floor."

"What?" This was rather unusual. New cadres would never quit their jobs unless they were demoted due to their involvement with the Gang. But Xi had the guts to ask for it. Was he bluffing? Anyway, Qiao called his bluff by saying, "Fine! I agree. In fact, respect doesn't come with an appointment. You have to earn it. Many people can be high fliers, some through their own efforts, while others are tossed up by the wind. I hope you're not looking for a wind like that again."

Xi sneered. "I don't know what wind you're talking about! If I were an opportunist I wouldn't have been suspended from my job. Twenty years ago I was an apprentice. I've been a worker, a group leader, a foreman, and when I was a little over thirty I became a deputy manager, a 'whiz kid,' as some of them called me. I'm willing to go down to the shop floor instead of holding on to the death like some others. Actually, those who once were officials still crave more power and promotion."

This was a bit too much—the old cadres blamed Qiao for favoring the young, whereas the new ones insinuated that he was a bureaucrat.

Tong offered Qiao some food, afraid he might lose his temper. But Qiao relaxed, mulling over what Xi had just said.

Xi knew that Qiao would never give him sympathy if he pleaded with him, but might soften if he were tough. A coward would never win his respect. Better to be tough with him.

"When will we Chinese rid ourselves of one-sidedness?" he went on. "During the Cultural Revolution nearly all the cadres were attacked and removed from their offices. Now, though we talk about drawing a lesson from it, all new cadres are being dismissed. Of course, there are some followers of the Gang among the new cadres, but they are only a handful. Most of them were fooled into believing that they were following the party line. If you're active in one political movement, you'll be a victim in the next. The safest way is to sit on the fence and do nothing. Once a movement starts everybody higher than a foreman is investigated. When a new man takes over the leading position, he puts in his own men and kicks out all the others. This is practiced right down to the small units. People are divided into factions. The cadres spend all their time and energy on hurting people with whom they don't see eye to eye. In work they can't cooperate with each other. If things go on like this, despite all your high sounding slogans, modernization will never be achieved."

Hearing this, Qiao, now alert, said, "Come off it, Xi. You sound like a theoretician. Our country has suffered enough from too many critics, too much empty talk. What we need are hard working and selfless people." He had imagined only the old cadres needed to vent their anger and had never expected such a complaint from a new cadre. It would be extremely damaging if the two forces clashed head on.

VI

Qiao went into action the following day. First, he had all nine thousand workers and staff sit for the exam and had an appraisal made of their work. All those who were judged as lazy, careless or unqualified were transferred to form a service team. After this, production began to pick up speed. The whole plant was stimulated by the new competitive spirit.

The workers felt that Qiao was a man of action. Once he had decided on something he would go all out for it. As he had promised, a fine building for a kindergarten was soon completed. He had said that bonuses would be awarded if the production quota were reached, and so in August the workers got them for the first time. All the skilled, hardworking workers said that there could be no better manager than Qiao. At the same time he was hated by some of the service team members, who were furious at having been transferred.

He dismissed the one thousand temporary workers who had been engaged in building and transportation. Their work was taken over by the service team. Qiao made a capable man, Li Gan, who was head of the finance office, the team leader and gave some of the temporary workers' wages to this team as a material incentive. Though they suffered no cut in wages, the young workers in it felt insulted and humiliated. Du Bing, for one, felt strongly about it. His girl friend had jilted him since he wasn't even a qualified lathe operator. He felt desperate and miserable.

But Qiao had other enemies. Worst were those angry cadres who had been sent to the service team. They in turn demanded that all the managers should take the exam too. Unperturbed Qiao went to the auditorium with a few deputy managers to sit for the exam.

The news soon got around and the workers, having ended their day shift, rushed to the hall which was soon packed. They fired all sorts of questions at Qiao, who answered with ease, but Ji Shen did badly, muddling up the answers to even some of the most basic questions. The veins on his forehead pulsating in anger at the workers' mocking laughter, Ji struggled to control himself, inwardly cursing Qiao for laying what he considerd to be a nasty trap, set with the aim of making a fool of him in public.

Ji found being a deputy manager was rather demanding. Moreover, he resented being at the beck and call of others, especially so before the workers. Now that he had failed the exam, jealousy and resentment pushed him to join the opposition. Qiao's deputy only in name, he started causing numerous problems in the plant. Wherever there was a problem in production he had a hand in it. Yet he was too careful to be caught. Qiao had to watch him constantly and at the same time solve the problems he'd already initiated. Ji was a damn nuisance.

Qiao made up his mind to send Ji to the service team and asked him to take charge of construction, unaware that the service team was already a keg of gunpowder and that Ji's appearance would certainly spark an explosion. It was Shi who foresaw the impending trouble. Qiao, however, ignored his warning. Even more surprising, he promoted Xi to be the deputy manager in place of Ji. Those who were capable were promoted; Qiao followed this rule regardless of personal likes or dislikes. Xi, a personal enemy of Qiao, had become his assistant.

As Shi predicted, only a few days after Ji's transfer, grumbling in the service team became open protests, with threats to overthrow Qiao.

Though Qiao was up to his neck in all sorts of contradictions and problems, he had not had time to deal with this movement to overthrow him. What preoccupied him most was preparing for the next year's production. He hoped to get the output up to two million kilowatts, but the power company did not like the idea. They preferred to import equipment from abroad. Besides, there were problems with fuel and raw materials, so Qiao decided to do some diplomatic spadework himself.

Unfortunately, being ignorant of the gap that existed between his wonderful plan and reality, Qiao met with ignominious defeat. Disorder and corruption made it impossible to reach his goals and he felt at the end of his rope. He needed a large amount of supplies, but the suppliers would not listen to him. He wanted raw materials and fuel but did not know how to get them. He was unaware of the unwritten rule that if you want something, you had to give something in return. It was called "mutual exchange." So it wasn't just a matter of clinching a deal. Anyway, Qiao learned something new: It was not important whether or not a manager knew anything about metallurgy or mechanics. What was essential was to develop a good relationship with others.

VII

The first thing Qiao did when he returned was to see Shi Gan. Shi, surprised by his sudden appearance, stuffed some papers into his drawer. But Qiao, concentrating on other things, failed to notice this. They sat down and began talking when Li, head of the service team, broke in. Seeing Qiao, he exclaimed joyfully, "Ah, Qiao, you're just the man I'm looking for!"

"What is it?" Qiao asked eagerly.

"The peasants are refusing to let us start building our apartment block. Xi is surrounded by them. There may be a scuffle."

"But the city planning bureau has given us permission. We've paid the money."

"They want five tractors in addition."

"The same old story!" Qiao bellowed. "We're producing electrical machinery! Where in hell's name can we get tractors?"

"But Ji Shen promised them."

"Shit! Where's Ji? Go and get him."

"He's been transferred, leaving everything in a mess," Li complained.

"What?" Qiao turned to look at Shi.

"Three mornings ago," Shi explained, "he came to say goodbye to me. That same afternoon he went to the Foreign Trade Bureau. He knew a certain big shot there who pulled some strings to get Ji the job. He didn't even say a word to the party committee. But his file's with us. He's still on our payroll."

"He can take his file with him. We won't pay him for doing nothing." Then he gestured to Li, "Let's go and have a look."

Problem after problem! There was no end to them. Since it was almost the end of the year and the workers were busier, problems were more likely to occur. Qiao feared that this new problem might mess up everything.

As they entered the workshop they saw the foreman pleading with Tong Zhen. Calmy shaking her head, she was not budging. She was especially meticulous about technical questions. She was as stubborn as a mule and the man's patience was beginning to wear out. Suddenly the exasperated man spotted Qiao. He dashed over to him, thinking he was the only person who could change Tong's mind.

"Qiao," he groused, "we were certain to fulfill this year's quota eight days ahead of schedule. We can do even better next year. But we've got a slight problem. You see, the failure rate of the lower coil of a rotor is no more than one percent. That's really nothing serious. But Tong insists we rewind the coil. Earlier this year coils with a failure rate around thirty or forty percent were passed. So it's a lot better now."

"Have you found the cause of it?" Qiao broke in.

"Not yet."

"Yes, we have!" Tong butted in. "I've told you twice about it. All I'm asking you to do is to erect a plastic covering and take measures to protect the generators from dust. But you think it's too troublesome."

"Troublesome?" Qiao said in a mocking tone, "It's easy to turn out rejects, but aren't they troublesome to the country? What about quality? You did fairly well in the exam. Theory is one thing and practice is another, right? Do it again! No bonus for you and your workers this month."

The man was upset.

"You don't have to be so harsh, Qiao," Tong pleaded. "They're bound to finish the work in time even if they do it again. Why cut their bonus?"

"It has nothing to do with you," Qiao said coldly without even looking at her. "Just think of the time and materials wasted because of their carelessness!" Then he and Xi walked out of the workshop.

With a wry smile the foreman said to Tong, "The service team wants to smash him, and we do everything possible to support him. I can't understand why he's so hard on us."

Tong said nothing. She was concerned with the technical side and had no say in such things. All she could do was try to console the angry man.

Tong bought four tickets for a Beijing opera, "The Forsaken Wife," to try and cheer up her husband. The other two were for Xi and his wife. Xi did not turn up in time so the three of them set off first, leaving a ticket for Xi.

Just as they were about to enter the theatre, Li Gan appeared out of the blue. Seeing him in such a flurry, Qiao sensed that something must have gone wrong. He asked the two women to go in first while he followed Li to a quiet place.

"What's up?" Qiao asked quietly. The look of authority in his eyes calmed Li down.

"Some people on the service team are out to make trouble."

"Who?"

"Du Bing. He's backed by Baldy Wang. They're making noises about Ji Shen supporting them. Du's been absent for three days, so he's probably in touch with those involved in the sit-in. He appeared this afternoon and talked with a few of his cronies and then wrote some posters. He said they were going to put them up on the wall of the municipal government building and even threatened to go on a hunger strike."

"Are you scared?" Qiao asked, sizing up this clever, capable man.

"Why should I be? It's you they're gunning for."

"Don't worry about me," Qiao said with a smile. "You just stick to the rules. Cut the wages of those who stay away from work without good reason. If they don't want to work here, fair enough. They can go somewhere else."

A leader must be firmer than his subordinates. Encouraged, Li grinned, "Watch out when you go home after the opera. They may mug you on the way. I must go now."

Qiao found his seat and sat down just as the bell rang. Some dignitaries entered and took their select seats in the middle of the row in front of Qiao. Ji Shen was one of them. With his sharp eyes he'd already spotted Qiao and Tong. Having sat down, he turned around and nodded to Tong. Then he proffered his hand to Qiao, saying, "So you're back, Qiao. How are things? A man like you always gets what he wants!"

Qiao just shook his head. He hated to talk loudly in public places.

Ji said condescendingly, "If you come to our bureau, look me up. I'm always at your disposal."

Qiao swallowed, feeling disgusted. Why was he so smug? Was it his promotion? Was he mocking him?

Indeed, Ji now felt superior to Qiao of whom he'd been so jealous only a few months ago. He'd never commit himself to boost production the way Qiao did or throw himself into a political movement. That was madness! To him, modernization was just another political movement, and Qiao was so stupid as to stake everything on it. He was on the brink of a precipice and could fall any minute. Now the electrical machinery plant was already in turmoil. Ji was proud of his prudent decision to leave the plant when he did. Meeting Qiao tonight in such a situation made him feel on top of the world. He seemed to enjoy the opera, discussing it with the people on either side of him.

But despite his efforts, Qiao could not concentrate on the performance. He racked his brains to find a good excuse to leave the theatre so as not to disappoint the two women.

Xi groped his way to his seat with the help of an usher's torch. The two women inquired why he was so late and if he had eaten anything. He mumbled a few words, nodding his head. Then casting a sidelong glance at Qiao, he whispered, "Manager, how can you sit still? Let's get the hell out of here!"

Agreeing, Qiao followed Xi and took his leave. But Tong ran after them and caught them in the lobby.

Xi hastily explained to her, "I have to talk to him. He has the full support of the Ministry of Machine Building and has some orders for generators from the Ministry of Electric Power. Our problems now are materials, fuel and the cooperation among the factories concerned. Contracts, documents and Qiao's firmness aren't enough. This is where the deputy manager should come in."

Qiao had not expected Xi to be willing to do such a job himself. Since he had failed, he couldn't bring himself to ask a deputy to try. Besides, he doubted whether Xi could succeed. Guessing Qiao's thoughts, Xi was upset.

"Are you leaving tomorrow?" Tong asked. "Why the hurry?"

"I've just discussed it with the party secretary. He agrees too. We've sent someone to buy the train tickets. We'll probably leave tonight." Though Xi talked to Tong, he intended Qiao to hear. "As a manager of a big factory, Qiao has a fatal weakness. He knows nothing about human relationships. It's different from the war years or even a few years ago. Unlike robots, men have feelings and thoughts. And it's most difficult to influence men's thinking." Abruptly turning to Qiao he went on, "You know how to run a big modern factory. When there is important business in the bureau or ministry, you should go yourself because you've a reputation and your words carry greater weight. As for public relations, leave that to the deputy managers or chiefs of departments. If things get out of hand you can smooth them out. But if you do everything yourself and get into a fix, what can we do?"

"OK," Qiao said, "but stop giving me all your fine theories! With you it's always theory before practice. I'm sick of it all." He asked Xi to accompany the two women while he went to see Shi.

Tong watched her husband as he walked away. She knew that he often covered up his anxiety and weakness and that he secretly tried to overcome them. He never showed a trace of depression or hesitation at home. He had to be tough for he shouldered a heavy load. Now the plant was improving. If he backed out at this moment the plant would collapse. He must not show softness or fear.

"When you two get together," Tong complained, "I'm always afraid you'll come to blows!"

"Never!" Xi said cheerfully. "Frankly there aren't many people as good as Manager Qiao around. Haven't you noticed how many of our cadres are following his example? They'll do well under Qiao's leadership. I confess I don't exactly like him, but I do admire his guts. Though he has a lot of charisma, I'm resisting him with all my might. I won't give in to him completely. He despises cowards."

He looked at his watch and exclaimed, "Hell! I'm afraid I have to go too. Being his deputy isn't easy."

VIII

Under a lamp Shi was carefully reading letters of accusation against Manager Qiao which had been forwarded from the plant's party committee, the municipal party committee and even from the Central Party Committee. He felt a mixture of indignation, fear and shame. All the letters attacked Qiao. Not a single one criticized him, the party secretary. On the contrary, he was described as a victim of Qiao's despotism, as only a figurehead, a living mummy. It was true that Shi had become very quiet and that quite often he pretended to be deaf, not answering certain questions. He had rather prided himself on his sophistication, but now he regretted it deeply and was angry with himself. He had never meant this behavior of his to blacken Qiao and whitewash himself. Sometimes he had been fired by Qiao's enthusiasm and very often his feelings overcame his common sense. On certain important issues he sided with Qiao by saying nothing or simply acquiescing. He sometimes thought if all cadres worked like

Qiao, China would have a new look and the party would recover its vitality. But the letters were like a deluge threatening to swamp Qiao for good. Shi's heart ached. He had no idea what to do with the letters. He feared that Du Bing and his mob would gang up with some hooligans to turn the plant upside down.

While he was thinking he heard someone call him. Opening the door, he saw Huo Dadao.

Huo looked around and asked, "So Qiao isn't here?"

"No."

"Well?" Huo sipped the tea Shi had poured him. "When I heard he was back, I went to see him right after supper. Unfortunately his door was locked. I guessed he might have come here."

"He and Tong have gone to an opera."

"Then I'll wait for him. I'm pretty sure he won't sit through it all no matter how good it is! It's a pity that he has to disappoint Tong again." Huo chuckled softly.

"But he's a Beijing opera fan."

"I know. But I bet he's going to walk through that door any minute now."

Huo, in high spirits, seemed unaware of Shi's bad mood. "What he's really keen on is his plant, his work," he added as if talking to himself. Glancing at the letters on the table, Huo asked indifferently, "Does he know about those?"

Shi shook his head.

"How was his trip? How is he?"

Shi shook his head again. He was about to say something when Qiao pushed the door open. Huo chortled and slapped Shi on the shoulder.

Qiao was puzzled by the laughter.

Shi immediately tried to hide the letters, but Qiao noticed him. Walking to the table, he picked up a letter.

Huo urged Shi to show them all to him.

After reading some of the letters, Qiao was enraged and swore, "The dirty bastards!" He paced up and down the room, his left cheek twitching, then went over to Huo who appeared engrossed in reading a newspaper. So he turned to Shi and asked, "So what will you do?"

Shi hesitated for a moment and answered, "It's time you left this plant for the bureau. This year's quota will be fulfilled. I'll stay and stick it out. I won't leave while there's trouble."

"What are you talking about?" Qiao roared. "You want me to run away? What about the plant?"

"But what about you? If you're disgraced, a lot of people will be hurt. Who else will take up this job?" Shi meant this also for Huo's ear.

Huo looked at them calmly, not uttering a word.

Qiao, still pacing, snapped, "I'm not afraid of dirty slanders. As long as I'm the manager, I'll run the plant my way!"

Shi appealed to Huo, "What do you think, Huo?"

"A few letters and you're scared out of your wits?" Huo asked quietly. "Still you're his loyal friend. You tell him to get out first and then you'll follow later, eh? A good idea! I must say you've made great progress."

Shi's face became very red.

Smiling, Huo turned to Qiao and said, "Qiao, you've only been back for half a year, and one of your achievements is that you've turned this deaf and dumb fellow into a high-ranking official. We had to drag Shi here to be the party secretary. Now he wants to be the manager as well! Come, Comrade Shi, there's no need to blush! I'm only speaking the truth. Now you're like a real party secretary. But one thing I must criticize you for is Ji Shen's transfer. Why did you let him go without first consulting the bureau?"

Shi was very embarrassed. Old as he was, he had never got such a dressing down from his leaders.

Huo rose to his feet and went over to Qiao. "You know I like the saying, 'Better to die fighting than in your bed!' Please tell me, how do you spend your time?"

"Forty percent on production, fifty percent on wrangles and ten percent on slanders," was Qiao's prompt reply.

"What a waste of time! You should spend eighty percent of your time on production and the rest on research."

He suddenly became very serious, "Modernization doesn't mean technique alone. You'll have to offend some people. Of course it's safest to do nothing, but that's criminal. As for misunderstandings, slanders, accusations, sneers, never mind them. Ignore them! If you want to achieve something, demand a free rein. We're racing against time. The curtain has just risen on our modernization drive. The real drama is yet to follow."

Seeing their faces brighten up, Huo continued, "the Minister rang me up yesterday and told me that he was very interested in the way you are running the plant. He asked me to tell you to be even bolder. Experiment with some new methods. Gain experience. Know what our problems are. Next spring he wants us to go abroad to have a look. China's modernization will be realized, but first we must study the experience of other countries."

The three men sat down and calmed themselves with a cup of tea. Huo suddenly suggested to Qiao, "You're good at singing Beijing opera. Sing us an aria."

"OK!" Qiao drank some tea, tilted his head and began to sing.

General, You Must Not Do This!

YE WENFU

Reportedly, a top-ranking general, who came into power again after being cruelly persecuted by the Gang of Four, recently ordered a kindergarten to be demolished to make way for his new mansion, which he lavishly furnished with modern facilities, costing the country a total of several hundred thousand RMB. And I...

What can I say?
And how shall I say it?
You, my honorable elder
And I, years your junior
Between you and me
Lie the gunsmoke years—
The nineteen-thirties
And forties.

To criticize you
Is something
I never imagined,
Because perhaps
It may have been your hand
That held the machine gun
Which aimed deadly shots
At the Old World.

It might have been your hand
That snatched away
The whip from my back—

You held me
In your blood-stained bosom,
As your teardrops fell
You touched the scars
Over my body,
Your thick lips trembling.

You said: "My child,
We are not liberated—"
And so I, bare-footed,
Small-footed, treading
In your giant footprints
Walk into a New China...

No! General,
Even if it were so
This I have to say
And with all the more reason!

Do you remember that year,
Crossing the Luding Bridge?
From behind: soldiers pursued us
On the opposite bank: a fire!
The snarling waves threatened
The iron suspension.
The fate of the revolution
Is dangerous—
Will this mighty Dadu River
Extinguish the flames
Of Jinggang Mountain?

You stared with bloodshot eyes
And tucked your Mauser pistol
In your waist;
You made your heroic entrance
Into history;
Your cry was like thunder!

General, what were your thoughts?
Were you thinking of
"Working toward happiness
For generations to come!"
And you said: "The hardest tasks
To me! To me!"

How sad, my battled-tired General
That forty or more years later
Your heroic stature should turn
To a limping gait,
Your achievements
And thunderous voice
Washed and shrunken
By the tide of time
To a weak note:
"To me....To me...."

Give you the Moon
But you say it's too cold,
Give you the Sun
But you say it's too hot!
You want the whole World
In one embrace, everything
To pick and choose...
For your amusement
Everything, you want all.
But why did you deny the oath
You swore to the party?

And why have you discarded
The mark of the true proletarian?
Must the flames of Jinggang Mountain,
Which even the Dadu River could not tame,
Be smothered by the cups of maotai
That adorn your banquet table?
And must the Red Boat,
That came through the storm
On the South Lake, be anchored in
Your comfortable armchair?
Must a member of the CCP
Create history as tragic as Niu Jinxing?
Must generation after generation
Start revolutions and pledge their lives
Only so you and your family
Can live in paradise?

If this be true, General
How can you do justice
To the last slain comrade
Who died in your arms?

And how can you do justice
To the whitehaired author
Of the *Communist Manifesto?*

General, go put on your old
Red straw sandals.
Go kiss the land
For which you once shed blood—
Inch after inch of land
Snatched from the enemies' hands,
Inch after inch of land
Redeemed from the abyss of suffering,
Inch after inch of land
That bears the mark of the Revolution,
Inch after inch of land
That nurtured the Red Army,
The New Fourth Army
And the Liberation Army!
Think of the woman who fed you
Millet soup at Taiheng, who
Stirred the wild herbs
With a wooden spoon.
And she who bandaged your wound
In Loyang; three generations
Huddled together in a square room,
Her bed occupied by the cooking pan....

My high and mighty General,
Tell me exactly for what cause
You have committed your lifetime
To battle! And why you turn a deaf ear
To the people's suffering,
Don't you, a member of the CCP,
Feel pangs of conscience
When you are rebuked by Truth?
Or do you really believe
That the Law is a card
Forever held in your hand,
Or at most the gentle breeze
Blowing on a summer's night?

Can it be that Premier Zhou Enlai's
Good teachings no longer penetrate
The pores of your skin?

For your own "modernization"
You tear down the kindergarten
And send the children away!
Do you know, hoary-headed one,
Your happy years are few.
The children hold the future,
Yes, it is the children
Who hold the future!
Disown them, and who will be left
To carry your ashes?

Perhaps you proudly say:
"I have my son..."
Yes, you have your son—
If your son is a revolutionary
He will angrily stay away
From your mansion; If your son
Is a good-for-nothing parasite
The accusations that you reap
From the people will forever
Weigh upon his delicate hands!

Imagine how sad a friend of mine
Will feel, when he learns
Of your generous deed—
When working as a buyer
He learned that
The downy hair inside
The ear of an ox
Could bring in foreign money,
Diligently, he cuts, cuts away
One hair after another
He accumulates more than ten catties
In just a few years....

Like silkworms in spring
Patiently yielding their threads,
Our people gather wealth
For the nation.
Then what right have you
To squander away so relentlessly
The blood of our valiant martyrs,
The trust our people bear toward the party,
The sweat of our hard-working laborers?

Can this be true?
That the Four Modernizations
Declared by Premier Zhou Enlai,
Those Four Modernizations
Which we are all striving for
Before the furnace; in the fields
Sweating and bleeding.
The pains of the past ten years
Can they be merely so much cooking oil
From your gluttonous stomach?
What misfortune, my General!

On the first Long March
You conquered the Dadu River
But as the new Long March
Begins, what are you contemplating today—
Fall back one step
And your end will be: the Dadu River!

No! Niu Jinxing's tragedy
Certainly will not happen again
Because the people
Will not remain silent!
And so may my lines
Become like thunder and with heroic force
Pound into your ears and heart,
while on our new Long March
Those who march after you,
And the Law, which also marches along,
Loudly join in unison: "General,
You must not do this!"

The Eye of Night

WANG MENG

(Translated by Janice Wickeri)

The street lamps above came on of course, but Chen Gao always felt as though the streams of light shot out in opposite directions from the top of his head. The street was an endless river of light. A large elm tree added its shadow to those of the people waiting for a bus.

He saw trucks and cars, trolley buses, and bicycles. He heard the shriek of whistles and the high-pitched din of voices talking and laughing. To Chen Gao, the city truly showed its peculiarities and vitality at night. He noticed people with permanent-waved hair and naturally straight hair, women wearing sleeveless dresses and shoes with spiked heels or pumps. He smelled the strong scents of perfume and face powder. Chen Gao was interested in everything and everyone he saw. He had not been to the city in over twenty years. He had spent those years living in a tiny village in a remote province where only a third of the street lights were turned on at night.

He didn't know whether this was due to forgetfulness or to technical mishaps, but it was not a major problem because the people there lived more or less according to the old rural system of waking at sunrise and sleeping at sunset. No sooner was it six P.M. than all the offices, factories, shops and canteens closed down. In the evenings the people all stayed indoors, caring for children, smoking, washing clothes and talking of things soon forgotten.

The bus arrived. The conductor was speaking into a megaphone while the passengers swarmed off the bus and Chen Gao and others crowded on. It was packed and there were no seats, but the people seemed not to mind. The conductor was a ruddy young woman with a smooth, resonant voice. In Chen Gao's remote village, such a young woman was sure to be chosen as an announcer for the cultural troupe. She flipped the switch and the small shaded lamp used to check the tickets lit up. When she had torn up a few tickets — snap — it went out again. Street lights, shadowy trees, buildings and pedestrians swept past. As the bus neared another station the melodious voice announced the stop. The light went on again and people pushed and shoved once more.

Two young men dressed as workers got on. They were talking animatedly "...Democracy is the key, democracy, democracy...." Chen Gao had been in the city just one week and everywhere he heard people discussing democracy. Discussion of democracy was as common in the city as discussion of mutton in his remote village. He thought this was probably because the food supply was more adequate in the city and people didn't have to worry about mutton. Chen Gao smiled enviously.

But he did not think democracy and mutton were contradictory. Without democracy, the mutton one was about to eat might be stolen. And a democracy that didn't help people in remote villages get more and meatier mutton was only extravagant prattle. Chen Gao had come to the city to participate in a discussion about writing short stories and drama. He had published five or six short stories since the fall of the Gang of Four. Some people heaped excessive praise on him for writing more maturely and with a broader scope than in his past works, while an even greater number said he still hadn't recovered his standard of twenty years before. He recognized the fact that the craftsmanship of writers who overemphasized mutton deteriorated easily. Still, he thought understanding the importance and urgency of mutton production to be a big step forward. As he was coming to the meeting, the train had stopped over at a small station for an hour and twelve minutes because a man there — a man who had mutton but no home and was selling his mutton at a high price — had been crushed to death by the train. In order to sell off his mutton as soon as possible, he had gone so far as to forget his own safety and walked in front of the train as it was coming to a stop. As a result the brakes jammed, the train slid, and the poor man was finished. This incident left Chen Gao feeling heavy-hearted throughout the trip.

At past meetings Chen Gao had always been the youngest member present; now he was one of the oldest. Furthermore, he was noticeably rustic, dark-skinned and coarse. Those tall, broad-shouldered, clear-eyed younger comrades expressed many bold, fresh ideas which were enlightening and arousing. However, the result was that literary questions weren't taken up. Despite the fact that those chairing the meeting did their utmost to guide everyone toward the central task, what people discussed most was the Gang of Four's dependence on a foothold in the countryside, anti-feudalism, democracy, ethics and the legal system. They discussed how there were more and more young people gathering in the public parks for social dancing to the accompaniment of electric guitars, and how the park authorities had fought against this disaster by broadcasting every three minutes the announcement that this kind of dancing was forbidden; violators would be fined and the parks closed as a consequence.

Chen Gao also spoke at the meeting. Compared to others, his remarks were low-key, "We must proceed bit by bit and begin with what's under our own feet, begin with ourselves. If half, no a fifth, no even a tenth of the statements made at this meeting became reality, we will have achieved our goal. This fact excited Chen Gao, but it made him apprehensive as well.

The bus reached the terminal but there were still many passengers on board. Everyone seemed relaxed. No one took any notice of the conductor's angry appeals to collect or check tickets. Like all out-of-towners, Chen Gao had happily held up his ticket early on, but the conductor hadn't even glanced at him. He had then very correctly taken the initiative to put it into her hands himself, but she hadn't even taken it.

He took out his little address book, opened the ash-blue cover, looked up an address and began to make inquiries. He asked one person the direction to the address he had written down, but there were a good many people who pointed it out to him. On this point only did he feel that the people of this big city retained the tradition of "courtesy." He said his thanks and left the bright lights of the bus terminal, made several turns and entered the maze of a new residential area.

To say it was a maze is not to say it was complex, but that it was a simple unit of six two-story residential buildings, each no different from the others. They were thickly dotted with balconies packed with confused piles of belongings. Windows shone with green fluorescent lights and the yellow gleam of ordinary light bulbs. Even the noises floating out of each building's windows varied little. There was an international soccer match on TV. The Chinese team scored a goal and the spectators on the field and those in front of the flickering TV screens cheered together. People were shouting wildly. The sound of applause and cheering rose like a torrent. The popular old sports announcer

Shang Shi was yelling for dear life knowing that at such a time commentary would be superfluous. From other windows came the sounds of hammering, of vegetables being chopped, of children quarreling and of adults threatening each other.

So many sounds, lights, and objects all seemed heaped together in each matchbox-like, blank building. Although this kind of cramped life was alien to Chen Gao, even a bit laughable, the shadowy trees, each one as tall as a building, cast a veneer of mystery over everything. In his remote village the evening sound heard most often was the barking of dogs. He was familiar with these dogs' barks to the point where he could distinguish, from a chorus of barks, which sound came from what color dog and who its master was. Then there were the sounds of trucks hauling goods. Their glaring headlights left one dazed. All the houses in the street shook in the wake of the trucks' rumbling.

Walking in this maze of residential buildings, Chen Gao had some regrets. He really shouldn't have left that bright main street and that noisily happy, crowded bus with everyone traveling down the road together. That had been good, but now he felt alone. It would have been even better if he had just stayed in the hostel and not come out at all. He could have argued the night away with those younger friends, each one clamoring to present his prescription for curing the ills of Lin Biao and the Gang of Four. They would have discussed Belgrade, Tokyo, Hong Kong and Singapore. After dinner they could even have bought a plate of deep-fried shrimp chips and boiled peanuts with a litre of beer to dispel the heat and to enliven the conversation. Now, however, he had inexplicably taken a very long bus ride to hunt for an unknown address to find a mysterious person to do a bewildering thing. Actually, the thing wasn't a bit bewildering; it was quite normal, quite proper, it was only that it was inappropriate for him to do it, and that was that. It would be better for him to get up on the stage and dance the role of the prince in "Swan Lake," though he had a bit of a limp when he walked, rather than do this. Of course, his limp wouldn't be noticed unless one were looking for it; it was a little souvenir from the "Clean Up All Ghosts and Demons" campaign.

A feeling of having no appetite reminded him of the time he had left this city over twenty years ago. Then too he felt sad for leaving the crowd behind. He had published several novels which were criticized for being excessive and now inadequate. Because of this, his standing swung back and forth for a long time between being part of the majority of good people or part of the minority of bad people. It was a dangerous game.

According to what people had said, the building he was looking for was not far. Why did they build here? It looked as if they
were going to put in some pipes; no, not just pipes; there were
bricks, tiles, lumber and stone as well. Maybe they were going to
build another couple of two-story buildings, a canteen, perhaps.
Of course it might also be a public toilet. In any case there was a
wide ditch which he probably couldn't leap across. Before being
"swept clean" he could have done it, but now he must find a
bridge, a plank. So he anxiously walked up and down along the
ditch, but in the end found no plank. All that walking in vain.
Should he go around or jump across? No, he couldn't bow to old
age yet; he backed up a few steps, one, two, three... No, it was no
good, one foot seemed to be bogged down in the sand. He had already begun to jump, but he didn't rise into the air; he fell into
the ditch. Luckily there was nothing hard or sharp at the bottom,
but it took him close to ten minutes to recover from the pain and
fright. He laughed and lamely crawled out. Wouldn't you know it;
just as he was climbing out, he stepped into a puddle with his
other foot. He pulled it out, but his shoe and sock were soaked.
His foot felt very gritty like the texture of sandy rice. He raised
his head and saw a red-orange light bulb on a crooked pole fixed
to the side of the building. This light bulb's existence here was
like a tiny question mark or say, an exclamation point, drawn on
a huge blackboard.

He walked toward the light bulb, now question mark, now exclamation point. A cacophony of shouting and whistling floated
out of the windows again; probably the foreign team had scored
another point. He drew near the door, carefully examined the
character above it, and decided that this was the place he was
looking for. Still, he wasn't satisfied, and stood in the doorway
waiting for someone to come by so he could inquire once more.
At the same time he felt quite embarrassed.

Just before he left, a leading comrade from his village, whom
he knew and very much respected, came to see him and gave him
a letter, asking him to meet the head of some company when he
arrived in the city. "We're old comrades-in-arms," Chen Gao's acquaintance had said, "I've already put it all down in the letter.
The only car in our organization, a Shanghai model, has broken
down. The supervisor and the driver have already been to a number of garages and it looks as if there's no place in this province
that can do a good job on it. They all lack the needed parts. This
old friend of mine is in the auto repair trade. He promised me a
long time ago that 'If it's anything to do with repairing cars, leave
it to me.' Look him up and when you've worked things out, then

send me a telegram."

It was just such a run-of-the-mill matter as this: Find one leader with position and power, one's own man, an old friend, to fix a state-owned car belonging to the unit of another leader with position and power who in his locality commanded respect. There was no reason to refuse this old comrade's request, and Chen Gao, who understood the importance of mutton, had not formed any opinions about the necessity of bringing the letter and finding the man. This incidental handling of a bit of business for his local unit was, of course, a duty to which he should give priority. But ever since he had taken on this responsibility, he felt it was a bit like putting on a pair of shoes that didn't fit, or putting on a pair of socks only to discover that each one was a different color.

The comrade in his remote village seemed to have read his mind. No sooner had he arrived in the city than he received a telegram urging him to do something about the matter as soon as possible. Anyway, he thought, I'm not doing this for myself. I have never ridden in that Shanghai car and I never will. He had urged himself on, upon the road with its river of street lights, out of the terminal with its theatrical brightness and warmhearted passengers. He had walked around and around, had fallen into a ditch and climbed out, clothes soiled, foot muddy. Now he had finally arrived.

At last, having had two children verify the building and apartment number, he walked quickly to the fourth floor. First he gave himself a few minutes to calm down and regulate his breathing, and then, as gently as possible, in a civilized yet sufficiently loud manner, he knocked on the door.

There was no movement, but a slight tinkling sound which seemed to come from within. He put his ear to the door. There seemed to be some music playing. So he had no choice but to brush aside the disheartening yet relieved impulse to say, "Ai...no one's home," and firmly knocked again.

After the third knock he heard footsteps, then the sound of the lock being turned. The door opened. It was a young man with disheveled hair whose torso and thighs were bare. From head to toe he wore only a pair of white undershorts and white plastic slippers. His flesh glistened. "What do you want?" he asked, a bit impatiently.

Chen Gao gave the name on the envelope. "I'm looking for Comrade X."

"He's not here." The young man turned and would have closed the door, but Chen Gao took a step forward. He introduced himself in the most polite manner, taking care to use the pronunciation most standard in that city. He asked, "Are you one of Comrade X's family?" (He judged that this was Comrade X's son, and actually the polite phrases were completely unnecessary for one as much his junior as this young man.) "Can you hear me out and relay my business to Comrade X?"

He couldn't see the young man's expression in the darkness, but his intuition told him that the young man frowned and hesitated for a moment before he finally said, "Come in," and he turned and went in with no greeting for his guest, in the manner of a nurse in a dental hospital telling a patient to come and have his tooth extracted.

Chen Gao followed the young man's footsteps—in the pitch black corridor. They passed a number of doors, one on the left, one on the right. There were so many doors behind the first. One door was open and a soft stream of light, the lovely sound of singing, and the mellow aroma of liquor wafted out.

There was a spring bed with an apricot silk-covered quilt, not folded but piled like a big, overturned dumpling. There was a floor lamp which gave out a brightness that could repel someone a thousand miles away. The door of the cabinet at the head of the bed stood half open, exposing the marbled top shelf. So many good friends in his remote village had entrusted Chen Gao with buying cabinets for them, but he hadn't bought any yet. There too, the production of these large free-standing cabinets was just coming into its own. He scanned the room again. It was furnished with rattan chairs and deck chairs and a round table. The table was covered with pages from the text of the model revolutionary play *Tale of the Red Lantern,* depicting the living room at Pigeon Mountain in the fourth act. There was a pocket-size tape player with two speakers, imported, from which came the voice of a Hong Kong singing star. It was a mellow, delicate voice with crisp enunciation. As he heard it he couldn't keep from smiling. If he took this tape and played it in his remote village, it would frighten the people living there more than an invading infantry. The only thing that made Chen Gao feel at home was half a glass of water sitting on top of the cabinet at the head of the bed. It was like finding an old acquaintance in the midst of strangers. Even if the friendship had not been deep or if there had been ill feelings in the past, in that instant they became the best of pals.

Chen Gao discovered a broken stool in front of the door, brought it over and sat down. His clothes were filthy. He began to give his reasons for coming. After a couple of sentences he paused, hoping the young man would turn down the music a bit.

He waited several moments, but seeing that the young man had no intention of lowering the music, he continued. It was strange that Chen Gao, who had always been considered a good talker, seemed to have lost his tongue; he spoke in fits and starts, in disconnected phrases. Some phrases he used inappropriately. For example, he had meant to say, "I'd like to ask Comrade X to help us make the contacts," but it came out, "Please give it your kind consideration," as if he had come to apply for a subsidy from the young man. He had originally intended to say, "I thought I'd come to see him first," but he said instead, "I've come to make contact." Furthermore, his voice had changed. It wasn't his own, but more like a blunt saw cutting wood.

After he finished he brought out the letter, but the young man, tilted back in the deck chair, didn't move. Chen Gao, who was probably twice his age, had no choice but to walk over and hand it to him. In so doing he got a clear look at the young man's conceited face, a face full of weariness, stupidity, and acne.

The young man opened the letter and glanced at it. He laughed once, a laugh full of contempt. His left foot began to beat time to the song. The sound of the tape player and its Hong Kong singing star was something new for Chen Gao. He certainly wasn't opposed to this style of singing, but he didn't find it very interesting either. A disdainful smile appeared on his face without his being aware of it.

"This X," (he was speaking of the leader of Chen Gao's remote area) is an old army buddy of my father's?" (Note that until now he hadn't introduced himself and theoretically there was still no way to verify who his father was) "How come I've never heard my father speak of him?"

Chen Gao felt as if he had been insulted. "You're young, perhaps your father never told you..." Chen Gao was no longer being polite either.

"But he did tell me that as soon as a vehicle needs fixing, everybody is his old friend!"

Chen Gao flushed, his heart began to pound and sweat appeared on his forehead. "Do you mean to say that your father doesn't know Comrade X, head of the remote area? He went to Yenan in 1936, last year he even published an article in *Red Flag*...his brother is the commander of Z Military Camp!"

When Chen Gao unexpectedly began talking like this, especially when he mentioned the big shot, the commander of Z Military Camp, he turned pale and dizzy and poured out sweat.

The young man's response was another contemptuous smile twenty times as big as the first. He even laughed out loud.

Chen Gao felt like crawling into a hole. He bowed his head.

"Let me put it this way." The young man stood up, assuming an air of finality. "There are two main conditions for getting something done. The first is you must have something to exchange. What have you got to offer?"

"What have we got to offer? We have...mutton..." He said as if to himself.

"Mutton is no good." The young man laughed again. His contempt was too great, and turned to pity. "The second condition depends on your ability to pull it off—your ability to con people...why is my father the only one you can ask? Once you have the goods, there will be someone who can handle it for you. Just use whatever name you need to use." Then he added, "My father has been sent to the seaside resort at Beidaihe... He's convalescing."

Chen Gao was bewildered. Just as he got to the door, he stopped a moment. He couldn't help inclining his ear to real music, by the Hungarian composer Lehar, which was now coming from the tape. It brought to mind a tableau of fluttering leaves and a jade-green lake surrounded by snow-capped mountains. His remote village was beside a high mountain lake. A wild swan often swam on the water.

He was back in the pitch black corridor again. Chen Gao, running and stumbling as if drunk, charged down the stairs. He didn't know if the tap-tapping sound was the sound of his footsteps or of his heart pounding against his sides. As soon as he got out the door he looked up. Heavens, that tiny question mark exclamation point of a faint light bulb suddenly turned red. It looked like the eye of a monster.

Such a frightening eye — it could change a bird into a rat, a horse into a grasshopper. Chen Gao, still running wildly, effortlessly cleared the ditch in one leap. The soccer game had ended. In a soft, intimate voice the TV announcer was giving tomorrow's weather. He reached the bus terminal in a flash. There were still just as many people waiting for the bus. There was a group of young women workers going to the night shift at the factory. They were all talking at once, discussing the workshop awards. There was a young couple holding hands; another wrapping their arms around each other's waists. He thought that if certain people had seen this, they would certainly have been shocked. Chen Gao got on the bus and stood near the door. This conductor was no longer young. Her body was so frail her bony shoulder blades seemed to be sticking out of her blouse. In twenty years of frustration and transformation, Chen Gao had gained a lot of precious knowledge, but had also lost a few things which should never have been lost. Yet he still loved the lamp light, loved people on the night shift, loved democracy, rewards, mutton,....the bell rang. There was one sound and then another, the three doors weren't completely closed. Shadows from the trees and lights began to recede. "Is there anyone without a ticket?" The conductor asked once, but left before Chen Gao had a chance to get out his small change. She thought that everyone on the bus was a night shift worker with a monthly ticket.

1979

"In the Archives of Society"

(A FILM SCENARIO)

WANG JING

(Translated by Ellen Klempner)

Prologue

A BORDER AREA IN SOUTHERN CHINA. A RAINY NIGHT. Someone is stepping carefully through the mud, weaving his way through the jungle with difficulty. A bolt of lightning suddenly illuminates him, revealing a thin youth, about twenty years old, a look of exhaustion on his face.

Breathing heavily, he climbs up a hillside and wipes the rainwater off his face with the back of his hand as he looks out at the terrain. Another lightning flash reveals the boundary river and a border marker. His face now takes on an expression of relieved elation.

In the jungle, a People Liberation Army border trooper spots him and begins to monitor him closely.

As he approaches the boundary river, he prepares to cross it when suddenly a tight, semi-suppressed voice in the forest ahead of him barks out an order: "Don't move!"

Several border troopers leap out and surround the young man. Taking a disappointed look around him, he turns dejectedly back under the pitch black muzzles of the soldiers' guns.

A BORDER GUARD STATION. The youth's things are spread out

102

on a table: a penlight, a military cap, a piece of hardtack now soaked and swollen by the rain, a paratrooper knife, a military set square and a green, plastic diary. There is also a copy of *On War* by Klausewitz and *The Diary of Che Guevara*.

An officer opens up the Guevara diary and glances at the name written on the title page. Then, looking closely at the youth standing in front of the table, he opens up a copy of the "Border Circular" and says, "This is already the third time you've tried to sneak across the border." The youth calmly nods his head.

Officer: "Do you realize this is traitorous behavior?"

Youth: "But the working class has no motherland!"

Officer: "What were your motives in attempting to cross the border?"

"You wouldn't understand," answers the youth reservedly.

Knitting his brow, the officer gestures to the soldiers to take the youth away. Then he gathers up the things on the table, puts the books and the diary in a briefcase and seals it, writing on the seal the date: June 25, 1971.

A HIGHWAY IN THE SAME BORDER AREA. The youth's face can be seen through the window of a jeep as it speeds down the road.

AN URBAN TRAIN STATION. A train pulls in and the youth is escorted off by two military men.

THE SAME CITY. THE DUTY ROOM OF A GOVERNMENT OFFICE. Hanging up the telephone, a cadre hands the bookbag and briefcase to the youth. "O.K., you may go now," he says.

Having won his freedom again, the youth walks out of the duty room. Disappointed and upset, he glances around at his surroundings, then strides over to a small high-level cadre residence in the dormitory area, where he hesitates with his hand on the doorknob, unable to come to a decision.

In the distance a large Red Flag limousine can be seen approaching along the driveway. As he turns his head, the youth sees the car and hurriedly leaves the building, heading down another road.

A RIVERSIDE IN AN ADJACENT CITY DISTRICT. The youth sits on the bank in the shade of some willow trees, deep in thought, with the green plastic diary in his hand. After a short while he puts the diary away with a sigh and takes up *The Diary of Che Guevara*. Turning a few pages, he soon becomes agitated and casts the book aside.

The sound of human voices can be heard coming from behind the youth. Turning around, he sees four people walking in his direction along the river, a girl with a cigarette dangling from her lips in the lead. The girl has dark rings under her deep-set eyes and wears an expression of cold indifference on her pale face, but one can tell that she had been a striking young girl at one time. Three young hoodlums are following behind, humming a nondescript tune.

Barely aware of what he is doing, the youth stands up and takes a good look at the girl. The girl sees the youth, too, and is stupefied at first, then an extremely complex look passes over her face.

Stepping up onto the riverbank, the youth quickly strides toward the girl.

A CITY HOSPITAL. An ambulance races up to the entrance, its siren blasting. The youth, now unconscious and covered with blood, is carried into the emergency room by several nurses.

Scene 1

AN OFFICE IN A PUBLIC SECURITY BUREAU. A cleaver, two three-edged plastering knives and a file-sharpened iron pipe are displayed on a large table. All are bloodstained.

"...Judging from the weapons, all four of them were directly involved in the crime. According to the plant nursery worker who was there at the time, it was the girl, Li Lifang, who was holding the cleaver. Of the male suspects, Zheng Xiaoliu and Liang Qi were carrying the plastering knives, and Sun Sheng was holding the pipe." Chen Jie, a young public security officer, is giving his report to an old detective, Shang Qi, who is standing in front of a window, smoking.

Shang Qi is pushing fifty and looks it. Fatigued, he walks over to the table and examines the cleaver and plastering knives which he has placed together, comparing the bloodstains through squinted eyes. "What about the victim?" he asks.

Chen Jie opens up a file and removes some papers: "The victim's name is Wang Hainan. We found this on him. It's a pass indicating that he's a dependent of someone in a government bureau. As we understand it, his father is..." Chen Jie points silently upwards. Shang Qi takes his hint: "Let's interrogate Li Lifang first."

Li Lifang is brought in and sits down without being asked, an expression of indifference still on her face.

Chen Jie: "Are you Li Lifang?"

"I'm sure the police wouldn't arrest the wrong person!" Li Lifang's voice sounds hoarse and harsh.

Chen Jie: "How many times have you seen the inside of a public security bureau now?"

Li Lifang: "Oh, this would be my fourth glorious time around!"

"Hmph! And it shows, too!" Chen Jie snorts with disdain, then more severely: "All right! Let's have a clear account of the crimes you've committed today."

"What crimes? What are you asking ME for?"

Bam! Chen Jie strikes the table in anger. "None of that stuff! Give me a straight answer! Do you know Wang Hainan?"

The corners of Li Lifang's mouth twitch a bit as she hears Wang Hainan's name. "Could you give me a cigarette?" she murmurs.

"And how about a piece of candy too?" Chen Jie asks with a cold, sarcastic smile. "Answer!"

"I don't have anything to say." Li Lifang, now sitting with arms folded arrogantly across her chest, recovers her indifferent expression and yawns widely, eyes closed.

Shang Qi, who has remained silent all this time, is now staring at her head. Suddenly he asks, "Where did you get the scar?" Chen Jie's attention now turns to Li Lifang's forehead, where he can vaguely make out a faint scar.

Li Lifang is struck dumb with panic at first, then glares at Shang Qi, eyes bulging.

"Don't you want to see more?" she says, hissing in a voice so tight it seems to squeeze past her clenched teeth. As she speaks, she wrenches open her collar, revealing a scar on her white chest that extends from her collarbone to the top of her breasts. Shang Qi carefully scrutinizes what is obviously a knife scar.

"Still interested? I've got more here!" She pats her belly and suddenly lets out a bizarre, dissolute laugh.

Shang Qi walks over to Li Lifang and coolly lifts her head with his hand. Struggling unsuccessfully to free herself, she raises both fists as if to strike at him. Shang Qi doesn't try to dodge, but turns her head around and examines the scar, pressing on it with his fingers before letting her go. Then he walks back to the table where he presses a buzzer. A policeman enters and leads out Li Lifang, whose face is now contorted with hate.

Shang Qi seems to be talking to himself and to Chen Jie at the same time: "Li Lifang was involved in this case, all right," he says, "but she didn't directly assault the boy."

Chen Jie: "How do you know?"

Shang Qi: "The bloodstains on the cleaver and the plastering knives were left on different occasions."

Chen Jie compares the two lethal weapons: "Should we interrogate Zheng Xiaoliu next?"

Shang Qi seems absorbed in thought for a moment: "I think we ought to investigate further before we rush this case off to trial."

Scene 2

MORNING. A HOPSITAL ROOM. An electric fan is blowing.

Wang Hainan is lying stiffly in bed, bandaged head to foot. His bookbag is hanging at the head of the bed.

A doctor leads Shang Qi and Chen Jie to the room: "He just came to yesterday," he says. "Don't talk to him too long." Shang Qi nods and they enter the room.

"We're from the public security bureau. This is Comrade Shang Qi. My name is Chen Jie." Chen Jie speaks from a seat by the bedside. Shang Qi is looking Wang Hainan over carefully. The youth's face is ghastly white due to loss of blood and he is staring blankly at the ceiling.

Chen Jie: "Do you know the people who attacked you?"

Wang Hainan (weakly): "I only know Li Lifang."

Chen Jie flips a notebook open. "Could you tell us how you got to know Li Lifang? Just the important points. You can be brief, but start at the beginning."

Wang Hainan pauses a bit, facial muscles twitching, then slowly begins his story: "The first time I met her was in the summer of 1969, when I went to the seaside convalescent home to see my father..."

FLASHBACK: Wang Hainan, dressed in a rather rustic, uncouth fashion, is standing at the entrance guard house of a seaside rest-home. A guard comes out and speaks to him very politely: "I've just called up for you. He says to let you in. I'm really sorry about what happened just now! It was a misunderstanding. Let me show you in."

Wang Hainan: "Never mind. I'll find it myself."

Li Lifang, dressed in a military uniform, walks through the gate carrying a stethoscope, blood pressure measuring cuff and other common medical instruments. She looks much different than in her first appearance in the film — fresh, pretty, full of grace; but her manner and bearing are a bit proud and aloof.

The guard sees her and immediately says, "Little Li, would you show this comrade in on your way up?"

Li Lifang looks Wang Hainan over, then nodding her head ever so slightly, turns around and goes straight in. Wang Hainan follows her promptly. "Sorry to bother you," he says politely.

Li Lifang turns her head and casts Wang Hainan a cold look. Taking the hint, Wang Hainan tactfully slows down his pace.

Walking single file they pass through a garden with a fountain in it. A pretty little vacation house, facing a golden, sandy beach can be seen through the trees.

A tall, thin young man pushes open the screen door of the house and languidly strolls out. He only sees Li Lifang at first. "Hey, Little Li," he says, "how come you didn't go swimming with me yesterday?"

"Had a cold." Li Lifang answers coolly, turns on her heels and goes straight into the building. The young man watches her go in out of the corner of his eye, then shrugs his shoulders. Seeing Wang Hainan enter, he walks down the steps to greet him. "Hainan!" he says, feigning surprise. "How did you get here?"

"Oh, it's you, Little Jing. I've come to see dad about something."

"Dad's upstairs waiting for you." The young man gives Wang Hainan the once over as he speaks, then adds, "Why don't you change your clothes first. I've got some other things here you could wear." Then he abruptly turns around and heads out toward the beach. Seven or eight young people in gaily colored bathing suits can be seen in the distance waving to him.

A LUXURIOUS BEDROOM ON THE SECOND FLOOR OF THE HOUSE. Li Lifang is taking the blood pressure of a man who appears to be a high official. Next to the sofa there is a little tea table piled with documents. A huge, two-toned red and blue pencil is resting on top of the papers. Wang Hainan walks in. "Hello, Dad," he says.

The official slowly turns his head around: "Why didn't you let me know you were coming ahead of time?"

"It was too urgent, I didn't have time to write you." Wang Hainan sits down, scrutinizing his father as if preparing to pass judgment on him.

"And what kind of urgent business would *you* have?" Raising his head, the official looks at his son with disgust and dissatisfaction.

I wouldn't have come here if I hadn't thought about it over and over," answers Wang Hainan harshly.

Li Lifang stands up, saying: "I'll come back a little later."

"Oh, you're not in the way!" laughs the official. "This is our family's 'democratic personage,' a regular Jia Baoyu! He's been openly cursing me for over two years."

"I can't stand the way you do things, and I certainly don't understand your revolution!" says Wang Hainan bluntly.

Official: "Oh? Aren't you a Red Guard? You were yelling 'Rebellion!' pretty fiercely at one time."

"And I'm still rebelling now, just a little more carefully then before, that's all!" Wang Hainan glares at the official in irritation. "Do you still think you can give anyone who opposes you a life-sentence?"

Feeling a little uncomfortable now, the official tries to explain his son's unseemly behavior to Li Lifang. "Tough isn't he?" he says with a laugh. "What kind of son would ever talk like that to his father?" Then to Wang Hainan, "All right. So tell me what you've come here for."

"I want to join the army." Wang Hainan rubs his calloused hands together as he speaks.

"I wanted to send you into the army in the first place! But no! You said that was 'going through the back door!' Too dishonorable! So you insisted on settling down in the countryside instead. *Now* what's going on in that head of yours?"

"Don't think you can always control me, keep me in the palm of your hand. It's different this time! I want to serve on the northern front!"

The official frowns: "Why?"

"The Zhenbao Island battle is just beginning. I want to go there!"

"You didn't start that fight, did you? What sort of weird nonsense are you up to now?"

The official pushes Li Lifang to one side and begins to pace unhappily about the room; "There are plenty of ways to die, if that's what you want!"

Greatly embarrassed, Li Lifang stares at the official and his son. Without a word Wang Hainan stands up and walks over to a window facing the sea.

THE BEACH. Little Jing and a few friends are lying on the sand, listening to foreign music on a tape recorder. A nurse brings them some towels.

A young man lying next to Little Jing gives him a push: "Who was that country bumpkin standing by your house just then?"

"My older brother. Haven't you heard of him?"

"Oh! That was him!" The young man snickers with contempt. "A real celebrity, that one. Didn't he write a big character poster about your dad and go back to your hometown in the country?"

Little Jing takes off his sunglasses: "Writing a big character poster about my father was nothing! He even put up one on Vice Chairman Lin Biao! That really put our family in a bad position! If it weren't for the fact that my dad is close to Vice Chairman Lin...Hmph! That freak!" Little Jing tosses down a bottle of soda, throws away the bottle and looks off into the distance where a number of people are swimming: "Certainly a lot of people on the beach today. How disgusting!"

BACK IN THE HOSPITAL ROOM. The doctor enters and says to Chen Jie and Shang Qi, "Let the patient rest awhile."

Wang Hainan closes his eyes in exhaustion as Shang Qi and Chen Jie leave the room.

Shang Qi: "Doctor, you've got to do everything you can to save him."

Doctor: "I hear his father is..."

Shang Qi interrupts: "I was thinking in terms of my work."

Scene 3

AN OFFICE IN THE PUBLIC SECURITY BUREAU. Chen Jie pushes open the door and walks in, folder in hand. "I've had the files of Li Lifang, Zheng Xiaoliu and the others transferred over from their street association," he says. "Nothing much in them, really. None of them has been assigned work yet."

Shang Qi: "Start off by telling me about Li Lifang."

Chen Jie opens the folder: "Li Lifang's mother passed away a long time ago. Her father's an older worker in a machine tool factory. She's also got a younger sister who hasn't been given a job yet due to illness. Li Lifang herself entered the army in 1968 from Hong Guang Middle School and was demobilized in 1970. After that, she was sent to work in the machine tool factory where she married the factory's clinic doctor, Zhao Qing last year, but was divorced soon after. Then six months later she was dismissed. Well, that's about all there is in the file."

Shang Qi: "She married awfully young!"

"That was because her husband was quite a bit older than she. If you average their ages it comes out in accordance with the marriage requirements."

Shang Qi puts out his cigarette: "O.K. Let's start at the beginning then — Hong Guang Middle School."

Scene 4

HONG GUANG MIDDLE SCHOOL. Just a sprinkling of students here and there. There isn't one unbroken window in the entire school and the place looks bleak and desolate.

A student carrying a big club over his shoulder leads Shang Qi and Chen Jie over to a tiny room under a stairway in the class-room building. "Hey, you old biddy! Come on out!" he shouts to-ward the little, makeshift room.

An old, white haired woman, head bowed, comes out and bends over to pick up a broom and dustpan in the corner.

"Who told you to pick up that stuff?" The student pokes her with his club and then turns to speak to Chen Jie and Shang Qi: "Why don't you ask her. She was the old bourgeois principal of our school." The student swaggers upstairs, club cradled in his arms.

Chen Jie: "We're from the public security bureau here on an in-vestigation. What's your name?"

"My name's Wang." Bewildered, the old woman straightens up, one hand pressing on her lower back, and fixes her gaze on the two officers. "But my mind's no good anymore," she con-tinues. "Can't remember much of anything."

Shang Qi: "We'd like to know something about a former stu-dent here — Li Lifang. Do you still remember anything about her?"

"Oh! Li Lifang! Didn't she join the army?"

Chen Jie: "Tell us a bit about how she did in school first."

Principal Wang pauses to gather her recollections a bit. "Li Li-fang's student number was one when she started here," she says. "That means she had the highest grades in her class that year. She was good in everything, but had a special love for literature and art. She was a member of the song and dance team of the children's palace also. Later she was criticized as a 'budding revi-sionist' in a mass movement — " Wang sighs slightly, then lowers her voice: "No one would recommend her when the army came back in '68 to recruit people for an army performing arts troupe, but I found an opportunity to tell the army comrade about her even though my own situation wasn't good. So that's how she was asked to take the exam..."

FLASHBACK: A LARGE CLASSROOM. A youthful Li Lifang is

singing a melodious folksong. Her full, sweet voice has attracted quite a few students, who are crowding outside the room watching. Principal Wang, broom in hand, is also drawn to the room when she hears Li Lifang, listening to her sing as she sweeps the floor.

Finishing her song, Li Lifang begins to perform a lovely dance number, humming her own accompaniment, lithely spinning, whirling.

Several People's Liberation Army cadres exchange satisfied looks. One of them puts a red mark next to Li Lifang's name on a list of student candidates.

The exam completed, Li Lifang bursts out of the classroom. Seeing Principal Wang, she rushes over to her, full of excitement: "Principal! The Liberation Army comrades have said they've already decided to take me!" A look of maternal benevolence appears on Principal Wang's face: "Oh that's good! You're so fortunate! You know, you're really going to have to work hard and serve the people now."

"Hey! Principal Wang, come on over to my house!" Li Lifang merrily takes the broom from Principal Wang's hand as she speaks and grasps her arm as if to lead her off. Suddenly someone behind them snaps an order: "What do you think you're doing? It's not permitted to mess around with 'black gang' people!" The speaker is none other than the club-wielding student of the previous scene.

Li Lifang's dark eyes flash fire, but Principal Wang pushes her away, picks up the broom from the floor and begins sweeping again, head bowed meekly.

BACK IN THE PRESENT.

Principal Wang: "I never saw her again after that. Did something happen to her?"

Shang Qi: "Was Li Lifang ever injured at school?"

Principal Wang (with wide-eyed uneasiness): "Did Li Lifang have some sort of accident? Please, tell me!"

Shang Qi doesn't answer.

Seeming to have a premonition of disaster, Principal Wang hangs her head dejectedly: "No, she was never injured at school..."

Scene 5

THE HOSPITAL ROOM. Wang Hainan continues to relate his

story to Chen Jie and Shang Qi, who are sitting by his bedside: "Later, dad agreed to my demand to join the army and told me to wait. I saw Li Lifang everyday while I was waiting for news, but we never spoke to each other in the beginning. Then one day..."

FLASHBACK: Wearing the same clothes he had on the first day he showed up at the sanitorium, Wang Hainan walks into the little house where he discovers a tense, annoyed Li Lifang, arms piled with medical instruments, trying to dodge Little Jing, who is pestering her. "Now what do you want?" she says angrily. "Can't you see I've got work to do?"

"What work? The old man won't die! Come on in for awhile!" Little Jing refuses to let Li Lifang go and tries to force her into his room. Indignant, Wang Hainan steps forwards and grabs his brother by the shoulder: "Don't you have any sense of shame?" Li Lifang struggles free and runs off. Shaking off Wang Hainan's hand from his shoulder, Little Jing stalks furiously back into his room, slamming the door behind him.

Wang Hainan stands there helplessly fuming for awhile, then goes into his room to fetch Klausewitz's *On War*, which he takes to the beach with him. Once there he climbs a breakwater, walks out to its end and sits down facing the sea. Having calmed down a bit, he takes up the book and begins to read.

Li Lifang has also gone down to the beach and is gazing out at the sea, furtively dabbing at her eyes as she walks slowly over to the breakwater.

Hearing the sound of footsteps behind him, Wang Hainan turns around and is surprised to see Li Lifang climbing up the breakwater, head down. "What are you doing here?" he asks.

Li Lifang sees him sitting there and says, not a little unhappily, "What's it to you? Anyway, this is my place."

"You mean this is your territory? Sorry!" Wang Hainan shifts over to one side. Li Lifang takes out a handkerchief and spreads it out on the rock. Then sitting down, she begins to carve out a line on the reef with a small sharp stone. Not until this point does Wang Hainan notice that she has already scratched out quite a few lines there. He can't stop himself from asking, "Is something bothering you?"

Looking at the sea, Li Lifang says abruptly, "You ought to be with them having fun."

Wang Hainan looks in the direction of the swimming area and sees Little Jing taking a group of young men and nurses into the changing rooms. He can't help laughing coldly, "You could be out there with them having fun too, couldn't you?"

Li Lifang reacts as if she has been stung. Whipping her head around, she looks fiercely at Wang Hainan, saying with curt finality, "I can't stand the sight of those people, or rather, you people. You all make me sick!"

"I don't like them either. But then again, that 'them' may include you as well."

"But I'm not the same as they are!" Li Lifang protests indignantly.

"And neither am I! Understand!" Wang Hainan starts to get angry.

With this, the conversation ends abruptly and the two of them proceed to gaze silently at their own little section of the sea.

After a long silence, Li Lifang begins to speak again, this time in a softer tone of voice: "You really do seem to be different. As a matter of fact, you don't even look like your brother."

"Nothing strange about that. We didn't have the same mother." There is little emotion in Wang Hainan's voice as he speaks. When he sees the look of astonishment that appears on Li Lifang's proud, yet childlike face, he adds very naturally, laughing: "That's pretty common in some cadre families." My parents got divorced after Liberation and my father married a university student. Little Jing is their son...but never mind all that now. What I'd like to know is how come someone as young as you has got such a head full of worries?"

Li Lifang answers with a sigh, "What do you think it would be like if a person couldn't integrate his ideals with reality?"

Wang Hainan casts a searching look at Li Lifang, but doesn't answer.

Li Lifang continues to speak as she looks apathetically out at the ocean: "I'm supposed to be in a PLA performing arts troupe, but was assigned here as a nurse almost as soon as I put on my army uniform. The only time I get to dance or sing is during solo performances for senior cadres and some of them are really bad-tempered! But, after all, senior cadres are senior cadres. What gets me is, I even have to wait on you, well maybe not you, but your brother and all of their sons, too. The leadership says it's part of our job...I'm a worker's child, you know. I never thought that the family life of some cadres was like that. And then there was Principal Wang, the principal of our school. She urged me to work hard to serve the people, even though she herself had been locked up in some little dark hole-in-the-wall. She said I was so fortunate, but..." Tears well up in Li Lifang's eyes as she speaks. "I want to transfer out of here, but the leadership won't approve."

"What school were you in before?"

"Hong Guang Middle School."

Wang Hainan laughs bitterly, "That Principal Wang you're talking about is my mother!"

"What! Principal Wang is your mother! Really?" Li Lifang opens her eyes wide in surprise. Seeing Wang Hainan nod his head in confirmation, she immediately feels she has met someone she can trust and moves closer to him. Wang Hainan raises himself slightly at the same time as if to shift over in her direction. Li Lifang laughs bashfully, "I was wondering why you didn't have the same last name as your father. How is your mom nowadays?"

Foamy white water tickles their feet as the waves gently push and slap against the breakwater.

THE HOSPITAL ROOM. A nurse enters. "Comrade Shang," she says, "The public security bureau just called. They want you to return to the office."

Wang Hainan struggles to lift his hand. Then pointing at the bookbag at the head of the bed, says with great effort, "There's a book with a green cover inside. It's my diary. You may take it."

Shang Qi opens the bookbag. All the things Wang Hainan had taken with him when he tried to cross the border are still there. Taking a quick look through the contents of the bag, Shang Qi noiselessly removes the diary. "Did Li Lifang have a scar on her head then?" he asks the boy.

Wang Hainan shakes his head: "She wasn't like that before. Comrade Shang, you've got to save her!"

Giving no indication of what he is thinking, Shang Qi silently exits, followed by Chen Jie.

Scene 6

IN THE JEEP. Chen Jie asks Shang Qi, "Old Shang, why are you so interested in the scar on Li Lifang's head?"

"You could say that scar is the key to this case." Shang Qi yawns and shuts his eyes.

THE PUBLIC SECURITY BUREAU. Shang Qi and Chen Jie enter the office of the military representative, who is on the telephone: "...Yes, we'll definitely wrap up the case as soon as possible...Of course, the assailant has to be severely punished...Right! O.K.!" The military representative hangs up the phone. To Chen Jie and Shang Qi: "I've had you come here primarily to ask you a few questions about how things are going on this case. Have you been to the hospital yet?"

Shang Qi nods his head as Chen Jie opens his notebook and begins his report: "An examination of the patient indicates seven wounds on his body made by two different types of weapons. Three of the wounds are in vital places and the patient is still in critical condition."

Military representative: "Li Lifang is the oldest. Moreover, she's been detained four times before. She quite clearly feels no remorse despite repeated warnings, so we ought to book her as ringleader. But with three wounds made by two different weapons, it's obvious that two people were involved in directly assaulting the victim. That second person ought to be the principal, the other one the accessory. Generally, the situation is pretty clear. Well, what do you think? Can we wind up this case?"

Shang Qi doesn't answer.

Chen Jie speaks up: "But according to the analysis made of the blood found on the weapons, Li Lifang didn't lay a hand on Wang Hainan."

The military representative objects: "Just now Hainan's father's secretary called and said that the ministries concerned are taking this case very seriously and hope that it can be wrapped up as soon as possible with a public trial."

Shang Qi thinks to himself for a moment: "From a legal point of view, I know that the office of the procuratorate has been abolished, but we still ought to understand criminals' motives before prosecution. Vicious crimes like this happen constantly these days. I think we should really check into the background of this case and not just take it at face value."

The military representative mulls this over a bit and says, "Alright. You may continue the investigation. But realize that the nature of this case is very serious. Even though Wang Hainan has become estranged from his family, the question of his personal background is still a consideration. I'll give you a week's time then."

Scene 7

Night envelops the city. The lights of countless homes glimmer through the darkness. Shang Qi sits by his desk, chain smoking, as he concentrates on Wang Hainan's diary. Wang Hainan's voice can be hear off-camera: "...Li Lifang and I have grown closer to each other since that day, though it's probably because we're both alone..."

FLASHBACK: DUSK. The sun is sinking into the sea. The silhouettes of Wang Hainan and Li Lifang can be seen on a reef. They are sitting very close to each other.

"Hainan, how come you're always reading that book?" asks Li Lifang as she takes up Klausewitz's *On War.*

"Funny, isn't it?" answers Wang Hainan with a forced laugh. Li Lifang doesn't laugh, but gazes at him with respect and admiration.

Wang Hainan: "I never had ideas like that before. I lived at our unit's school when I was little because I didn't get along with my stepmother. Then, later, my real mother sent me to an ordinary school. Every summer vacation I'd either go back to our home county to work or go to a factory to learn industrial skills. I was really close to the masses then and felt that our life's goal was clearly to build socialism. But nowadays things have changed so much that I can't understand anything. It seems as if the most glorious thing you can do is persecute somebody....My mom was taken into custody and is doing forced labor now, but dad's up in Central. When I'm at my mother's, people cursed me as a son of a bitch, but when I'm with dad, all of a sudden I'm 'Red Posterity.' I really don't know what I ought to do with myself. But I'm young! I'm burning with righteous ardor and it gives me so much energy! If I don't use it on the battleground, then where am I going to use it?..."

A sea breeze begins to blow, causing Li Lifang to shiver slightly. Wang Hainan takes off his jacket and places it gently over her shoulders. "My father's rise has been positively meteoric during these years," he continues, "but there's something I've seen quite clearly — that is, the more people are knocked down, the higher he rises. I'd just be a parasite if I stayed with him and kept leading this privileged life. So I left home. I've had many dreams and have tried a lot of different things, but I've failed in all of them..." Wang Hainan pauses, heaving a deep sigh.

Li Lifang looks at Wang Hainan: "I used to read all these revolutionary memoirs," she says sighing lightly, "And I always felt so much respect and affection for those old cadres. So when I first came here, I thought that working alongside senior officials would be really meaningful. But who would have thought there were high cadres like your father? I mean, what can I say? I didn't have the slightest mental preparation for it. I just can't take it! But the leadership says it's my job. I didn't even have someone I could really talk to either...before you came here, that is. I couldn't stand you at first, you know. But later on I found that you were different from them, that you respected me..."

A bell rings in the sanitorium. Standing up, Li Lifang returns the jacket to Wang Hainan and says sadly, "Well, time for me to make another appearance." Then, resigned, she walks down the breakwater.

(Wang Hainan's voice, off-camera) "Li Lifang and I meet on the reef everyday now. Each time she cuts another line in the rock."

THE SENIOR OFFICIAL'S BEDROOM. Li Lifang is taking the official's blood pressure as he lies across his bed, twirling a big red and blue pencil in one hand. Wang Hainan walks in and says, "Did you call me, Dad?" (Li Lifang and Wang Hainan act as if they barely know each other in front of other people.)

The official nods: "Really getting itchy waiting this past month, aren't you? I've already arranged everything for you, but don't tell your mother."

"Where will I be stationed?"

"My, my! Very picky, aren't we! I've got it set up for you to enter the Army Medical School."

This comes as a surprise to Wang Hainan: "Me? At Army Med? " he asks, astonished.

"What's the matter with that?" The official abruptly stops playing with the pencil and touches the desk with it, point down. Almost drawling, he continues, "Vice Chairman Lin has come out with a directive — got to cultivate kids like you, you know. Anyway, there aren't any other universities that you can go to at the present."

"No! I want to go to the northern front! I wouldn't have come here to see you if it weren't for that!"

"Look, even if I agreed to let you go to the northern front, who do you think would fix you up anywhere later on? Hasn't that ever occurred to you?"

"Then I'm not joining the army!" With that, Wang Hainan stands up and moves toward the door.

"You come back here!" The official's manner suddenly becomes quite serene. "Now what do you want to go and do that for?"

"What for? Because I have no other way left! I want to go and fight!"

"What nonsense! Why are you so bent on going to war? It can't be that there are no other alternatives for you!" The official shakes his head.

"But where can I go? And who can I go with?" Wang Hainan

begins to feel indignant. "Should I go with mom? She's been locked up. Go work in a factory? They're all divided into warring factions. Go back to our home county? It's turned into a disaster area and no one cares. No one's doing anything. They're giving out certificates in the production teams, letting everybody go out and beg! Go along with a rebel faction? I'm not too enthusiastic about that. Then who should I go with? Looks like the only alternative is to let myself be carried in a sedan chair into the army, into the party, into a university and then into a nice position. But what century is this that all this stuff is still going on? I have no respect for the road you've chosen. I want to go my own way — a way that'll set my mind to rest when I die!"

Unable to restrain his fury, the official grabs a glass fish from a cabinet at the head of the bed. He is about to throw it at Wang Hainan when Li Lifang catches his hand, stopping him. "Your health!" she says. "Think of your health." Then she shoots a look at Wang Hainan indicating that he should go.

The official sits down, huffing and puffing, "This is just too much!"

BY THE SEA. A full moon shines down on great, billowing waves as they roll in one after another. Li Lifang comes up quietly, sits down beside Wang Hainan on the breakwater and attempts to soothe his anger. "Hainan, don't be like this. These few years have been tough for me, too, but I always think to myself — just wait, everything'll turn out for the better."

Wordlessly, Wang Hainan cups his hands around Li Lifang's hand.

"I can understand you," she continues, "but fighting a battle at the front is not the only thing left for you." She lets out a soft sigh. "I'm going in two days!" says Wang resolutely. "I have a few old classmates in an army reclamation farm. I can join them."

"Can't you stay?"

"No. This is one battle I have to fight!" Wang Hainan is speaking with great resolve, but then he notices how sick at heart Li Lifang looks. "What are you planning to do?" he says, sighing, almost apologetically.

"Me? I'm going to ask to be demobilized. Hainan, in the future, I..." Eyes brimming with tears, Li Lifang buries her head in Wang Hainan's chest: "Don't forget me!"

The night grows deeper and the moon rises to the center of the sky. Li Lifang lifts her head: "But what am I doing? This is not the time to be depressed! You're going to be leaving soon! Come!" She takes Wang Hainan by the hand and leads him off the breakwater. "Sit here." She presses him down gently, forcing him to sit down on the sand, then taking a few steps back, she removes her army cap and lets down her long, long braid. "I haven't danced the way I like since I came here. But tonight, I going to dance for *you*." As she finishes speaking, she starts to hum a pretty tune, then ever so gracefully she proceeds to dance...

Wang Hainan can see the teardrops in Li Lifang's eyes as she whirls in the moonlight... Too moved to remain seated, Wang Hainan suddenly stands up and takes a step towards Li Lifang. Instantly, Li Lifang realizes what has happened, abruptly stops dancing and throws herself into Wang's arms. Wang Hainan's voice is again heard off-camera: "And that's how I left Li Lifang — off in search of my ideals. And spilling my blood to defend the motherland's borders seems about the only way left to realize those ideals. What else is there for youth like me to do nowadays? We can't study, we can't work. What is there left for us to do?"

ON A NORTHBOUND TRAIN. Wang Hainan opens a Soviet military science textbook entitled *Military Strategy*. On the title page he has scrawled the maxim: "Know the enemy and know yourself, and you can fight one hundred battles without a defeat."

BY A RIVER NEAR THE NORTHERN BORDER. Wang Hainan and other army reclamation unit fighters are lying face down in a snow shelter in a forward position closely watching the other side of the river. One finger of Wang Hainan's gloveless right hand rests tensely on the trigger of his rifle.

IN AN OBSERVATION TOWER. Wang Hainan is sweeping his eyes alertly along the border when another comrade appears below, energetically waving a letter in his hand, shouting, "Hainan! You've got another letter from the seaside!" Wang Hainan casts a cursory glance downwards, nods his head in acknowledgement and continues to hold to his post.

NIGHT. Wang Hainan reads Li Lifang's letter under the light of an oil lamp. Li Lifang's gentle, warm voice is heard off-camera. "Hainan, if the leadership approves of my request to demobilize, I'll be joining you this spring and be a real soldier...with you together — together for the rest of our lives...." Taking a furtive glance at his soundly sleeping comrades, Wang Hainan quickly plants a kiss on the letter.

EARLY SPRING. The vast stretches of the northern borderland

are still covered with silvery white snow. There is little sign of life anywhere because all the animals, great and small, are sleeping deeply under the heavy snow. One can tell that spring has arrived only from a 1971 calendar hanging on a wall.

In the remaining light of the setting sun, a messenger hands a letter to Wang Hainan, who is lying on a homemade military sand table practicing tactical operations. As he hurries to open the letter, Li Lifang's voice is again heard off-camera: "Hainan, don't write to me after you receive this letter. Just listen to the dictates of fate — we must part with each other. It may be very painful for you now, but you'll get over it as time passes. And you have your cause. Take good care of yourself...and forget me. Don't try to look for me. I've gone to a place you'll never find!" Wang Hainan's mood changes from incomprehension to pain and then to anger. He rushes outside and, oblivious of everything, dashes up a hill where he stands knee deep in snow, a look of panic and agitation on his face...

NIGHT. Wang Hainan returns from his post and sits pensively on his bed. Accidentally, his hand brushes a book which is by a roommate's pillow. He picks it up without thinking — *The Diary of Che Guevara*.

LATER THE SAME NIGHT. Wang Hainan is in bed, wrapped up in his blankets, feverishly writing a letter to Li Lifang by flashlight. Finished with that, he proceeds to draw up a rough draft of a telegram. A strange, nervous smile flashes across his grief-wracked face...

(Wang Hainan's voice off-camera): I've written so many letters and sent too many telegrams, but nothing in return. After losing Li Lifang, I've sunk into such a mire of suffering and depression. And now in the midst of all this pain and meaninglessness I know I must leave here and seek out a new life...."

A FEW DAYS LATER. Wang Hainan burns Li Lifang's letters and finishes packing his bags. Several comrades see him off.

ON A SOUTHBOUND TRAIN. Wang Hainan concentrates on a map of southern China, his finger tracing the southern boundary line....

Wang's off-camera voice continues: "Yes, I've failed time and time again. And what's shameful about it is not just my failures, but that I still can't escape my father's "protective umbrella." Will I never be able to take responsibility for my own actions?

Can I never choose a path of my own?."

IN THE PRESENT. Shang Qi finishes reading Wang Hainan's diary and opens a letter he found tucked between the pages, Li Lifang's last letter to Wang Hainan. He reads it over very carefully, then lights a cigarette and begins to pace back and forth, lost in thought. After a short while he suddenly returns to the desk, where he goes back through the diary, page by page, almost obsessively, as if searching for some inaccessible secret.

THE SEASIDE SANITORIUM. A public security bureau jeep is parked outside the gate. Shang Qi and Chen Jie walk out of the pretty little vacation cottage that once housed Wang Hainan's father. Crossing the beach, the two men stop at the breakwater where Shang Qi examines the concave marks left in the rock by Li Lifang. The last etched furrow is noticeably deeper than the others. Shang Qi counts the number of lines and stands up.
"What does this all add up to?" asks Chen Jie, perturbed.
Shang Qi doesn't answer his question. "This is a pretty nice place," he says, pointing out at the sea. "Sure beats the mud puddles of the cadre school. Come on! Let's go for a little swim!" Taking of his clothes, he dives into the water. Chen Jie jumps in after him and the two men have a good, hearty swim.
Doing the breast stroke one minute, free style the next, Shang Qi cuts a vigorous path through the white, frothy waves. Sometimes he even dives underwater...he appears to be enjoying the exercise immensely, even though it is clear that he is searching for something hidden beneath the surface.

Scene 8

A WORKSHOP IN A MACHINE TOOL FACTORY. Li Lifang's father is making a pipe to dispel his boredom. He works slowly and a bit fitfully, stopping frequently to examine his work...
A cadre leads Shang Qi and Chen Jie over to Li. "People are here to see you about someone," he says, "say they've got a few questions to ask you."
"Questions?" says Li, lifting his head. "Uhhh, then you would be...?"
"We're from the public security bureau," answers Chen Jie. "We'd like some information concerning your daughter."
Li's face darkens instantly. "You guys are really busy, huh? Why don't you play cards if you've got nothing to do?" he says, shooting a contemptuous look inside the workshop where a group

of young men are engaged in a raucous game of poker.

"Well, I guess it's our turn to be busy if you're not," laughs Shang Qi, a bit apologetically. Li grins wryly. "Have a seat!" he says.

The three men sit down on a tool box. "We're primarily interested in what happened to your daughter after she left the army," Chen Jie speaks first, opening up his notebook.

Li removes some tobacco from a pouch and stuffs it into the new pipe. "All right," he says. "I'll start from the beginning then. You know how people get into the People's Liberation Army these days — straight through the back door. But not Lifang. She got in on her ability alone, and I can tell you everyone in the factory was glad for her too. Who would've guessed that she would leave the army after only two years? But then it was just one of those things — she got sick, says it was rheumatism or something like that. Wouldn't you know it! Afterwards she came to work here in the factory. The old worker who taught her the ropes was quite satisfied with her, but I was more worried about who she would marry than anything else. As for those young guys in the plant — forget it! I just knew there would be trouble the way those damn pests followed her all over the place. So I was really concerned about finding her someone more suitable..."

FLASHBACK: Li Lifang, now dressed as a worker, returns home from a day at the factory. Her father comes out from the inner room and clears his throat. "So what's your decision?" he asks. Li Lifang, now busy preparing the evening meal, doesn't answer.

"Don't you like Doctor Zhao?" says Li, somewhat annoyed. "The man may be a little old for you, but he's honest and solid. Besides, what else do you think you can get nowadays? Remember, he was the one who knocked my high blood pressure down, and when your teacher in the shop got sick, who was it that stayed by his bedside for three days and nights without closing his eyes? And wasn't he the one who cured you when you were ill? And whenever any of the old ladies and housewives have problems, Dr. Zhao's the man they look for. He cares about us; he's so close with us — and he's a university graduate yet!" Seeing that Lifang is not answering, Li continues: "Normally, this is the sort of thing you should be able to decide for yourself, but I was afraid you'd fall for one of those good-for-nothing jerks. Those boys choose wives the way you buy fruit at a peasant market — if it's good-looking, grab it! But if you go with one of them it won't last long, let me tell you."

Li Lifang is washing rice. "I don't even want to think about it right now," she says, a bit impatiently. "So don't bother yourself arranging anything."

"Look at her, will you! So now fathers are unnecessary, optional! Well, to tell the truth, I'm a little afraid the man's not going to like YOU! He's got a skill, character, a comfortable home. So what are you being so picky about? So he's a little older than you, but then that means he'll be giving in to you all the time. There won't be any difficulty at the marriage registrar that way, either."

"But, I ..." Lifang appears to want to say something, but stops herself.

"Your mom died young, so I'm the one who has to make this decision for you. You just listen to dad and you'll be all right." Lifang's father heads for the door. "I'm going to get him now," he says, on his way out. "You don't have to make anything special for dinner. He doesn't care much about that kind of thing."

A single teardrop rolls down Li Lifang's face. The rice, still in the pot, flows with the water into the sink, slowly, grain by grain....

FLASHBACK: THE WEDDING BANQUET. Li Lifang and Zhao Qing, dressed in new clothes with bright red flowers adorning their chests, are seated by a table surrounded by noisily celebrating friends and relatives.

Li Lifang's younger sister, Li Xiaofang, is dangling a piece of candy on a string in front of the bride and groom. "Have some candy, you two!" she urges impishly.

Li Lifang gives her sister a shove. "Don't make such a fuss!" she says, hanging her head.

Seeing Li Lifang's mortification, Zhao Qing quickly leans over and grabs the candy between his teeth.

"Why did you have to be in such a hurry?" Li Xiaofang shouts, pounding the doctor playfully on the shoulder. The guests burst into loud laughter.

At this point several apprentices enter the room. Li Lifang's father hurries to greet them. "O.K. you punks, you can eat, but no trouble making!" he says, jovially issuing candy to each of them. "Here! Fill your mouths with this!"

A young apprentice wearing a green PLA cap takes Li by the arm. "Hey, master worker Li," he says, "What does Dr. Zhao here have that I don't?" Li playfully pretends to give the young man a slap across the face. "The last thing I want for a son-in-law would be a dumb pest like you!" he says. "By the way, didn't you have to make a trip to the public security station lately for a little talk with the police?"

"Don't bring that up now, O.K.?" says the apprentice with an embarrassed laugh. "What good is there in talking about that sort of thing on such a joyous occasion?"

Another burst of laughter from the guests....

BACK IN THE MACHINE TOOL SHOP. Li bangs the pipe against the sole of his shoe.

"Later they got divorced," he continues. "And you can bet that bunch of youngsters made my life miserable afterwards. It caused such a scandal I can't raise my head and look people in the eye around here anymore."

"Why did they get a divorce?" Chen Jie asks.

Right at this moment a man appears at the shop door. "Let's go, boys!" he shouts. "The meeting's about to begin!"

"I can't really give you the reason for that," says Li, standing up. "You'd better go ask Dr. Zhao."

Shang Qi also stands up. "One other thing before we go — do you know how your daughter got the scar on her head?"

"I asked her. She said she'd choked on some water swimming and bumped her head on a rock," Li answers off handedly.

Shang Qi nods his head. Chen Jie looks at his superior somewhat disappointedly. "If there's anything else you're not clear about, ask my other daughter — she's at home. Well, I'll be going now." Li is about to make an exit when he suddenly turns around and pulls something out of his pocket. "This is the key to the front gate of our house," he says with a gesture. "I lock her in everyday."

"O.K.," says Shang Qi, taking the key. "Thanks a lot for your help! We'll go see Dr. Zhao now and then your daughter."

Scene 9

THE FACTORY CLINIC. Zhao Qing is sitting at a table across from Shang Qi and Chen Jie. He seems reserved and withdrawn. "This whole thing was arranged by master worker Li — from our first meeting down to the wedding," he says. "I don't have any complaints about old Li, though. He's got his share of aggravation from it too. There are a few apprentices in our factory who get their kicks out of following him around, ribbing him about how he had supposedly 'palmed off used goods for new.' I think you probably know what they man by that. I guess I just take things too seriously, plus I'm a physician. Or maybe I know too much for my own good. Maybe I just think too much...."

FLASHBACK: THE WEDDING NIGHT. Zhao Qing, his shirt over his shoulder, is pacing intensely back and forth.

Li Lifang's eyes are brimming with tears as she finishes dressing.

"I beg of you," she pleads. "Please forgive me! It wasn't because..."

"Who was he?" Zhao Qing asks stubbornly. "Tell me!"

Li Lifang collapses on the table, head buried in her arms, crying. Zhao Qing walks over to her side of the table. "We're husband and wife now," he says urgently. "You ought to trust me. I just want to know who he was!"

Stricken with grief and remorse, Li Lifang begins to sob, causing Zhao Qing to lose his composure. "Tell me!" he shouts suddenly grabbing her. "Who was he? I can't take it!" Li Lifang's entire face is now wet with tears. "I...I..." she stammers.

Zhao Qing shakes her roughly by the shoulders. "Tell me who he was! Tell me! Tell me!" he demands relentlessly.

Li Lifang: "I...I can't..." She bites her lip so hard it seems as if the blood may flow at any minute.

"Phonies! You're all a bunch of phonies!" shouts Zhao Qing. "Get the hell out of here!"

Wracked with grief, Li Lifang pushes her way past Zhao Qing and rushes out the door. "Lifang, Lifang!" Regretting what he has done, Zhao Qing quickly chases after her.

A group of young apprentices who have just gotten off the night shift stand there watching the spectacle, exchanging puzzled comments. The sound of mocking laughter can be heard amid their whispers.

BACK IN THE CLINIC. "After Lifang ran back home," Zhao Qing continues, "her father came to see me. He was furious! I had no other choice but to tell him the truth—that Lifang simply wasn't a virgin. Afterwards she insisted on a divorce, and that's how we parted."

"How much do you know about what happened later?" asks Chen Jie.

Zhao Qing bows his head sorrowfully. "I saw her in a restaurant once afterwards. She was with a bunch of suspicious looking characters. I don't know why, but she ran right out...."

FLASHBACK: DUSK. A SMALL RESTAURANT. Three young hoodlums are sitting at a table in a corner with Li Lifang, making her drink glass after glass of wine in an attempt to get her drunk. Li Lifang can't hold her alcohol and falls over onto the table.

Other customers in their end of the room cast them contemptuous glances.

Entering the restaurant, Zhao Qing sees Li Lifang and stands there, glued to the spot.

A young hoodlum wearing a snap-brim cap lifts Li Lifang's head by the chin and examines her face closely. She is hopelessly intoxicated. "I...I...want to go home," she stammers.

"Home? What home? Didn't you say you were homeless? Come on, have another drink. In a little while I'll take you where we can have some *real* fun!"

Li Lifang wretches noisily. Just as the three young hoods are about to lead her out of the restaurant, Zhao Qing walks over to stop them. "Get out of way!" snaps the young man with the cap, deliberately colliding with Zhao Qing.

The three hooligans forcibly escort Li Lifang out of the restaurant and stagger into a narrow alley. Zhao Qing follows them from a distance.

Finally, they come to a halt at a deserted work site. Zhao Qing hurriedly ducks into a shed. Hearing the gang members break into argument, he stretches his head out to observe, only to see the one with the snap-brim cap suddenly wallop one of his companions across the face, thus bringing on a full-scale battle. In an attempt to stop the bloodshed, the third hood releases Li Lifang, who stands there weakly clasping an upright post, head drooping low.

The hooligan with the cap is thrown onto a pile of bricks in the scuffle, bloodying his face badly. His opponent is just about to continue the attack when he is grabbed by the third youth. Leaping to his feet, the hood suddenly pulls a three-edged plastering knife out of his jacket, frightening the other two into rapid retreat. He laughs wickedly: "Let's see who wants her now!" and falls upon Li Lifang, thrusting the knife into her lower abdomen. Li Lifang screams horribly and topples over.

Zhao Qing, who has witnessed the entire scene, is paralyzed with terror and covers his eyes with his cupped hands. Legs giving out from under him, he sprawls on the ground.

BACK IN THE CLINIC. Zhao Qing is in tears. "It's all my fault!" he cries, striking his head with his fist. "I hate myself!"

Shang Qi's face remains expressionless as he silently, savagely draws on his cigarette. "Don't do this to yourself, Dr. Zhao," Chen Jie says, attempting to console the physician. "That's all we'll talk about for today."

Scene 10

THE FACTORY'S RESIDENTIAL AREA. Shang Qi looks at the number on the door, then up at the window, which is tightly boarded up. He gestures silently at Chen Jie to open the door.

Li Xiaofang thinks her father is returning and comes out to greet him, but is stunned to find two strangers at her door.

"Don't be afraid. We're from the public security bureau," explains Shang Qi, dangling the key in front of her. "Your father said we could come."

"We'd like to ask you a few questions about your sister," adds Chen Jie.

Finally relaxing her guard, Li Xiaofang asks them to sit down and starts to prepare tea.

"Why did your sister leave home?" Chen Jie asks.

"After Lifang came running home that night, dad went to see Zhao Qing," Xiaofang answers. "I don't know why, but when dad came back he was terribly angry. "Who was it? Who was it?" he kept asking her. But Lifang just cried. So dad started whipping her with his belt — and hard, too! After Lifang and Dr. Zhao got divorced, just about everyone in the factory was talking about it. Then one day dad came home really drunk...."

FLASHBACK: Li Lifang's father returns home quite drunk. As he enters the room, he finds Xiaofang trying to console Lifang who is sobbing uncontrollably on the bed. "Shameless hussy!" he curses, pulling Xiaofang out of the way. "Because of you I have to take insults every day at work! Very funny! They say I peddle used goods! You have ruined the good name of the entire Li family!" Then, roughly grabbing his older daughter: "Tell me! Who did it? I'll chop him in two! Tell me!" The tears flow down Li Lifang's face as she struggles weakly to free herself.

"Dad, don't..." says Xiaofang, in a timid attempt to mediate. "Dad..."

Rudely shoving Xiaofang aside, the old worker grabs Lifang again and pulls her off the bed. "Are you going to tell me or not?" he roars. Turning around, he picks up a wooden stool and is about to smash it over Lifang's head when she throws herself on her knees at her father's feet, pleading: "Daddy, don't hit me! I, I..." Seeing that Lifang still will not give him the information he is looking for, Li swings down the upraised stool. Xiaofang clasps her arms around her father, pinning his arms to his sides. "Lifang!" she shouts to her sister, "get out! Quick!"

Li Lifang struggles to her feet and with tear-filled eyes casts a look of utter mortification at her father and sister. Then, turning around, she painfully staggers out the door....

BACK IN THE LI HOME. Xiaofang: "Lifang never came home again after that. And she didn't go back to work either. I heard she had been detained several times by the police. Then she got fired from her job at the factory. Dad felt really sorry about it all and had me go look for her. One day on the street..."

FLASHBACK: OUTSIDE A FIRST-CLASS DOWNTOWN RES-TAURANT. Li Lifang, a cigarette dangling impudently from her mouth, ambles out the front door accompanied by several young male hoodlums, laughing and joking. Leading the group is a bushy-haired young man; he is followed by three others—Zheng Xiaoliu, Liang Qi and Sun Sheng. The five of them all reek of liquor.

Li Xiaofang, who is standing on the other side of the street, spots her sister. "Lifang!" she cries, trying to run across the road. She is blocked, however, by a steady stream of traffic.

Hearing her sister's shout, Li Lifang ducks into an alley with the four hoods. Xiaofang casts a quick look at her surroundings and chases after the little band, making several turns before finally catching up with them in an out-of-the-way alley. Xiaofang plants herself squarely in her sister's path, pleading: "Come home with me, Lifang. Dad wants you to come home too!"

"I don't know you," Lifang says indifferently. "Get out of the way!"

"Lifang!" the tears well up in Xiaofang's eyes.

Biting her lip, Lifang shoves the younger girl aside.

The bushy-haired hoodlum walks over to Xiaofang and pinches her on the chin, laughing strangely. "Heehee! You two sisters really look alike!" he says, hiccupping. In a panic, Xiaofang begins to retreat, but the hooligan catches up with her in one step, grabbing her by both arms. "Don't be afraid!" he says, "Come along with big sister! Heehee!"

"Lifang!" Xiaofang cries out again. Lifang does not move. Her back pressing against the wall behind her, Xiaofang gazes at her older sister in terror. Zheng Xiaoliu and company grin hideously. Suddenly Li Lifang steps forward, grabbing the bushy-haired youth by the shoulder. "Haven't you had enough?" she asks.

Spinning around, the young delinquent shoots Li Lifang an angry look. "What the hell do you want!" he curses, smacking her across the face. Then with a cold laugh he turns and embraces Xiaofang, who shouts and struggles to free herself, and kisses her savagely.

Li Lifang grabs the youth by the hair and yanks him roughly backwards, then places herself between Xiaofang and the still-reeling youth, protecting Xiaofang with her own body.

The young hoodlum goes wild. Pulling out a long knife, he threatens Lifang: "Stinking bitch! You looking for trouble?" Zheng Xiaoliu and the others quickly attempt to restrain him: "Forget it! Forget it!"

"Get lost! This is none of your business! When somebody gets me mad, there's no stopping me!" Viciously pushing his cohorts out of the way, he turns to face Li Lifang, snarling savagely, "Step aside or I'll carve you up!" At first Li Lifang is taken aback by his threat and retreats to the wall next to Xiaofang. Then, suddenly she ferociously pounces on the wild-haired youth, wrenching the knife from his clumsy hands. Quickly leaping out of the way, the youth joins Zheng Xiaoliu and the others who have all whipped out concealed weapons. The five young men turn on Li Lifang, eyeing her voraciously like a pack of wolves stalking its prey.

"Didn't you say you wanted to carve me up?" spits Li Lifang, full of wrath. Little Momma'll do it for you!" Taking a step forward, Li Lifang rips open her collar, and with one swift motion slashes down across her chest. The bushy-haired boy is startled at the sight of the fresh, red blood rapidly staining Li Lifang's blouse and quickly retreats several steps. Zheng Xiaoliu and the others stop dead in their tracks.

"Ha! You're going to get it this time!" Li Lifang stands there, hands on her hips, ignoring the blood as it flows down her chest. "What are you doing just standing there like a bunch of idiots?" she yells at Zheng and the others. Immediately Zheng Xiaoliu and the other hoods spin around to attack the bushy-haired hood, who takes to his heels at once.

Watching them go, Li Lifang laughs wildly, then suddenly her body starts to sway, almost tottering over. With one hand on the wall for support, she slowly slides into a squat. Then grabbing a handful of earth from the ground, she rubs it on her chest over the wound. As Lifang turns her head around she sees her sister who has rushed to her side, and quickly stands up. "Beat it!" she screams harshly, almost insanely, cracking Xiaofang across the face. "Get lost!" Li Lifang screams again at Xiaofang, deliberately tripping the younger girl with one sweep of the leg, leaving her on the ground, as she staggers off.

Li Xiaofang remains prone on the ground. "Lifang! Lifang!" she cries, holding the bloodstained earth in her hands.

THE LI HOME. "I never saw her again," continues Xiaofang, dabbing her eyes with her fingers. "Dad stopped telling me to go look for her. And now he keeps me locked up here all day long."

Agitated, Chen Jie turns his face away. "O.K.," says Shang Qi, standing up calmly. "That's about all for today. When your father comes back, tell him we came by. In the meantime, why don't you take the key?" Turning around, Shang Qi takes a look at the boarded up window and suddenly starts to tear away the nailed planks almost as if they represented some sort of terrible affront to his personal dignity. Li Xiaofang and Chen Jie stand to one side watching, astonished by his behavior.

Finished pulling down the boards, Shang Qi walks straight out without looking back.

Scene 11

THE PUBLIC SECURITY BUREAU. Shang Qi is still studying Wang Hainan's diary. Chen Jie is flipping through a pile of papers.

The military representative enters. "Anything new to report?" he asks.

"We're right in the middle of our investigation," answers Chen Jie. "The problem is Li Lifang refuses to answer every time we interrogate her."

"I wouldn't be at all surprised if you found this case hard to handle," says the military representative self confidently. "The whole thing goes well beyond the bounds of an ordinary criminal case."

"I would agree with you on that," says Shang Qi, joining the conversation.

"The Cultural Revolution is intensifying," says the military representative, looking at Shang Qi. "And the class struggle at present is quite complex. If the son of a senior cadre is assassinated, wouldn't you think there might be a political motivation."

Shang Qi: "There's no basis to say that as yet."

"What's the matter, Old Shang?" the military representative laughs. "A few years at cadre school knock the spirit out of you? Got to continue the Revolution, remember?"

Shang Qi laughs noncommittally, rubbing his furrowed brow with his right hand.

"All right then, continue the investigation," says the military representative, turning to leave. "But you've got to pick up the pace."

Shang Qi makes a decisive gesture towards Chen Jie: "Let's interrogate Zheng Xiaoliu!"

THE DUTY OFFICE OF THE BUREAU LOCKUP.

"How's Zheng Xiaoliu been lately?" Shang Qi asks a guard.

"We've tried to reason with him several times," he answers, "but with no result. Now he's pretending to have gone nuts. He must have slapped himself across the face a hundred times since yesterday! And he eats his quilt. Says he wants to be sent to a hospital on the outside for treatment."

Chen Jie laughs coldly: "If he's demanding treatment outside, that shows he's not crazy."

"I'll go get him," says the guard, also laughing.

Zheng Xiaoliu is brought in. He looks about the room idiotically, pretending not to care in the least about anything.

Shang Qi begins the interrogation. "How old are you?" he asks.

"Almost eighty-nine!"

"How much schooling did you have?"

"Eight years of junior middle school!"

Shang Qi hesitates for a moment, then continues. "Why didn't you go on to senior middle school?" he asks.

"Don't tell me you don't know the answer to that?" the youth answers lightheartedly. "There's nothing left to study!"

"Then where did you learn how to handle a knife and fight?" Shang Qi asks sarcastically. Momentarily stuck for an answer, Zheng Xiaoliu suddenly plunks himself down on the ground where he begins to box his own ears and rub dirt in his face.

Ignoring this performance, Shang Qi picks up an old copy of a magazine entitled *New Youth* from out of the files. On the cover is a photograph of Zheng Xiaoliu and a group of classmates making model airplanes together. They all have red flowers pinned to their chests.

Shang Qi waits til Zheng Xiaoliu seems bored with his own antics, then thrusting the magazine in his face, he asks him, "Do you still remember this?" Zheng Xiaoliu hangs his head at the sight of the photograph on the cover.

"That was a long time ago!" he sighs, returning to the chair.

"Do you know the party's policy on captured criminals?" asks Shang Qi, severely now. Seeing the youth nod his head, Shang Qi continues: "Then do yourself a favor and get on the right track! Give me the facts as they happened!" Zheng Xiaoliu is about to speak, but is stopped by Shang Qi. "Think before you open your mouth!" he warns.

Zheng Xiaoliu bows his head despondently. "I'll confess," he says. "I'll confess everything. It all started that morning..."

FLASHBACK: A SMALL SHOP IN THE SUBURBS. Customers are few and far between. Zheng Xiaoliu and Li Lifang are leaning on the counter pretending to buy things. As they ask to see different objects on display, Sun Sheng, who is standing there with Liang Qi, takes advantage of the sales clerk's turned back and whips out a collapsible television antenna from his sleeve, the tip of which had been dipped in glue, and probing into the cash register, quickly pulls out a ten *yuan* note. By the time the clerk turns back to face them, the antenna has already disappeared and Sun Sheng is standing there, whistling innocently, as if nothing had happened. This process repeats itself several times; each time Sun Sheng rolls up the bills and passes them on to Zheng Xiaoliu. After awhile, Sun Sheng and Liang Qi leave the store.

Suddenly another gang of hooligans dash out into the street, intercepting Sun Sheng and Liang Qi. Seeing what is happening, Zheng Xiaoliu and Li Lifang immediately rush to the defense.

"Got some fresh bills there? What're you waiting for? Divvy it up!" says a member of the opposing gang, speaking in street slang.

"Whose dough you want to divvy up, man?" Zheng Xiaoliu cuts in.

The hooligans spot Li Lifang and break into malicious smiles. "Hey, baby," says one, "You sure got a pretty face!"

A faint, icy smile creeps across Li Lifang's harsh, indifferent face as she stands there, arms crisscrossed over her chest. A cigarette in one hand, she quietly unties the bookbag under her arm. Grinning cheekily, the opposing gang members move in. Zheng Xiaoliu tilts his body slightly to one side, preparing to pull out a weapon, when Li Lifang shoots him a look, temporarily stopping him. "Call me Momma first!" she says, taunting them.

"The hell we will, you bitch!"

In a flash, Li Lifang whips out a chopping knife from the bookbag and slices down on the first hooligan's head. Cupping his hands over the wound, he falls with a scream, frightening the rest of the gang into flight.

Several trucks can be seen approaching from a distance. "Meet in the usual place!" shouts Zheng Xiaoliu. Li Lifang and the others run off, dispersing in opposite directions....

ZHENG XIAOLIU: "We got together again by the river in the afternoon of the same day. Almost as soon as we'd gotten there, we bumped into that person. Li Lifang called him Wang Hainan. She told us to wait, then went over by herself to talk to him...."

FLASHBACK: Wang Hainan and Li Lifang stand facing each other. "Lifang!" Wang Hainan cries, overwhelmed with conflicting emotions.

Li Lifang doesn't answer, but for an instant, a spark of vitality flashes across her face.

"But, you're..." Wang Hainan looks Li Lifang up and down, astonished at what he sees.

"I'm what?" queries Li Lifang, biting her lip, suddenly feeling resentful.

Wang Hainan looks over at Zheng Xiaoliu and the others. "You're hanging around with that sort now?" he asks.

Li Lifang recovers her expression of indifference. "Yeah," she answers. "They're my brothers!"

Zheng Xiaoliu walks over and taps Li Lifang on the arm. "Who's this guy?" he asks.

"He would have been your dear brother-in-law!" says Li Lifang, breaking suddenly into loud, dissolute laughter.

Zheng Xiaoliu begins to fiddle contemptuously with Wang Hainan's cuffs and collar. Wang violently pushs him aside: "Lifang. I wrote you so many letters and tried to find out where you were so many times...But I never imagined you would be..."

"There's a lot of things you never imagined!" counters Li Lifang, grimacing.

Then turning around, she shouts, "Xiaoliu! Let's go!"

Zheng Xiaoliu gives Wang Hainan a mocking salute. "Bye-bye, brother-in-law!" he says, following Li Lifang.

Wang Hainan hesitates for a moment, frowning, then chases after them.

Without even turning back to look, Li Lifang walks quickly to a nearby plant nursery where she comes to a halt, out of breath.

Several workers stand there quietly watching.

As Zheng Xiaoliu catches up with the rest of the gang, Liang Qi turns his head and looks behind him. "Hey Xiaoliu, old buddy," he says. "That jerk is still following us!"

Li Lifang shoots Liang Qi an angry look. "Who are you saying is a jerk!" she snaps, startling him into silence.

Running briskly, Wang Hainan catches up.

The bookbag still tucked under one arm, Li Lifang faces him. "Stand still!" she commands.

"I've been looking for you all this time, Lifang," Wang Hainan says, his clear voice full of misery. "But you..."

Li Lifang: "Why were you looking for me?"

"I..." Wang stammers, lifting his head. "Don't you know the answer to that question yourself?"

"All right! Why don't you join our gang then!" says Li Lifang, making a queer face.

"No! You ought to come with me!"

"What for? Still off fighting your little wars?"

"Yes! I'm still fighting!" Then suddenly remembering his numerous defeats: "I tried to go over the border several times," he says, sighing. "I'd planned on joining a foreign communist guerilla band. And I'm going to keep trying even though I've failed so far! Lifang! Come with me the next time!"

"Didn't they arrest you?" Li Lifang asks curiously.

"Yes, they picked me up, but they sent me home each time and released me."

"Oh right! Your dad's a big official!" she says derisively. "Hey, if you joined up with us, they'd let you go every time you got taken in! Fantastic!"

Wang Hainan fixes his eyes on Li Lifang. "Don't tell me you're saying that too!"

"What else should I say, *young master*?" Li Lifang answers acidly.

"You...You've degenerated!" returns Wang Hainan, somewhat indignantly.

A cold, callous expression comes over Li Lifang's face. "Degenerated? Who? Me? Or is it you? You and your kind? I hate you! I hate you all! If I ever run across you again, I'll..." Grinding her teeth in fury, Li Lifang whips out from her bag the still bloody knife.

"You think you can intimidate me with that?" asks Wang Hainan, brows locked in a frown.

Li Lifang laughs wickedly: "You can try me if you'd like," Then putting away the knife, she turns around and stalks off.

Sorrowfully watching Li Lifang as she walks further and further away, Wang Hainan suddenly shouts, "Lifang! Come back! Lifang!" and goes off in pursuit.

Hearing Wang Hainan's cry, Lifang comes to a stop.

"What'll we do?" asks Zheng Xiaoliu.

"Go give him a lesson," answers Li Lifang, eyes shut wearily. "But don't overdo it."

Zheng Xiaoliu, Liang Qi and Sun Sheng wheel around and begin their attack. Wang Hainan falls beneath a rain of blows and kicks despite his resistance. Then crawling back to his feet, he is forced into a corner. "What are you doing? Don't get any closer!" he warns. Not to be outdone by this foul-mouthed, snickering mob, Wang Hainan pulls out the paratrooper knife from his belt as the hooligans close in for the final attack.

Uttering a strange cry, Zheng Xiaoliu flashes a razor, as does Liang Qi. Sun Sheng catches up with the group, sharpened pipe in hand....

Li Lifang does not turn her head around when she hears the sharp cry of pain that follows, but merely stands there, eyes squeezed tightly shut. Two lines of hot tears trickle slowly down her face.

Several workers from the nursery rush immediately to the scene.

Turning around, Li Lifang walks back to the fallen Wang Hainan, now lying in a pool of blood, and stands there motionless, resigned to her fate, arms dangling helplessly at her sides.

BACK IN THE LOCKUP DUTY ROOM. Zheng Xiaoliu's face is covered with sweat. "That Wang Hainan didn't die, did he?" he asks plaintively.

Shang Qi waves his hand curtly and Zheng Xiaoliu is led off.

The telephone begins ringing urgently. "Yes?" says Shang Qi, picking up the receiver. "...Speaking...All right. I'll be there right away."

THE HOSPITAL GATE. The bureau jeep flies through at full speed.

Shang Qi and Chen Jie walk rapidly down the hallway followed by a doctor: "Wang Hainan has just taken a turn for the worst...."

"Have you informed the family yet?" asks Chen Jie.

"His brother is here."

Little Jing, dressed in military attire, is waiting for them at the entrance of the emergency room. "Are you from the public security bureau?" he asks Shang Qi, stopping him at the door. "My brother's case has been under investigation for quite a few days. How come you haven't...."

Shang Qi ignores him completely. "Go get Mrs. Wang as fast as you can!" he says to Chen Jie.

A look of disgust appears on Little Jing's face as he steps over to one side. Walking into the emergency room, Shang Qi takes a close look at Wang Hainan, who is lying on an operating table — dead.

Shang Qi raises his head, fixing his eyes on the doctor who is helplessly wiping his glasses, head bowed.

"What did he say before he died?" Shang Qi asks

"He said he COULDN'T die," answers a nurse. "He said that if he died, it would get someone called Li Lifang into trouble. He wanted you to know that Li Lifang wasn't like that before, that she had to be saved...Also, he kept on repeating a name, something like..." the nurse pauses to think, "Right! It was Guevara. He didn't say anything else."

The nurses are just about to wheel Wang Hainan's corpse out of the emergency room when Chen Jie comes running in, accompanied by a breathless Mrs. Wang.

Comprehending at once what has happened, Mrs. Wang collapses, one hand pressed over her heart. Nurses rush to her aide immediately.

As Mrs. Wang regains consciousness, Chen Jie helps her over to the operating table. At the sight of her son's dead body, she begins to weep silently, tears pouring out of her eyes.

Shang Qi gestures to a nurse to help Mrs. Wang to one side. Covering Wang Hainan with a sheet, another nurse wheels him out of the room.

Quivering with emotion, Mrs. Wang grabs Shang Qi by the arm. "Tell me!" she cries, "Who killed Hainan? Who killed him?"

Shang Qi answers in his usual tranquil tone of voice: "It was your student, Li Lifang."

"What?" That's impossible! Impossible! the old woman is stunned, almost beyond words.

"Yes, it should have been impossible!" says Shang Qi. Then turning to Chen Jie: "Have all persons involved in the case come down to the bureau," he says, striding out of the emergency room.

THE BUREAU INTERROGATION ROOM. "...And that's how it all happened." Finishing his report, Chen Jie sits down, closing the file. He is taking a sip of water.

Mrs. Wang, Li Lifang's father, Xiaofang, Dr. Zhao, the emergency room doctor, Little Jing and the military representative are all present. Not a sound can be heard from the table where they are sitting.

Sweeping his eyes over the group, Shang Qi is the first to break the silence: "Now that everyone involved is present, I'd like to inform you that, as the military representative has pointed out, this is definitely not a simple criminal case. My own personal opinion is that the social environment was critical." Looking fixedly at Mrs. Wang, he says, "Mrs. Wang, as an educator with many years of experience, do you really think that teaching students only about the bright side of human affairs and ignoring the dark side can provide them with the ability to deal correctly with contradictions? Don't you see how weak and vulnerable this makes them when they go out into the world?" Dabbing her eyes, Mrs.

Wang bows her head.

Turning to Lifang's father, Shang Qi continues: "Comrade Li, you're a worker. So could you tell me, then, how is it that you could have taken up the whip and beaten your daughter like an old-fashioned overseer?" Unable to answer, Li heaves a heavy sigh.

"And you, Dr. Zhao," he continues, "do you mean to say that your understanding of the joys of marriage boils down to the simple right of possession on the first night?" Zhao Qing, conscience stricken, is on the verge of tears.

Facing Little Jing, Shang Qi merely looks at the young man coldly without saying anything. Then, addressing the military representative: "I don't know if I'm correct or not," he says, "but as public security officers, I think our main responsibility is to trace the social roots of crime and to take measures to eliminate them." Sitting back in his seat, the military representative coughs noncommittally.

"Of course, we also have to take some of the responsibility ourselves," Shang Qi goes on, self mockingly. "We allowed ourselves to be thrown over so easily; we all gave up so easily the responsibility the party invested in us to uphold the dictatorship of the proletariat. And then with criminal elements active everywhere, some parents lock up their own children as if *they* were the criminals. Don't you find this a bit strange?"

Clearing his throat again, the military representative interrupts: "Comrade Shang Qi! This is not the appropriate occasion!"

Ignoring him, Shang Qi presses a buzzer on the table.

Li Lifang is brought in. As soon as she recognizes the company gathered, a look of hatred and spite comes over her face, which is even paler than in the previous scene.

Shang Qi: "This is Li Lifang as she is today — a criminal, an instigator to murder. But did she really have to become a criminal? Or is it that all those present here today pushed her onto the road of crime, step by step?"

Everyone in the room hangs his head shamefacedly. Li Lifang remains seated, expressionless.

"Of course, I'm not going to fix the blame on anyone of you," continues Shang Qi. "But I certainly am going to investigate the original crime that caused this incident in the first place."

Little Jing and the military representative exchange whispers. "Old Shang!" shouts the representative, looking very unhappy.

Acting as if he hasn't heard anything, Shang Qi turns to address Li Lifang. "Lifang!" he says, severely. "Don't you think you ought to confess?"

Li Lifang stares blankly at the ceiling. "I have nothing to confess," she says hoarsely.

Opening up the file, Shang Qi takes out a green plastic notebook: "This is Wang Hainan's diary. Everything is in it, from the day you first met to your final separation. Do you still remember how you danced for him on the beach?" Li Lifang's expression changes slightly. Shang Qi removes a letter from the diary. "This is the last letter you wrote to Wang Hainan. Do you remember writing it?" he asks. Li Lifang stares at the letter. "And this is part of a letter Wang Hainan wrote you as he was preparing to go join a foreign communist guerilla band," he continues. "Wouldn't you like me to read it to you?"

Li Lifang bites her lip savagely.

As Shang Qi picks up the diary, Wang Hainan's voice can be heard off-camera: "Lifang, I am starting a journey down a new road today. If only you would go with me — how wonderful that would be! But even if you hadn't left me, I wouldn't have made that demand on you because the road I've chosen may only bring destruction. But the way I feel now, I'd rather go to the ends of the earth than go home. At this moment, I have one desire — to see you once more. But where are you? What are you doing? I wish so much that you could be genuinely happy!..."

Li Lifang's lips begin to twitch, then suddenly she breaks into hysterical laughter.

Watching her, Shang Qi smiles, then he too starts to laugh — and loudly. Everyone in the room looks at them in shocked amazement.

Li Lifang immediately stops laughing, the confusion showing in her eyes. Shang Qi slowly walks over to her side. "I can tell you now,' he says. "Wang Hainan is dead."

"What!" shouts Li Lifang, getting up from her seat. Shang Qi stands there motionless, eyes fixed on the girl who has now fallen back into her chair, weeping with both hands over her face. Tears trickle out between her fingers. "I've killed him!" she cries hoarsely, and begins to wail.

As if in a violent fury, Shang Qi suddenly shouts, "Do you think it's right for you to take the blame in this case? Tell me!" he says, cupping Li Lifang's chin in his hand. "How did you get that scar on your head?" Lifang struggles to free herself, but Shang Qi refuses to release his hold: "This scar wasn't left by any rock! There are no rocks in beaches designated for swimming! There's only one thing that could have left a scar like that!"

Wrenching herself free from Shang Qi's grasp, Li Lifang stares at him with panic stricken eyes.

"On the day you carved out the deepest line in the reef just before you wrote Wang Hainan for the last time, what was it that left that scar on your head...And who left it? Tell me!"

Li Lifang buries her head in her arms, reacting as if struck by lightning. Her eyes are filled with grief, indignation, terror. Amazed at what they are witnessing, everyone stands up. Little Jing tugs on the military representative's sleeve and the two men hurry out of the room.

Now weeping convulsively, Li Lifang cries out, "It was him! It was them!" She points upward with her hand as she speaks.

FLASHBACK: THE SEASIDE SANITORIUM. A bolt of lightning slashes across the velvety night sky. The sea is seething, churning, creating great billows.

The doctor on duty puts down the telephone receiver and gently shakes Li Lifang, who has been sleeping head down on the table.

Li Lifang goes outside, walking against the wind, in the direction of the same lovely vacation cottage of the previous scenes, a bag of medical instruments under one arm.

Presently, the shadows of the senior official and Li Lifang can be seen on the back-lit second floor curtain. The official stands close to the girl. Then suddenly the light goes out and a startled cry can be heard.

Poking his head out of his bedroom door downstairs, Little Jing looks upstairs, listening attentively....

A bolt of lightning illuminates the official's bedroom. Someone is pressing Li Lifang down onto the bed. A look of humiliation on her tear-soaked face, Lifang struggles with all her might, resisting...

A hand picks up the glass fish from out of the cabinet at the head of the bed and savagely brings it down on Li Lifang's head. The glass falls onto the carpet, shattered....

On the desk is a pile of documents awaiting approval. The camera closes in on the large red and blue pencil....

Clothes in disarray, Li Lifang walks woodenly down the stairs, flecks of blood still visible on her head. As she passes Little Jing's door, a hand suddenly reaches out and grabs her, dragging her inside....

THE BEACH. Braving the rain, several doctors and soldiers with flashlights in their hands are following footprints in the sand, searching....

Li Lifang is sitting on the breakwater in a daze. Her tangled hair blows in the wind as she gouges out a last furrow in the rock, weeping violently....Then, finishing her work, she leaps into the great sea....

BACK IN THE PUBLIC SECURITY BUREAU. Chen Jie's pencil snaps in two, making a cracking sound. Everyone in the room is in a state of shock except for Shang Qi, who is smoking tranquilly.

Leaning back in her chair, Li Lifang sobs weakly and dryly, beyond tears. She is clutching several tufts of her own hair in her hand.

Shang Qi presses the buzzer and a guard enters.

Automatically, Li Lifang slowly rises to her feet, staring dully at Shang Qi.

"Li Lifang, you are hereby under arrest for instigation to murder!" announces Shang Qi coldly, crushing out his cigarette. Stepping forward, the guard adroitly places handcuffs on Li Lifang's wrists. She stands there mutely, head bowed low.

Horror stricken, Lifang's father and Mrs. Wang stand up simultaneously, their faces wet with tears. "Lifang!" they cry out together, almost as if by prior arrangement.

Li Lifang, now drained of all emotion, casts them a brief look. Then, turning around, she walks haltingly out the door.

Chen Jie picks up his notebook. "What are we going to do with the records of this interrogation?" he asks Shang Qi, agitated and full of emotion.

"Destroy them," Shang Qi answers without the slightest hesitation.

"What?" Chen Jie's eyes are open wide.

"That is their only possible fate — destruction," Shang Qi says slowly, looking at Chen Jie. "However, the record of this particular crime, and of all other crimes, is written in the archives of society, inscribed in the hearts of the victims. That's something no one can destroy!"

"But that's not fair!" cries the emergency room doctor, standing up. "You mean the real criminals are going to get away with it?" Anger and indignation filling his breast, the physician turns to Shang Qi, expecting the officer to provide an answer.

Shang Qi lights another cigarette and inhales deeply, strenuously breaks the silence: "That question ought to be answered by you, by all of you..."

Shang Qi has hardly finished speaking when the door is thrown open with a bang and the military representative charges in, leading a group of soldiers. Making no attempt to hide his anger, the representative thrusts an arrest warrant in Shang Qi's face.

Crying out in alarm, everyone present tries to gather protectively around Shang Qi but are prevented from doing so by the soldiers. Looks of anxiety, agitation, and indignation flash across their faces.

Quite unruffled, Shang Qi puts down his cigarette. "There's nothing else to do here today. You all can go home," he says, taking the warrant and calmly signing it.

"Comrade Shang Qi" cries Chen Jie, grasping the older man's hand. Pushing him aside, Shang Qi takes off his hat and removes the insignia — the national emblem. An extremely complex look appears on his face. Solemnly, he then hands the gleaming insignia over to Chen Jie, looking the younger man up and down. Chen Jie meets Shang Qi's meaningful glance and nods his head slightly.

Shang Qi picks up his cigarette, taking a deep drag. As he lifts up his head, a smile can be seen on his face for the first time—a bitter smile.

Escorted by several soldiers, Shang Qi walks peacefully down the long, long corridor to the main exit. Li Lifang trails after him haltingly, a dull look in her eyes.

Heading towards the light at the end of the hallway, Shang Qi casts a long shadow on the bright, clean floor....

Middle Age

SHEN RONG

Chapter 1

Were those stars she saw twinkling overhead in a night-sky? Or was she somehow on a boat rocking on the sea? Lu Wenting, an ophthalmologist, lay on her back in the hospital, unable to speak, unable to see. Circles of hazy, flickering light danced before her eyes. She felt as if she were enveloped in a cloud, drifting....

Was she dreaming or dying?

She remembered vaguely going to the operating room that morning, putting on her gown and walking over to the wash basin. Ah, yes, Jiang Yafen, her good friend, had volunteered to be her assistant. Having acquired their visas, Jiang and her family would soon leave for Canada. This was their last operation as colleagues.

Together they washed their hands. They had been medical students in the same college in the fifties and after graduation had been assigned to the same hospital. As friends and colleagues for more than twenty years, they found it hard to part. This was no mood for a doctor to be in prior to an operation. To ease their sadness, Lu turned to Jiang and inquired, "Have you booked your plane tickets, Yafen?"

After a long silence, Jiang asked, "Think you can manage three operations in one morning?" Her eyes seemed red as she spoke.

Lu couldn't remember what she had answered. She had probably gone on scrubbing her nails in silence. The new brush hurt her fingertips. She looked at the soap suds on her hands and glanced at the clock on the wall, strictly following the rules, brushing her hands, wrists and arms three times, three minutes each. Then minutes later she soaked her arms in a pail of antiseptic, seventy-five percent alcohol. It was white — almost yellowish. Even now her hands and arms were numb and burning.

From the alcohol? No. It was unlikely. They had never hurt before. Why couldn't she lift them?

She remembered that at the start of the operation, when she was injecting novocain behind the patient's eyeball, Yafen had asked softly, "Has your daughter got over her pneumonia?"

What was wrong with Jiang today? Didn't she know that when operating a surgeon should forget everything, including herself and her family, and concentrate on the patient? How could she inquire after Xiaojia at such a time? Perhaps, feeling miserable about leaving, she had forgotten that she was assisting at an operation.

A bit annoyed, Lu retorted, "I'm only thinking about this eye right now."

She lowered her head and cut with a pair of curved scissors.

One operation after another! Why three in one morning?

She had had to remove Vice-minister Jiao's cataract, transplant a cornea on Uncle Zhang's eye and correct Wang Xiaoman's squint. Starting at eight o'clock, she had sat on the high operating stool for four and a half hours, concentrating under a lamp. She had cut and stitched again and again. When she had finished the last one and put a piece of gauze on the patient's eye, she was stiff and her legs wouldn't move.

Having changed her clothes, Jiang called to her from the door, "Let's go, Wenting."

"You go ahead." She stayed where she was.

"I'll wait for you. It's my last time here." Jiang's eyes were watery. Had she been crying?

"Go on home and do your packing. Your husband must be waiting for you."

"He's already packed our things." Looking up, Jiang called, "What's wrong with your legs?"

"I've been sitting so long, they've gone to sleep! They'll be fine in a minute. I'll come to see you this evening."

"All right. See you then."

After Jiang left, Lu moved back to the white tile wall, supporting herself with her hands for a long time before going to the changing room.

She remembered putting on her grey jacket, leaving the hospital, and reaching the lane leading to her home. All of a sudden she was exhausted, more tired than she had ever felt before. The lane became long and hazy; her home seemed far away. She felt she would never get there.

She became faint. She couldn't open her eyes, her lips felt dry and stiff. She was thirsty, very thirsty. Where could she get some water?

Chapter 2

"Look, Dr. Sun, she's come to!" Jiang cried softly. She had been sitting beside Lu all the time.

Sun Yimin, head of the Ophthalmology Department, was reading Lu's case history and was shocked by the diagnosis of myocardial infarction. The grey haired man shook his head and pushed back his black-rimmed spectacles. Lu was hardly the first middle-aged doctor in his department to fall ill with heart disease. She had been a healthy woman of forty-two. How could this have happened?

Sun turned his tall, stooping frame to look down at Lu's pale face. She was breathing weakly, her eyes closed, her dry lips trembling slightly.

"Dr. Lu," Sun called softly.

She didn't move; her thin, puffy face remained expressionless.

"Wenting," Jiang urged.

Still no reaction.

Sun raised his eyes to the oxygen cylinder which stood at a corner of the room and then at the EKG monitor. He was reassured when he saw a regular QRS wave on the oscilloscope. He turned back to Lu, waved his hand and said, "Ask her husband to come in."

A good looking, balding man in his forties entered. He was Fu Jiajie, Lu's husband. He had spent a sleepless night at her side and was reluctant to leave when Sun sent him to lie down on the bench outside the room.

As Sun made way for him, Fu fixed his eyes on the familiar face, now so pale and strange.

Lu's lips moved again. Nobody except her husband understood her. He said, "She wants some water. She's thirsty."

Jiang gave him a small teapot. Carefully, Fu avoided the rubber tube leading from the oxygen cylinder and put the pot to Lu's parched lips. Drop by drop the water trickled into the dying woman's mouth.

"Wenting, Wenting," Fu called but she didn't respond.

Chapter 3

Eyes. Eyes. Eyes....

So many eyes. Eyes of men and women, old and young, big and

small, bright and dull, all kinds, blinking at her.

Ah! These were her husband's eyes. In them she saw joy and sorrow, anxiety and pleasure, suffering and hope. She could see through his eyes to his heart. His eyes were as bright as the golden sun in the sky. His love had given her so much warmth. It was his voice, Jiajie's voice, so endearing, gentle and far away, as if from another world:

> "I wish I were a stream,
>
> .....
>
> And my love
> were tiny fish ,
> frolicking
> In my frothy waves."

Where was she now? It was...yes, in a park covered with snow! There was a frozen lake, clear as crystal, on which red, blue, purple and white figures skated. Laughter resounded in the air while they moved arm in arm, threading their way through the crowds. She saw none of the smiling faces around her, only his. They glided on the ice, side by side, twirling, laughing.

In the snow the ancient Five Dragon Pavilions were solemn, tranquil and deserted. Wenting and Fu leaned against the white marble balustrades while snowflakes covered them. Holding hands tightly, they defied the severe cold.

She was young then. She had never expected this love or happiness. Her father had deserted her mother when she was a girl, and her mother had had a hard time rearing her alone. All she remembered from her bleak childhood was her prematurely old mother who, night after night, sewed under a lamp.

She boarded at her medical college, rising before daybreak to memorize new English words, going to classes and filling scores of notebooks with neat little characters. In the evenings she studied in the library and then worked late into the night doing autopsies. She never regretted spending her youth studying.

Love had no place in her life. She shared a room with Jiang Yafen, her classmate, who had beautiful eyes, bewitching lips and who was tall, slim and lively. Every week Jiang received love letters. Every weekend she dated. Lu, ignored by everyone, stayed home.

After graduation she and Jiang were assigned to the same hospital which had been founded more than a hundred years earlier. Their residency lasted four years, during which time they had to be in the hospital all day long and agree to remain single.

Secretly Jiang cursed these rules, while Lu accepted the terms willingly. What did it matter, being in the hospital twenty-four hours a day? She would have liked to be there forty-eight hours if possible. No marriage for four years. Hadn't many skilled doctors married late or remained single all their lives? She threw herself into her work heart and soul.

Then Fu Jiajie entered her quiet, routine life.

She never understood how it had happened; nor had she ever tried to. He had been suddenly hospitalized because of an eye disease, and Lu who by chance had been assigned to his case, cured him. Perhaps it was under her conscientious care that his feelings had developed into love, a passionate love that would change their entire lives.

Winter in the north is always very cold, but that winter he gave her warmth. Never having imagined love could be so intoxicating, she almost regretted that she hadn't found it earlier. She was already twenty-eight, yet she still had the heart of a young girl. With her whole being, she welcomed this late love.

> "I wish I were a deserted forest,
>
> ......
>
> If my love
> Were a little bird,
> She'd nest and twitter
> In my dense trees."

It seemed incredible that Fu Jiajie, who was doing research on a new material for a spacecraft in the Metallurgical Research Institute, and who Jiang regarded as a bookworm could read poetry so well.

"Who wrote it?" Lu asked.

"The Hungarian poet Petofi."

"Does a scientist have time for poetry?"

"A scientist must have imagination. Science has something in common with poetry in this respect. What about you? Do you like poetry?"

"Me? I don't know anything about it. I seldom read it."

Lu smiled. "The Ophthalmology Department does operations. Every stitch, every incision is strictly laid down. We can't use the slightest imagination...."

Fu cut in, "Your work is a beautiful poem. You can make people see again...."

Smiling, he moved over to her, her face close. She felt bewildered and unnerved; something was going to happen. Putting his arms around her, he embraced her tightly.

Heart thumping, head raised, she closed her eyes in embarrassment, moving away instinctively in the face of his irresistible love.

Beihai Park in the snow was just the right place. Snow covered the tall pagoda, Qiongdao Islet with its green pines, the long corridor and quiet lake. It also hid the sweet shyness of the lovers.

To everyone's surprise, after her four-year residency had ended, Lu was the first to get married. Fate had decided Fu Jiajie's intrusion. How could she refuse his wish that they marry? How insistently and strongly he wanted her, preparing to sacrifice everything for her!...

> "I wish I were a crumbling wall,
>
> ......
>
> If my love
> Were green ivy,
> She'd tenderly entwine
> Around my lonely head."

Life was good, love was beautiful. These recollections gave her strength, and her eyes opened slightly.

Chapter 4

Under the influence of a large dose of sedative, Dr. Lu had fallen into a lethargic state. The Director of Internal Medicine had come in to examine her personally. He looked over her electrocardiogram and case history and then warned the doctor on duty to watch out for any abnormalities of heart function and possible complications.

As they stepped out of the ward, the Director of Internal Medicine said to Sun Yimin: "She's very weak. I remember she was quite strong when she first came to our hospital."

"How true!" sighed Sun Yimin, shaking his head. "It's been eighteen years since she came to join us. She was in her early twenties then."

Eighteen years ago Sun Yimin had already enjoyed a high reputation as an eye specialist. His superior skill and conscientious attitude toward his work had gained him the respect of every doctor in the department. In the prime of life, the professor felt himself duty-bound to help guide young doctors to maturity. Every time new medical graduates were assigned to the hospital, he insisted on interviewing them one by one. He wanted to establish his hospital's Department of Ophthalmology as the nation's finest and so began by choosing the most promising candidates.

He could still recall clearly what happened that morning he had chosen the twenty-four-year-old Lu Wenting.

That morning Director Sun had already interviewed five of the medical graduates newly assigned to the hospital and he felt very much disappointed. Some of them were obviously fit for ophthalmic work, but they held it in disdain. The others preferred ophthalmology on the assumption that work in this department would be simple. When he took up the sixth dossier and saw Lu Wenting's name on it, he did not expect too much. He was a bit tired and was thinking about the need to improve instruction in the medical schools to give the students a better outlook on ophthalmology.

The door opened. Looking up, Sun Yimin saw a slim girl wearing a cotton suit with threadbare knees and a patch on one sleeve. Slender and small, she had an oval face, a head of black, neatly bobbed hair, and looked no older than a schoolgirl.

As usual Director Sun asked several questions related to the medical profession. The girl gave direct and relevant answers without touching upon any other topics.

"Would you like to serve in the Department of Ophthalmology?" asked Sun, wearily massaging his temples. He had decided to end the interview quickly.

"Yes. I was interested in ophthalmology even at medical school." Lu Wenting responded with a light southern accent.

This answer pleased Sun Yimin. He changed his mind right away and decided to carry on the conversation seriously.

"Why are you interested in ophthalmology?" he asked.

It might have been an awkward question for her, but to his surprise, the girl answered calmly, "Our country is too backward in ophthalmology..."

"Good! Tell me, where do you think this backwardness lies?"

"Well, I can't exactly put my finger on what's wrong. But it seems that we are still unable to do some of the operations which are common practice in foreign countries. For example, healing detached retinas with lasers. I think we should have a try at it."

"Perfect!" Again, he asked, "And what else? Any more suggestions?"

"Eh...well...cataract removal by freezing should be popularized...Anyhow, I think there are still many other fields in which we should conduct research."

"Ah! Well spoken. Can you read foreign material in the original?"

"Yes, but only with the aid of a dictionary. I like foreign languages."

"Excellent!"

It was indeed very rare for Director Sun to shower praises on a candidate during an interview. Several days later Lu Wenting and Jiang Yafen were the first two to be assigned to the Department of Ophthalmology. Jiang was chosen for her intelligence, enthusiasm and shrewdness while Lu was chosen for her frugality, perceptiveness and depth of intellect.

Their first year in the Department of Ophthalmology they performed extraocular operations and studied general ophthalmology. Their second year was devoted to intraocular operations and the study of refraction and eye muscles. In their third year they were able to perform such delicate operations as cataract removal. It was in this year that Director Sun had singled out Dr. Lu for special commendation. She had, after going the rounds of the wards with Director Sun and other doctors, aired an opinion which ran counter to the diagnosis of a senior doctor and was proved to be correct. Now, a rigid hierarchy existed in this hospital. Junior doctors had to obey senior doctors and opinions given by professors were supposed to be irrefutable. Dr. Lu's courage had won her the high esteem of all. "She's a very promising doctor, I should say," was the judgement of Director Sun.

Eighteen years elapsed. Doctors like Lu Wenting and Jiang Yafen had become the backbone of the Department of Ophthalmology. They should have long been promoted to the rank of director if promotions were based on ratings in competitive examinations. As it was they had been ordinary residents all these eighteen years. The Cultural Revolution blocked the avenue of promotion, and changes made after the Four's fall had not yet had an effect at the hospital.

"As lean as a blade of grass!" murmured Sun Yimin. Compassion welled up in his heart as his eyes rested with concern on Lu Wenting, who appeared to be growing worse. Turning to the Director of Internal Medicine, he asked, "Do you think she is in immediate danger?"

The Director of Internal Medicine heaved a sigh as he glanced at the ward and shook his head, saying, "Let's hope she'll pull through, Old Sun."

A fit of melancholy such as he had never known before seized him as he looked out of the window at the yellow leaves falling. The thought of losing two of the best doctors of his department tortured him. One was gravely ill, the other leaving. They were the two pillars of his department. What would happen to the hospital if these two pillars crumbled or disappeared?

Chapter 5

She seemed to be walking along an endless road, not a winding mountain path which urged people on, nor a narrow one between fields of fragrant rice. This was desert, quagmire, wasteland, silent and empty. Walking was difficult and exhausting. She wanted to lie down and rest. The desert was warm, the quagmire soft. The ground wouldwarm her rigid body, the sunshine caress her tired limbs. Death called softly, "Rest, Dr. Lu!"

Lie down and rest. Everlasting rest. No thoughts, feelings, worries, sadness or exhaustion.

But she couldn't! At the end of the long road her patients were waiting for her. She seemed to see one patient tossing and turning in bed with pain in his eyes, crying quietly at the threat of blindness. She saw many eager eyes waiting for her. She heard her patients calling to her in despair, "Dr. Lu!"

This was a sacred call, an irresistible one. Dragging her numb legs she trudged down the long road from her home to the hospital, from the clinic to the ward, from one village to another with a medical team. Day by day, month by month, year by year, she trudged on...

"Dr. Lu!"

Who was calling? Director Zhao? Yes. He had called her on the phone. She remembered putting down the receiver, handing over her patient to Jiang, who shared her consulting room, and heading for the director's office.

She hurried through a small garden, ignoring the white and yellow chrysanthemums, the fragrance of the osmanthus and the fluttering butterflies. She wanted to finish her business with Zhao quickly and return to her patients. There were seventeen waiting that morning and she had only seen seven so far. Tomorrow she was on ward duty and she still had to make arrangements for some of the out-patients.

She remembered walking right in without knocking. A man and woman were sitting on the sofa. She halted. Then she saw Director Zhao in his swivel chair.

"Come in please, Dr. Lu," Zhao greeted her.

She walked over and sat down on a leather chair by the window. The large room was bright, tidy and quiet, unlike the noisy clinic where the children sometimes howled. She felt odd, unused to the quietness and cleanliness of the room.

The couple looked cultured and composed. Director Zhao was always erect and scholarly in appearance, with well groomed hair, a kind face and smiling eyes behind his gold-rimmed spectacles. He had on a white shirt, a well pressed light grey suit and shining black leather shoes.

The man sitting on the sofa was tall and greying at the temples. A pair of sunglasses shielded his eyes. Leaning back against the sofa, he played with his walking stick.

The woman in her fifties was still attractive and well dressed.

Lu remembered how the woman had sized her up, with a look of doubt and disappointment.

"Dr. Lu, let me introduce you to Vice-minister Jiao Chengshi and his wife, Comrade Qin Bo."

A vice-minister? Well, in the past ten years and more, she had treated many ministers, party secretaries and directors. She had never paid attention to titles. She simply wondered what was wrong with his eyes. Was he losing his sight?

Director Zhao asked, "Dr. Lu, are you in the clinic or on duty in the ward?"

"Starting tomorrow I'll be on ward duty."

"Fine. Vice-minister Jiao wants to have his cataract removed."

That meant she had been assigned to the task. She asked the man, "Is it one eye?"

"Yes."

"Which one?"

"The left one."

"Can't you see with it at all?"

The patient shook his head.

"Did you see a doctor before?"

As she rose to examine his eye, she remembered he had named a hospital. Then his wife, who was sitting beside him, politely interrupted.

"There's no hurry, Dr. Lu. Sit down, please. We ought to go to your clinic for an examination." Smiling, Qin Bo turned to Director Zhao. "Since he developed eye trouble I've become something of an oculist myself."

Though Lu didn't examine him, she stayed a long time. What had they talked about? Qin had asked her many personal questions.

"How long have you been here, Dr. Lu?"

Lu hadn't kept track of the years. She only remembered the year she graduated. "I came here in 1961."

"Eighteen years ago," Qin said.

Why was she so interested in this? Then Director Zhao chipped in, "Dr. Lu has a lot of experience. She's a skilled surgeon."

Qin went on, "You don't seem to be in good health, Dr. Lu."

Lu was so busy caring for others that she had never given any thought to her own health. The hospital didn't even have her case history. And none of the leaders had ever inquired after her health. Why was this stranger showing such concern? She hesitated before answering, "I'm very well."

Zhao added again, "She's one of the fittest. Dr. Lu hasn't missed a day's work in years."

Lu made no answer, wondering why all this was of such importance to Qin. She was eager to get back to her patients. Jiang couldn't possibly cope with so many alone.

Her eyes fixed on Lu, the lady smiled and pressed, "Are you sure you can remove a cataract easily, Dr. Lu?"

Another difficult question. She had had no accidents so far, but anything could happen if the patient didn't cooperate well or if the anaesthetic were not carefully applied.

She couldn't recollect whether she had made a reply, just Qin's big eyes staring at her with doubt. Having treated all kinds of patients, she had got used to the difficult wives of high cadres. She was searching for a tactful answer when Jiao made an impatient gesture and turned his head to his wife who stopped and averted her gaze.

How had this trying conversation finished? Oh, yes, Jiang had come to tell her that Uncle Zhang had come for his appointment.

Qin said politely, "You may go, Dr. Lu, if you're busy."

Lu hurriedly left the large, bright room. How suffocating it was! She felt as if she could hardly breathe.

Chapter 6

Shortly before the day ended Director Zhao hurried over to the internal medicine ward.

"Dr. Lu has always enjoyed good health, Dr. Sun. Why should she have this sudden attack?" Zhao asked as they headed for Lu's ward. Eight years Sun's junior, Zhao looked much younger.

He shook his head and went on, "This should be a warning to us. Middle-aged doctors are the backbone of our hospital. Their heavy responsibilities and daily chores are ruining their health. If they collapse one by one, we'll be in a fix. How many people are there in her family? How many rooms does she have?"

Looking at Sun who was depressed and worried, he added, "What...Four in a room? So that's how it is! What's her wage? ...56.50 yuan! That's why people say better to be a barber with a razor than a surgeon with a scalpel. Why wasn't her salary raised last year?"

"Not enough to go around. You can't raise everyone's," Sun said.

"I hope you'll talk that problem over with the party branch. Ask them to investigate the work, income and living conditions of the middle-aged doctors and send me a report."

"What's the use of that? A similar report was sent in 1978," Sun retorted politely, his eyes on the ground.

"Stop grumbling, Dr. Sun. A report's better than nothing. I can show it to the municipal party committee, the Ministry of Health and whomever else it concerns. The Central Party Committee has stressed time and again that talented people and intellectuals should be valued and their salaries increased. We can't ignore it. The day before yesterday at a meeting of the municipal committee, it was stressed that attention should be paid to middle-aged personnel. I believe their problems will be solved." Zhao stopped when they entered Lu's room.

Fu Jiajie stood up as Zhao entered. He waved his hand in greeting and walked over to Lu, bent down and examined her face. Then he took her case history from her doctor. His status had changed instantly from administrator to physician.

Zhao, a noted thoracic expert, had returned to China after Liberation. Very enthusiastic politically, he was praised for both his political consciousness and his medical skill. He joined the party in the fifties. When later he was made director, he had to take part in so many meetings and do so much administrative work that he seldom found the opportunity to see patients except for important consultations. During the Cultural Revolution he had been detained illegally and made to sweep the hospital grounds. The last three years, as director again, he had been so tied up with daily problems that he had practically no time or energy for surgery.

Now he had come especially to see Lu. All the ward doctors had gathered behind him. Having read the case history and looked at the EKG monitor, he told the doctors to note any changes and watch out for complications. Then he asked, "Is her husband here?"

As Sun introduced Fu to Zhao, the director noticed immediately that this otherwise pleasant-looking man was going bald; deep lines already creased his brow. Apparently, a man who didn't know how to look after himself couldn't look after his wife either.

"It won't be easy," Zhao told him. "She needs complete rest. She'll need help for everything, even to turn over in bed. Help twenty-four hours a day. Where do you work? You'll have to ask for leave. You can't do it all by yourself, either. Is there anyone else in your family."

Fu shook his head. "Just two small children."

Zhao turned to Sun, "Can you spare someone from your department?"

"For one or two days, maybe."

"That'll do to begin with."

His eyes returning to Lu's thin, pale face, Zhao still couldn't understand why this energetic woman had suddenly collapsed.

It occurred to him that she might have been too nervous operating on Vice-minister Jiao. Then he dismissed the thought. She was experienced and it was highly improbable that an attack had been brought on by nervousness. Besides, myocardial infarction often had no obvious cause.

But he couldn't dismiss the notion that there was some kind of a link between Jiao's operation and Lu's illness. He regretted having recommended her. In fact, Jiao's wife, Qin Bo, had been reluctant to have her right from the start.

That day, after Lu's departure, Qin had asked, "Director Zhao, is Dr. Lu the vice-head of her department?"

"No."

"Is she an attending doctor?"

"No."

"Is she a party member?"

"No."

Qin said bluntly, "Excuse my outspokenness. Since we're all party members, I think it's rather inappropriate to let an ordinary doctor operate on Vice-minister Jiao."

Jiao stopped her by banging his walking stick on the floor. Turning to her he said angrily, "What are you talking about, Qin Bo? Let the hospital make the arrangements. Any surgeon can operate."

Qin retorted heatedly, "That's not the right attitude, Old Jiao. You must be responsible. You can work only if you're healthy. We must be responsible to the Revolution and the party."

Zhao quickly butted in to avoid a quarrel, "Believe me, Comrade Qin, although she's not a party member, Lu's a good doctor. And she's very good at removing cataracts. Don't worry!"

"It's not that, Director Zhao. And I'm not being too careful, either." Qin sighed. "When I was in the cadre school, one old comrade had to have that operation. He was not allowed to come back to Beijing. So he went to a small hospital there. Before the operation was through his eyeball fell out! Jiao was detained by the followers of the Gang for seven years! Don't you realize he has just resumed work. He can't do without his eyes!"

"Nothing like that will happen, Comrade Qin. We have very few accidents in our hospital."

Qin still wasn't appeased. "Can we ask Dr. Sun, the department head, to operate on Jiao?"

Zhao shook his head and laughed. "Dr. Sun's almost seventy and has poor eyesight himself! Besides, he hasn't operated for years. He does research, advises the younger doctors and teaches. Dr. Lu's a better surgeon than he."

"How about Dr. Guo then?"

Zhao stared. Dr. Guo. She must have made a thorough investigation of the department.

She prompted, "Guo Ruqing."

Zhao gestured helplessly. "He's left the country."

Qin wouldn't give up. "When is he coming back?"

"He's not."

"What do you mean?" This time she stared.

Zhao sighed. "Dr. Guo's wife returned from abroad. Her father, a shopkeeper in Southeast Asia died and left his store to them. So they decided to leave."

"To leave medicine for a store? I can't understand it." Jiao sighed too.

"He's not the only one. Several of our capable doctors have left or are preparing to go."

Qin was indignant. "I don't understand their mentality."

Jiao waved his stick and turned to Zhao, "In the early fifties intellectuals like you overcame many difficulties to return here to help build a new China. But now the intellectuals we've trained are leaving the country. It's a serious lesson."

"This can't go on," said Qin. "We must do more ideological work. After the Gang was smashed, the social status of intellectuals was raised a lot. Their living and working conditions will continue to improve as China modernizes."

"Yes. Our party committee holds the same view. I talked with Dr. Guo twice on behalf of the party and begged him to stay. But it was no use."

Qin, who was about to continue, was stopped by Jiao who said, "Director Zhao, I didn't come to insist on having an expert or a professor. I came because I have confidence in your hospital, or to be exact, because I have a special feeling for your hospital. A few years ago, the cataract in my right eye was removed here. And it was superbly done."

"Who did it?" Zhao asked.

Jiao answered sadly, "I never found out who she was."

"That's easy. We can look up your case history."

Zhao picked up the receiver, thinking that Qin would be satisfied if he got that doctor. But Jiao stopped him. "You can't find her. I had it done as an out-patient. There was no case history. It was a woman with a southern accent."

"That's difficult." Shao laughed, replacing the receiver. "We have many women doctors who speak with a southern accent. Dr. Lu also comes from the south. Let her do it."

The couple agreed. Qin helped Jiao up and they left.

Was this the cause of Lu's illness? Zhao couldn't believe it. She had performed this operation hundreds of times. She couldn't be so nervous. He had gone over before the operation and found her confident, composed and well. Why this sudden attack, then?

Zhao looked again at Lu with concern. Despite the seriousness of her condition, she looked as if she were sleeping peacefully.

Chapter 7

Lu was always composed, quiet and never flustered. Another woman would have retorted or shown her indignation at Qin's insulting questions or, at very least, felt resentful afterwards. But Lu had left Zhao's office as calm as ever, neither honored to be chosen to operate on Vice-minister Jiao nor humiliated by Qin's questions. The patient had the right to decide whether or not he wanted an operation. That was all there was to it.

"Well, what big official wants you this time?" Jiang asked softly.

"It's not definite yet."

"Let's hurry." Jiang steered her along. "I couldn't persuade your Uncle Zhang. He's made up his mind not to have the operation."

"That's nonsense! He's traveled a long way to get here and spent so much money. He'll be able to see after the transplant. It's our duty to cure him."

"Then you convince him."

Passing by the waiting room, they smiled and nodded at the familiar patients who stood up to greet them. Back in her room, while examining a young man, Lu was interrupted by a booming voice calling her name.

Both Lu and her patient looked up as a tall sturdy man advanced. In his fifties, he was broad shouldered, wore black trousers and a shirt and had a white towel around his head. The people in the corridor quickly made way for him. A head taller than everyone else and almost blind, he was unaware that he attracted so much attention as he groped his way toward Lu's voice.

Lu hurried forward to help him. "Sit down, please, Uncle Zhang."

"Thank you, Dr. Lu. I want to tell you something."

"Yes, but sit down first." Lu helped him to a chair.

"I've been in Beijing quite a while now. I'm thinking of going home tomorrow and coming back some other time."

"I don't agree. You've come such a long way and spent so much money...."

"That's just it," Uncle Zhang cut in, slapping his thigh. "So I think I'll go home, do some work and earn some more workpoints. Although I can't see, I can still do some work and the brigade's very kind to me. I've made up my mind to leave, Dr. Lu. But I couldn't go without saying goodbye to you. You've done so much for me."

Having suffered from corneal ulcers for many years, he had come to the hospital to have a transplant, a suggestion proposed by Lu when she had visited his brigade with a medical team.

"Your son spent a lot of money to send you here. We can't let you go home like this."

"I feel better already!"

Lu laughed. "Since you're so strong, when you're cured you can work for another twenty years without help from the brigade."

Uncle Zhang laughed. "You bet I will! I could do anything when my eyes are good."

"Then stay and have them treated."

Zhang confided, "Listen, Dr. Lu, I'll tell you the truth. I'm worried about money. I can't afford to live in a Beijing hotel."

Stunned, Lu quickly told him, "I know you're next on the list. Once there's a donor, it'll be your turn."

He finally agreed to stay. Lu helped him out of the room. Then a little girl of eleven accosted her.

Her pretty, rosy face was marred by a squint. Dressed in hospital pajamas, she called timidly, "Dr. Lu."

"Why don't you stay in the ward, Wang Xiaoman?" She had been admitted the previous day.

"I'm scared. I want to go home." She began to cry. "I don't want an operation."

Lu put one arm around her. "Tell me why you don't want an operation."

"It'll hurt too much."

"It won't, you silly girl! I'll give you an anaesthetic. It won't hurt at all." Lu patted her head and bent down to look with regret at the afflicted eye. She said, "Look, won't it be nice when I make this eye look like the other one? Now go back to your ward. You musn't run around in a hospital."

When the little girl had wiped away her tears and left, Lu returned to her patients.

There had been many patients the last few days and today was no different. She must make up for the time she had lost in Zhao's office. Forgetting Jiao, Qin and herself, she saw one patient after another.

A nurse came to tell her she was wanted on the phone.

Lu excused herself.

It was the kindergarten nurse informing her, "Xiaojia has a temperature. It started last night. I know you're busy, so I took her to the doctor. He gave her an injection. She's still feverish and is asking for you. Can you come?"

"I'll be there in a minute." She replaced the receiver.

But she couldn't go immediately since so many patients were waiting. She rang her husband but was told that he had gone out to a meeting.

Back in her office, Jiang asked, "Who called? Anything important?"

"Nothing."

Lu never troubled others, not even her supervisors. I'll go to the kindergarten when I'm through with the patients, she thought as she returned to her desk. As she began to work, an image of her daughter crying and calling "mamma" appeared before her. This vision was soon supplanted, however, by the very concrete image of her patients' eyes. Not until she had seen the very last one did she rush off to the kindergarten.

Chapter 8

"Why did it take you so long?" the nurse complained.

Lu walked quickly to the isolation room where her little daughter lay, her face flushed with fever, her lips parted, her eyes closed, her breathing difficult.

She bent over the crib. "Mummy's here, darling."

Xiaojia stirred and called in a hoarse voice, "Mummy, let's go home."

"All right, my pet."

Bundling Xiaojia in her arms, Lu quickly took the child back to the hospital to see a pediatrician.

"It's pneumonia," the sympathetic doctor told her. "You must take good care of her."

She nodded and left after Xiaojia had been given an injection and some medicine.

In the hospital everything came to a stop at noon. The out-patients left, the in-patients slept and the hospital staff rested. The spacious grounds were deserted except for sparrows flying among the trees. Nature had to compete with men in this noisy center of the city where tall buildings crowded in the polluted air. In the hospital all day, Lu had never been aware of the birds before.

She couldn't make up her mind where to take her daughter, hating to leave the sick child alone in the kindergarten's isolation room. But who could look after her at home?

After some hesitation she steeled herself and headed for the kindergarten.

"No. I don't want to go there," Xiaojia wailed on her shoulder.

"Be a good girl, Xiaojia...."

"No. I want to go home!"

They had to go along a busy street with recently posted billboards of the latest fashions. Lu never so much as glanced at the costly goods in the shop windows or the produce the peasants sold in the streets. With two children it was hard to make ends meet. Now, carrying Xiaojia in her arms and worrying about Yuanyuan at home, she was even less eager to look around.

Arriving home at one o'clock, Lu found a pouting Yuanyuan waiting for her. "Why are you so late, mummy?" he asked.

"Xiaojia's ill," Lu answered curtly, putting Xiaojia on the bed, undressing her and tucking her in.

Standing at the table Yuanyuan fretted, "Please cook lunch, mummy. I'll be late."

In frustration, Lu shouted at him, "You'll drive me crazy if you go on like that!"

Feeling wronged, Yuanyuan was on the point of tears. Ignoring him, Lu went to stoke up the fire, which had almost gone out. The pots and cupboard were empty. There were no left-overs from yesterday's meals.

She went back into the room, reproaching herself for having been so harsh on the poor boy.

In the past few years, keeping house had become an increasing burden. During the Cultural Revolution her husband's laboratory had been closed down and his research project scrapped. All he had needed to do was to show his face in the office for an hour in the morning and afternoon. He spent the remainder of his day and talents on domestic chores, cooking and learning to sew and knit, thereby lifting the burden entirely from Lu's shoulders. After the Gang was smashed, scientific research resumed and Fu, a capable metallurgist, was busy again. Lu once more shouldered most of the housework.

Every day at noon, whatever the weather, Lu Wenting would rush home, where exchanging her white physician's coat for a blue apron, she would begin another battle for time. Everything had to be done within fifty minutes, or else both Lu and her husband would be late for work and Xiaojia would be late for school.

On days like today, the entire family would be faced with the danger of going hungry. Sighing, Lu took some change out of a drawer and gave it to her son. "Go and buy yourself a bun, Yuanyuan."

He turned back halfway, "What about you, mummy?"

"I'm not hungry."

"I'll buy you a bun too."

Yuanyuan soon came home with two buns and gave one to his mother. He left for school immediately, eating his on the way.

Biting into the cold hard bun, Lu looked around at her small room.

She and her husband had been content with a simple life, living in this room since their marriage without a sofa, wardrobe, or a new desk. They had the same furniture they had used when they were single.

Though they owned few material possessions, they had many books. Aunt Chen, a neighbor, had commented, "What will the two bookworms live on?" But they were happy. All they had wanted was a small room, some clothes and three simple meals a day.

Treasuring their time, they put their evenings to good use. Every night, when their neighbor's naughty children peeped into their small room to spy on the new couple, they invariably found them at work: Lu at their only desk studying foreign material with the help of a dictionary and taking notes, while Fu, who would be perched on a pile of boxes, would pore over the reference books he had spread out on the bed.

The evening was not wasted when they could study late quietly and undisturbed. In the summer their neighbors sat cooling themselves in the courtyard, but the smell of tea, the light breeze, bright stars, interesting news and conversation...none of these could lure them from their stuffy little room.

Their quiet life and studious evenings ended much too soon.

Lu gave birth to Yuanyuan and then to Xiaojia. Their lovely children brought disorder and hardship as well as joy to their lives. When the crib was later replaced by a single bed and the tiny room filled with children's clothes and pots and pans, they could hardly move about. Their children's laughter and tantrums shattered the peace.

What could an oculist achieve without keeping up with foreign developments in the field? Lu had no choice but to isolate herself behind the home-made curtain Fu had hung up to provide a little privacy and study late into the night.

When Yuanyuan began school he had to use their only desk. Only when he had finished doing his homework was it Lu's turn to spread out her notebook and the medical books she had borrowed. Fu came last.

Lu fixed her eyes on the little clock: five past, ten past, fifteen. Time to go to work. What should she do? Lots of things needed to be finished before she went to the ward tomorrow. What about Xiaojia? Should she call her husband? There was no public telephone nearby, and anyway, she probably could not reach him. Since he had already wasted ten years, better not to disturb him.

She frowned, at a loss what to do.

Perhaps she shouldn't have married. Some claimed that marriage ended love. She had naively believed that though it might be true for some, it could not happen to her. But she couldn't help thinking that if she had been more prudent, she would not have ended up weighed down by the burdens of marriage and a family.

One-twenty. She must turn to her neighbor Aunt Chen, a kind-hearted woman who had helped on many occasions. Since she would not accept anything for her services, Lu was reluctant to trouble her.

Still, she had to this time. Aunt Chen was most obliging, "Leave her to me, Dr. Lu."

Lu put some children's books and building blocks beside Xiaojia, asked Aunt Chen to give her the medicine and hurried to the hospital.

She had intended to tell the nurse not to send her too many patients so that she could go home early, but once she started work she forgot everything.

Zhao called up to remind her that Jiao was to be admitted the following day.

Qin called twice asking how Jiao and his family should prepare for the operation.

Lu was hard put to give an answer. She had performed hundreds of operations and no one had ever asked her that before. So she said, "Oh, nothing special."

"Really? But surely it's better to be well prepared. What if I come over and we have a chat?"

Lu quickly told her, "I'm busy this afternoon."

"Then we'll talk tomorrow in the hospital."

"O.K."

When the trying conversation had ended, Lu returned to her office. It was dark before she had finished her clinic.

Arriving home, she heard Aunt Chen singing an impromptu song:

"Grow up, my dear,
To be an engineer."

Xiaojia laughed happily. Lu thanked Aunt Chen and was relieved to find Xiaojia's temperature down.

She gave her an injection. After Fu returned, Jiang Yafen and her husband, Liu, stopped by.

"We've come to say goodbye," said Jiang.

"Where are you going?" Lu inquired.

"We've just got our visas for Canada," replied Jiang, her eyes fixed on the ground.

Liu's father, a doctor in Canada, had urged them to join him there. Lu had not expected them to go.

"How long will you stay? When will you come back?" she asked.

"Maybe for good," Liu shrugged his shoulders.

"Do you have to go?" Lu Wenting asked softly.

"Do I have to go? I've argued with myself I don't know how many times." Liu Xueyao swirled his half-full glass of red port and added, "With more than half a lifetime behind me, how much longer can I expect to live? It doesn't make sense to have my ashes thrown onto foreign soil."

Everybody listened as Liu Xueyao expressed his feelings of sadness. He stopped suddenly to drain his glass, then blurted out: "Alright, go ahead and berate me. Undoubtedly I deserve it."

"Don't talk like that, Old Liu. We know what has happened to you all these years," Fu Jiajie said after refilling Liu's glass. "The long night has come to an end. Day is breaking. Everything will be all right."

"That I believe." Liu Xueyao nodded. "But when will the golden sun reach my doorstep? When will it shine upon my daughter? I can't wait forever."

"Let's talk about something else!" From what he said Lu Wenting gathered that his only daughter was the reason Liu Xueyao wanted to leave. Judging it wise to change the topic, she said,

"You know I never drink. But since you're going away, let me drink a toast to you two!"

"No, no. Allow me to drink a toast to you!" said Liu Xueyao. "You're the mainstay of our hospital, a newborn star in the sky of our medical world."

"Why didn't you let me know earlier, Yafen?" Lu turned to her friend.

"I was afraid that you would try to stop me. I was afraid I'd change my mind." Jiang avoided her eyes, staring hard at the ground.

From his bag Liu produced some wine and food and said in high spirits, "I bet you haven't cooked yet. Let's have our farewell banquet here."

Chapter 9

It was an unhappy banquet. Xiaojia was in bed and Yuanyuan had gone to a neighbor's to watch television. Liu Xueyao raised his glass, looked at the wine and said with deep feeling: "As a child, I liked literature and I hankered after literary fame. But, as fate would have it, I became a doctor like my father. Before I knew it, thirty years had gone by. My father is a prudent man. His adage is: 'He who talks too much will come to grief.' I'm sorry to say that this is where I made my fatal slip. One false step brings everlasting grief. I was free with my tongue and you know what happened to me. I was made a target in every political movement. When I graduated in 1957 I came close to being branded as a rightist. I'm a Chinese. I'm patriotic. I do hope my country will grow prosperous and powerful. Little did I expect that I, a man going on fifty, would come to leave my homeland."

"You must be drunk!" Lu Wenting smiled.

"No, I'm not."

Jiang Yafen, who had remained silent for a good while, raised her glass and said, "Wenting, I do want to drink to your health, to our friendship of more than twenty years' standing and to your future career as an eye specialist!"

"Who do you think I am?" said Lu Wenting.

"Who are you?" It looked as if Liu Xueyao were really drunk now. He went on bitterly, "You're a doctor who lives in a hole like this, who works hard with no desire for personal fame or gain. You're what Lu Xun called 'a willing ox.' You feed on grass but you give milk to the people. Am I right, Fu Jiajie?"

Fu Jiajie, who had been drinking in silence, gave him a nod.

"But there are plenty of people like that," remarked Lu Wenting, smiling all the time. "I am not alone."

"It's for this very reason that our nation is a great nation!" Liu Xueyao drained another glass.

Jiang Yafen glanced at Xiaojia lying fast asleep in her bed and said sentimentally, "So it is."

Liu Xueyao stood up and refilled the glasses.

"In other words, she would gladly give up her life in order to save mankind," Liu Xueyao commented.

"Why are you showering praises on me like that?" Lu Wenting smiled and pointed her finger at her husband. "Just ask him. I'm the most selfish woman in the world. I've banished by husband to the kitchen, I've neglected my own children. To tell the truth, I'm neither a good wife nor a good mother."

"But you're a good doctor!" cried Liu Xueyao.

Fu Jiajie put down his glass. "In this regard," he said, "I have a lot of complaints about your hospital. Doctors have their families and children, haven't they? Doctors' children get sick too. It seems that no one is interested in them." He paused for a moment, then continued, "Whenever she left with the mobile medical team for the countryside, she just dumped the two children in my lap. If I didn't go into the kitchen, who would? Thanks to the Cultural Revolution, I had plenty of time to get myself into shape. I became a man of many talents."

Ordinarily, Fu Jiajie seldom touched alcohol. "Look at me. I've been transformed into a househusband...."

Lu Wenting felt bad to hear their bitter jokes. As they dwelt on the sufferings of middle-aged cadres, Jiang Yafen, who had been silent for some time, nudged her husband. "Cut it out, will you?" said she. "It simply doesn't make sense!"

"Sense? This is a social phenomenon!" Liu Xueyao waved his hand and said. "Middle age, middle age. Everybody says middle-aged cadres are the backbone of the country. It's the middle-aged doctors who perform major operations. It's the middle-aged scientists who conduct important research. It's the middle-aged workers who have the toughest jobs in the factory. And it's the middle-aged teachers who give the principal courses in schools. Everybody says they are the backbone of society but who's concerned about their welfare?...."

Lu Wenting was listening with a heavy heart. "A pity so few realize this," she said.

"Old Liu," Fu said, pausing to re-fill his friend's glass. "You shouldn't be a doctor or a man of letters. You ought to be studying sociology!"

"No thank you!" said Liu with a wry smile. "When you study sociology you have to study society's maladies as well. I'd end up labeled a big 'rightist' for sure!"

"But you can't have social progress until you've found those maladies and corrected them. That's what I call being really leftist, not rightist!"

Liu Xueyao rested his elbows on the table. "I'm really interested in the problem of middle age." He talked on and on in a flow of eloquence. "In the old days we had a saying: 'When one reaches middle age, he is tired of earthly life.' It faithfully reflected the conditions prevailing in the old society. When one reached middle age, he felt that he no longer had a future. He could attempt nothing and accomplish nothing. But now, when one reaches middle age, there is still too much to be done. Right? A man around fifty has sufficient knowledge and experience. He is in the prime of his life. He should be able to shoulder heavy responsibilities. Unfortunately, the harsh reality is that during the years of upheaval when Lin Biao and the Gang of Four rode roughshod over the people, we lost forever the best years of our lives. Now, we feel unequal to the task of Four Modernizations that has been placed on our shoulders. Our intelligence, our energy and our physical strength all fall short of the demands of the times. This is the greatest tragedy of our generation."

The way he talked gave Lu Wenting the impression that it was probably not for the sake of his daughter alone that he wanted to leave. He wanted to leave for his own sake as well.

Once again, Liu Xueyao raised his glass and in a loud voice said, "Come, let's drink a toast to middle age!"

Chapter 10

After their guests had gone and the children were asleep, Lu washed up the kitchen. In their room she found her husband leaning against the bed, deep in thought, his hand on his forehead.

"A penny for your thoughts, Jiajie." Lu was surprised to see him looking so depressed.

Fu asked in reply, "Do you remember Petofi's poem?"

"Of course!"

"I wish I were a crumbling ruin..." Fu removed his hand from his forehead. "I'm a ruin now, like an old man. Going bald and grey. I can feel the lines on my forehead. I'm a ruin!"

He did look older than his age. Upset, Lu touched his forehead,

"It's my fault! We're such a burden to you!"

Fu took her hand and held it lovingly. "No. It's not your fault."

"I'm a selfish woman who thinks only about her work." Lu's voice quavered. She couldn't take her eyes away from his forehead. "I have a home but I've paid it little attention. Even when I'm not working, my mind is preoccupied with my patients. I haven't been a good wife or mother."

"Don't be silly! I know more than anyone how much you've sacrificed!" said Fu, fighting back the tears.

Nestling up against him, she said sadly, "You've aged. I don't want you to grow old...."

"Never mind. 'If my love green ivy would be, she'd tenderly entwine around my lonely head.'" Softly he recited their favorite poem.

In the still autumn night Lu fell asleep against her husband's chest, her lashes moist with tears. Fu put her carefully on the bed. Opening her eyes she asked, "Did I fall asleep?"

"You're very tired."

"No. I'm not."

Fu propped himself up and said to her, "Even metal has fatigue. A microscopic crack forms first and it develops until a fracture suddenly occurs." That was Fu's field of research and he often mentioned it. But this time, his words carried weight and left a deep impression on Lu.

A dreadful fatigue, a dreadful fracture. In the quiet of the night, Lu seemed to hear the sound of breaking. The foundations of overloaded bridges, old bricks and the ivy-covered ruins...all these were breaking.

Chapter 11

The hanging lamp in the room was off now and the wall lamp shed a dim blue light.

Dots of light flickered in her eyes like fireflies on a summer night. Lu lay there, entranced, staring at the wall.

Qin had been warm and kind when she summoned Lu to Jiao's room the morning he entered the hospital. "Sit down please, Dr. Lu. Old Jiao has gone to have his EKG done. He'll be back in a minute."

The room was in a quiet building with red-carpeted corridors reserved for high cadres. Qin had risen from her chair. She asked Lu to sit in the other armchair, then walked over to the locker beside the bed and got out a basket of tangerines which she placed on the sidetable between the chairs.

"Have a tangerine."

Lu declined.

"Try one. They were sent to me by a friend in the south. They're very good."

Qin took one and offered it to Lu, who accepted but held it in her hand without eating. Qin's new friendliness sent a chill down her spine. She was still conscious of the coldness in Qin's eyes when they had first met.

"What actually is a cataract, Dr. Lu? Some doctors told me that an operation is not suitable for all cases." Qin's manner was humble and ingratiating.

"A growth which progressively covers the eyeball, destroying the sight." Looking at the tangerine in her hand, Lu explained, "It can be divided into stages. It's better to have the operation when the cataract is mature."

"I see. What happens if it isn't done then?"

"The lens shrinks as the cortex is absorbed. The ligament becomes fragile. The difficulty of the operation increases because the lens is more liable to be dislocated."

Qin nodded. She had not understood nor tried to understand what she had been told. Lu wondered why she had bothered to ask the questions. Just passing time? Having started her ward duty only that morning, she had to familiarize herself with her patients' cases and attend to them. She couldn't sit there making small talk. She wanted to check Jiao's eyes if he returned soon. After all, he was a patient too.

Qin had more questions. "I heard there was an artificial lens abroad. The patient needn't wear a convex lens after an operation. Is that right?"

Lu nodded. "We're experimenting on that too."

Qin inquired eagerly, "Can you put one in for my husband?"

Lu smiled. "I said it's still in the experimental stage. I don't think he'd want one now, do you?"

"No." Of course she didn't want him to be a guinea pig. "What is the procedure for his operation?"

Lu was baffled. "What do you mean?"

"Shouldn't you map out a plan in case something unexpected comes up?" As Lu looked blank, she added, "I've often read about it in the papers. Sometimes surgeons form a team to discuss and work out a plan."

Lu couldn't help laughing. "No need for that! This is a very simple operation."

Disgruntled, Qin looked away. Then she turned back and

pressed her point patiently with a smile, "Underestimating the enemy often leads to failure. This has happened before in the history of our party." Then she got Lu to describe certain situations which could cause the operation to fail.

"One has to think twice about patients with heart trouble, hypertension or bronchitis. Coughing can create problems."

"That's just what I feared," Qin cried, striking the arm of her chair. "My husband's heart isn't good and he has high blood pressure."

"We always examine the patient thoroughly before an operation," Lu counseled her.

"He has bronchitis too."

"Has he been coughing lately?"

"No. But what if he does on the operating table? What shall we do?"

Why was she so anxious, Lu wondered, looking at her watch. The morning was almost gone. Jiao, a blue and white terry cloth gown around his shoulders, was helped in by a nurse.

Qin commented, "It's taken you a long time!"

Jiao shook Lu's hand and flopped down exhausted in the armchair. "There were lots of examinations. I had a blood test, an X-ray and an EKG. The staff were all very kind to me. I didn't have to wait my turn."

He sipped the cup of tea Qin handed him. "I never thought an eye operation involved so many tests."

Lu read the reports. "The X-ray and the EKG are normal. Your blood pressure's a bit high."

Qin piped up. "How high?"

"One-fifty over a hundred. But that doesn't matter." Then she asked, "Have you been coughing recently, Vice-minister Jiao?"

"No," he answered lightly.

Qin pressed, "Can you guarantee that you won't cough on the operating table?"

"Well..." Jiao was not so sure.

"That's important, Old Jiao," Qin warned him gravely. "Dr. Lu just told me that if you cough, the eyeball can fall out."

Jiao turned to Lu. "How can I be certain I won't cough?"

"It's not serious. If you are a smoker, don't smoke before the operation."

"O.K."

Qin pressed again. "But what if you should cough? What will happen?"

Lu laughed. "Don't worry, Comrade Qin. We can sew up the incision and open it again after he stops coughing."

"That's right," said Jiao. "When I had my right eye operated on, it was sewn up and then opened again. But it wasn't because I coughed!"

Curiosity made Lu ask, "Why then?"

Jiao put down his cup and took out his cigarette case, but put it away again remembering Lu's advice. With a sigh he related, "I'd been labelled a traitor and was having a difficult time. When the sight went in my right eye I had an operation. Soon after it started, the rebels came and tried to force the surgeon not to treat me. I nearly choked with indignation, but the doctor calmly sewed up the incision, threw the rebels out and then removed the cataract."

"Really?" Stunned, Lu asked, "Which hospital was that?"

"This one."

A coincidence? She looked at Jiao again to see whether she had seen him before, but could not recognize him.

Ten years earlier, she had been operating on a so-called traitor when she was interrupted by some rebels. That patient's name was Jiao. So it *was* he! Later, the rebels from Jiao's department, collaborating with a rebel in the hospital, put up a slogan claiming that "Lu Wenting has betrayed the proletariat by operating on the traitor Jiao Chengshi."

No wonder she hadn't recognized him. Ten years ago Jiao, sallow and depressed, dressed in an old cotton-padded coat, had come to the hospital alone as an ordinary patient. Lu suggested an operation and made an appointment, which he kept. When she began operating she heard the nurse saying outside, "No admittance. This is an operating theatre."

Then she heard shouting and noises.

"What do you mean operating theater? He's nothing but a renegade! We won't tolerate anyone operating on a renegade!

"There's no way we'll allow a stinking intellectual make things easier for a renegade!

"Force open the door!"

Jiao, indignant, said on the operating table, "Let me go blind, doctor. Don't do it."

Lu warned him against moving and quickly sewed up the incision.

Three men charged in, while the more timid ones hestitated at the door. Lu sat there immobile.

Jiao said the doctor had thrown them out. As a matter of fact, Lu had not. She had sat on the stool by the operating table in her white gown, green plastic slippers, blue cap and mask. All that could be seen of her were her eyes and her bare arms above the rubber gloves. The rebels were awed perhaps by her strange appearance, the solemn atmoshpere of the operating theatre and the bloody eye exposed through a hole in the white towel covering the patient. Lu said tersely from behind her mask, "Get out, please!"

The rebels looked at each other and left.

When Lu resumed work, Jiao told her, "Don't do it, doctor, they'll only blind me again even if you cure me. And you may get involved."

"Keep quiet." Lu worked swiftly, not uttering another word til she had finished bandaging Jiao. "I'm a doctor," she said.

The rebels from Jiao's department, coming to the hospital to put up a big poster denouncing her for curing a traitor, had created quite a sensation. But what did it matter? She was already being criticized for being a bourgeois expert. These charges and this operation had not left much impression on her. She had forgotten all about it, until Jiao brought it up.

"I really respect her, Dr. Lu. She was a true doctor," Qin sighed. "Pity the hospital kept no records then. I can't find out who she was. Yesterday I expressed my wish to Director Zhao to have her operate on my husband." Lu's awkward expression made her add, "I'm sorry, Dr. Lu. Since Director Zhao has confidence in you, we will too. I hope you won't let him down. Learn from that doctor. Of course, we've a lot to learn from her too, don't you agree?"

Lu had no alternative but to nod.

"You're still young," Qin said encouragingly. "I heard you haven't joined the party yet. You must strive for it, comrade."

Lu told her frankly, "I don't have a good class background."

"That's not the way to look at things. You can't choose your family but you can choose what you do with your life."

Qin was eloquent and enthusiastic. "Our party does pay attention to class origins, but not exclusively. It's your attitude that counts. When you draw the line between yourself and your family, get close to the party and make contributions to the people, then the party will open its doors to you."

Lu crossed the room to draw the curtain and examine Jiao's eye. Then she told Jiao, "If it's all right with you, let's do the operation the day after tomorrow."

Jiao answered briskly, "All right. The earlier the better."

It was already after six when Lu took her leave. Qin hurried out after her. "Are you going home, Dr. Lu?"

"Yes."

"Shall I arrange for Jiao's car to take you?"

"No, thank you." Lu declined with a wave of her hand.

Chapter 12

It was midnight. The ward was very quiet. A single wall lamp cast a pale blue light on an intravenous bottle from which the medicine was dropping, as if it were the only sign of Dr. Lu's life.

Fu, sitting at the side of the bed, stared blankly at his wife. It was the first time that he had sat alone with her since her collapse, probablythe first time that he had looked at her so intently for the past dozen years.

He remembered that once he had fixed his eyes on her for a long time and she had asked, her head on one side, "Why do you look at me like that?" Sheepishly he had turned his eyes away. That was when they were courting. But now she could neither move her head nor speak. Vulnerable, she was unable to raise a protest.

Only then did he notice to his great surprise how old and frail she had gotten. Her jet-black hair was flecked with grey; her once firm, sleek skin had become flaccid; her forehead, at one time smooth as silk, had become deeply lined. And her mouth (what had happened to her lovely mouth?!), now drooped at the corners. Fu simply could not understand how his once vigorous wife could have become so weak overnight.

But she was not a weak woman; he knew that well. Despite her slim build, she was in fact, fit and strong. She had silently endured the hardships and sudden misfortunes of her life without complaint or growing discouraged.

"You're a tough woman," he had often said to her.

"Me? No, I'm timid. Not tough at all." Her answer was always the same.

Only the night before she had fallen ill, she had made, as Fu put it, another "heroic decision"—that he should move to his institute.

Xiaojia had quite recovered by then. After Yuanyuan had done his homework, the children went to bed. At last there was peace in the small room.

Autumn had come, the wind was cold. The kindergarten had asked parents for their children's winter clothes. Lu took out the cotton-padded coat Xiaojia had worn the previous year, ripped it apart, made it bigger and sewed on a new pair of cuffs. Then she spread it out on the desk and added a layer of new cotton padding.

Fu took his unfinished article from the bookcase and, hesitating for a brief second beside the desk, sat down on the bed.

"Just a moment," Lu said without turning her head, hurrying,

"I'll soon finish."

When she removed the coat from the desk Fu remarked, "If only we could have another small room. Even six square metres, just big enough for a desk."

Lu listened, lowering her head, busy sewing. After a while, she hastily folded up the unfinished coat and said, "I've got to go to the hospital now. You can have the desk."

"But why? It's late," he queried.

While putting on her jacket she said, "There will be two operations tomorrow morning and I want to check the patients. I'll go and have a look at them."

She often went to the hospital in the evening. Fu always teased her, saying, "Though you're here at home, your heart's still in the hospital."

"Put on more clothes. It's cold," he urged.

"I won't be long," she said quickly. With an apologetic smile she continued, "I've got two funny patients, you know. One's a vice-minister. His wife's worrying about the operation and making an awful fuss. So I must go to see him. The other's a little girl. She told me today that she had a lot of nightmares and slept badly."

He smiled. "O.K. Get going and come back soon!"

When she returned he was still burning the midnight oil. Not wanting to disturb him, she said, "I'm going to bed first."

He looked around, saw she was in bed and again buried himself in his papers and books. But soon he sensed that she had not fallen asleep. Was it perhaps the light? He bent the lamp lower, shielded the light with a newspaper and carried on with his work.

After a while he heard her soft, even snoring. But he knew that she was faking. Many times she had tried to pretend she slept well so he could feel at ease studying late. In fact he had long since seen through her little trick, but he had no heart to expose it.

Some time later he got to his feet, stretched and said "All right! I'll sleep too."

"Don't worry about me!" Lu said quickly. "I'm already half asleep."

Standing with his hands on the edge of the desk, he hesitated, looking at his unfinished article. Then he made up his mind and said, closing all the books, "I'll call it a day."

"How about your article? How can you finish it if you don't make full useof your nights?"

"One night can't make up for ten years."

Lu sat up, threw a sweater over her shoulders and said in earnest, "Guess what I've been thinking just now?"

"You oughtn't to have thought of anything! Now close your eyes. You've got to cure other people's eyes tomorrow."

"It's no joke. Listen, I think you should move into your institute. Then you'll have more time." Fu stared at her. From her expression he could tell she was very pleased with the idea.

She went on, "I'm serious. You have things to do. I know the children and I have been hampering you."

"Come off it! It's not you...."

Lu broke in, "Of course it is! We can't divorce. The children need their father and a scientist needs his family. However, we must think of some way to turn your eight working hours into sixteen."

"But the children and the housework will all fall on you. That won't do!"

"Why not? Even without you we can manage."

He listed all the problems, which she answered one by one. Finally she said, "Haven't you often remarked that I'm a tough woman? I can cope. Your son won't go hungry, your daughter won't be ill-treated."

He was convinced. They decided to have a try the next day.

"It's so very difficult to do something in China!" Fu said undressing. "During the war, many old revolutionaries died for a new China. Now to modernize our country, again a generation has to make sacrifices though hardly anyone notices it."

He kept talking to himself like this. He put his clothes on the back of a chair and when he turned to get into bed, he saw that Lu had fallen asleep. With the faint smile on her face she looked pleased with her proposal, even in her dreams.

Chapter 13

The operations were successful, though Lu's private little plan failed.

That morning, when she had entered the ward ten minutes early as usual, Dr. Sun was already there waiting for her.

"Good morning, Dr. Lu," he greeted her, "we've got a donor's eye today. Can we fit in the corneal transplant?"

"Excellent! We've got apatient who's anxious to have the operation done as soon as possible."

"But you already have two operations scheduled for this morning. Do you think you can manage a third?"

"Sure," she replied, straightening up as if showing him that she was perfectly capable.

"O.K., it's settled then."

Holding the arm of Jiang, who had just arrived, Lu headed for the operating room.

The operating rooms of this hospital, occupying a whole floor, were large and impressive. When a wheeled stretcher bearing a patient was pushed through the double glass door, his relatives remained outside, anxiously looking at the mysterious, perhaps even frightening place, as if death were lurking about inside.

But, in fact, the operating theatre was a place of hope. Inside, the walls along the wide corridor were painted a light, agreeable green. Here were the operating theatres for various departments. The surgeons, their assistants, anaesthetists and theatre nurses glided silently to and fro. No laughter, no chatter. This was the most quiet, most orderly area of the large hospital into which more than a thousand patients poured every day.

Vice-minister Jiao was brought into one of these theatres and then put on a high operating table. His head was covered by a sterilized white towel. There was an olive-shaped hole in it revealing one of his eyes.

Lu, already in her gown, sat on a stool near the operating table, her gloved hands raised. Lu, being small, had to raise the height of the adjustable stool whenever she operated. But today it had already been adjusted. She turned and glanced at Jiang gratefully, realizing she had done it.

A nurse pushed the surgical instrument table nearer to Lu. The adjustable plate was now placed above the patient's chest within the surgeon's reach.

"Shall we start now?" Lu asked, watching Jiao's eye. "Try to relax. We'll first inject a local anaesthetic. Then your eye will feel numb. The operation won't take long."

At this Jiao suddenly cried out, "Hold on!"

What was wrong? Both Lu and Jiang were taken aback. Jiao pulled away the towel from his face, striving to raise his head. He inquired, pointing at Lu, "It was you, Dr. Lu, who operated before on my eye?"

Lu quickly raised her gloved hands lest he touch them. Before she could speak, he went on emotionally, "Yes, it was you. It must have been you! You said the same words. Even your tone and intonation are the same!"

"Yes, it was me," Lu had to admit.

"Why didn't you tell me before? I'm so grateful to you."

"Never mind...." Lu could not find anything else to say. She cast a glance at the towel, beckoning the nurse to change it. Then she said again, "Shall we start, Vice-minister Jiao?"

Jiao sighed deeply, unable to calm his turbulent emotions. "Don't move!" said Lu in a commanding tone. "Don't speak! We're starting now."

She skillfully injected novocain into his lower eyelid and began the operation. She had performed such operations countless times, but every time she picked up her instruments she felt like a raw recruit on the battlefield. Lu held out two tapering fingers to pick up a needle holder which looked like a small pair of scissors. She fixed the needle to the instrument.

"What's the matter?" Jiang asked softly.

Instead of answering, Lu held the hook-shaped needle up to the light to examine it.

"Is this a new one?"

Jiang had no idea, so they both turned to the nurse.

"A new needle?"

The nurse stepped forward and said in a low voice, "Yes, a new one."

Lu had another look at the head of the needle and grumbled, "How can we use a needle like this?"

Lu and some other doctors had complained many times about the poor quality of their surgical instruments. However, faulty ones appeared from time to time. Lu could do nothing about it. When she found good scalpels, scissors and needles, she would ask the nurse to save them for her.

Even though all the surgical instruments had been replaced by new ones that day, there was unfortunately one bad needle among them. Whenever such things occurred, Lu's good-natured expression would change and she would reprimand the nurse. The young nurse, though innocent, perhaps, could not defend herself. There was nothing to say in the circumstances. A blunt needle not only prolonged the operation, but also increased the patient's suffering.

Frowning, Lu said quietly, so that Jiao could not overhear, "Bring me another!"

It was an order. The nurse picked out an old needle from a sterilizer.

The theatre nurses respected Lu, but at the same time feared her. A doctor's authority was established through his scalpel. A good oculist could give a blind man back his sight, while a bad one might blind him permanently. Lu had no position, no power, but through her scalpel she wielded silent authority.

The operation was almost complete when Jiao's body jerked

suddenly.

"Don't move!" Lu warned him.

"Don't move!" Jiang repeated quickly. "What's the matter?"

"I...want to...cough!" A strangled voice sounded from under the towel.

This was just what his wife had feared would happen. Why choose this moment to cough? Was it psychological? A conditioned reflex?

"Can you control it for a minute?"

"No, I...can't." His chest was heaving.

There was no time to lose! Lu hurriedly took emergency measures, while calming him down, "Just a second! Breathe out and hold your cough!"

She was quickly tying up the suture while he exhaled, his chest moving vigorously as if he would die of suffocation at any moment. When the last knot was done, Lu sighed with relief and said, "You can cough now, but not too hard."

But he did not. On the contrary, his breath gradually grew even and normal.

"Go ahead and cough. It won't matter," Jiang urged again.

"I'm awfully sorry," Jiao apologized. "I'm all right now. Carry on with the operation, please."

Jiang rolled her eyes, wanting to give him a piece of her mind. A man of his age should know better. Lu threw her a glance, and Jiang bit back her resentment. They smiled knowingly at each other. It was all in the day's work!

Lu snipped off the knots and started the operation again. It continued without a hitch. Afterwards Lu got off the stool and sat at a small table to write out a prescription while Jiao was moved back onto the wheeled stretcher. As it was being pushed out Jiao suddenly called to Lu. Like a kid who had misbehaved, his voice trembled slightly.

Lu stepped over to him. His eyes had been bandaged. "Anything I can do?" she stooped to ask.

He reached out, groping. When he caught hold of her hands, still in their gloves, he shook them vigorously. "I've given you so much trouble on both occasions. I'm so sorry...."

Lu was stunned for a moment. Then she consoled him, looking at his bandaged face, "Never mind. Have a good rest. We'll take off the bandage in a few days."

After he was wheeled out, Lu glanced at the clock. A forty-minute operation had lasted an hour. She took off her white gown and rubber gloves and immediately donned another. As Lu turned to let the nurse tie the gown at the back, Jiang asked,

"Shall we continue?"

"Yes."

Chapter 14

"Let me do the next operation," Jiang begged. "You take a short rest, then do the third."

Lu shook her head and said smilingly, "I'll do it. You're not familiar with Wang Xiaoman. The child's scared stiff. We became friends during the last few days. Better leave her to me."

The girl wearing a white gown a size too large, did not come into the operating theatre the ususal way on a wheeled stretcher; she was almost dragged in.

"Aunt Lu, I'm scared. I don't want the operation. Please tell my mother."

The sight of the doctors and nurses in their bizarre-looking outfits terrified her. She tried to wrench away from the nurses, and pleaded with Lu for help.

Lu walked toward the table and coaxed her with a grin, "Come on, little girl. Didn't you promise to have this operation? Be brave! There's nothing to fear. You won't feel any pain once you've been given some anesthetic."

Xiaoman sized up Lu in her funny clothes and gazed at her kind, smiling, encouraging eyes. Then she climbed up onto the operating table. A nurse spread a towel over her face. Lu motioned the nurse to tie the girl's hands. As the little patient was about to protest, Lu said, "Xiaoman, be a good girl! It's the same for all patients. Really, it won't take long. I'm going to give you an injection and soon your eye will feel nothing at all."

Lu took the scissors, forceps and other instruments which Jiang handed to her, all the while keeping up a running commentary for the benefit of the girl. When she severed the straight muscle which caused the squint, a nerve was affected and Xiaoman became nauseated.

"You feel a little sick?" Lu asked. "Take a deep breath. Just hold on for a minute. That's better. Still sick? Feeling any better? We'll finish the operation very soon. There's a good girl!"

Lu's words lulled Xiaoman into a trance while the operation continued. When the girl had been bandaged and wheeled out of the room, she remembered what her mother had told her to say and called out sweetly, "Thank you very much, Auntie."

Everyone burst out laughing. A half hour had passed.

Perspiration beaded Lu's forehead. Wet patches showed under

her armpits. She was surprised because it was not hot. Why had she perspired so profusely? She slightly moved her arms, which ached from being raised for the duration of the operation.

When she removed the operating gown again and reached out for another, she suddenly felt dizzy. She closed her eyes for a minute, shook her head several times and then slowly eased one of her arms into a sleeve. A nurse came to help her tie the gown.

"Dr. Lu," the nurse exclaimed suddenly. "Your lips are so pale!"

It was true. There were black rings under Lu's eyes. Even her lids were puffy. She looked like a patient herself.

Seeing that Jiang's startled eyes remained fixed on her, Lu grinned and said, "Stop fussing! It'll soon be over."

She had no doubt that she could carry on with the next operation. She had worked like this for years.

"Shall we continue?" the nurse asked.

"Yes, of course."

The donor's eye could not be stored too long, nor the operation delayed. They had to go on working.

"Wenting," Jiang suggested. "Let's have a break for half an hour."

Lu looked at the clock. It was just after ten. If they postponed it for half an hour, some colleagues would be late for lunch, while others would have to rush home to prepare a meal for their children.

"Continue?" the nurse asked again.

"Yes."

Chapter 15

Doctors from a number of hospitals undergoing further training had been given special permission to to see Lu operate. Now they crowded the doorway.

Uncle Zhang, helped by a nurse, clambered onto the operating table, still talking and laughing. The table was a bit too small for him and his feet and hands dangled over the sides. He had a loud voice and talked incessantly, joking with a nurse, "Don't laugh at me, girl. Before the medical team came to our village and persuaded me to have this operation, I would have died before I let you cut my eye with a knife. Just imagine! A steel knife cutting into my flesh, ugh! Who knows if it will do me any good or not? Ha! Ha!..."

The young nurse tittered and said softly, "Uncle, lower your voice please."

"I know, girl. We must keep quiet in a hospital, mustn't we?" he boomed. "You can't imagine how I felt when I heard that my eye could be cured. I didn't know whether to laugh or cry. My father went blind in his old age and died a blind man. I never dreamed that a blind man like me could see the sun again. Times have really changed, haven't they?"

The nurse giggled while covering him with a towel. "Don't move again, Uncle!" she said. "This towel's been sterilized. Don't touch it."

"All right," he answered gravely. "Since I'm in the hospital, I should obey the rules." But he attempted to raise his strong arms again.

Worried about his restlessness, the nurse said, "I'll have to tie your arms to the table, Uncle. That's the rule here."

Zhang was puzzled, but soon chortled. "Truss me up, eh?" he joked. "O.K., go ahead! To be frank, lass, if it were not for my eyes, I wouldn't be so obedient. Though blind, I go to the fields twice a day. I was born a lively character. I like to be on the go. I just can't sit still."

This made the nurse laugh, and he chuckled too. But he stopped immediately when Lu entered. He asked, cocking up his ear, "Is that you, Dr. Lu? I can recognize your steps. It's funny, since I lost my sight my ears have grown sharp."

Lu took her seat, preparing for the operation. As she picked up the precious donor's cornea from a vial and sewed it onto a piece of gauze, Zhang piped up again, "So an eye can be replaced? I never knew that!"

"It's not replacing the whole eye, just a filmy membrane," Jiang corrected him.

"What's the difference? It takes a lot of skill, doesn't it? When I return to my village with a pair of good eyes, the villagers'll say I must have met some good fairy. I'll tell them I met Dr. Lu!"

Jiang tittered, winking at Lu who felt a little embarrassed. Still sewing, she explained, "Other doctors can do the same."

"That's quite true," he agreed. "You only find good doctors in this big hospital."

Her preparation over, Lu parted his eyelids with a speculum and said, "We'll start now. Just relax."

Zhang was not like other patients, who only listened to whatever the doctors said. He thought it impolite not to answer. So he said understandingly, "I'm perfectly all right. Go ahead. I don't mind if it's painful. Of course, it hurts to be cut with a scalpel or a pair of scissors. But don't worry about me. I trust you. Besides...."

Jiang had to stop him, still smiling. "Uncle, don't talk any more."

Finally he complied.

Lu picked up a trephine, small as a ballpoint cap, and lightly cut out the clouded cornea. Cutting a similar disc of clear cornea from the donor's eye, she transferred it to Zhang's eye. Then she began the delicate task of stitching it with a special needle. The suture was finer than a hair.

The operation went smoothly. When Lu had finished, the transplanted cornea was perfectly fixed on the surface of the eye. Except for a few tiny black knots, one could never tell it was a new cornea.

"Well done!" the doctors around the operating table quietly exclaimed.

Lu sighed with relief. Deeply touched, Jiang looked up at her friend with feeling. Silently she put layers of gauze over Zhang's eye....

As he was wheeled out, Zhang seemed to awaken from a dream. He became animated again. When the wheeled stretcher was already out the door, he cried out, "Thanks a lot, Dr. Lu!"

The operations were over. Lu found her legs had gone to sleep. She simply could not stand up. After a little rest she tried again and again until she finally made it. There was a sudden pain in her side. She pressed it with her hand, not taking it seriously for it had occurred before. Engrossed in an operation, sitting on the little stool for hours at a time, she was aware of nothing else. Now she felt utterly exhausted, too tired even to move.

Chapter 16

Early that morning Fu, at his wife's suggestion, had rolled up his bedding, put it on his bicycle and taken it to his office to begin his new life. By noon, however, he was wavering. Would Lu finish her operations in time? Imagining her dragging herself home to prepare lunch for the children, he suddenly felt a pang of guilt. He jumped on his bicycle and pedalled home.

Just as he turned down the lane, he spotted Lu, propping herself up against the wall.

"Wenting! What's wrong?" he cried out, leaping off his bike.

"Nothing. I'm just a bit tired." She put an arm over his shoulder and moved slowly towards home.

Fu noticed that she was very pale and that beads of cold sweat had broken out on her forehead. He asked uneasily, "Shall I take you to the hospital?"

She sat down on the edge of the bed, her eyes closed, and answered, "Don't worry. I'll be all right after a short rest." She pointed to the bed, too weak to say anything. Fu took off her shoes and coat.

"Lie down and get some sleep. I'll wake you later."

"No need. I can't sleep. But lying down will help."

He went to boil some water in a saucepan. When he came back to fetch noodles, he heard her say, "We ought to have a rest. Shall we take the children to Beihai Park next Sunday? We haven't been there for more than ten years."

"Fine. I'm all for it!" Fu agreed, wondering why she should suddenly want to go there now.

He gave her an anxious glance and went to cook the noodles. When he returned, food in hand, she had already fallen asleep. He did not disturb her. When Yuanyuan came home the two of them sat down to eat.

Lu began to groan. Fu put down his bowl and rushed to the bed. Lu was deathly white, her face covered in sweat.

"I can't fight it," she said in a feeble voice, gasping for breath.

Frightened, Fu took her hand asking, "What's wrong? Have you any pain?"

With a great effort Lu pointed to her heart.

Panicking, Fu pulled open a drawer to look for a pain killer. On second thought, he wondered if she needed a tranquilizer.

Though in great pain, Lu was clear-headed. She signaled to him to calm down and said with all her remaining strength, "I must go to the hospital!"

Only then did Fu realize the seriousness of her illness. For more than ten years she had never seen a doctor, though she went to the hospital every day. "I'll go and get a taxi," he said, hurrying out.

He rushed to the public telephone on the corner. He dialed quickly and waited, then heard a cold voice say, "No taxis at the moment."

"Look, I've got a very sick person here!"

"Still, you'll have to wait half an hour."

Fu began to plead, but the man hung up. He tried to call Lu's hospital, but no one seemed to be in the office of the Ophthalmology Department. He asked the operator to put him through to the vehicle dispatch office.

"We can't send you a car without an official approval slip," was the answer. Where on earth could he track down the necessary officials to get an approval slip?

"But this is urgent! Hello!" he shouted into the receiver. The line had already gone dead.

Next, he phoned the political department. Surely they would help him, he thought. After a long time a woman answered. She listened patiently and said politely, "Would you please contact the administration department?"

He had to ask the operator to put him through to the administration department. Recognizing his voice, the operator demanded impatiently, "Who exactly do you want?"

Who? He was not sure himself. Pleading, he said he wanted to speak to anyone in the administration department. The telephone rang and rang. Nobody answered.

Finally, Fu abandoned the idea of finding a car. He headed for a small workshop in the lane which made cardboard boxes, hoping to borrow a pedicab and trailer. The old lady in charge, hearing of his predicament, sympathized with him, but unfortunately could do nothing; both her pedicabs were out.

What was to be done? Standing in the alley, Fu was desperate. Sit Lu on the bicycle carrier? That was impossible.

Just then Fu saw a van coming. Without hesitation, he dashed into the middle of the road to stop it. The van came to a halt, and the driver poked his head out, staring in surprise. But when he heard what was happening, he beckoned Fu to get in.

They went straight to Fu's home. When the driver saw Lu being dragged toward the van, by her husband, he hurried to help. Then carefully he drove them to the emergency entrance.

Chapter 17

Lu had never slept so long, never felt so tired. Her whole body ached and she felt terribly weak. Yet her recent forced rest had allowed her to utterly relax for the first time in a long time.

For years she had simply had no time to pause, to reflect on the hardships she had experienced or the difficulties lying ahead. Now all physical and mental burdens had been lifted. She seemed to have plenty of time to examine her past and to explore the future. But her mind had switched off; no reminiscences, no hopes. Nothing.

Perhaps it was only a dream. She had had such dreams before....

One evening when she was only five, her mother had gone out, leaving her alone at home while the north wind howled outside. Soon it was very dark but her mother had not returned. For the first time, Lu felt lonely, terrified. She cried and shouted, "Mama...mama..." That scene had often appeared in her dreams. The howling wind, the door blown open by a sudden gust, the pale light of the kerosene lamp remained vivid in her mind. For a long time she could not tell whether it had truly happened or had been a dream.

This time it was not a dream.

She was in bed, ill, and Jiajie was attending her. He looked exhausted too. Dozing, half lying on the bed, he would catch cold if not awakened. She tried to call him but no sound came out. It was as if there were something in her throat choking her. She wanted to pull a coat over him, but her arms felt as though they belonged to someone else.

She glanced around and saw she was in a single room. Only serious cases were given special treatment. She was suddenly seized by fear.

The autumn wind rattled the door and windows. Darkness gathered, swallowing up the room. Lu felt clearer despite her cold sweat. It was real, she knew, not a dream. This was the end of life, the beginning of death.

So this was dying. No fear, no pain, just life withering away, the senses blurring, slowly sinking, like a leaf drifting on a river.

All things come to an end inevitably. Rolling waves swept over her chest. Lu felt she was floating in the water....

"Mama...mama...." She heard Xiaojia's call and saw her running along the bank. She turned back, reaching out her arms.

"Xiaojia...my darling daughter...."

But waves swept her away, and Xiaojia's face grew vague, her hoarse voice turned into sobbing.

"Mama...plait my hair...."

Why not plait her hair? The child's one desire in all her six years was to have pigtails. Whenever she saw other girls with pig-tails adorned with silk ribbons, admiration overwhelmed her little heart. But Lu didn't even have the time to satisfy that one little request.

Mother had no time for that. On Monday morning the hospital was crowded with patients and, for Lu, every minute counted.

"Mama...mama...."

She heard Yuanyuan's call and saw the boy running after her along the bank. She turned back, stretching out her arms.

"Yuanyuan...Yuanyuan...."

A wave swept over her. When she struggled to the surface, there was no sign of her son, only his voice in the distance.

"Mama...don't forget...my white gym shoes...."

A kaleidoscope of sports shoes whirled around. White and blue sneakers, sports boots, gym shoes, white shoes with red or blue bands. Buy a pair for Yuanyuan, whose shoes were already worn out. Buy a pair of white gym shoes and he would be in raptures for a month. But then the shoes disappeared and raining down were price tags: 3.1 *yuan*, 4.5 *yuan*, 65.3 *yuan*.

Now she saw Jiajie chasing after her, his running figure mirrored in the water. He was in a great hurry, his voice trembling as he called, "Wenting, you can't leave us like this!"

How she wished that she could wait for him! He held out his hand to her, but the ruthless current surged forward and she drifted away helplessly.

"Dr. Lu...Dr. Lu...."

So many people were calling her, lining the banks. Yafen, Old Liu, Director Zhao, Dr. Sun, all in white coats; Jiao Chengshi, Uncle Zhang and Wang Xiaoman in pajamas. Among the other patients, she only recognized a few. They were all calling to her, calling!

I cannot leave. No! There are so many things I still have to do. Xiaojia and Yuanyuan shouldn't be motherless. I must not bring Jiajie more sorrow. He can't afford to lose his wife so young. I can't tear myself away from the hospital, the patients. Oh no! I can't give up this miserable yet dear life!

I won't drown! I must fight! I must remain in the world. But why am I so tired? I've no strength to resist, to struggle. I'm sinking, sinking....

Ah! Goodbye, Yuanyuan! Goodbye, Xiaojia! Will you miss your mother? In this last moment of life, I love you more than ever. Oh, how I love you! Let me embrace you. Listen, my darlings, forgive your mummy who did not give you the love you deserved. Forgive your mummy who, time and again, refrained from hugging you, who pushed away your smiling faces. Forgive your mummy for leaving you while you're still so small.

Goodbye, Jiajie! You gave up everything for me. Without you I couldn't have achieved anything. Without you, life had no meaning. Ah, you sacrificed so much for me. If I could, I would kneel down before you begging your pardon since I can never repay all your kindness and concern. Forgive me for neglecting you. I often thought I should do more for you. I wanted to end my work regularly and prepare supper for you. I wanted to let you have the desk, hoping you would finish your article. But it's too late. I've no time now.

Goodbye, my patients! For the past eighteen years, my life was devoted to you. Whether I walked, sat or lay down, I thought only

*of you and your eyes. You don't know the joy I felt after curing an
eye. What a pity I shall no longer feel that....*

Chapter 18

"Arrhythmia!" The doctor monitoring the screen exclaimed.

"Wenting! Wenting!" Fu cried out, fixing his eyes on his wife
as she struggled for breath.

The doctors and nurses on duty rushed into the room.

"Intravenous injection of lidocaine!" The doctor snapped an
order.

A nurse quickly injected it, but before it was finished, Lu's lips
went blue, her hands clenched, her eyes rolled upwards.

Her heart stopped beating.

The doctors began massage resuscitation. An artificial respira-
tor was placed over her face; it made a rhythmic sound. Finally,
the defibrilator went into action. As the machine struck Lu's
chest, her heart began to beat once again.

"Get the ice cap ready!" The doctor in charge ordered, his fore·
head sweating. An ice cap was put on Lu's head.

Chapter 19

The pale dawn could be seen outside the window. Day had broken at last. Lu had lived through a critical night.

A day nurse came into the room and opened the windows, letting in fresh air and the birds' merry singing. At once the pungent
smell of medicine and death was dispelled.

Another nurse came to take Lu's temperature, while a medical
orderly brought in breakfast. Then the doctor on duty dropped in
on his ward rounds. An air of hope seemed to have returned to
Lu's room.

Wang Xiaoman, still bandaged, pleaded with a nurse, "Let me
have a look at Dr. Lu! Just one peep."

"No. She nearly died last night. No one's allowed to see her for
the time being."

"Aunt, perhaps you don't know, but she fell ill because she
operated on me. Please let me go and see her. I promise not to say
a word to her."

"No, no, no!" The nurse scowled.

"Oh, please! Just one glance." Xiaoman was close to tears.
Hearing footsteps behind her, she turned and saw Old Zhang

coming, led by his grandson.

"Grandpa," she rushed to him, "will you have a word with the nurse? She won't let me...."

The little girl dragged Zhang, with his eyes bandaged, over to the nurse.

"Sister, do let us have a look at her."

Now with this old man pestering her too, the nurse flared up, "What's the matter with you people, fooling around in the wards?"

"Come off it! Don't you understand?" Zhang's voice was not so loud today. He went on humbly, "We've a good reason, you know. Why is Dr. Lu ill? Because she operated on us. To be frank, I can't really see her, but to stand beside her bed for a while will calm my nerves."

He was so sincere that the nurse softened and explained patiently, "It's not that I'm being mean. Dr. Lu's seriously ill with heart trouble. She mustn't be excited. You want her to recover very soon, don't you? It's better not to disturb her at the moment."

"Yes, you're quite right." Zhang sighed and sat down on a bench. Slapping his thigh, he said regretfully, "It's my fault. I urged her to do the operation as quickly as possible. But who would've thought....? What shall I do if anything happens to her?" He lowered his head in remorse.

Before starting his work Dr. Sun hurried to Lu also, but was stopped by Xiaoman.

"Dr. Sun, are you going to see Dr. Lu?" she asked.

He nodded.

"Will you take me along? Please."

"Not now. Some time later. O.K.?"

Hearing Sun's voice, Zhang stood up and reached out for him. Tugging Sun's sleeve, he said, "Dr. Sun, we'll do as you say. But may I have a word with you? I know you're extremely busy. But I still want you to listen to what's been bothering me."

Sun patted Zhang on the shoulder and said, "Go ahead."

"Dr. Lu's a very good doctor. You leaders ought to do your best to cure her. If you save her, she can save many others. There are good medicines, aren't there? Give them to her. Don't hesitate. I hear you have to pay for certain precious medicines. Lu's got two children. She's not well off. Now she's ill. I don't expect she can afford them. Can't this big hospital subsidize her?"

He stopped, holding Sun's hands and slightly cocking his ear towards him, waiting for his answer.

Sun was rather stiff and reserved, seldom showing his feelings.

But today he was moved. Shaking Zhang's hands, he said emotionally, "We'll do everything possible to save her!"

Zhang seemed satisfied. He called his grandson to come nearer and groped for a satchel which was slung across the boy's shoulder.

"Here are some eggs. Please take them to her when you go in."

"It's not necessary," Sun replied quickly.

This got Zhang riled up instantly. Gripping Sun's hands, he raised his voice, "If you don't take them to her, I won't let you go!"

Sun had to accept the satchel of eggs. He would ask a nurse to return it later and explain. As though guessing what was in Sun's mind, Zhang continued, "And don't ask someone to bring them back."

Forced to acquiesce, Sun helped Zhang and Xiaoman down the stairs.

Qin, accompanied by Director Zhao, approached Lu's room. "Zhao," the woman talked rather excitedly while walking, "I've been acting like a bureaucrat. I didn't know it was Dr. Lu who had operated on Old Jiao. But you should have known, shouldn't you? Luckily Jiao recognized Lu. Otherwise we'd still be in the dark."

"I was sent to work in the countryside at that time," Zhao replied helplessly.

Shortly after they had entered the room, Sun arrived. The doctor on duty gave a brief report of the emergency measures taken to save Lu the previous night. Zhao looked over the case history, nodding. Then he said, "We must watch her carefully."

Fu, seeing so many people entering, had stood up. But Qin, unaware of his presence, quickly sat down on the vacant stool.

"Feeling better, Dr. Lu?" she asked.

Lu's eyes opened slightly but she said nothing.

"Vice-minister Jiao has told me all about you," Qin said warmly. "He's very grateful to you. He would have come himself if I hadn't stopped him. I'm here to thank you on his behalf. Anything you fancy eating, anything you want, let me know. I can help you. Don't stand on ceremony. We're all revolutionary comrades."

Lu closed her eyes.

"You're still young. Be optimistic! As long as you're sick, you might as well take the opportunity to get a good rest. Besides..."

Zhao stopped her by saying, "Comrade Qin Bo, let her have some rest. She's only just regained consciousness."

"Fine, fine. Have a good rest," Qin said, rising to her feet. "I'll come again in a couple of days."

Out of the ward, Qin frowned, "Director Zhao, I must give you a piece of my mind. Dr. Lu's a real treasure. If you had been more concerned about her, she wouldn't have become so ill. The middle-aged comrades are the backbone of our country. It's imperative to value talented people."

"Right," was Zhao's reply.

Gazing after her receding figure, Fu asked Sun in a small voice, "Who's she?"

Sun looked over the frame of his spectacles at the doorway and answered, frowning, "Madame Marxism-Leninism!"

Chapter 20

That day Lu was slightly better and could open her eyes easily. She drank two spoonfuls of milk and a sip of orange juice. But she lay with her eyes blank, staring at the ceiling. She wore a vacant expression as if indifferent to everything, including her own critical condition and the unhappiness of her family. She seemed weary of life.

Fu stared at her in mute horror. He had never seen her like this. He called to her again and again, but she only responded with a slight wave of her hand, as though not wishing to be disturbed.

Time passed unheeded. Fu, sitting at her bedside, had not slept for two nights. Dozing, he was suddenly awakened by a heart-rending scream which shook the whole ward. He heard a girl wailing next door, "Mama! Mama!" and a man's sobbing. Then there came the sound of footsteps as many people rushed to the room. Fu hurried out too. He saw a wheeled stretcher, on which lay a corpse covered with a sheet, being pushed out of the room. Then a nurse in white pushing the stretcher appeared. A girl of sixteen with disheveled hair stumbled out, shaking, and threw herself at the stretcher. Clutching at it with trembling hands, she pleaded, tears streaming down her cheeks, "Don't take her away! Please! My mother's asleep. She'll soon wake up! I know she will!"

Visitors made way for the wheeled stretcher. In silence they paid their respects to the deceased.

Fu stood frozen in the crowd. His bloodshot eyes began to fill with tears. Clenching his fists, he tried to contain his trembling. Unnerved by the girl's shrill cries, he wanted to cover his ears.

"Mama, wake up! Wake up! They're taking you away!" the girl

screamed madly. Had she not been held back by others, she would have pulled off the sheet. The middle-aged man following the stretcher repeated, sobbing, "I've let you down! I've let you down!"

The man's desperate cries pierced Fu's heart as he stared at the stretcher. All of a sudden he dashed towards his wife's room. He went straight to her and threw himself on the bed. He murmured with closed eyes, "You're alive!"

Lu stirred, awakened by his heavy breathing. She opened her eyes and looked at him, but her eyes didn't seem to focus.

He felt a shiver of fear and cried out, "Wenting!"

Her eyes lingered on his face indifferently, making his heart ache. Fu did not know what to say or do to encourage her to hold on to life. This was his wife, the dearest person in the world. How long ago was it since he had read poems to her in Beihai Park that winter? During all these years, she had always been his beloved. Life without her was unthinkable.

Poetry, he thought. Read a poem to her as he had done then. It was poetry which had helped him to win her before. Today he would recite the same poem to remind her of sweet memories, to give her the courage to live.

Half kneeling beside her bed, he began to recite with tears in his eyes:

> "I wish I were a stream,
> ......
> and my love
> were tiny fish
> frolicking
> in my frothy waves."

The verse seemed to have touched her. She turned her head toward him, her lips moving slightly. Fu leaned over and listened to her indistinct words: "I can no longer...swim...."

Choking back his tears, he continued:

> "I wish I were a deserted forest,
> ......
> If my love
> Were a little bird,
> She'd nest and twitter
> In my dense trees."

She murmured softly, "I can no longer...fly...."

His heart ached. Steeling himself, he went on, in tears:

"I wish I were a crumbling wall...

......

If my love
Were green ivy
She'd tenderly entwine
Around my lonely head."

Blinding tears silently poured down her cheeks and fell on the white pillow. With an effort she said, "I can't...climb up!"

Fu threw himself onto her, weeping bitterly. "I've failed you as a husband...."

When he opened his tearful eyes he was astonished to see that Lu did not seem to respond to his entreaties. She lay there quietly, eyes fixed on the ceiling. She seemed unaware of his weeping, his appeals, unaware of everything around her.

On hearing Fu's sobbing, a doctor hurried in and said to him, "Dr. Lu's very weak. Please don't excite her."

Fu said nothing more the whole afternoon. At dusk Lu seemed a little better. She turned her head to Fu and her lips moved as if she wanted to speak.

"Wenting, what do you want to say? Tell me," Fu asked, holding her hands.

She spoke at last, "Buy Yuanyuan...a pair of white gym shoes...."

"I'll do it tomorrow," he replied, wiping away tears with the back of his hand.

Lu, still watching him, uttered a few words after a long time. "Plait...Xiaojia's hair...."

"Yes, I will!" Fu promised, still sobbing. He looked at his wife, his vision blurred, hoping she would be able to tell him all that was worrying her. But she closed her lips as if she had exhausted her strength.

Chapter 21

Two days later a letter came for Lu, posted at Beijing International Airport. Fu opened it and read:

Dear Wenting,

I wonder if you will ever receive this letter. It's not impossible that this won't reach you. Though you're very ill, I believe you'll recover. You can still do a lot. You're too young to leave us.

When my husband and I came to say goodbye to you last night, you were still unconscious. We'd wanted to see you this morning, but there were too many things to do. Yesterday evening may have been the last time we meet. Thinking of this, my heart breaks. We've been studying and working together for more than twenty years. No one understands us as well as we do each other. Who would imagine we would part like this?

I'm now writing this letter in the airport. Can you guess where I'm standing at this moment? At the arts and crafts counter on the second floor. There's no one about, only the shining glass counter in front of me. Remember the first time we traveled by air, we came here too? There was a pot of artificial narcissus with dew on their petals, so lifelike, so exquisite! You told me that you liked it best, but the price was far too steep. Now I'm before the counter again, alone looking at another pot, almost the same color as the one we saw. Looking at it, I feel like crying. I don't know why. Now I realize suddenly, it's because of all that has passed.

When Fu had just met you, I remember once he came to our room and recited a line by Pushkin, "All that has happened in the past becomes a sweet memory." I pursed my lips and said it wasn't true. I even asked, "Can past misfortunes become sweet memories?" Fu grinned, ignoring me. He must have thought inwardly that I knew nothing about poetry. But today I understand. Pushkin was right. It reflects my mood now exactly. It's as if he wrote the line for me. I really feel that all the past is sweet.

A jet has just taken off, its engines roaring. Where is it going? In an hour I'll be climbing up the steps into the plane, leaving my country. With only an hour left I can t help weeping, and my tears wet this letter. But I've not time to rewrite it.

I'm so depressed; I suddenly feel as if I've made the wrong decision. I don't want to leave everything here. No! I can't bear to leave our hospital, our operating theatre, even that little desk in the clinic. I often grumbled that Dr. Sun was too severe, never forgiving a mistake. But now I wish I could hear his criticism again. He was a strict teacher. If not for him, I wouldn't be so skilled.

The loudspeakers have just wished passengers bon voyage. Thinking of boarding the plane in a moment, I feel lost. Where will I land? What lies in store? My heart's in my throat. I'm scared! Will we get used to a strange country which is so different from ours? How can my mind be at peace?

My husband is sitting in an armchair brooding. Busy packing the last few days, he had no time to think. He seemed quite firm about the decision. But last night when he stuffed the last coat into the suitcase, he said all of a sudden, "We'll be homeless after tomorrow!" He hasn't spoken since then, and I know his mind is still divided.

Yaya was most happy about this trip. She was nervous and excited, but now she's standing at the glass door watching the planes landing and taking off, as if reluctant to leave.

"Won't you change your minds?" you asked that night when we were at your place.

I can't answer that question in one sentence. Liu and I have been discussing it almost every day for the past few months. Our minds have been in turmoil. There are many reasons, of course, urging us to leave China. It is for Yaya, for Liu and myself. However, none of those reasons can lessen my pain. We shouldn't leave when China has just begun a new period. We've no excuse for avoiding our duties.

Compared with you, I'm weak. I had less trouble than you did over the last ten years, but I couldn't bear it as well as you. I would always lose my temper whenever I was viciously slandered or attacked—better to die than be humiliated, I thought. But there was Yaya to think of. It's surprising that I was able to function at all those years when Liu was illegally detained as a "suspect enemy agent."

Of course, all these are just bitter memories of the past now. Fu was right when he said, "Darkness has receded and day has dawned." The trouble is, all the prejudices of those years can't be eradicated overnight, and government policies take an awfully long time to reach the people. So there's still a lot of resentment that won't be easily removed. And you know how rumors can destroy a person. I dread the repetition of the nightmare of the past. I lack your courage.

I remember how you and I were cited at that meeting as bourgeois experts. When we left the hospital afterwards I said to you, "I can't understand all this. Why should people who have worked hard in their field be crushed? I'll refuse to attend such meetings as a protest!" But you said, "Forget it. If they want to hold a hundred such meetings, let them. I'll attend. We'll still have to do the operations. I'll study at home." I asked you, "Don't you feel wronged?" You smiled and said, "I'm so busy, I've no time to care." I admired you very much. Before we parted you warned me, "Don't tell Fu about this. He's in enough trouble himself." We walked a block in silence. I noticed that you looked very calm, very confident. No one could shake your faith. I knew that you had a strong will which enabled you to resist all kinds of attacks and go your own way. If I had half your courage and will power, I couldn't have made such a decision.

Forgive me! This is all I can say to you now. I'm leaving, but I'm leaving my heart with you, with my dear homeland. Wherever I go, I'll never forget China. Believe me! Believe that I'll return. After a few years, when Yaya's grown up and we have achieved something in medicine, we'll come back.

I hope you'll soon recover. Learn a lesson from your illness and pay more attention to your health. I'm not advising you to be selfish. I've always admired your selflessness. I wish you good health to make full use of your talents.

Goodbye, my dearest friend.

With love,
Yafen

Chapter 22

A month and a half later Dr. Lu was almost fully recovered and was permitted to go home.

It was a miracle. Lu, several times on the brink of death, had survived.

That morning Fu jubilantly helped her put on a cotton-padded jacket, a pair of woolen trousers, a blue overcoat, and wrapped around her neck a long fluffy beige scarf.

"How are things at home?" she asked.

"Fine. The comrades of your party branch came yesterday to help clean the room."

Her thoughts immediately turned to that small room with the large bookcase covered with a white cloth, the little alarm-clock on the windowsill and the desk....

She felt feeble and cold, though so warmly dressed. Her legs trembled when she stood up. With one hand gripping her husband's arm, the other touching the wall, she moved forward, leaning heavily on Fu. Slowly, she walked out of the ward.

Zhao, Sun and her other colleagues followed her, watching her progress along the corridor toward the gate.

It had rained for a couple of days. A gust of wind sighed through the bare branches of the trees. The sunshine, extraordinarily bright after the rain, slanted in through the windows of the corridor. Fu, supporting his wife, plodded toward the sunlight and the wind.

A black car waited at the steps. It had been sent by the administration department at Zhao's request.

Leaning on her husband's shoulder, Lu walked slowly toward the gate....

Between Human and Demon

LIU BINYAN

(Translated by Lu Yunzhong and Gu Tingfu)

PART ONE

The Party Committee of Bin County

The courtyard of the Party Committee of Bin County of Heilong-jiang Province had always been a gathering place for the popu-lace of the county. For ten years or so after land reform, when people came here on market days or on errands, they would look in on cadres who had been members of the work team stationed in their villages to talk things over. But as time wore on, the wall around the courtyard seemed to grow higher and thicker until it took on a secretive and awe-inspiring look. People passing by would seldom pop their heads in to look about. By the early six-ties the sweet enticing smell of meat, oil and steamed bread would frequently assail the nostrils of passers-by, some of whom would crack bitter smiles, grumbling: "Well, they're doing quite well, this bunch of officials!"

One day in November 1964, a jeep pulled into the courtyard of the Party Committee, attracting a crowd of people outside its gate. For a long time rumor had it that a new party secretary would soon be assigned to Bin County and people were eager to see what he looked like. Their curiosity was mixed with anxie-ties; three secretaries had fallen before him. How would the new-comer fare?

Since then, the new secretary, Tian Fengshan, a stalwart stranger with ruddy complexion, had become an object of the

195

local people's scrutiny. Before long their comments could be heard: "This guy is a different communist altogether."

Bin County had just recovered from the effects of three years of economic hardship during which the common people had suffered a great deal. There were many problems the party leaders needed to ponder seriously in order to reappraise the situation. However, either at the meetings of the standing committee of the County Party Committee or at the study classes for party members held at Mount Erlong, the preferred topic of discussion was women.

The leading group taken over by Tian Fengshan was rotten to the core. When the people had to live on ersatz food made from the starch of crushed maize leaves and corn cobs, the children of the county party secretary were throwing steamed bread stuffed with meat at the dogs for fun. With nothing but coarse dried food to fill their stomachs, peasants had once walked a distance of over thirty miles to present a petition to the County Party Committee, only to be met with cold, stony stares. After that, few people liked to go to the County committee to get their problems solved, preferring to go instead all the way to Harbin*. As a result, the County Party secretary as well as members of the standing committee had nothing to do but lounge on the sofa and engage in chitchat.

Tian Fengshan, however, liked to receive petitioners in person and he did look into ten major cases, the investigation of which had been deliberately delayed for years. People would come by in the morning before he had even gotten out of bed. Chewing dried food, he would listen to their complaints. He used to visit every restaurant and shop in the county town in order to check on the quality of goods and services. When he revoked the designation "advanced enterprise" which had been bestowed on the foodstuffs factory every year, he said, "I see you can make tens of thousands of *yuan* in a year and save tens of thousands of catties of rice, oil and sugar, but you're simply squeezing the common people. What sort of 'advanced enterprise' are you running?" Then, after inquiring into housing conditions, he lowered the rent. In addition, he led cadres down to the rural areas and helped improve remarkably conditions in the more backwards production brigades.

But the time allowed him by history was only two short years. In November 1966, the red guards stormed into the courtyard of the Party Committee, and in less than two hours the man known

*Capital city of Heilongjiang Province

as "Just Judge Tian" was swept off the historical arena of Bin County.

When the stalwart Tian Fengshan fell, a new star majestically appeared over Bin County—Commissioner Yang. Though lean, small and plain-looking, Yang soon became all-powerful, with the destiny of the 500,000 people of Bin County in his hands—this, thanks to that military greatcoat of his. To this day, thirteen years after his rise, the consequences of his work as commissioner can still be seen in the county. Even today he is a frequent topic of discussion. His image in the minds of the people forms a strong contrast with that of Tian Fengshan who is greatly missed.

At first what impressed the people most was his husky voice and his agitated speech. Then the people began to take a closer look. One thing was conspicuous—when Commissar Yang drove past in his jeep, raising a cloud of dust, people could not but wonder: How come Commissar Yang keeps company with *that* woman?

The woman sitting beside him on the jeep was none other than the shock the whole country.

"Leftist" Wang Shouxin Mounts the Stage

On the eve of the storm*, things were a bit too quiet in the small coal company of Bin County. The personnel of the company consisted of a few dozen staff and workers. Party Secretary Bai Kun and Manager Teng Zhixin, who were platform workers in the old days, kept things in good order. To learn from Lei Feng** was the order of the day. Cadres were unselfish, putting the public interest above everything else. But looking back through the historical clouds of the past thirteen years, one can not say everything was all right. A case in point concerned Zhou Lu, the designated successor to the party secretary (A Party Secretary should be elected. Whether it is appropriate to designate one is not our primary concern here) and Liu Changchun, who was generally believed to be ideologically backward. The former was to become an accomplice of the notorious grafter and embezzler Wang Shouxin, while the latter was to wage a long and bitter struggle against her.

---

*Reference is to the Cultural Revolution.

**Lei Feng, a PLA martyr who was regarded as an heroic embodiment of all communist virtures.

At that time, Wang Shouxin was an energetic cashier of the company. Unfortunately, she was energetic only when she was out of the office. She had a knack for suddenly disappearing during office hours. She would find out before anyone else who was having a scrap with whom in the street or which couple in the neighborhood was contemplating divorce or what new commodities the local department store had just put on display. Then she would spread the news throughout the company, sowing discord among her colleagues with her wagging tongue.

As the upsurge of the Great Cultural Revolution set in, no one knew what passion it had kindled in her, bringing into full play her political initiative. At first she attempted to establish ties with various commercial units, but ran into snags. Then she tried to get in touch with the students, but with little success. It was not until she sought out Commissar Yang at the military department that she got the support she had been looking for. As soon as she came back to the company she took steps to set up an organization but no one would join. Then she approached Zhang Feng, who had once been a bandit in the old days. "Let's gang up and pull them down," she said. "Let's call ourselves the 'Black Lair-Storming Fighting Force'!"

Nudging Zhou Lu's rib with her elbow and dragging this party member aside, she said, "You were oppressed in the past. What are you waiting for?" She continued in an intimate tone, "Why not rebel?"

Zhou Lu was a coward despite his burly appearance. Rebellion might get him into trouble, but he would be worse off if he did not follow suit. Wang Shouxin, as matters stood, would soon be one of Commissar Yang's valuable assistants. He had to convince himself that the old cadres in power, like Bai Kun, would never be able to stage a comeback. In desperation he made up his mind to join Wang. Wang used to prattle to him, "If you marry a hawk, you'll have meat for dinner; if you marry a duck, you'll have to eat its watery droppings!"

It so happened that Liu Changchun, formerly a handicraft weaver and now the planner and statistician of the company, was the very first person to stand in Wang's way. Liu had a large family to support: five sisters and brothers, his wife and son. With the meager pay he was given, he could barely feed the whole family. So after a day's work, while his colleagues would either rest at home or enjoy a play at the theatre, he had to weave socks to make some extra money or sell bean sprouts he had grown himself. This would only fetch him a few *jiao* each night. Sometimes he would buy a piglet from the market to raise at home. He would lose money, however, because of his inexperience in pig raising. In short, he was neither servile nor fawning, nor was he willing to steal. Instead he chose to rely on his own resources to survive. Never had he complained to Heaven for its prejudice, nor was he likely to pull a long face. As a matter of fact, he always seemed to be content with his lot.

Probably because of his poor childhood or because of a contrary disposition shared by handicraftsmen, Liu Changchun never bowed to his superiors, nor did he hesitate to speak his mind. Besides, he had to work on his private plot in order to make ends meet. No wonder he had fallen out of favor with the leadership.

It was not long before Wang Shouxin's Black Lair-Storming Fighting Force challenged Liu Changchun's Red Rebellion Corps to debate. Not conscious of the influence Wang now wielded, Liu regarded her more as an individual than as an adversary. That was where his mistake lay — he had underestimated his enemy.

At the debate a thin man, short of stature, was seen to step onto the platform. He had his hands behind his back, his chest thrown out and his shoulders squared. Liu was at first taken aback, thinking the man to be a leader from Harbin. But when he looked closer, he burst out laughing. "That rat," he cursed. "He has been rebel chief for only three days and there he is, putting on airs."

The man was none other than the commander-in-chief of the "United Command to Defend Mao Zedong Thought," Wen Feng by name. He spoke with a resonant voice and clear enunciation, showing his eloquence, which had fallen into disuse over the years. What counted most was the slogan he put forth in conclusion, which stunned the audience: "Closely follow Commissar Yang and boldly make revolution!"

Also on the platform was Wang Shouxin. With her hair cut short she looked smart and young for her forty-five years.

On the platform a staff officer from the troops sent by Commissar Yang could be seen. What he said counted.

"...Liu Changchun, you and the Red Rebellion Corps have never denounced the cadres in power. You grasp production to hold down revolution. And what's worse, you have discussed production matters with the cadres in power. You are no rebel!...You are right-deviationists. Your general orientation is wrong. Dissolve your corps at once today!"

Liu flew into a rage. He was an avid reader of newspapers and liked to dig out the truth. He prided himself on being able to understand policies and act according to them. So he leapt onto the platform. A booklet of "Sixteen Points" and a pamphlet of "The Latest Instructions" in hand, he cleared his throat and struck a pose, ready to argue things out. He was too naive to realize that the old books and pamphlets were already out of date. Deafening shouts and slogans broke out and people started swinging and kicking. This modern and peculiar way of "debating" in our ancient civilized land was very effective — and Wang Shouxin's political opponent was "refuted" in no more than two minutes.

Liu Changchun, however, refused to capitulate no matter how many meetings were held to repudiate him. Even with his head forced down, he would still look around as if to joke with the audience or to throw in an ironic remark. Zhou Lu, the chairperson, had shouted himself hoarse, only to find Liu struggling to raise his head and say, "Damn you, what a blockhead you are. You don't have to scream your head off!"

Zhou Lu was embarrassed but the audience was greatly amused.

On the second day after the debate, Wang Shouxin, seeing nobody else around, put her face close to Liu's and said in a gentle voice, "Changchun, let's stand together. I'm poorly educated. I'd like to have you as my military counselor. You'll be my second-in-command, what do you say?..."

"You better give up that absurd idea altogether!" he said angrily. "I'd rather be a groom for a true man than the ancestor of a coward. You and I are not made for each other."

He was a man who would not turn back even when he was forced up against the wall. But because quite a number of people had changed sides, Wang's strength grew and the Red Rebellion Corps fell into disarray. But Liu was still giving pep talks to those who had not yet given in. "Don't be afraid. I'll bring you meals if you are taken into custody!" he told them.

To no one's surprise, however, Liu Changchun himself was handcuffed and thrown into prison as "an active counter-revolutionary" who opposed the army.

A Situation Turned Upside Down

In regions that were poor and backward, political power was very exciting. If this were not the case, Wen Feng, the rebel boss, would not have shouted the slogan "Closely follow Commissar Yang" before anyone else and would not have profited by it. Commissar Yang, to be fair, was surprised at first to hear that slogan himself. "What's he shouting?" Yang asked a man standing near him. "Aren't you the man sent by Chairman Mao's Headquarters?" replied the man, eager to enlighten him. "It's only natural that we must all follow you closely." "Well, well, in that case let them follow," said the commissar, nodding his approval.

In the wake of "Closely follow..." came "Love and reverence..." It so happened that Commissar Yang went to work one day and left his keys at home. Without being prompted, his secretary went by bus immediately to fetch them. At the same time his chauffeur returned to Commissar Yang's residence for the same purpose. As each tried to hide his mission from the other so as to get hold of the keys, a heated argument ensued. In the end they could not but appear before the commissar at the same time and make equal contributions.

In brief, Commissar Yang was enjoying the greatest possible prestige in Bin County. When Wang Shouxin came to one of the local communes at night accompanying the commissar on his inspection tour, and said that Yang's favorite dish was boiled lean meat with sour cabbage and blood sausage, the commune cadres were eager to oblige. By this time Wang Shouxin had begun to have a taste for power. She liked it no less than this famous dish of the northeast.

It was on one of those days in August 1968 that the commissar hurried into the office of the planning group for the Revolutionary Committee of Commerce in Bin County. No sooner had he got inside than his eyes swept the group members who had stood up to salute him. The words he uttered in his habitual, firm tone shocked them all: "Wang Shouxin must be admitted into the leading group of this Revolutionary Committee!"

All the members gazed at each other dumbfounded until at last one of them plucked up his courage to ask in a whisper, "Is it proper to let her in?" The question implied that she was a loose woman of ill fame and little education.

The commissar was pacing up and down in the office when he heard the objection. He stopped abruptly, knitted his brows and said, "She must be admitted as vice director rather than as an ordinary member!"

It was clear that this was at once an order as well as a resolution, and was adopted immediately by the whole planning group. That's the way things were those days. Everyone was afraid of what there might really be behind Yang's frown. He could very well be thinking: "You diehards! What are you up to? You want to oppose the army, eh? Do you really want revolution or not!"

In fact, Commissar Yang had difficulties of his own that he did not like to mention. Since 1967 Wang Shouxin had been begging him to grant her a title. She insisted on being made chairman of the Women's Representative Congress. This baffled the highest authority: How could that be done when she was not even a committee member? So Wang was greatly disappointed and displeased. Since she first "rebelled," she had been bustling about with Commissar Yang and for the first time in her life she had come to know the pleasures of wielding power. Many people obeyed and flattered her, showering material benefits and praises. How many times more respectable than being the wife of a police officer or a landlord (something she had yearned for in the old days)! So disappointed was she that she began grumbling behind Yang's back: "Commissar Yang be damned. He's a good-for-nothing. All the members of the Women's Representative Congress are merely a pack of loose women, bitches!"

The next thing the commissar did was to order the Revolutionary Committee to admit Wang Shouxin into the party. Quite a few of the committee members did not agree and even Zhao Yu, director of the Revolutionary Committee who had resolutely opposed Tian Fengshan and firmly stood for overthrowing him (In those days to oppose or not to oppose Tian Fengshan was the line of demarcation between "revolutionaries", and "counterrevolutionaries"), found it hard to "closely follow" the commissar anymore. So they got a dressing down from Yang:

"Needs fostering, you say? In what way do you think she must be fostered? Isn't the Great Cultural Revolution the best way to put a person to the test? To my way of thinking, she is the only person in the whole county qualified for party membership."

One month later in his admonitory talk given at the Workers' Representative Congress he said in the presence of more than five hundred people: "Some of you have a grudge against the rebels. You find fault with them and turn a blind eye to the general orientation. Look at those genuine rebels here waiting to be recruited into the party and yet all you do is recruit docile and uncontentious persons!"

In the end, despite the opposition of seventy percent of the party members, Wang Shouxin became a party member "specially approved" by Commissar Yang.

All this took place in September 1969, when comrade Zhang Zhixin, an outstanding member of the Chinese Communist Party, was arrested in Liaoning Province by the Public Security Bureau, under the direct leadership of the same Chinese Communist Party. So, one goes up and another goes down: Tian Fengshan falls while Commissioner Yang ascends; Zhang Zhixin is expelled from the party and Wang Shouxin is admitted. But were these events merely insignificant coincidences as far as the party organization was concerned?

Ten years were to pass before this upside-down situation was acknowledged as a problem...

The Interchange System

The first day Wang Shouxin took office as manager and concurrently party branch secretary of the Bin County Coal Company (later changed to Bin County Fuel Company), she found workers busy digging pits and laying oil pipe, while several members of the county work team were playing chess in the house. This made Wang Shouxin flare up. "Damn you," she scolded them at the top of her voice. "Playing chess while the others are hard at work. What a work team!"

Zhou Lu (now promoted to the post of assistant manager) was as much surprised as he was puzzled: She had never before called others names. Little did he realize that someone else was watching—Bai Kun. Perplexed at the changes in Zhou Lu, the old party branch secretary thought to himself: "Zhou Lu is no professional, veteran driver! He could lose a wheel while driving and not even know it. That much is clear, but I thought he was of fine moral character—I was bringing him up as a successor! How could he have changed so much in only a few days? He fawned on Wang Shouxin and was ready to throw in a word or two of flattery whenever that woman talked. Was this the way he had approached me before? Was I fooled by his flattery? Why on earth have I failed to see through him after so many years?"

There were other things he could not quite see through. For one thing, Wang Shouxin was no longer what she used to be. She had always been languid and listless, but now she was always the first to show up in the office and the last to leave. Even the way she dressed had changed—now she wore an ordinary cotton blouse and a pair of rubber shoes. All day long she would be bustling in and out, taking care of this and that. When the workers were unloading coal or cleaning up, she would lend them a helping hand from time to time.

Wang Shouxin had known this small fuel company like the palm of her hand and had come to be disgusted with it. Since she became the boss here, however, everything seemed to take on a new look and a kind of splendor appeared everywhere. Heaps and heaps of jet-black coal dust and coal lumps—what a sight!

She was no longer indifferent to those who were busy unloading or weighing coal or collecting bills. All these people were now her subordinates and would do anything at her bidding.

Wang Shouxin certainly thought that she was serving the people. But the people she served all had different grades of authority. The first thing she did by way of reform was to sell coal in accordance with rank and importance. Coal of the best quality was picked out and packed in flood-control straw bags before it was delivered by trucks to the houses of the county party secretary and all the members of the standing committee. This kind of coal caught fire easily, burned well and was just what was needed to cook dumplings for the Spring Festival. Payments? No hurry!

As for the people's armed forces, that went without saying. In the scales of Wang Shouxin's mind, the military cotton-padded coat outweighed everything else and the people's military ranked number one in the hierarchy. Next to it was the organization department. The best coal was delivered to them by special trucks. And next were those in charge of personnel, finance and labor.

Wang Shouxin was a sentimental woman with strong likes and dislikes of her own. The local brewery, bakery and confectionery were in her favor and were always stocked with coal for the production of liquor, pastry and candy. Not that Wang Shouxin was a gluttonous woman. To her the sweet smells could be used to entice the nose of each higher-up in the province, the prefecture and the county. For this reason those factories had a constant supply of quality coal at a reasonable price. As to the ball-bearing factories and ceramic mills, she never troubled herself about them. They produced nothing but hard gadgets. (Who would like to have those things for presents?) So these works and mills could only get inferior coal at marked-up prices. What if they lost money or went bankrupt? She didn't give a damn!

In January that year the county hospital ran out of coal. A man from the hospital came to see Manager Wang. After glancing over the letter of introduction she asked the man with a raised brow:

"Why hasn't your leading cadre come?"

"He's busy and couldn't take the time out to..."

"A certain Gao Dianyou of your hospital has informed against my son. No coal for you."

The man begged and implored but Wang Shouxin turned a deaf ear. She continued: "Gao Dianyou has accused my son of adultery. Two months have passed since the County Party Committee started the investigation. Isn't my son still vice director of Xinli Commune? Don't think Old Lady Wang is utterly in the dark. As far as my son's case is concerned, Director Rong of the commune health department was the culprit behind the scenes. The letter of accusation was penned by Fang Yongjiu of the commune and Gao Dianyou served as the mouthpiece."

When Gao Dianyou learned of this he immediately wrote to the county leadership, "...Obviously there is something fishy. Otherwise how could Wang Shouxin get to know in detail what I had written about her son, Liu Zhimin...I hope the county committee will see to it that the culprits are dealt with sternly and guarantee the informer's safety."

It was neither the first nor the last time a written accusation fell into her hands. And it was neither the first nor the last time Wang Shouxin used her coal as a weapon to exact vengeance and made no secret of it.

Trucks were also powerful weapons she could have recourse to when necessary. Now it was customary for the local people to go up into the mountains every year to gather firewood for winter to exchange for autumn vegetables. In a town with a population of 30,000 there was a great demand for trucks. So when it was time to borrow trucks, every household would have an ordeal to go through.

Yang Qing, an inspector of the county commission for discipline, asked that year for a driver to go into the mountains to gather wood for him. The family had prepared a banquet—no easy task for a man making forty *yuan* a month. It was nearly dark when the truck was heard pulling up. The whole family rushed out, only to find an empty truck. The driver, very displeased, informed them. "The road was impassable." With that he drove the truck away. Husband and wife could only stare at the dishes which were getting colder by the minute. How would they pass the winter?

Who lent them a helping hand at this moment of despair? It was Old Lady Wang. Shouldn't the whole family feel grateful?

Wang Shouxin was constantly bothered by the difficulties of the local people. The county cadres' wages had remained unchanged for more than ten years. Every family had to shoulder a heavy burden. As a result, many of the cadres had borrowed from the public fund to the tune of over one thousand *yuan*. In 1975, according to instructions from above, the local party committee set a deadline for payment. Now Wang Shouxin was the "Goddess of Wealth." She had a fat bankbook and at any moment she could reach her hand into the drawer of her desk for some ready cash. Those who were useful to her need not even open their mouths. She would approach them on her own accord. "Hard up for money, eh?" she would ask. Not only Wen Feng the rebel boss and his buddies, but also some section chiefs with real power had borrowed from Wang Shouxin, who had appropriated part of the public fund. Through this misappropriation of money belonging to the state, Wang Shouxin personally became the creditor in place of the state. She did not mind if they returned the money or not. As a matter of fact, she would rather have them keep the money and not pay it back, as they would then not only owe her money but would have to repay her an obligation someday. Even if they did repay the money, they would still feel obliged to her. So the best recompense was to provide her with all kinds of favors and conveniences by using or abusing the power in their hands. This would satisfy both sides: The debtor would lose no material goods and Wang Shouxin would get her favors.

This was the barter system through which the functions of power were exchanged. For instance, this interchange system This was the barter system through which the functions of could find expression in the supply of goods and materials. Wang Shouxin raised a lot of pigs. Where did the fodder come from? (The pigs were intended for another round of interchange — pork was used to repay the functions of power that other parties performed.) A call to the vice director of the grain bureau would secure thousands of catties of maize, bran, soybean and chaff. She needed plenty of flour and rice and bean oil since she was in the habit of throwing parties and sending gifts. Within a year over ten thousand catties of rice, flour and bean oil came into her possession. In return the vice director could "borrow" money or bricks from Wang Shouxin or buy full cartloads of coal on credit. No payment was required. As a matter of fact, no payment was ever demanded.

The local organ of the "Dictatorship of the Proletariat," the county's public security bureau had been working in the interests of Wang Shouxin's "socialist" enterprise. When Wang Shouxin intended to ship loads of meat, fish, grain, oil and vegetables to Harbin, she had to bypass the law which forbade these commodities to be taken out of the county. The section chief of industry and commerce, second-in-command of the rebels, came to her rescue. He signed the necessary documents. Since 1973 all her trucks had free passage. In return he received a "loan" of six hundred *yuan* and a variety of gifts. As a result, Wang Shouxin had to hold back part of the cash which should have been turned over to the national treasury. The deputy chief of the finance section, one of her fellow rebels, let her open a special account, No. 83001, at the bank. She needed the cash to engage in illegal purchasing and building activities. This way the sum of more than one hundred thousand *yuan* in cash was at her disposal. Thanks to the deputy chief, everything was in order and furthermore the money would never be frozen. To pay back this kindness, Wang had his son-in-law, a day laborer, turned into a regular worker and had his son admitted into the "settlement for educated youths" she had set up. Later, after tampering with his credentials, she had him sent to college.

For years this kind of power interchange took place between Wang Shouxin and dozens of cadres of the county, the prefecture and the province. In order to set up a non-staple food base Wang Shouxin wanted a large area of excellent land belonging to Song-jiang Brigade of Niaohe Commune. This stirred up the resentment of the commune members. The director of the office for agricultural affairs as a rule was not authorized to approve the taking over of land, but he and Wang Shouxin went about selling the idea to the cadres of the commune, the brigade and the production team. They entertained the peasants at dinner and led them to believe that the County Revolutionary Committee had encouraged the negotiation and acquiesced to this illegal deal. In the end a good tract of cultivated land was given to Wang.

This kind of "socialist" interchange was indeed superior to the capitalist one: The two parties involved need not own any capital. They need not give up any personal effects and there was no risk of loss or bankruptcy. As a result of this interchange each party got what he wanted.

It was clear that no interchange of this kind was possible without trespassing on party policy. It would either do direct damage to public property or invalidate the discipline of the party and the laws of the state. Eventually it would harm the socialist system and discredit party leadership. In the course of these interchanges, cadres of the party and the government degenerated into worms which swallowed the fruits of the people's labor and ate into the socialist system. It was only natural that the relationship between the party and the masses would deteriorate.

One Hand Tied Behind His Back

When Commissar Yang referred to Wang Shouxin's family as a "red family," he meant to compliment the family. When the people, however, mouthed the same phrase, they meant to curse the family. Everybody in her family had either joined the Party or won promotion, or both. In the eyes of the people, they all rose to power and position without meriting them.

Her eldest son Liu Zhimin was a loafer. He was seldom sober and chased after women all the time. Could he have become a party member and vice director of Xinli Commune in his own right? Once he tried to rape a girl, but was dealt with leniently and transferred to the County Party Committee "to study policies." Her second son joined the party at the cadre school during a time when it was illegal to recruit new members. Her youngest son was a good-for-nothing. Why was he promoted to the post of assistant manager of a photo studio? Her younger sister, strangely enough, joined the party immediately after she was expelled from the youth league....

The people loved the party. Could they have remained indifferent when they saw those persons of dubious character sneak into the party? Since 1972, whenever a movement was launched, people would come to the County Party Committee continually to put up big character posters exposing Wang Shouxin and her "red family."

But the party leadership had to be improved before the party organization could be expected to change for the better. An opportunity presented itself in 1970. At the beginning of that year Commissar Yang was transferred to the party committee of Heilongjiang Province to take up the post of chief of the group for special cases. The man who stepped into Yang's shoes was an old cadre named Zhang Xiangling. He was a sturdy middle-aged man with calloused feet. In 1945 he had walked all the way from Yanan to Baiquan County in Heilongjiang Province. Now, with his thick-soled feet he would measure the land of Bin County. Despite severe stomach cramps he sometimes managed to cover a distance of thirteen miles a day.

But it was not long before he discovered that he was incapable mittee. Commissar Yang refused to clear out of Bin County for several months after the transfer order had reached him. In the meantime he reorganized the county administation so that all important posts above section chiefs were now held by "rebels." Most of the former leading cadres who had been relegated to the countryside or placed under house arrest were yet to be "liberated."

Whenever Zhang Xiangling intended to liberate a certain cadre, the Cultural Revolution group would inform him that a meeting to criticize and repudiate that cadre was to be held the next day and that he was requested to attend. Now this Cultural Revolution group excercised the same authority as its counterpart in Beijing. Its deputy leader happened to be a woman, too —

Wang Shouxin's daughter-in-law.

She was in her early twenties, delicate and pretty but not very tall. She showed a pair of canine teeth whenever she grinned, making herself all the more attractive. As a typist at the County People's Committee, she behaved fairly well. But since Commissar Yang came and appointed her deputy leader of the Cultural Revolution group, this woman of ordinary education and limited ability had changed into quite another person.

Nothing was more likely to induce delusions of grandeur than power. Once vested with great power she began to imagine herself equal to the task required of her. The vanity, narrow-mindedness and jealousy lying dormant in the typist's heart were awakened overnight. Her lovely eyes now flashed suspicion, envy and hatred, ready to ferret out all potential enemies. The more tears she shed as she bade farewell to Commissar Yang, the more hostility she felt toward Zhang Xiangling. Every time she went to Harbin to attend a meeting, she always paid a visit to the commissar, who could thus manipulate the affairs of Bin County by long distance.

For a time Zhang Xiangling seemed to have no power except that he could refuse to attend meetings of criticism and repudiation. This was somewhat like the case of the patriotic county magistrates under the reign of the Manchukuo puppet regime in the early 1930's when power fell into the hands of the Japanese. The only difference lay in the fact that there was only one Japanese power at that time, while the county was now overrun with "Japs." Rebels who held deputy posts wielded greater power than even chiefs like Zhang Xiangling.

I shall describe in some detail what these rebels in Bin County were like so that there will be no misunderstanding. The red guards formed by local students had been charged long ago by the United Command to Defend Mao's Ideology of "opposing the army" and disbanded. The faction in power then called themselves Red Guards and wore red bands on their arms. They were, however, all adult cadres, some of them in their late forties and old enough to be grandpas and the parents of former Red Guards. But it was not only a matter of age. First, they were all family men and their interest in money matters was much greater than the youngsters. Secondly, having been officials for years, quite a number of them rose in rebellion either because they had failed to gain admittance into the party or because they had not won the promotion they thought they deserved. Driven by strong desires for worldly goods and for power and influence, they stopped at nothing to gain their ends.

What worried Zhang Xiangling most was that not only the leading group, but also party members at all levels were now open to contamination. A couple who joined the party in 1969 at about the same time as Wang Shouxin once quarreled with each other. Let's listen to what they had to say: "You've got nothing to be cocky about. Everybody knows you bought your party membership with a few bottles of hard liquor."

"Damn you, you are even worse. You couldn't have joined the party without your pretty face."

It was at the risk of being ousted that Zhang Xiangling had at last succeeded in removing a few of the most hated rebel chiefs from office. In 1970 the County Party Committee passed a resolution to reinvestigate the scoundrels who had sneaked into the party in 1969. In spite of all his hard work he had to admit sadly when he left Bin County in 1972 that he had failed to restore the balance of political power there. The same notorious rebels who had been dumped two years before had all returned to power. As for the resolution to clear the bad elements out of the party, it had never been put into effect.

Zhang Xiangling left behind a few newly built factories in Bin County. It had never occurred to him that these factories would lose money year after year and would contribute little to the national treasury. They provided a happy hunting ground for the grafters and embezzlers and those in power.

A Heroine of Our Time

Different people would make different comments on Wang Shouxin's character and morals. "Old Lady Wang is candid and straightforward. She speaks without reservation." "Wang Shouxin is a hypocrite." "Old Lady Wang is kindhearted, cordial and solictious." "She's cruel and drives people into a corner." These comments were all true. She could be truthful one moment and hypocritical the next. Two months ago you could have been her favorite, and two months from now she would persecute you like mad. But she was not a confused woman as we shall see.

Once she came upon a worker eating sugar behind her back. She rushed over to him and boxed his ears. After a while, however, she asked him, "How come you're so gluttonous? No sugar at home? Take this bag of sugar with you!" She had changed her attitude abruptly in only a few minutes, but she was no hypocrite. What she wanted was servility on the part of her subordinates and what she liked even better was to flaunt her authority.

Wang Shouxin had experienced many ups and downs in her life. Her father, a horse dealer by profession, owned no property and had been engaged in dishonest work. He was bullied by men in power and dreaded by honest men. As a small girl Wang Shouxin was afraid of the Japanese invaders, and of policemen and wealthly landlords. But as a good-looking woman with little sense of shame she learned to defend herself and to attack others. She had learned not to be shy with strangers and to deal with people of high standing. At the same time, having experienced sordid poverty, she was equally capable of living on good terms with people at the lowest social stratum. All this was to play an important role in the seventies when her life began to take a radical turn.

Since 1970 a number of factories had been built in Bin County. Coal consumption took a jump as a result. Since the output of coal remained unchanged, Wang Shouxin now had an opportunity to put her talent to good use.

To cope with the coal shortage it was necessary for her to go to the prefecture and the province to fight for more coal, more barges to transport the coal and the appropriation of more funds. She felt completely at ease when she met the high-ranking officials for the first time. She would not hesitate to make a show of what little charm a woman of fifty still possessed, hoping against hope that the other party would not be disgusted.

"I say," she would begin, "Secretary Wang (or Manager Fang or Secretary-General Nie, as the case might be), we people in Bin County are in trouble. We have to line up for a small basket of coal. If you don't give us a bigger allotment, we'll have to burn our legs soon...."

She would fawn on you, cuddle up to you and pester you for coal in more ways than one. She would laugh one moment and cry the next; she was really earnest. Nothing doing? Well, she had still another trick. She would undo her waistband and let you have a look at the scar on her belly to show you how she was fighting for coal for the benefit of the people in spite of her illness. Well! If you wanted her to fasten up her pants, you'd better oblige her immediately! You'd be angry, upset; you'd want to get rid of her as soon as possible. But on second thought you could see that she was working for the people after all. Besides, that woman's local flavor, her vulgarity, her earnestness (with her pants let down halfway) and her intimacies did somewhat charm the opposite sex of her age.

"Sure, we'll allot you 2,000 tons."

What difference did it make whether coal was sold to Bin

County or to Hulan County? Old Lady Wang would leave in high spirits.

A few days later gifts of all sorts would start coming in: fish, pork, eggs and bean oil. At first you would have no idea where they came from. Nevertheless, as the old saying goes, "No officials are offended by gifts." Besides, these were special commodities no longer obtainable on the market.

"How much do I owe you? How much in all shall I pay for it?"

"No hurry," would be her messenger's smiling reply. "We'll figure it out later."

At first the gifts were bought at high prices. Wang Shouxin did not give a damn. She even had an underground storage bin built to keep the goods in good condition. Later, she procured some of the foodstuffs on a barter basis. For example, a commune or a brigade would be supplied with the coal it needed for its kilns in exchange for pigs, and not just ordinary pigs—they had to be thin-skinned fattened ones weighing at least 265 pounds each. As Wang's scope of interchange widened and her need increased by leaps and bounds, she had to somehow expand the source of goods and reduce the cost. As a result her property grew larger. Fishery teams of four men and a net each were set up, only to be topped by a pig farm and a non-staple food base which took up as much land as a production team. Old Lady Wang was not yet satisifed. In order to construct a large fish pond she had even borrowed a bulldozer which rumbled all day long as it cleared the land.

In the meantime the County Party Committee entrusted her with the task of getting cement and chemical fertilizer as well as tractors for the county. This called for greater efforts. She must now associate with more officials, especially with the very top ones. Was there any other way, besides sending gifts, to bring their initiative into full play?

Wang Shouxin probed into the life, thought and requirements of the leading cadres both inside and outside the county. "What's constantly on their minds, besides food?" she asked herself. "Now I know," the clever woman cried out at last, slapping her thigh. "Their sons and daughters! They are doing everything possible to keep their children in towns, to get them out of the countryside as soon as possible; or to get them into college, or a good job!" Why shouldn't her fuel company set up a Settlement for Educated Youths in the name of a production brigade, now that these settlements could be found everywhere in the rural areas? She could make it a revolving door for cadres' children, and with her connections that extended in all directions, she could dispose of dozens of them.

Then she decided to locate the new settlement in Songjiang Brigade, Niaohe Commune in which some ten tile-roofed houses were built for that purpose. The children of the leading cadres of the county, the prefecture and the province arrived one after another. Some did not come, but she had their names put on the register and let them draw a monthly salary of forty to fifty *yuan*. The daughter of Commissar Yang, who had her name put on the register, never worked there once. She managed to join the party before she was "transferred" back to Harbin.

Yet amid the laughter there was crying.

Letters of accusation like this one were posted by the peasants of the Songjiang Brigade over the past years:

> "...For years worms like Wang Shouxin have bullied us because of their powerful connections or position. They have forcibly bought or occupied the cultivated land and destroyed the forests of our four production teams. We have lost so far 870 *mu** of land altogether. Since she supplies the kilns of our Songjiang Brigade with coal, she could throttle us if we refuse to give her the land. We have grown pine trees laboriously for ten years and now about ten thousand pine trees have been chopped down. The one hundred fifty *mu* of terraced land has been turned into her melon patch. We've had to neglect our own land in order to take care of Wang's land. They have sunk a well near the terraced land, but have locked it up to prevent the peasants from using it. With our good land seized and our manpower taxed, we have been so cruelly exploited that our income has dwindled to no more than sixty *fen*** a day. Furthermore, they never pay agricultural tax and keep all the proceeds for themselves. Everything they produce is used to corrupt the cadres. They give dinners and send gifts to curry favors..."

But Wang Shouxin seemed to have a clear conscience, for she had worked entirely "in the interests of the public." Otherwise why would the secretaries of all the previousCounty Party Committees praise her so profusely? "Old Lady Wang is simply terrific!" said one of them. "The amount of coal she has! What a competent manager!" another approved. "Of all the five counties along the river, Bin County is the one which has procured the largest amount of coal."

The question was: Where did she get so much money?

There were two kinds of coal: The coal from the state-run coal mines came under the category of "planned supplies." The selling

*870 mu = 145 acres
**Sixty fen = $.40

price of this kind of coal was fixed on the principle of "high price in, high price out; low price in, low price out." The coal from small pits came under the category of "unplanned supplies" with incidental expenses borne by the consumers. In 1972 it occurred to Wang Shouxin that she could easily make pots of money by passing part of the state coal off as small-pit coal. Since then she had employed this device to her great advantage. Two separate invoices were made out, one of the amount calculated at the original price and the other for the transportation and miscellaneous expenses (five to ten *yuan* per ton). The latter would not be entered in the account books and the money would be pocketed.

Only two men shared Wang Shouxin's secret. One was her accomplice, Director of the Baishi business department of the fuel company, Ma Zhanqing. The other was an accountant named Sun Xiyin. Both of them were party members recruited by Wang Shouxin. Formerly a small trader, the only human relationship Sun Xiyin understood was that between a shopkeeper and his assistant, or between the Japanese and a conquered people. He was as submissive and as loyal to Wang as he used to be to the shopkeeper and was forever grateful to Secretary Wang because it was she who had recruited him into the party. By order of Wang Shouxin, extra income from small-pit coal was put aside and not turned over the state. The second invoice for the incidental expenses was to be destroyed. It was certainly not difficult for Sun Xiyin to carry out the secretary's instructions, for he held four posts concurrently: He made out invoices, collected payments, kept accounts and handed over the coal. One day after Sun Xiyin received instructions from Wang Shouxin, she cornered him, saying: "Wait a minute! I've heard that you are going to remarry. Is that true? Aiya, you're already an old man on the wrong side of fifty. Why remarry? Forget it!"

It was also an order. But Sun Xiyin believed the advice was well intentioned: The secretary was concerned with his well-being. As a matter of fact, his wife had been dead for nineteen years, and it was only after careful consideration that he had made up his mind to take an old woman as his wife.

What Wang Shouxin was interested in was the security of her secret. One more pair of ears and one more mouth could do her harm. Who knew what kind of woman Sun Xiyin would take as his wife? What if the woman should turn out to be a chatterbox like herself?

Her Party

Even years later when Wang Shouxin had been placed in detention, she still bragged, "You guys go to Bin County and find out for yourselves. Old Lady Wang has always been most zealous in caring for the public welfare!" And that was true. She always saw to it that fuel and food were delivered to the doorsteps of her staff and workers. When the New Year and other festivals came around, they were rewarded with extra food and drink. Take the Mid-autumn Festival for instance: Everyone could expect to have two catties of mooncakes. She usually handed over the gift by herself so that the recipient was likely to think that he was the only one favored and therefore feel particularly grateful. Once when Wang Shouxin went to Guangzhou for medical treatment, she made it a point to present everyone with an acrylic sweater when she returned. In Bin County the fuel company boasted that there were more residential quarters for its staff and workers than any other unit.

When dealing with people Secretary Wang had another artifice she would resort to. No one could rival her in taking someone to task. Her words would touch people to their very souls and at the same time reduce her opponents to tears. Take for instance tall and burly Zhou Lu, second-in-command: Wang Shouxin sometimes scolded him as if he were her son. To use a local term he was abused "like a small garlic" or "like an eggplant." When the workers started in the morning, they could tell whether Secretary Wang was in or not by studying the face of Zhou Lu. If he were looking after things in a friendly, informal manner, then Wang Shouxin must be out. If he handled affairs in a meticulous way and kept a straight face, then Wang Shouxin must be in. Zhou Lu himself once said, "It all started because I was afraid. In her presence I am like a cake of beancurd dropped on a pile of ash. You can neither flip it over nor blow the ash away...I pin my last hope on her age. I think: How many more days can this candle of hers burn? As soon as it goes out, I'll start all over again."

Despite the terror she inspired in people, Wang Shouxin still could not set her mind at ease. She was always suspicious that someone might somehow find an excuse to crush her. She had at her disposal a very sensitive intelligence net. No longer able to put up with her arrogance Zhou Lu once wanted to quit his job as vice manager and go back to driving. The very next day Wang Shouxin found out and gave him hell. "Zhou Lu, so you want to quit, eh? If you must go, I'll give you permission right away. On your way, this very minute!"

Naturally she took great pains to build up her intelligence net. After drawing some people in and pushing others out she could have complete faith in the majority of the workers of the fuel company. Meanwhile, Wang Shouxin set up a party organization which she could absolutely rely on.

She would say to someone she found obedient and to her liking. "Enthusiasm alone won't do. You've got to come over to the party." The first one she recommended for party membership met with disapproval at the meeting for party members. Wang Shouxin flew off the handle.

"He's better than any one of you, I must say, because he stood up to the test of the Great Cultural Revolution. Just look at the bunch of you, you party members. You're either capitalist-roaders or royalists. Not one of you is any good. If he is not qualified for membership, not one of you is."

If she said O.K., then no more need be said and that was that. Ma Zhanqing was the next one she recommended. "Ma Zhanqing is good at hauling coal. He is a hard worker who never spares himself. And he is never wicked. He always keeps an eye on public property. I think he is qualified." When someone took exception, her face instantly fell and she snapped, "If all of you in our fuel company followed his good example, I'm sure things would take a turn for the better." With that she picked up her tobacco pouch and left. This signified that the candidate was admitted and the meeting was over.

Thus, Wang Shouxin singlehandedly recruited eleven new party members. Have patience, my dear readers, and we shall see of what special timber these new members were made.

Her chauffeur: docile and honest. When he drove on gift-sending missions he was also honest. Obviously there were things he couldn't understand, but he kept mum and stuck to one article of faith: "No one is to question what Secretary Wang does."

A carpenter: hard-working, honest and obedient. Seeing that Wang Shouxin was having a house built for her sister, he sawed a pine gangplank which was public property into six sections and sent it all by truck to the building site. He did this because he was eager to qualify for party membership.

Another carpenter: hard-working, honest and obedient. He took care of practically all the woodwork in Wang Shouxin's house. He was also good at running gift-sending errands.

With the exception of one, all three of the new members were "hard-working, honest and obedient" to Wang Shouxin, of course! In the light of the logic that to follow closely the secretary is to follow the party and to safeguard the secretary is to safeguard the party, were they to blame?

In short, Wang Shouxin had a dependable rear base — the fuel company. In the County Party Committee as well as the County Revolutionary Committee, more than thirty "rebel buddies" swarmed around her. She enjoyed the complete confidence of the members of the standing committee of the County Party Committee and the party secretary of the county. And she won high praises from them all. What more could she ask for? Her career entered a period of prosperity.

Of course, whenever she called to mind those 40,000-odd brand-new ten *yuan* banknotes in her secret treasury, she could not help getting a little scared. At moments like this, an image never failed to surface in her mind, boosting her courage. "Bah! Come to think of it, what do we small fry think we are. Aren't the leading cadres in the province grabbing their share?"

She was referring to Vice-manager Guo Yucai of the provincial fuel company. Since 1971 she had been in touch with him from time to time whenever she applied for a coal allotment. She was always generous with the presents she sent him — chickens, fish, meat, eggs and what not. She ended up by inviting him to Baishi's port facilities where she threw a grand dinner party in honor of this distinguished guest. After being wined and dined Guo Yucai lay down on the brick bed and said, "Well, these two trucks I have got for you...I'm none the better for it." Wang Shouxin readily took the hint and wrapped up three hundred *yuan* for him. The next time they met he said among other things, "I went to Beijing on business and found my pockets empty!" This time he found himself a few hundred *yuan* richer. Over a period of four years Guo Yucai accepted bribes to the tune of two thousand *yuan*. In return he allotted to Bin County six trucks, one refueller and plenty of coal.

This was just what Wang Shouxin wanted. She was afraid that other communist party members were not like her. The bigger the official and the more gifts he accepted, the happier she would be. Through the good offices of Guo Yucai, she got to know the vice-director of a certain bureau of the Ministry of Commerce and she asked him to dinner. Before he left, Wang Shouxin presented him a set of sofas with teapots to match, a bedside cupboard, three cubic meters of timber and several sacks of soybeans. All these were accepted. Now Wang Shouxin was more reassured than ever. "Well, this kind of cadre is found even in Beijing. What I gave away wasn't my family property. He must have known that."

The fall of the Gang of Four frightened Wang Shouxin and her rebel comrades-in-arms. One long-distance journey she undertook in 1978, however, convinced her that even then nearly two years since the fall of the Gang of Four, the status of Old Lady Wang was not only as secure as ever, but strangely enough, was actually improving.

In particular, the assistant secretary-general of the Heilongjiang Province Economic Committee chose this time to stage for her benefit a show of strength and devotion. Evidently, she had pulled enough strings to arrange for his children to get out of the countryside and land jobs in the city. Out of gratitude he booked her passage to Guangzhou and sent his son to accompany her. When Wang left Harbin, three department heads from the provincial government drove her to the airport and saw her off. After her arrival in Guangzhou, three units there accorded her a cordial reception. In Shanghai she was taken to a high-class guesthouse.

Wang Shouxin now had reached the acme of prosperity and honor. Her growing influence, the automobiles of officials from the province, prefecture and county parked before her house and the things she got for her county boosted her social status considerably. By dint of this status and her strong backing, she became all the more arrogant and domineering. Who was there to fear in little Bin County?

All-around Dictatorship

In the winter of 1975 Wang Shouxin, accompanied by some workers, went into the mountains in Gaoleng to gather lumber, carrying along quantities of meat, spirits, cigarettes and soda. Whenever her trucks stopped at a checkpost, Old Lady Wang would go in to negotiate while her assistants would start giving away exotic presents. At some checkposts Old Lady Wang would drop her carryall on the table and say in tones at once generous and intimate, "I've heard that you folks here are running short of battery cells. We've brought you some and here are some flashlights. They form complete sets."

In the mountains they greased the palms of the lumber inspectors. Old Lady Wang charged ahead of her men, nimbly climbing up to the top of the log piles covered with slippery snow. She picked the best logs, making a rough estimate of the total cubic meters of lumber they had gathered. When her trucks laden with logs drove back, all the checkposts on their way home let them pass unhindered. Thus, they paid a little more than five hundred *yuan* for over fifty cubic meters of quality pine.

This was a happy occasion which called for celebration. Little did Wang Shouxin suspect that bad news was awaiting her at the county office. Inspector Yang Qing from the County Commission for Discipline came to see her and divulged that a member of the standing committee had received an anonymous letter accusing her of corruption and illegal activities. That very evening Wang Shouxin called on Yang Qing, carrying along two bottles of Binzhou liquor. That night she asked for the letter of accusation. She wanted to identify the handwriting of the culprit.

The next day, as soon as she arrived at the company, she tossed the letter to Zhou Lu and started yelling, "Damn! I have been away for only twenty days gathering lumber in Gaoleng and things at home are topsy-turvy...How the hell were you managing things? Didn't I tell you to keep an eye on those guys?"

Inspector Yang Qing (later promoted to be vice-director of the commission for inspecting discipline) also came over. He and Zhou Lu tried to identify the handwriting by comparing it with that on some of the big character posters. But, to their disappointment, nothing came of it. Yang Qing took the letter back and said to Wang Shouxin, "Never mind who wrote it, I say. Anyway, it's in my hands now. Let's leave it at that."

His remarks were a hint, a promise. He had it in his power to protect criminals. He was offering that power for sale on the market. He had found his buyer.

Demurely Wang Shouxin announced, "All right. This letter was directed against me. I'm the secretary, aren't I? Forget it. If it had been directed against someone else, he'd have plenty of questions to answer."

Yang Qing kept his promise and that letter vanished into thin air.

But Wang Shouxin didn't let it pass so easily. She sent three cables in succession, requesting chauffeur Qu Zhaoguo be sent back at once from Jixi Colliery for reasons of national security. Qu came back that night. Before he had time to take of his cotton-padded jacket, Wang Shouxin shouted at him, "So it was you who wanted to seize my power. And you who wanted to plant a detonator under my ass to blast me to pieces!"

Qu was flabbergasted. For years he had been her chauffeur and carried out the task of sending gifts. He used to call himself the Old Lady's adjutant. Each parcel, be it large or small, was personally delivered to the recipient by this "adjutant." He had to make sure that nothing got mixed up, but he was not supposed to find out the contents. Qu could only be a silent observer. Wang

Shouxin came to suspect that he had pried into her secret and she was right at that. Once when they went to the provincial fuel company to apply for coal allotments the accountant there queried her on the possibility of getting five thousand *yuan*. He also heard Wang Shoxin reply, "Only five thousand, you say? I'll let you have ten thousand." The accountant asked, "You can disburse that much?" And Wang Shouxin said, "No need to disburse. We have enough cash at Baishi." Qu was taken aback but he pretended to have heard nothing. That was the first time the secret was let out — that there was a secret treasury at Baishi. Nearly four years later an investigation team appointed by the county party committee stationed itself in the fuel company. But even after three months of hard work, the team still failed to uncover Wang Shouxin's secret.

Wang Shouxin now ordered that study classes be conducted for the entire staff. The two long articles by Zhang Chunqiao and Yao Wenyuan were to be studied first. This was the correct approach. Here Wang Shouxin exercised dictatorship but she was not dictatorial enough. Her dictatorship should have been all-encompassing. Next, everyone was required to study Xiao Jin Zhuang* and write critical articles. Wang Shouxin collected their articles afterwards and scrutinized them to find out who wrote that damning letter of accusation.

Next on the program was a "poetry contest" to follow the example of Xiao Jin Zhuang. The opening remarks or pep talk given by Wang Shouxin were, as usual, vivid and vigorous: "Our fuel company has produced a Fu Zhigao!** she began, passing her hand through her jet-black hair. She fancied herself to be Jiangjie.*** "What's wrong with this company of ours? Even if there were something the matter, couldn't we tackle it among ourselves? Was it necessary to write a letter of accusation? I'm well over fifty. So why am I still working from dawn to dusk, I ask you? Everyone knows how I go on working despite illness. I..." With that she began to undo her waistband. Some males in the audience knew what was to follow so they lowered their heads immediately. Perhaps she was over-excited today. She failed to undo the waistband, fumbling with it. "Tell me, when did I, Wang Shouxin, let you down?" she continued, alternating tears with curses. "The writer of that letter will come to a bad end! If he has two sons, may both of them die! If he has two daughters,

*A fake "model commune" established by Jiang Qing.
**A traitor in the novel, *Red Crag*.
***Heroine of the novel, *Red Crag* and a revolutionary martyr.

may both of them die also! Let him die childless!"

The atmosphere of the "poetry contest" was charged with tension and drama. Drums began rumbling and it looked as if Zhang Fei was ready to jump out any minute. A handkerchief was passed round as the drumbeats rolled. The one who had it in his hand would pass it on to the next fellow with lightning peed as if the handkerchief were on fire. Whoever was caught with the handkerchief in his hand when the drumbeats stopped had to improvise a poem. Apples and candy were laid out on the table, but no one was in the mood to taste them.

The first batch of poems were directed against Lin Biao and Confucius. What ensued did not appeal to refined taste. Even a swineherd would be offended by what was being said. The following doggerel was considered comparatively civilized:

> "A Jap for a mother, his uncle's
> A Soviet revisionist,
> American imperialist bones
> And the flesh of an Israeli,
> If you ask the name
> of this baboon —
> His last name is Wan and his
> first name gigolo!"

Wang Shouxin sniggered and the ice was broken.

The next poet obviously knew what Wang Shouxin had in mind. So he made a caricature of Qu Zhaoguo:

> "One meter seventy in height,
> a big mouth like his ma's.
> A knife-shaped face and a
> pointed chin,
> A tortoise's neck
> and long legs.
> Cracking a smile he
> works but accomplishes
> nothing.
> Notebook in hand, he jots
> down everything;
> Useful when a political movement
> comes around, appealing to
> the higher authorities for help or
> lodging a complaint
> He is bent on paralyzing the
> Party branch to walk upon
> his capitalist road!"

Every stanza gratified Wang Shouxin. She grabbed an apple

and a handful of candy and gave them to the poet. As soon as the recitation came to an end, she pulled a long face and snapped, "Qu Zhaoguo, come out here!"

Qu dragged his one meter seventy carcass to the center of the meeting-place.

Wang Shouxin went on, "A man with a virtuous wife at home never goes astray. Lu Yaqin, you little coquette, stand by his side!"

Lu Yaqin refused to budge. Wang Shouxin again shouted, "Fetch the militia! Don't you know the saying, 'Maintain an army for a thousand days to use it for an hour'?" But the militiamen would not budge either. "So you sympathize with her, is that it?" She turned to confront Qu, a pleasant expression suddenly coming over her face.

"Zhaoguo, you wrote it. You must confess."

"I never wrote it, so what am I supposed to confess to? Besides, it wasn't a reactionary slogan or a vicious attack and it wasn't directed against the central authorities either. What if I had written it? What should I be afraid of?"

The drumbeats resumed and the poetry contest went on. These people handled coal all day long. They were no poets. Some of them racked their brains, sweated all over and got fed up. They would shudder at the mention of poetry for the rest of their lives. If you refused to compose a poem and fling dirt at somebody, you would be suspect—and that was nothing to be trifled with. Someone would sneak up behind your back and see what you were writing. Those not blessed with culture could only stand up and recite slogans or let loose a torrent of abuse...

Oh, motherland! Are *they* supposed to be the masters of the People's Republic? Masters of the Dictatorship of the Proletariat? Is this our working class?

Wang Shouxin—is she a member of the Communist Party, the vanguard of the working class?

This chapter of our history — how should we proceed to write it?

PART TWO

Weakening of the Backbone—An Epochal Illness

The fuel company was only two hundred meters from the County Party Committee. If the cursing of Wang Shouxin and the crying of the workers could not reach them, could they have heard the drumbeats? What about those big character posters and letters of accusation? What about those written complaints passed on to them by the provincial and prefectual party committees? Had they seen and heard nothing?

If you leafed through the minutes of the meetings of the standing committee from 1972, all sorts of issues would well up in your mind! The things they discussed included a variety of problems—conscription, family planning, criminal sanctions, sowing plans—in short, everything that had to do with the fate of the people. The one thing they seldom touched upon was the problem relating to the party itself. The Communist Party administered all public affairs with the sole exception of governing its own members.

It was a year of crucial importance in the modern history of China. In Bin County, the practice of extravagant eating and drinking and general corruption among the leading cadres reached high tide. It was in that year Wang Shouxin took to large-scale corrupt practices. It was also in that year that the County Party Committee officially resumed functioning. At this time Liu Zhen came to Bin County to assume office as head secretary of the first County Party Committee since the Cultural Revolution.

Before he moved in, Wang Shouxin had wooden partitions fixed up in his residence. Quantities of jet-black coal and, later, rice of fine quality were carted to his house. Being her neighbor, Liu sometimes came into contact with Wang Shouxin. But there was no evidence that he had gone along with her in her evil deeds. There was no evidence either that he had deliberately condoned her criminal activities. As he left for another post in 1976, he even warned the woman who succeeded him as secretary, "Be careful when you deal with Wang Shouxin. That woman isn't straight."

This proved that Liu Zhen was a keen observer and an educated man. There was, however, a major fault in his personality.

He was too kind. Whether he was addressing a meeting, receiving guests or walking in the street, he was always radiant with smiles. He had unctuous gestures, voice, manner and gait. It seemed as though he wanted to remind others constantly—"I've nothing against you. Don't get me wrong, please. I won't offend or do harm to anybody." Even those who nursed grievances would not lose their temper when they talked with Secretary Liu because they could see the deep sympathy which he manifested behind his rimless spectacles. He would listen to your appeal with utmost care and patience. It seemed as though he would do his best to meet your demands, whatever they might be. As a consequence, he was never able to solve a single problem.

Before long he came to be nicknamed, "Old Lady Official." Another nickname was "Liu Ha Ha." He had formed the habit of nodding his head and saying, "Fine, fine, fine" at everything. Once his wife told him sorrowfully that pest infestation had swept away all their chickens. "Fine, fine, fine," came the usual response.

Was he born with this kind of disposition? Not necessarily. If it were a disposition native to the county, how could you account for the fact that three of the members of this County Party Committee had been dubbed "sly" and "wicked?"

As it happened Liu Zhen had been secretary of the County Party Committee of Shuancheng at the outset of the Cultural Revolution. His soul (together with his body) was "touched" a bit too ruthlessly, which left a deep scar. Before he took up his post in Bin County he was warned, "The situation there is rather complicated. Few ever come out unscathed once they poke their noses into local affairs. In Bin County you can't make a thorough investigation of anything." And he had learned long ago through hearsay that violence and unjust verdicts had accounted for more deaths in this county than anywhere else in the whole prefecture.

When handing over his work, the former secretary of the County Party Committee, Zhang Xiangling, dwelt on the state of affairs of the "rebels." He specifically told Liu that the few chiefs like Wen Feng should not be relied on.

Liu Zhen kept on nodding while listening, but he kept his own counsel. "I know you have offended a lot of people," he thought. "If I don't make friends with the 'rebels,' how can I hold my ground? Isn't it as clear as glass?"

Not long afterwards he helped the grumbling Wen Feng to his feet. Wen Feng had been demoted to the town of Binzhou by Zhang Xiangling. Liu made Wen Feng a member of the standing committee of the County Revolutionary Committee. The other ringleaders were also properly provided for.

In 1972, shortly after the County Party Committee resumed functioning, those on the standing committee pointed out: The greatest problem confronting the party leaders at present was failure to combat harmful trends and pacifism. The secretary and members of the standing committee even raised these clarion calls: "Work energetically and change rapidly!" "The county headquarters must be the first to change!" "Whether we can change or not depends on the headquarters!"

Three years later the standing committee of 1975 came down to check on work again. The same old problem existed: People dared not fight. And the reason? "Afraid to get bogged down...afraid to offend others...afraid to stir up a hornet's nest..."

Another four years elapsed. In early 1979 Wang Shouxin was finally indicted. Members of the standing committee came down again to check up. They were confronted with the same old problem: People would not speak up.

Was it because they had accepted bribes? Had they been bought by Wang Shouxin? In fact, nine out of the eleven members of the standing committee had accepted gifts from Wang Shouxin. But not all the leading cadres accepted gifts. Consider the director of the Commission for Inspecting Discipline—she was clean. Among the two hundred-odd persons Wang Shouxin had approached, she was the only one who resisted temptation and remained uncontaminated. She had joined the revolutionary ranks in 1946. An honest and upright cadre, she would frown in disapproval at flattery and favors. She felt very unhappy when she observed that during these last few years people seemed to make no distinction between good and evil. "Doing one's job is easy but building good relations with the masses is difficult. When can we ever solve this problem?" she asked herself anxiously. However, she failed to understand that she herself must fight to solve this problem. She had nearly all the fine qualities a good cadre should have—modesty, prudence, diligence, conscientiousness and a willingness to work and lead a simple life. But she had no fighting spirit.

Though the Gang of Four had fallen, the leading group of the County Party Committee was as weak and timid as ever in front of the rebels. The "expose-criticize-investigate" campaign was not launched until 1978. Wen Feng felt obliged to criticize himself this time. Well, come to think of it, that criticism meeting did make a lasting impression on the cadres and masses in the county. The first session of the meeting turned out to be a farce. Wen's language, tone and chosen subject matter gave one the impression he was giving a speech, not a self-criticism. Then there was Secretary Guan who chaired the meeting—everyone had expected him to make his position known. But he did no such thing! At the second session, Wen Feng's self-criticism was substantially the same. And Secretary Guan still did not declare where he stood. The whole thing was rather out of the ordinary. In Bin County they were all veteran campaigners. Recalling all their previous campaigns, they thought it customary for the chairman to exert a little pressure. But there was no pressure!

The third session was a mystery. It was announced that Wen Feng had been temporarily relieved of his post in order to make a self-examination. It was then somebody else's turn. Wen Feng was sitting in the back row when the session started. Secretary Guan did something strange. He sent someone from the personnel department to invite Wen Feng to come up to the platform. Wen Feng felt embarrassed and the fellow could not budge him. To the surprise of everyone (including Wen Feng himself), Secretary Guan came down from the platform, walked through the audience to the back row like the emperor himself going out to battle. He insisted that this good-for-nothing should go up to the platform and take a seat. He would not take no for an answer. At last Wen Feng complied with his wish. At that moment, the bewildered audience burst into an uproar. "Isn't this going against the will of the people?" "Isn't he trying to boost the morale of Wen Feng's gang? " "Old Guan, Old Guan, what are you up to? Are you not afraid of losing face before the people of the whole county?" Everyone was despondent and hurt. Old Guan had risen from the ranks during the land reform campaign in Bin County. In the old days he had been famous for his courage and resoluteness in fighting the enemy and had been nicknamed "Ruthless Guan." What a glorious name it was! He was generally believed to be an upright fellow, a cadre to be trusted in the County Party Committee. After the Wang Shouxin affair became known, the local people started talking among themselves. They all agreed that "no matter how many people in that building of the County Party Committee get involved, Ruthless Guan won't be one of them. Now he had lost face and let everybody down.

Members of the standing committee and party secretaries sometimes made no attempt to conceal the reason why they were so soft on the rebels including Wang Shouxin. One of them confessed that as the "United Command to Defend Mao's Ideology" had liberated him and then "united" him, he felt very much indebted. Things were entirely different with another secretary. The rebels had once made him suffer. He did not want others to think that he was vengeful so it was only natural that he dared not fight them. But the basic truth was that the rebels remained a political force not to be trifled with.

In other words, they were afraid to offend everybody except the "masters" of the People's Republic!

Of all the secretaries of the previous County Party Committees, one should be singled out here for special mention. His was a special case.

Among the members of the County Party Committee during the period from 1972 to 1976, Wei Gao was one of the three secretaries and members of the standing committee with better qualifi-

cations and records of service. They were all equally "sly" and
had irresistible cravings for alcoholic drink. At a meeting of the
standing committee in 1972, the appraisal given of his style of
work was that he was evasive when confronted with problems
and slow in making known his position. He was a smooth fellow,
eager to please everybody. Toward matters of principle he took
an equivocal attitude. To play it safe, he would rather step back
so as not to bungle matters. However, to his credit, he was very
thoughtful and adept in consulting with others.

He was then the secretary in charge of finance and trade. As
the immediate superior of Wang Shouxin he knew her like the
palm of his hand. After careful observation and consideration he
decided to have his daughter marry her son.

Wei Gao and his wife went to see the go-between. The wife did
all the talking. Would Old Lady Yu act as matchmaker for their
Xiaoxia and Wang's youngest son Liu Zhizhong? Old Lady Yu
did not like the idea. She said, "Secretary Wei, your lucky star is
shining bright. You don't need an old woman like me to introduce
anyone to your darling daughter. There is an abundance of eligi-
ble young men!"

Since the couple insisted, she added: "Don't you know the
background of that family? Wang and I came from the same native place, Manjing. She didn't behave herself when she was
young."

"That was long ago," Wei Gao interrupted. "She's old now and
won't do it again."

Old Lady Yu could not but agree, saying, "Well, if you insist,
I'll do the legwork."

Again, the couple took the initiative and called at Wang's residence with their daughter. Later the couple paid a visit to the
photo studio where their prospective son-in-law, who was vice-
director of the Revolutionary Committee, worked. Wang
Shouxin, however, was not very satisfied with the marriage because she thought the girl too plain.

It was a quiet wedding. Even some of the secretaries of the
county felt puzzled when they heard about it afterwards. Why
was Wei Gao so eager to marry his daughter into Wang's family?
They were not well-matched.

Li Yongguan, vice-director of the County Planning Committee,
once went to Harbin with Wei Gao to attend a meeting. He took
this opportunity to talk to Wei Gao about Wang Shouxin "As a
top-ranking official in this county," he said, "you should do a
good turn for your daughter's mother-in-law. She has quite a
name for giving parties and giving gifts. She throws money

around like water and makes a mess of things." Li cited numerous examples. closely watching Wei's face for any sign of reaction. There was none. However, he could see that Wei was aware of everything and only feigned ignorance.

"You think so?" answered Wei.

Li Yongquan regretted what he had said. He now realized that this was a man who lived up to his reputation—a sly old dog indeed. From what he had said you couldn't tell whether he denied the guilt of Wang Shouxin or confirmed it.

Perhaps because he was so sly, people were led to believe during all those seven years that it was Wang Shouxin who wanted to marry her son into his family in order to have a backer. Only six months later when Wang Shouxin's case came to light did people see the truth. Wei Gao had set eyes on Wang Shouxin's money.

The Root of the Matter

The case of Wang Shouxin shocked the whole country. How could a boorish housewife like her have such audacity and ability? How could such thinly veiled crimes have remained undetected for so long? Guided by common sense and intuition, people naturally focused their attention on the members of the County PartyCommittee. They were the roots of all this. They were her accomplices and sheltering umbrella!

So it would appear that Wang Shouxin's case was detached from the economic, political and social life of Bin County. But when Wang Shouxin and the crimes she committed were reconstructed again into a living organism with all the blood vessels and all the main and collateral channels connected, the whole thing assumed an entirely different look.

Thus if one shut his eyes to the secret treasury of Wang Shouxin which contained ready cash amounting to over half a million *yuan*, he would easily find that she and her activities would not have attracted so much attention and the whole thing would not have looked so shocking as it did when the whole truth came out.

One could see a simply dressed old woman, candid and hardworking, who was busy all day rushing about, in and around Bin County. It was her job to lay hands on coal, trucks, chemical fertilizer and cement for the benefit of the whole county.

She conducted her party-giving and gift-sending operation on a large scale, but which unit did not give parties or send gifts?

"Without oil the machine won't run," was a universal truth. Trucks carrying non-staple food from the fuel company sped on the Bin County-Harbin highway, and speeding on the same highway were special cars laden with Binzhou liquor from Bin County's brewery, and some laden with apples from the fruit company all heading for government departments. Even within Bin County itself, different economic departments found it necessary to "pay tribute" to each other. Wang Shouxin's non-staple food base, her sanitorium and the banquets of the Baishi business department were all famous. And nearly each section in Bin County had its own kitchenette, guest house and warehouse. Extravagant eating and drinking were common spectacles. Wang Shouxin proved herself to be the coal overlord in Bin County. But she was not alone. There was also an electricity overlord. The head of the power section behaved like a millionaire. His annual outlay in giving parties, sending gifts and extravagant eating and drinking amounted to twenty thousand *yuan*. Like Wang Shouxin's fuel company, the power department had to pay tribute to higher-ups regularly.

As far back as 1964, Secretary Tian Fengshan of the County Party Committee had decided to suppress extravagant eating and drinking once and for all, but people slipped back into their old ways. After 1970, Zhang Xiangling again renewed the fight, but during his tenure in office this practice spread. Their honesty and willingness to fight were unquestionable, yet both of them failed. After 1972, The County Party Committee even laid down the rule that in entertaining guests, no wine should be served and the number of dishes limited to four. This rule, however, never came into effect. The guest house run by the County Party Committee allocated one thousand *yuan* annually to defray entertainment expenses. All the guest houses run by the different sections of the County Revolutionary Committee used their income to subsidize the cadres who indulged in excessive eating and drinking. Eating alone could not satiate their greed. They grabbed. Not only did they grab, their dependents also grabbed. The County Party Committee had once ordered these guest houses closed down but to no avail.

It was true that Wang Shouxin used embezzled funds to build her house, but there were no telltale marks of corruption on the bricks or tiles. Besides, these were houses which had been built under false pretenses. It was corruption in disguise. The owners of these houses were leading comfortable lives without fear of being prosecuted. Secretary Yang, concurrently the director of the biggest towel factory in Bin County, owned such a house.

His house was originally a building attached to the factory. Since it was built for purifying water, the structure was simple and crude with a water tower on top. Secretary Yang ordered that the water tower be torn down and the house rebuilt and modernized, thus converting an industrial building into a private residence. Twenty-one tons of cement had been used as well as other materials.

Secretary Yang was different from Wang Shouxin in that he made use of state materials and labor and not public funds. But, ultimately, was there any difference? Thus it is clear that the corruption of social values, the gradual legalization of illegal activities, the tolerance toward this degeneration and other things all served to shield Wang Shouxin's criminal activities. Now it was no longer easy to tell what was legal and what was illegal. Where the line of demarcation between the legitimacy of a gift and the offering and accepting of bribes could be drawn no one seemed to know. Was dipping into public funds to pay for excessive eating and drinking or the covert seizure of public property (like taking samples of food or other commodities) any different from corruption and theft? The former was legitimate and was even considered above reproach morally, but as a matter of fact, it sometimes amounted to corruption and bribery. The appropriation of public property, moreover, often did more harm than corruption and bribery.

To return to Yang's residence, obviously the rebuilding work on his four-room apartment should not have required twenty-one tons of cement. He did this against the rules and had the walls plastered with a thick layer of cement, but even so, it was too much. It turned out that Section Chief Du of the industry section was then building his own residence. So a lot of cement and other materials disappeared from the work site of Yang's residence. The two residences were completed one after the other, and Yang and Du came to be on intimate terms.

We must pay close attention to this connection between Yang and Du. Section Chief Du protected and continued to protect Director Yang. In return, Director Yang supported and continued to support Section Chief Du. Yang had a weakness. From the time he started working in the county trade union in the sixties, he began to seek extramarital pleasure. He changed jobs several times before he took up the post in the towel factory. No matter where he worked he always managed to have his paramours. But not once was he caught red-handed. Why? Section Chief Du had the same weakness, but he employed different tactics. In order to satisfy his lust he would not hesitate to harm anyone who stood in the way or who was likely to tell on him. For instance, he was responsible for at least two cases of injustice. Thanks to him, it took a long time to right the wrong and exonerate the innocent victims. Why was he so powerful? Because he had backers and he knew how to pull the strings.

All of Bin County's cadres above the middle echelons had their roots in the countryside, having started their careers during the 1945 Land Reform Movement. By the late sixties and early seventies their children had become old enough to marry. Unfortunately, with a population of only 30,000, there simply weren't enough cadre families in Bin County of the proper social status to go around. Therefore, relations between in-laws, and even between in-laws of in-laws became more important, attaching a new layer of meaning to all the various other relationships among relatives, family, friends, old classmates and old colleagues. Even the type of relationship that exists between acquaintances who had performed mutual favors was affected. In short, relationships among in-laws served to double the scope of the feudal relationships already in existence. Equally important (if not more important), were the new layers of political relationships that were woven during the Cultural Revolution. Having protected each other throughout shared adversities, members of the same faction, once perfect strangers, became as close as brothers in a few short years. The relationship that ought to have existed among party members and revolutionary comrades paled in comparison with this new relationship.

People who had lived in Bin County for awhile would offer their own explanation to newcomers: "Its hard to figure out how people relate to each other here. It's as if there's a special connection that exists between people. But you don't discover it until you give somebody a yank and find that a whole lot of other people have moved along with him."

A member of the standing committee of the County Party Committee, who had come from another part of the country in 1972, gave vent to his feelings: "One has to uphold Marxism-Leninism. But when one goes in for it, he is faced with all sorts of obstacles. Why is it that human relationships have become so complicated? It's no longer easy to act in accordance with policies. You'll get involved, one way or another. You're likely to offend people at every turn and things often go wrong. Plenty of inexplicable problems!"

Nothing could be kept absolutely secret. Even members of the standing committee, who held confidential talks in such a top-secret place as the campaign room of the military department, could not maintain secrecy. As long as the talk involved someone, the one concerned would get wind of it somehow. This would lead to difficulties in handling matters of personnel. If the one concerned was to be transferred and he did not like the idea, he would lodge complaints and protests or he would seek the good offices of some influential friends. In the end the matter would be left unsettled.

In other words, if someone got into trouble, everyone related to him in some way would intercede on his behalf. What would you do if, for example, someone came to see you and said "Well, so-and-so and so-and-so have already promised to help. You're the only one left who hasn't." Would you stick to policy and insult everyone, or would you close your eyes and let it pass? Unless your party spirit was quite strong, it's fairly clear which choice you would make, isn't it? And it's precisely because of this that some people say, "It's the fear of insulting people that has made it so hard to do anything in China."

As a result, the same bizarre occurrence continues to happen: A serious, if not scandalous situation exists that has to be dealt with, but as soon as you send someone to investigate, it somehow disappears. For example, in 1972 people in Manjing had complained that someone by the name of Chen from the local supply and marketing cooperative frequently indulged himself in expensive bouts of feasting and drinking, and had a number of illicit sexual relationships with women. Clearly something had to be done, as the cooperative was in the process of being set up as a model unit for the entire province. So the secretary of the standing committee in charge set someone to investigate. But what was the upshot of his report? "No major problem." It took another seven years to reveal that this Chen was in fact guilty of graft and had engaged in illicit sexual relations for some time.

Political campaigns were launched every year in Bin County. But strangely enough evildoers seemed to be immune to these campaigns, otherwise known as class struggles. The more frequent the campaigns, the more comfortable the evildoers. Innocent people suffered instead. Some were framed while others fell victim to retaliation because they dared to expose and denounce evildoers and their deeds.

An intricate, dense net of overlapping human relationships was woven. If anything fell into the net, whether it were Marxist-Leninist principles or policies, it would quickly lose all its effectiveness. When an enterprise got entangled in the net, its socialist system would deviate completely from what had been originally intended; and when a legal case became entrapped it would result in the distortion of the meaning of the Dictatorship of the Proletariat. In short, right and wrong were confused, reward and punishment reversed, truth yielded to falsehood and good submitted to evil.

"Why is it that good people are on the bottom, and bad people are on top?" That thesis was the topic of discussion for a Bin County Party Committee Standing Committee meeting. Actually, it wasn't really a question of who was in what position. As the masses like to put it: "In Bin County, good people get bullied, and bad people do the bullying."

Take for example, that Zhao Chun, who had been caught red-handed countless times and still had gone scot-free. After having wormed his way into the party through the "rebel faction" in 1969, Zhao Chun had on numerous occasions, stolen materials belonging to the state and had gotten caught each time. But no action was ever taken against him despite all the documented evidence. Then even though there was a County Party Committee regulation forbidding people who owed money to the state from building their own homes, Zhao Chun went and built himself a house with state construction materials despite his own debt, ignoring the fact that he already was living in public housing. And to do this, he had stolen rocks that had been set aside for use in case of war. Plus, when the tractor he had borrowed turned over, killing the driver, he simply wrote off the cost of providing compensation to the dead man's family and repairing the machine to the state's account. If that were not enough, he later privately sold off the scaffolding and pocketed all the money.

To this day, you can still see Zhao Chun charging around like mad in a local car. Sometimes he will deliberately head straight for Han Cheng, the security cadre, braking at the last minute. This is his way of threatening and venting his resentment on Han, the man who had handled his case—"You little creep! I could run you over any time I please!" Of course, verbal abuse is even more common.

And what about Han Cheng? Not only did he not receive any support, but he was stripped of the position of security cadre as well. You can still see him, with files concerning Zhao's offenses in hand, trying to seek redress from all the relevant authorities. He has had no success to date.

Could there be any injustice more obvious and infuriating than this? In fact, Han Cheng's case is hardly the only example of security cadres being bullied by bad people in Bin County.

Why is it that in socialist Bin County, under the leadership of the Communist Party, nearly three years after the collapse of the

Gang of Four, this upside-down situation has not yet been righted?

The answer is quite simple: Zhao Chun knows the right people. In addition, to his old "rebel faction" buddies, he also has a valuable uncle—Vice Director Lu of the County Party Committee's Organization Department, who is in the same clique as Section Chief Du.

We already are familiar with the relationship between Du and Director Yang of the towel factory. Han Cheng had been under the supervision of Director Yang, and it had been Yang who had been responsible for stripping Han of his security post. All of Zhao's various offenses had been committed in connection with the factory, and it had been Director Yang who had given permission to write off the costs of repairing the tractor and giving compensation to the driver's family.

Relationships based on gross common interests have, in fact, been established under the guise of brotherly loyalty, gratitude and feelings of goodwill among family members and friends. This seemingly innocent practice of returning favor for favor has, in effect, created conditions favorable for a constant exchange of material benefit, with personal power as the lever.

This was the social condition which formed a protective screen around Wang Shouxin and continued to do so with other malefactors.

Nobodies Who Defied Somebodies

In Bin County there were two nobodies who showed contempt for this omnipotent net and dared to challenge it.

One of them was Liu Changchun, whom we've talked about. Wang Shouxin used to look down upon Liu and often sneered at him behind his back. "Take a look at that carcass of his!" she would say and then spit. She never realized that Liu's small and emaciated carcass could be so tough. The tremendous pressure brought on him by the rebels and the army representatives did not crush him. Years of privation did not wear down his fighting spirit. Liu Changchun's part in finally bringing Wang Shouxin to justice could not be dismissed.

He was at first thrown into jail as an active counter-revolutionary on a charge of opposing the army. Later the charge against him was changed to "bad element," and he was transferred to the jail run by his own unit. After his release he was sent to do hard labor more than ten hours a day and received only twenty *yuan* a month to defray his living expenses. His wife was bedridden with serious heart disease. Wang Shouxin's son, Liu Zhizhong, vice director of Xinli Commune, instructed the hospital to deny her medical treatment. At last Liu Changchun was sent down to the countryside together with those cadres eliminated as "former personnel." Liu Changchun was now head over heels in debt and had no one to turn to for a loan. He had no alternative but to sell off his only property, a two and a half room house—at a sacrifice. The sale brought him a mere four hundred *yuan*. In the countryside his wife's condition took a turn for the worse and she passed away soon afterwards. He toiled on the farm for four and a half years and he was the the last among more than one thousand displaced cadres to be allowed to come back to Bin County.

Wang Shouxin was now a VIP in Bin County. Her tastefully-furnished residence and her way of life compared favorably with those of a party provincial secretary. Her house was usually swarming with people who had come to present gifts or ask her for favors. There were so many of them that she could scarcely attend to them all. Liu Changchun, alas, was all alone in the world. His wife was dead; he had nothing he could call his own.

Liu Changchun had come to this grief on account of his obstinacy. He was never popular during the ten-odd years before the Cultural Revolution. He liked to make comments or suggestions in front of anyone regardless of the consequences.

Back from the countryside, he caught sight of the new houses Wang Shouxin had built. "Where on earth did she get so much money?" he asked himself. With a view to probing the matter to the bottom, he sent for Qu Zhaoguo. The latter, a talkative fellow, blurted out that Wang Shouxin had once lent ten thousand *yuan* in cash to the provincial fuel company. Before leaving Qu sized up Liu Changchun and guessed what he had in mind. After weighing the capability of this man against that of Wang Shouxin, he asked, "Are you in a position to contend with her?"

"That depends on whether she is guilty or not!" Liu Changchun was just like his old self.

He sensed that Wang Shouxin was guilty of corruption but he needed conclusive evidence. Since he was once engaged in planning and statistical work, he was sure that by manipulating the supplementary wages alone she could not have grafted so much. He went to consult Old Wutou.

"By the way, when you marked up the price of coal not covered by the plan, how did you show that in your daybook?" he asked. "Could you tell how much small-pit coal had been sold on a particular day?"

"No. They only entered in the journal 24.80 *yuan* a ton. The additional 15.10 *yuan* was not shown at all," he said. "And in the accounting report they made out once every ten days, they usually put at the bottom of the report so many *yuan* received for small-pit coal transportation expenses. That's all."

What about coal invoices? A former salesman at Baishi told him that two separate invoices were made out, one for coal charged at the original price and the other for transportation and miscellaneous expenses. The latter was never handed in.

"You don't mean they grafted all this?" Liu Changchun was excited.

"Who knows? We were not supposed to ask..."

"That settles it!" Liu did mental arithmetic: ninety thousand tons sold in a year...suppose ten thousand of which were sold as small-pit coal, then an extra one hundred fifty thousand *yuan* could be gained. In five years' time seven hundred fifty thousand *yuan*! How to get to the bottom of the matter? It could be done. Let each enterprise in the county check back on the invoices they received for coal purchased.

This discovery gave an impetus to Liu Changchun's investigation. When vice-director Yang Qing of the Commission for Inspecting Discipline of Bin County CPC betrayed the informer to Wang Shouxin, it was found to be a voluntary task taken up by a non-party member. He was not after personal gain and subsequent events proved that he not only gained nothing but had come to a good deal of harm instead.

The other nobody was Shi Huailiang, a worker of the Bin County Drugs and Medicine Company. He did his share of stirring up the hornets' nest surrounding Wang Shouxin.

As early as 1972 Shi had put up a big character poster which began, "Wang Shouxin is the key to the solution of the problems in Bin County."

Shi Huailiang had a broad mind and was full of surprises. In 1972 he had a brainstorm to send ten *yuan* by mail to Chairman Mao. On the remittance slip he wrote: "Herewith my party membership dues—Shi Huailiang."

This was indeed something quite unusual and almost brought him great suffering. The remittance was rejected and the slip was returned. The leading cadres and party members of the Drugs and Medicine Company then brought him to account. "You are not a party member. That's as clear as daylight. Why send party membership dues to Chairman Mao?" They answered their own questions. "You are hopelessly crazy about joining the party!" "You're mad!"

Why was being crazy about joining the party looked upon as a crime? Probably because quite a few joined the party not for the good of the people, but for personal fame or gain. What grounds were there for assuming that Shi Huailiang really wanted to win promotion and get rich and not to dedicate himself to the cause of communism? It was like measuring another's corn by one's own bushel. Or was it possible that this way of thinking reflected the objective truth that joining the party could become a means to acquiring personal fortunes?

It had been many years since Shi Huailiang had sent his money to Chairman Mao. Even after he sent in his application for party membership, he could not understand many things. A fellow in Xindian Grain Depot was expelled three months after joining the party as a bourgeois element. He found out later that all of them in the depot had committed offenses before being admitted into the party. How come people like this could be recruited into the party? Once when he went to Harbin on business, he heard that many new party members had never been approved by the party organization. They were called the "specially approved" party members, admitted on the recommendation of certain big shots. "If things go on like this, and more of these people get into the party, won't the party degenerate?" Shi thought to himself. "It's a serious matter. How can I let Chairman Mao know?" A letter most probably could not reach him, and he would certainly get into trouble if the letter were passed back to his unit. He pondered over the matter for a long time and came to the decision to remit his "party membership dues" to Chairman Mao. He was sure that Chairman Mao would get the hint. He would think: "Why did he remit it to me instead of handing it over to the County Party Committee? Something must be wrong with the party there." If only Chairman Mao would see it his way and pass his slip on to the proper authorites with written instructions on it, then he could dispel all misgivings and report in full detail to the higher party committee how things worked with the party in Bin County.

But it was only wishful thinking and things went contrary to not look like a man who sought to do others harm. When he talwishes. He was criticized and denounced time and time again at public meetings, and the true state of affairs was never reported to the higher level. He was convinced, however, that something must be amiss with the party organization.

Compared to Liu Changchun, Shi Huailiang was even more reliable, straightforward and good-natured. He giggled often and did not look like a man who sought to do others harm. When he talked, he talked slowly. Given to hard thinking, he did not want to waste his energy on talking as others did. He often wondered why after so many years of socialism the individual at one end and the collective at the other end were as poor as ever.

Shi would study the works of Marx, Lenin and Chairman Mao every night. Unfortunately he could only afford to buy a few slim offprints, but he did manage to get a good grasp of Engel's *Anti-Duhring*. Actually there were plenty of people in Bin County who wrote better than Shi or whose theoretical understanding was on a higher level, but he was the only one for whom conducting investigative research on social problems was such a labor of love.

The first thing that struck him as strange was the leading group of the Drugs and Medicine Company. After his arrival in the company, Secretary Pan got together with a few cadres and formed small circles within the leading group. Old leading cadres were squeezed out one after another. Of the five new leaders, four were not even trade union members! When Secretary Pan first became secretary two years earlier, he still owed the public fund more than thirteen hundred *yuan*. Two years later he not only paid off his debts but added to his possessions high quality radios, clocks and watches. His son bought a light motorcycle, a shotgun, and other extravagances. His salary, by the way, was 54.50 *yuan* a month. Shi Huailing took a closer look at the relationship among cadres within the company and summarized his observations in a big character poster: "...It's really surprising that a certain leading cadre of our company is still dreaming the dreams of a feudal monarch of the eighteenth century, though he is living in a 20th-century socialist society. His doctrine is 'I am the State.' Whoever disobeys will be persecuted. Deprived of all civil rights, the workers of the Drugs and Medicine Company have become slaves at the mercy of the leading cadres, thus changing the nature of a company owned by the people..."

As Shi Huailing was putting up another big character poster directed against Wang Shouxin, someone tried to dissuade him. "Forget it, you're no match for them." He just laughed, saying, "That doesn't matter. It will go down in history that someone has opposed Wang Shouxin. That will help too."

On September 15, 1978 he wrote another poster and put it up inside the County Party Committee building. This was an unconventional poster, entitled "A Satellite of Social Science," the opening part of which read:

In the seventh decade of the twentieth century, leading cadres of successive party committees of Bin County succeeded in launching a social-bourgeois satellite*. Breaking all records, the launching brought about a great advance in our social sciences, furnishing our Academy of Social Sciences with valuable data for research and, in my view, all the socialist countries in the world could benefit from this reference data.

Wang Shouxin did not own any private means of production, such as factories, land, or stores. However, she had amassed 414,-800 *yuan* in cash and more than nine hundred different kinds of goods and materials. Her family must be rated as rich and powerful. In my view the emergence and growth of Wang Shouxin conformed to certain scientific principles, otherwise she couldn't have existed. For this reason a dissection and analysis of Wang Shouxin would serve to promote the development of human society and enrich our social sciences. May I, therefore, offer a piece of advice to the leading cadres of successive party committees (not including Zhang Xiangling), bureau directors and section chiefs implicated in the case of Wang Shouxin: Dispel your misgivings; do not consider your guilt and responsibility alone. Have at heart the destiny of our party and state and truthfully report the whole story to the provincial party committee and sum up the lessons to be drawn there from..."

This was a very significant and necessary big character poster.

Anxiety Amidst Joy

Bin County launched its "Double Strike" campaign in 1978. On August 1 the first one to put up big character posters directed at the corruption of Wang Shouxin was again Liu Changchun.

On August 5 the work team from the County Party Committee entered and stationed itself in the fuel company. It should be mentioned here thatthe Party Committee had made up its mind this time. The struggle had been crowned with success, but certain problems had just been brought to light.

Who would have believed that a work team sent by a county party committee to one of its enterprises to make investigations there would not be given support by the party organization in that enterprise! From start to finish not one party member came forth to expose Wang Shouxin before the work team.

*The term "launching satellites" was used to describe the achieving of new records in agriculture, industry, commerce, and other undertakings in China. The term is now somewhat discredited, being closely associated with the grossly inflated production figures of the 1958 "Satellite Fields" during the "Great Leap Forward."

Team leader Gu Zhou was an astute and capable cadre. He and many of his team members were so absorbed in work that they forgot food and sleep. But three months elapsed and they still failed to uncover any conclusive evidence necessary to nail Wang Shouxin for her crimes.

Comrade Gu Zhou admitted that during this period the only valuable and important information was provided by Liu Changchun. And he was also the only man who came of his own accord to offer the information. He told Gu Zhuo excitedly: "Wang Shouxin's den is in Baishi. (A secret treasury concealing stolen money amounting to hundreds of thousands of *yuan* was later ferreted out in Baishi Business Department.) She passed state coal off as small-pit coal and jacked up the price. I'd wager my head that she is guilty of corruption. Perhaps she is the biggest grafter and embezzler in our country."

"Nonsense!" Gu Zhou was thinking to himself disapprovingly. But it turned out that every word Liu Changchun said was true.

And what Liu said next really irritated Gu Zhou: "This is what I've told Secretary Guan and the leading cadres in the province and the prefecture. If you should fail to get to the bottom of this matter, I'll lodge a complaint against you."

Liu Changchun was not afraid to offend people and that made Gu Zhou mad. "You would just love to go to the County Party Committee and have me recalled. You think this is a cushy job, don't you?"

Gu Zhou remembered that Liu Changchun had once said, "If Wang Shouxin can't be overthrown, I'll won't rest even in the grave!" But why should he talk like that? Wasn't it merely out of personal spite? Gu never asked himself once: Why shouldn't one feel personal spite against evil-doers? The social forces represented by Wang Shouxin had broken up Liu Changchun's family. Why shouldn't the White-haired Girl hate Huang Shiren?* Of course those party members of the fuel company did not have a sense of "personal spite" against Wang Shouxin; they did not even have public spite against her. Comrade Gu Zhou was not to blame. For years a way of thinking had been prevalent—individuals by definition were thought to be at odds with the collective. Personal feelings and aspirations, no matter how proper and reasonable or even noble, were trampled upon as "individualism."

Because of this prejudice against Liu Changchun, the work team did not make a serious study of the information he brought forward. If only they had stormed the den in Baishi and interro-

*Two of the main characters in a revolutionary opera, the *White-haired Girl*.

gated Ma Zhanqing and Sun Xiyin, they could've cracked the case.

The work team and the County Party Committee had one shortcoming in common. They were both divorced from the masses, and consequently, from reality. The attitude adopted by the work team toward Section Chief Zhao Yu of the commerce section was ridiculous. Following its arrival in the fuel company, the team had come to look upon Zhao Yu as an important clue. He was expected to give them information concerning Wang Shouxin.

The relation between Zhao Yu and Wang Shouxin was an open secret. Because he had openly opposed Tian Fengshan, he was made number one man of the bureau of commerce by Commissar Yang in 1969, Wang Shouxin being second to him. He pigeonholed all the letters of accusation directed against Wang Shouxin. When Wang elbowed a great number of staff and workers out of the fuel company, he backed her up.

In 1976 Zhao Yu found himself in Wuhe Commune conducting education on the party line. He stayed at the guesthouse in the Baishi business department. Commune cadres, workers in Baishi and commune members in the neighborhood called his attention to the tyranny and irregularities of Wang Shouxin. He retorted and threatened, "Old Lady Wang is not to be trifled with! Don't look for trouble."

In 1977 the Party Committee of the commerce section started the rectification movement. Shi Huailiang wrote four posters exposing Wang Shouxin. Because these posters touched upon some crucial issues, Zhao Yu forbade him to put them up.

After Liu Changchun put up his poster exposing Wang Shouxin, Zhao Yu, knowing Liu was in for it, predicted, "That Liu Changchun is rather audacious, I should say. Among half a million people he was the only one to come out into the open to attack Wang Shouxin. Sooner or later he will get into trouble." When Shi Huailiang wrote posters to support Liu Changchun, Zhao Yu sent word to the work team stationed in the Drugs and Medicine Company to make it hot for him. They criticized and denounced him over ten times at mass meetings and group meetings and tried to brand him as counter revolutionary. Wasn't it strange that just when Zhao Yu instigated the work team in the Drugs and Medicine Company to brand Shi Huailiang as counter revolutionary, the work team in the fuel company should approach Zhao Yu and interrogate him about Wang Shouxin?

Nevertheless the case was finally solved. Hundreds of people had been mobilized to track down and recover the stolen money.

The whole story was as exciting as it was intriguing. Unfortunately, I can't go into details here because I have something more important to say: Zhao Yu at last made clean admission of guilt before the work team. He was Wang Shouxin's accomplice. After his confession he asked the work team to guarantee his security. "You will be held responsible for my safety." he told Gu Zhou. "If she finds out that I've confessed, she'll stop at nothing to have me killed...What if she knocks at my door in the dead of night to finish me off?"

That very evening Sun Xiyin confessed and the work team placed him under protective surveillance as well. He was rather relieved because protection was what he needed under this circumstance. He, too, feared Wang Shouxin might plot against his life.

Things were different with Liu Changchun. However, folks with the best of intentions came to warn him: "Take good care of yourself from now on. When you go out after dark be on guard. Wang Shouxin hates you to the very marrow of her bones. She would gladly pay ten thousand *yuan* to have you assassinated."

Even reporters and researchers who came out to Bin County to gather news and materials in connection with the case were duly warned: "If you come again you'd better watch your step. It is true that Wang Shouxin has been put behind bars, but the situation in Bin County is rather complicated."

The situation in Bin County was indeed complicated. How could it be otherwise? The ten persons implicated in the case and thrown into jail were all members of the CPC.

The former secretary of the County Party Committee in Bin County, Wang Shouxin's notoriously sly relative by marriage, was willing to conceal the stolen money for her. Later he advised her to "...get a big earthen jar, put the money inside at the bottom and put something else on top. Bury it as deep as possible."

Was Bin County the only place where the situation was complicated? Decidedly not. Liu Zhimin, the eldest son of Wang Shouxin, was undergoing examination in Harbin by the prefectural party committee of Songhuajiang. That he was guilty of corruption was not beyond doubt. Those buddies of his who had helped him in fixing up his and his wife's transfer from one post to another or in removing evidence from official files were still doing what they could to help him. (It goes without saying that they were amply repaid for their services.) During the period when he underwent interrogation Liu Zhimin could eat and drink to his heart's content and while the time away by playing chess or poker with his warders. He could even drive to Acheng more than thirty miles away to draw up a pact with an accomplice to shield each other in the judicial inquiry.

Wang Shouxin's corruption case had been cracked once and for all. But as for those social conditions favoring the emergence and growth of a Wang Shouxin—how much have things changed? Aren't there still countless Wang Shouxins, big or small, still nibbling at the foundation of socialism and corroding the organism of the party without being penalized by the Dictatorship of the Proletariat?

Be on guard, everybody! It's still too early to celebrate our victory.

Author's note: For obvious reasons, certain characters have been given fictitious names.

A Place Forgotten by Love

ZHANG XIAN

(Translated by Katherine Lu)

I

Although it was already the last year of the seventies, love was still too strange and mysterious to be mentioned by the young people of Paradise Commune. Hence, when the newly-arrived secretary of the Youth League used this word during the discussion on "Opposition to Mercenary Marriage" held at the auditorium, everyone was amazed. Shortly thereafter young men exchanged winks and chuckles while young women lowered their heads, blushing and giggling bashfully.

The only one who did not laugh was an elegant-looking girl sitting by the window at the far corner — Shen Huangmei, the team leader of the ninth squad of the Paradise production brigade. Her face paled and she turned toward the window, avoiding the gazes of others. Suddenly her eyelashes fluttered, trying hard to hold back her tears. The previously reprehensible word "love" now stirred the heart of this nineteen-year old girl. She felt shame, sorrow and an indescribable sense of fear. She sat thinking of her sister Cunni whom she at once missed and hated. Alas! Had it not been for that boy nicknamed Young Leopard, life would have gone well. Sister Cunni would now be sitting beside her, laughing boyishly. She would embrace her with her strong arms and after the meeting they would walk together to the supply cooperative to pick up some crimson thread for embroidering flowers on pillow cases later at home.

Cunni was the most fortunate among the five siblings. She was born in 1955, right after a bumper harvest. To celebrate her first month of life, her parents prepared a banquet dinner. Holding his precious daughter, all bundled up in a flowered blanket, the excited young father Shen Shanweng announced: "After I took Linghua to the delivery station, I went to the credit cooperative to deposit some money. When I went back to the station my little darling had already been born. The first delivery was so fast and smooth, someone suggested the name Shunni ("smooth girl"); but I thought, this being the first time for poor farmers like us to open a savings account at the bank, she should be called Cunni ("savings girl"). Just imagine the good days ahead for her when she grows up!"

His happiness radiated from his heart to every friend who came to congratulate him. At that time Shen was the vice chief of the Kao Shan Zhuang cooperative. He was optimistic, skillful and bold. The pear trees he grafted along the hillside brought a bumper harvest the very first year. After he had delivered the state's portion of wheat and maize, there was still plenty left. In this little village of twenty or so families, everybody was content and confident and looked forward to a good future.

Five years after Cunni was born things changed. The Kao Shan Zhuang cooperative had turned into the ninth squad of the Paradise production brigade. The name "paradise" was suggested by the secretary of the county party committee. This idea had its origin in the slogan "Communism is paradise, the commune its bridge." At the time everyone, including the squad leader Shen Shanweng, believed wholeheartedly that they were very close to "being in paradise." All they had to do was to chop down all the collective's pear trees, together with all the gingko and chestnut trees in the front and back of every house, and haul them to the commune-owned steel smelting factory for fuel. As soon as sparks of molten steel spurted out from the miraculous and howling furnace, they thought they would easily walk over "the bridge," arriving at the paradise of communism. Instead, that ugly iron mass which had turned thousands of tons of trees into ash was not put to use. Due to drought, maize and wheat were lost, including their seeds. Potatoes planted where pear trees used to grow were as slender as Cunni's fingers. When the pregnant Linghua finally came home from begging, she found out that Shen Shanweng had been fired from his job as a result of his attack on the "Great Iron and Steel Smelting Movement." Looking at his new-born and feeble second daughter, Huangmei ("little sister famine"), a bitter smile appeared on his swollen face: "What bad luck it is for her to be born at a time of famine!"

Cunni grew up to be a physically strong girl—it must have been due to the good nutrition she received in the womb and during breast feeding. She would put on flesh even if all she had to eat were tree leaves and cold water. By the time she had reached sixteen, Cunni had grown into a healthy, well-developed girl. Carrying a shoulder-pole of mulberry wood, she helped her father by taking over the work of her mother who had grown ill giving birth to three more daughters. She received the third highest work points for the hardest annual task—carrying pine lumber down the hill to the state-owned forestry center. She woke up before dawn every morning and came home when the stars were already shining. She would then gobble up a plate of either potato or maize paste and fall asleep as soon as her head touched the pillow. Although she couldn't save any money even when she received a bonus because the family was constantly in debt, she was always joyful and didn't succumb to sorrow. When she was happy she would embrace Huangmei, her full-grown breasts pressing against her sister's delicate body, while she hummed the tune of a folksong her mother used to sing as a young girl.

Everything would have gone well had Cunni not gotten involved with that boy Young Leopard.

Young Leopard's real name was Xiaobao. He was the only son of Uncle Jiaguei, who lived on the east side of the village. He and Cunni were the same age. This husky young man was full of energy, especially when it came to work. Once during a winter rainstorm when everyone was clearing the fields of fallen pine branches, Xiaobao's mother tripped and fell, breaking her shoulder pole in two. He picked his mother up and tied together two loads of pine lumber. Then stripping himself to the waist, he heaved the lumber on his shoulder, huffing and puffing and grinding his teeth all the way to his destination. The load on the steelyard was three hundred and five *jin**. Everyone said that Xiaobao was as powerful as a young leopard. Hence he was called Young Leopard.

One morning in the spring of 1974, all the cadres on the squads at the commune went to a criticism meeting on the writings of Confucius. At this time all the strong young hands were working on the construction of a dam. The storeman, Old Uncle Xiang, ordered Cunni to stay behind to help him clean out the warehouse. The old man complained as he gave directions to the girl:

"Those cadres come down here once a year. They point their fingers and say: 'Here!' Then we have to keep busy working our butts off for a whole year. Then, all of a sudden, torrents of water rush down the mountain to sweep away everything. When those

*One *jin* (or *catty*) is equivalent to 1.1 pounds.

cadres come again the following year, they point their fingers an-
dcommand: 'There!'... totally ignoring our situation."

"Haven't we been told to 'transform China in the spirit of the
Old Man who moved the mountain' "? Cunni casually asked.

"That is fine as long as our stomachs are full!...Come on over
here, sieve this pile first. Easy, don't spill any... Look at this sickly
maize grown around the roots of pear trees. I doubt if it will
sprout at all!" The old man was complaining about the maize
seeds now.

"Haven't we been told 'to take grain as the key link'?" The girl,
still casually coming up with questions, thought it more fun to
tote sand with young companions at the dam then to work with
this man, though the job was easy.

Suddenly the shadow of a strong man darkened the warehouse
door. "Find me something to do, Old Uncle Xiang."

"Young Leopard!" Cunni called joyfully. "I thought you
sprained your foot yesterday!"

Old Uncle Xiang urged him: "Go home and take the day off!"

"I'll be bored if I don't do anything." Young Leopard smiled
good-naturedly, "I'll be alright doing some light work!" He picked
up a wooden spade and started to sift seeds with Cunni.

Squatting down, Old Uncle Xiang delightedly lit a cigarette.
Then he remembered he had to fetch the carpenter to fix the
plow. He left shortly after briefing Cunni about the work to be
done. Cleaning up the warehouse and sifting seeds were nothing
to a couple of nineteen year-old youths. In no time the seeds were
packed into gunnysacks and dried sweet potatoes were spread
out in the courtyard. Young Leopard suggested: "Let's take a
break!" He then laid his cotton jacket on a gunnysack and lay
down on it.

Wiping her perspiration, Cunni sat down on a gunnysack opposite him. She had also taken off her cotton jacket. Beneath it
she wore an aqua sweater which had been her mother's dowry.
Although the sweater had been taken apart and reknitted many
times with a few other colored yarns added, it was still too tight
for her. But the sweater was still considered an enviable luxury
by the young women of the ninth squad.

Staring furtively at Cunni's rosy sun-lit complexion and full-
developed breats. Young Leopard felt a strange sensation well up
inside him, an agitated feeling he had never before experienced.

"There was a movie showing at Wu Zhuang Village the day before yesterday. Didn't you go?"

"Who would want to go? It's so far away!" Evading his eyes,
she lowered her head and started to pull out odd pieces of thread

from her sleeve.

Two mountains away was another commune called Wu Zhuang Village. It would have taken Young Leopard more than an hour to walk there. Although Wu Zhuang Village was not considered a rich commune, the thirty-eight cents pay its members received for ten work points was enough to make members of Paradise Commune envious. They admired even more the fact that the village was only thirty *li* away from a railway station. Last year, during his spring vacation, Young Leopard went there with a few others to watch the grain come in and out of the station. It took them most of the day to walk there and back. They waited for two hours before they finally saw a green passenger train speed by the tiny station. Still they felt satisfied since the majority of the commune members had never seen a train. As for riding on one, only accountant Xu, nicknamed Blind Xu, was so fortunate.

Young Leopard continued: "I didn't want to go to the movie either. 'Tunnel Warfare,' 'Mine Warfare,' 'Fighting North' and 'South on Many Fronts.' I've watched those films so many times I've almost memorized each line..." Stretching himself, he sighed: "But what else is there to do? We played poker so much, we ruined the deck. We've tried to bribe the manager of the supply cooperative for a new deck but nothing has come of it yet!"

Besides movies and poker there was nothing else for young people here to do after work. The one copy of the local newspaper ordered by the squad was read only by Blind Xu at meetings. Although he constantly mistook the words, "Confucius said" for "Confucius day," nobody would correct the only intellectual on the squad. In the past folksongs were popular. Now that they were considered "pornographic," they were banned....

Suddenly Young Leopard sat up: "Guess what? Blind Xu said he has seen foreign films. Isn't that great!" He tittered as he continued: "There was..."

"Yes?" she asked curiously.

"...I can't tell you," Young Leopard chuckled.

"There was what? Please tell me."

"If I tell you...you must not scold me!"

"Go on!"

"There was..." He laughed so hard that he had to bend over. Cunni more or less guessed what he had to say. She grabbed a handful of dirt. As expected, Young Leopard gathered enough courage to say: "There was a man and a woman embracing and kissing each other! Ha! Ha!..."

"Bull! Nonsense!" Cunni's face turned red and she threw dirt at him.

"That's true! That's what Blind Xu said." Young Leopard evaded the attack.

"Shame on you!" She threw another handful of dirt at him. Sand and maize stuck to his shoulders and neck. He threw a handful of dirt back at Cunni. It trickled down the open collar of her sweater. Making a long face, she rebuked him: "Damn it! You..."

Young Leopard laughed apologetically as he wiped the dirt on his muscular chest with his shirt. Pouting her lips, Cunni took off her sweater so she could shake off the dirt sticking to her breasts. All of a sudden, as if electrified, Young Leopard became transfixed. Staring at her, holding his breath, he felt the blood rush to his head. Cunni had accidentally pulled up her blouse while taking off her sweater, exposing half of her white, full-grown and bouncy breasts.

Leaping up just as a wild animal would from a ravine, Young Leopard sprang at her. Completely out of control, he held onto her tightly. Unprepared, she raised her arms to stop him. But as his hot and trembling lips touched hers, she felt a mysterious dizziness. Closing her eyes, she dropped her arms, and all of her attempts to resist him ceased. A primitive instinct was burning in their blood. Traditional ethics, dignity, the danger of violating the law, a girl's sense of shame, all were burnt to ashes in the fire of their passion.

II

The skinny maize seedlings sprouted only sparsely. After the first round of hoeing, fourteen-year-old Huangmei perceived a change in her older sister: No longer would she laugh and joke. Instead, she frequently sat on her bed alone as if in a trance. She didn't seem to hear what others said to her. Sometimes she lowered her head to wipe away the tears running down her face, while at other times she would blush and laugh to herself. The most peculiar incident occurred once when Huangmei woke up in the middle of the night and her sister was not in bed beside her. When Huangmei asked her sister about it, she nervously denied she had left her bed and insisted that Huangmei must have been dreaming.

At this time their mother's kidney disease recurred. While their father hastily left for Wu Zhuang Village to borrow money from their uncle and to find a doctor, everybody else in the family was too worried to notice the change in Cunni. Huangmei faintly sensed something terrible was about to happen to her sister.

Something terrible did occur. As a matter of fact, it was much worse than what Huangmei had anticipated.

By now the maize had grown halfway to the height of a man. After the day's hard work, the commune members were gathered together after dinner to hear Blind Xu read "Confucius day" under the kerosene lamp. Huangmei sneaked out of the meeting before it was over. She went home, put her three younger sisters to bed, and then lay down to sleep. She was soon awakened by loud voices mingled with the barking of dogs. Panic-stricken, Huangmei hurriedly turned on the light, only to find that the noises were drawing nearer until they were at the front door. Suddenly her sister rushed in, sloppily dressed with her hair disheveled. She threw herself onto the bed and began to wail. She was shortly followed by Young Leopard, naked to the waist with both hands tied behind his back. He was escorted into the house by the battalion commander of the people's militia. Bright flashlights illuminated the streaks of blood left by sapling lashes on his body. Straightbacked and shamefaced he knelt down in front of her angry father who began to slap him in the face. By this time, her mother had also gotten out of bed. Sitting wearily on a stool, she began to weep, her hands covering her face. It seemed as if everyone in the village, children and adults, were standing by the door. Finally, the shivering Huangmei came to realize that her sister had done the most shameful deed on earth. She broke down in tears, feeling humiliated. Her dearest sister had brought disaster to the whole family as well as to herself. As she cried she heard her own indistinct voice saying: "Shame on you!...You disgraced your family!...You disgraced our whole squad!...Shame! Shame!..."

Her crying lasted until late into the night.

Huangmei dozed off. In her sleep she seemed to hear the commander breaking up the crowd. Auntie and Uncle Jiaguei were begging her parents' forgiveness and Old Uncle Xiang was comforting and reminding them "Don't go too far. The young couple might take it hard!..." Her mother's abusive language had become disconsolate. Huangmei finally fell asleep on her wet pillow, but was constantly interrupted by nightmares. In her last nightmare she suddenly heard urgent screams: "Help! Help! Somebody please..."

She jumped out of bed. The sun was shining brightly outside. Cunni was not in bed, nor was her mother. Following the people in front of her, she ran barefoot to San Mou Dike by the edge of the village. There lay her sister. Some people had dredged up the body from the pond. She went away so fast! Just like that!

Holding the body, her mother cried shrilly. Time and again relatives tried in vain to pull her away. Her father sat by the dike in a daze, staring at the tranquil water. In his wooden stupor he looked like a dead tree trunk.

Rays of morning sunlight shone on Cunni's pale face, restoring a touch of color to it. Although Cunni had paid the highest price for her blind impulse, Huangmei thought she had atoned for her crime and shame. She thought her sister's death was pointless; but then, what had there been left for her in life? Before Cunni jumped to her death, she had remembered to take off the aqua sweater and hang it on a tree, bequeathing to her sister the only treasure she ever had.

After about two weeks cries of sorrow were heard from Uncle Jiaguei's house. Two public security officers arrested Young Leopard. The whole village was once again in shock. They ran from the fields and stood by the roadside staring at the shiny hand-cuffs on Young Leopard's wrists. Auntie and Uncle Jiaguei walked behind their only son, wailing and sniveling.

"Comrades! Comrades!" Shen Shanweng dropped his hoe and ran after them as he called. This brigade leader during the fifties had experienced life and seen the world. Although the death of his daughter had aged him ten years and made him indifferent toward life, his sense of responsibility urged him to talk to the officers: "Comrades, we aren't pressing charges!"

The officers gave him a cold stare and said in disdain: "Go away! With or without an accusation, he is being charged with rape and manslaughter."

Young Leopard remained calm. He raised his head to look around. Suddenly he stopped and then started to run towards the bare slope ahead.

"Stop! Where do you think you're going?" The two officers yelled and tried to catch up with him.

Young Leopard did not slow down. He ran through the weeds and brambles, finally falling down at Cunni's fresh gravesite breaking into sobs. With both hands he dug deeply into the wet soil. The two officers derided him. Then he knelt in front of the grave and respectfully kowtowed three times.

III

The meeting was over. Huangmei walked out of the commune auditorium with a heavy heart. Paradise Commune was situated in a remote corner of the county and the ninth squad of Paradise

Commune was the most remote squad of them all. Looking at the evening glow through the woods in the west, she knew she had to give up on the idea of shopping at the supply cooperative if she wanted to be home before dark. Once her mind was made up, she walked to a back street, passed by a wheat field and trotted along a path uphill.

"Wait for me, Huangmei! Let's walk together!" The voice of Rong Shuxu, branch secretary of the Youth League, called out from behind. He lived in the eighth squad, separated from the ninth squad only by San Mou Dike. Huangmei was naturally anxious to have someone walk with her up the long path, which was extremely desolate during the winter evenings. Neverthless, she didn't want a young man for company, especially not Rong Shuxu. She hesitated a little, then walked swiftly on. When Shuxu finally caught up with her at the other end of the wheat field, she cautiously moved farther apart from him, maintaining a distance of at least four steps between them.

The death of Cunni had bequeathed to Huangmei more than just an aqua sweater. The tragedy had given her an inextricable sense of humiliation and fear. The responsibilities of being the eldest child now fell heavily on her thin shoulders. Huangmei had acquired a pyschological burden as well—she had come to fear and hate young men. She refused to talk to them and tried to avoid them whenever possible, holding in contempt even other girls who didn't share her negative feelings toward young men.

In spite of her feelings her complexion was rosy and radiant; her eyebrows thick and the contrasting black and white of her eyes were brighter than ever. She could feel her breasts developing and the aqua sweater was already too tight for her. When she saw a blooming flower she could not resist picking it and tying it to her hair. When a bird chirped she thought it was such good music that she had to stop to listen for a while. Everything looked so beautiful: the leaves, the fields, the weeds and the dew. Often she secretly looked into her mother's broken mirror. She even enjoyed looking at her own reflection at the dike where she fetched water. She began to mingle with other girls and would go shopping with them hand in hand at the supply cooperative during the holidays. She still kept a distance from young men, although she did not think them so annoying anymore... Shuxu came into her life right at this time.

She had known him for a long time. Once when she was in first grade some boys were bullying her and Shuxu, an older boy about Cunni's age, came to her rescue. He wiped her tears with his sleeve. Later on when her mother gave birth to her youngest sister, Huangmei had to quit school. When Shuxu saw her carrying her little sister on her back while cutting greenfeed for hogs, he always left his friends quietly; taking the sickle from her hands, he would swiftly cut up a big bunch of greenfeed, throw them into her basket and leave in a hurry. Some years later, hearing the sound of gongs and drums, Huangmei took her sisters to see what was happening. She saw him dressed in a soldier's uniform, wearing a red flower, marching along the path by the San Mou Dike. He had joined the army.

It was not until the previous year at the meeting of the Youth League branch that she saw him again. He had just demobilized from the army. After walking into the conference room, he bashfully looked around and then took a seat in a corner of the room. At this moment several of the more active members surrounded him and insisted that he talk about his combat life. He blushed, and embarrassed, declined: "I was a soldier in peacetime without any fighting experience. I have little to say!..." He didn't have the kind of might and grandeur expected of a revolutionary soldier.

However, it was exactly his modesty that had won him Huangmei's favor. When he was nominated for the position of secretary of the Youth League branch, she bravely raised her hand, wishing that he would be elected.

When the next meeting approached, the newly elected Secretary Rong Shuxu put forward some controversial proposals, generating much disagreement from the former commander of the people's militia who was now the deputy secretary of the branch party committee.

In the past the only activity of the Youth League in Paradise Commune, besides holding meetings, was manual labor— collecting farmyard manure and carrying and moving rocks. The usual procedure was first to hold the meeting and then work. This kind of labor without pay was called the "exemplary role of the Communist Youth League" and was very time-consuming. Shuxu spoke out against this rule. He said, "Young people have their own ways of thinking. I suggest we all go to the movies!" Everyone was surprised. This was instantly followed by laughter and applause. He was considerate enough to have reserved some tickets at a nearby commune factory ahead of time. After the short meeting he led all the young people to the movie. They walked in groups, laughing, talking and even singing folksongs—as if it were a holiday. For the first time in her life Huangmei sat on a chair with a comfortable back and armrests to watch a film.

Also for the first time in her life a young man appeared in her dreams. He looked very much like the actor in the movie who had

led a crowd of people to repair a dam, but he bore a greater re-
semblance to the secretary of the Youth League branch. He
smiled and talked to her so intimately. When she woke up the
moon was shining by her bedside. For the first time in her life she
felt tenderness. This terrified her. "What's the matter with me?"
She was perplexed: "Thank goodness! It was only a dream!..."

Nevertheless, when she became the team leader of the squad,
Shuxu began to call on her rather frequently. As usual, Huangmei
was solemn and aloof. She never invited him to her house and
kept a distance of at least four feet from him. They talked about
meetings, never anything personal. After Shuxu had left she
would pretend to do some work outside and secretly watch him
walk away. How she wished he could talk a little more, stay a little longer, or even talk about something other than meetings; but
then she was afraid he might really do so. The more they met, the
more this contradictory feeling grew in Huangmei's heart. One
day she came home late. Her eleven-year-old sister told her:
"Shuxu was here!" Their mother, who had just walked into the
house, asked: "Him? Coming here again?" Their father replied:
"He came looking for me. He wanted to know how to graft pear
trees, how long before the trees will yield any fruit, and how
much he can profit from one acre of land. I asked him if that
wouldn't be capitalistic. He said that was not capitalism. He got
the idea from the newspapers! That kid...!"

Her father did not seem to agree with Rong Shuxu's ideas, but
Huangmei was pleased to sense that her father had a good impression of the young man. Nevertheless, her mother made a long
face and frowned: "He's not the well-behaved kind!"

Huangmei heard from others that Shuxu had quarreled with
the eighth squad leader, who happened to be his uncle, over the
issue of allowing commune members to raise their own chickens.
Some people criticized Rong for disobeying his superior. She had
never paid much attention to what people said about Rong Shuxu
until this moment when she heard what her mother had to say
about him. Huangmei got angry but as she was about to defend
him, her mother's suspicious look stopped her. She quietly swallowed her rice, pretending not to care. After dinner she overheard
her mother whisper, "There is already much gossip around.
We have to make sure she doesn't follow Cunni's footsteps!..."

Huangmei felt as if somebody had stabbed her in the heart.
She fell onto the bed and cried. She resented the disgraceful thing
her sister had done which could not be erased even by death; she
resented the fact that her mother did not understand her; and

most of all she resented herself for feeling a fondness for the young man. "How wrong and how shameful this is! Shame on you! How could you possibly like a man?...Shame! Shame!" She rebuked herself, hiding her face in the blanket so nobody could hear her cry.

She finally made up her mind that starting the next day she would not talk to him anymore. If he had to discuss anything with her, he would have to go through the vice team leader. Would he be surprised? Would he be humiliated? She could not worry about that anymore. She could not help it. He was a man!

After a while she actually began to hate Rong. She happened to hear Blind Xu say: "Guess what? Rong really has an exaggerated opinion of his abilities. This time he's fighting with the deputy secretary of the production brigade." Someone asked, "Over what?" Blind Xu sniffed, "He wanted to appeal for redress for Young Leopard."

"What?" Huangmei was so surprised she almost screamed. Young Leopard was sentenced for the crime he had committed. He deserved it. His case was not misjudged. Almost everyone agreed about Young Leopard's guilt and Huangmei was no exception. Because her sister had been involved, she hated Young Leopard all the more. She could not see why Rong, a party member and a respected secretary of the Youth League branch, supported Young Leopard. Auntie and Uncle Jiaguei must have bribed him...She was so agitated she shook all over. She decided to question Shuxu in person. However, her courage evaporated when she saw him at the San Mou Dike walking toward her with a smile. She did not know how to put her doubt into words, nor could she summon the strength to do so. She quickly turned around pretending she was going someplace else and took a roundabout route home. Soon afterwards she regretted what she had done...

She was angry with him, hated him and was aloof towards him, but couldn't help thinking of him. All these feelings came and went causing her much agony and unrest.

Although her feelings were far from being realized, Huangmei was experiencing love similar to the way most young girls of Paradise Commune did. Their attraction to young men remained secret and in most cases passed away without anyone's ever finding out. One day a distant relative or someone else would appear with an aqua- or crimson-colored sweater and come to an agreement with the girl's parents after much bargaining. Then on a chosen day this distant relative would return to the house accompanied by a young man. The young man and the girl, too timid even to look at each other, would be taken to Wu Zhuang Village to get their pictures taken. On a designated day the girl would leave her parents and her home.

This type of arrangement had in the past been the only proper way for a young couple to become engaged; but the speaker at the meeting had called this approach mercenary. He even talked about love! Was it the kind of love Cunni and Young Leopard had for each other, thought Huangmei. No! Their love was shameful and illegal. Then was there any alternative? Huangmei was perplexed.

She couldn't help thinking about Shuxu, who was now quietly following her. The other girls had all gone to the supply cooperative. There was nobody else walking on this quiet mountain path. She could even hear her own heart beating.

Suddenly Shuxu began to sing with a deep voice:

> My love is for the blue ocean,
> Wide is our motherland's sea!

Huangmei was amazed to hear his ardent voice. Turning her head, she gave him a smile of praise.

Smiling, he seemed to be speaking to himself: "This pine wood reminds me of the sea and those days spent on the naval vessel!" He continued: "The sea enables me to look farther. Wouldn't it be great if only our villagers could get a glimpse of the sea?"

She listened to him still smiling. Her vigilance was quietly slipping away.

"Huangmei, have you been to the main street? Eggs and vegetables are sold in the market now. Nobody will interfere anymore. Do you know that the farming policy is changing now? The hillside fields will become a pear orchard again. Uncle Shen, your father, is going to play his part again. He will start the tree seedlings on his private family plot!" He sounded disorganized but excited. "Since Auntie is not in good health, she can pull twigs off the trees to weave baskets at home in exchange for some pocket money. Your younger sister can probably start working next year. Your two little sisters can be shepherds...I have a comrade-in-arms who is a cadre at the commune. He told me that the central government will soon ratify a document that will let the peasants improve their living standards. Really! Don't you believe it?"

His eyes were filled with hope, his speech was a gurgling stream, so endearing and touching. Huangmei did not believe in what he had said. She had never thought of becoming rich. Ever since she was small, being rich was always linked with capitalism, which was to be criticized. What touched her, though, was that Shuxu knew so well and cared so much about her family. This was his answer to her indifference and distrust. She blushed with guilt.

"You see, if everyone lives in poverty, there is no future to talk about." He shook his head, "Let's take Young Leopard as an example. Was that all his fault? Being poor, backward, ignorant, stupid! On top of all that he had feudal ideas! An honest young man is now in jail. As for your sister, it was even worse!"

As soon as she heard him mention this, she felt humiliated. Looking him in the eye, she shouted, "Don't talk about that! Don't talk about my sister!..."

Trying hard to hold back her tears, she rushed up the mountain and ran away, leaving Shuxu totally baffled.

IV

It was completely dark when she came home. She had calmed down a little. Her youngest sister ran to her as she called. Her mother also welcomed her with a big smile, and this especially surprised Huangmei. Poverty, hardship and illness, had made her mother prematurely old. The death of Cunni had ruined her mother's already sad-looking face. She wondered what it was that had suddenly made her mother so happy.

"Hurry! Go look what's on your bed!" Her mother almost laughed.

It was a brand new sky-blue sweater, glowing softly and attractively under the dim kerosene lamp.

Before she could feel the softness and warmth of the sweater in her hands, she dropped it abruptly as if she had received a shock. Flabbergasted, she asked, "Whose is this?"

"Yours!" her mother replied as she ladled some sizzling maize congee from a pot. With radiating vigor, she continued: "It's from your auntie..."

"My auntie?!..." A shiver ran over her body and her legs started shaking. She sat down by the bed, completely dumbfounded. A short while back her auntie had dropped by. She and her mother chatted in a whisper for a longtime while she looked Huangmei up and down. At the time Huangmei could sense that something fishy was going on. As she had expected the sweater was now delivered.

Her mother sat by her. With an unusually tender voice, she said: "He also lives in the third squad of Wu Zhuang Village, as your uncle and auntie do. He is three years your senior. His brother is a worker at the North Pass railway station with a monthly salary of more than fifty *yuan!*

Huangmei could feel perspiration rolling down her spine. She was shivering all over. She could hear nothing but a buzzing sound.

"I don't want to!" she cried, throwing the sweater at her still smiling mother. "No! I don't want to!"

Linghua continued her attempt to convince her daughter: "You won't be married just yet! The other party will come here to meet you during the Double Fifth Festival and will bring some new clothing. Sixteen sets! Five hundred *yuan* more in cash will be sent over after the engagement.

"No! No! No!" She had never felt so humiliated. She was suffocating from horror. Not knowing what to do, she just let the tears of humiliation run down her cheeks. Angrily she pushed aside her mother's comforting arms and ran away.

Standing by the door were her sullen father and three wide-eyed sisters. Covering her face, she ran to the backyard. Leaning by the half tumbled-down wall of the pig shed, she let herself cry her heart out.

"What is the matter?" Her mother had followed right after her and was holding her hands. "Huangmei, you're a good girl, but we are poor. I am sick most of the time and your sisters must eat. Without money for feed, it is hard to raise pigs. We haven't even gotten back our principal after half a year of pig raising. We try to sell some eggs in the market, but we are being pushed around like thieves. We did not get a penny from last year's bonus because we had already overdrawn. I can't even afford to buy you a pair of socks."

As she talked, she began to weep. "Your sister died so young. We have nobody to depend on. We need new shingles for this house, but where can we find money to do this while we are still in debt? According to your auntie, as soon as we receive the five hundred *yuan*...."

"Money! Money!" The girl yelled hysterically, "You treat your daughter like a piece of merchandise!"

Her mother stopped short. She felt so terribly weak. Clinging to the half tumbled-down wall for support, she slid slowly to the ground. "You treat your daughter like a piece of merchandise." These words had hurt her, yet they sounded so familiar! The young girl who had said the same words as her daughter did, who was she? Aiyah! It was none other than herself!

It was during the winter when the land reform work team had moved to Wu Zhuang Village that Linghua met an honest and handsome young worker, Shenweng, for the first time at the opera house where *White Haired Girl* was being performed. Ever since that moment, the word "lover" in folksongs suddenly made sense to her. Not only did the nineteen-year-old Linghua bravely participate in the landlord-purging meeting, she also bravely met her lover that evening at the maize field. However, she was already engaged to be married to the young owner of a grocery store at North Pass Town, an arrangement that had been made by her parents. When her fiance heard the rumors of her romance, he sent fifty silver dollars, requesting that the wedding be held before the end of the year. Linghua wailed and whined, causing much commotion. She openly admitted that she had fallen in love with the poor young man at Kao Shan Zhuang and was willing to live with him in poverty for the rest of her life. She denounced her "old feudalistic" family. Exasperated, her parents cursed and beat her. She cried, screamed, rolled on the ground and threw the silver coins into the air, yelling: "You, you treat your daughter like a piece of merchandise!"

Those were the days when the fire of anti-feudalism had burnt down "parents' orders and match-maker's words" along with deeds and IOU's of landlords. Posters advertising marriage laws were posted on the walls of the county administration office. Liu Qiaoer on the stage and the child bride in her village set good examples for Linghua. The honest and handsome Shen Shanweng was waiting for her with a good and prosperous future. Linghua was full of the needed courage to break down the barrier of feudalism.

"They treat their daughter like a piece of merchandise!" The next day in the newly painted county administration office, just because of these words from Linghua, a person from the land reform work team, with a smile of approval, issued them a marriage license on which the picture of Mao Zhedong was imprinted.

Much to her surprise, thirty years later, her own daughter was accusing her of the same injustice others had once tried to inflict on her. "What is going on? Is life going backwards?" She was worried and scared, and raised her head slowly to look into the dark sky of the winter night. A few distant stars were twinkling with a solitary and faint light. Clutching her breasts as if struck by painful revelation, Linghua suddenly cried, "Retribution, retribution! What retribution!"

Tears of bitterness welled up in her old eyes. She hated Huangmei, Cunni and their father. She hated her misery and she hated this land on which she had toiled most of her life, but which had in return given her nothing but misery.

Now that Huangmei had calmed down, she began to comfort her mother: "Mom, do you know that on the commune streets you can sell eggs and vegetables again? You could break off twigs of the trees to weave baskets and sell them. My sisters can work as shepherds. Fields by the hillside may be used for planting fruit trees and dad is good at it. They want farmers to live better lives. That's what Shuxu said. The central government will soon ratify such a document!"

"Documents! Documents! Today this, tomorrow that! We've been through enough of these lies! Nothing has ever changed. We are still as poor as ever. Huangmei, I don't want you to live the way I have." Her mother was gradually calming down, but still weeping. "My baby, you are a good girl. I know that Shuxu is very fond of you and you like him too; but that is no use if you are constantly hungry. I regret....Aiyah! I am getting my retribution now!"

The wind had died down. Her mother leaned her feeble body against Huangmei. They were quietly absorbed in their own thoughts.

"Mom, why don't you go inside," Huangmei whispered. Her eyes were searching for a house in the distant village where the eighth squad was located. She said to her mother, "I have something to do!"

She then courageously walked toward San Mou Dike. She had suddenly matured and become more wise from what had just happened. All of a sudden it seemed to be a reasonable thing to redress the injustice done to Young Leopard. Before she had abhorred this idea. Now she believed that Rong Shuxu could explain this change in her heart. He knew so much. Why should Huangmei doubt it if he had so much faith in this document about better lives for the peasants? She was certain he could help her understand herself.

A breeze blowing over the surface of San Mou Pond warmed her for a moment, caressing the withered grass and drying her tears. "Has Spring really come?" she thought. "Has Spring finally come to this corner fogotten by love?"

"Can't the right side and the wrong side serve the same purpose? Can't comedy and tragedy express the same elevated thought? By analyzing the hearts of the shameless ones, couldn't we delineate the image of those with high ideals? Doesn't all this violation of law and discipline and scandalous behavior tell us the meaning of law, duty and justice?" — Gogol: *In Front of the Theatre Doors*

If I Were For Real

A Play in Six Acts

SHA YEXIN, LI SHOUCHENG, YAO MINGDE

CAST OF CHARACTERS:

Zhao *Director of the Drama Troupe*
Qian *Chief of the Political Branch of the Organization Department*
Sun *Chief of the Cultural Bureau*
Li *Li Xiaozhang, an "educated youth" now working on a state farm*
Zhou *Zhou Minghua, his girl friend; a cotton mill worker in the city*
Wu *Secretary of the Municipal Party Committee*
Zheng *Director of Haidong State Farm*
Juanjuan *Chief Sun's daughter*
Mr. Zhang* *Responsible cadre of the Central Party Disciplinary Commission*
Officer *Public Security Officer*
A,B,C,D,E *Theatre-goers*
Theatre attendants
Middle-aged man who answers phone
Restaurant Workers
First and Second Youths
Judge
Jurors
Public Prosecutor

*"Mr. Zhang" is a rather inappropriate way of translating the Chinese phrase used in the original, "Zhang Lao," a highly respectful term of address which carries much more weight than "Lao Zhang" (Old Zhang). For socio-political reasons, the term "Mister" has generally not been used in China since 1949 except for addressing foreigners and overseas Chinese.

261

PROLOGUE:

Drama is based on life. Our play comes out of real life experience; it begins with the actual conditions in which we find ourselves in.

Our loyal, beloved audience has poured into the theatre from all directions. Naturally, they know nothing about the play they have come to see. Some are sitting in their seats leafing through the playbill they purchased, hoping to understand something of the plot beforehand. Some are crowded in the lobby, chatting with their companions, talking about the content of the play...smoking, eating ice cream, content and carefree, unwilling to tax their brains over anything.

In a few moments, at the urging of a bell the audience will file to their seats. They will sit, some attentive, some casually waiting for the curtain to rise.

Finally it's curtain time! The lights fade, the music begins, the audience's eyes are fixed on the stage. Suddenly, the music stops, the lights come on again and the voice of Miss Zhao, director of the drama troupe, is heard from behind the curtain, shouting: "Close it, close it; wait a bit before you raise it." The main curtain, which was just raised a crack, closes again. In a few moments Miss Zhao comes to the front of the stage.

Zhao: Comrades, we're terribly sorry! Two leading comrades and an honored guest haven't arrived yet. I'm afraid we'll have to ask you to wait a bit longer. This often happens here; it's nothing out of the ordinary. But please don't worry, the play will go on. When they come we'll start immediately. We're terribly sorry, terribly sorry.

The troupe director finishes speaking and disappears behind the curtain. And how does the audience react? Do they voice impatient complaints, censures, scolding? Each audience has its own way of expressing how it feels about unfortunate events like this one.

After some commotion, the troupe director again sticks her head out from behind the curtain and looks toward the entrance. Suddenly her face begins to glow with pleasant surprise. Naturally, the audience follows her gaze.

There appears at the theatre entrance the wife of the secretary of the Municipal Party Committee, Section Chief Qian, a woman of uncommon bearing who is also a chief of the political section of the Municipal Party Organization Department, and the solemn, cautious Mr. Sun, chief of the Cultural Bureau. The audience is bound to think that these are the honored guests they have been waiting for, but they are mistaken. The cause of the delay is only a young man. At present his name is Zhang Xiaoli, but in actuality it's Li Xiaozhang. Chief Qian and Bureau Chief Sun behave courteously and humbly to Li Xiaozhang, saying, "After you! Please sit down," as they escort him directly to the three empty seats in the first row near the middle aisle. Once they are seated Zhao's voice is heard from behind the curtain, "They've arrived, let's get ready to begin."

The music starts again.

Suddenly two gun-toting public security officers enter the theatre, rushing straight to Li Xiaozhang's seat.

Officer: (to Li Xiaozhang) Li Xiaozhang, you're under arrest!

Qian: (greatly startled) What? His name's not Li Xiaozhang! You can't just arrest anyone you please.

Officer: Here's the warrant!
(The other officer handcuffs Li Xiaozhang.)

Sun: Let him go! You've made a mistake. Don't you know who he is?!

Officer: Who do you think he is?

Sun: His name's Zhang Xiaoli!

Qian: He's the son of a senior officer of the Central Committee!

Officer: No, he's an imposter!

Qian, Sun: Huh?

(Troupe Leader Zhao runs out to the front of the stage.)

Zhao: Aiya, What's this? What's this? How can we put on the play with this happening? (to the officer) Comrade, please explain this to everyone, what's going on here, after all?

Officer: All right!

(The two security officers, Li Xiaozhang, Section Chief Qian and Bureau Chief Sun all mount the stage.)

Officer: Comrades, I'm terribly sorry to bother you all, but this man is an imposter. His real name is Li Xiaozhang, alias Zhang Xiaoli. He really works on a state farm, but has been passing himself off as the son of a senior cadre of the Central

Committee and engaging in other fraudulent activity. We're here to arest him before he gets away.

Zhao: What! (to Li) Is this true?

Li: Aren't you putting on a play? Well, so am I. My play is finished now; but you can continue with yours.

Zhao: Huh?

Qian, Sun: You??!

Sun: Damn!

(Spotlights play over the faces of Li, Zhao, Sun and Qian, one after the other, then the lights go out.)

ACT ONE

Toward evening one day in the first half of 1979. The main entrance of a theatre. (If this play is fortunate enough to be performed in a theatre, then the scenery for this act would be exactly the same as the main entrance to that theatre, or, at least, very like it.) There is a large poster announcing the current play on one of the walls:

XX Drama Troupe Presents the Russian Satire
THE INSPECTOR GENERAL

There is also a picture of the author, Gogol, on the poster.

Obviously there are no seats left. A number of people are gathered at the door, hoping for tickets. They hold their money ready. When someone comes they ask eagerly, "Are you returning a ticket?" If there's a ticket available, a great crowd of people surges forward, competing for it. The successful ones are wildly happy, express their gratitude over and over and enter the theatre with pleasure. The losers are disappointed but don't give up, and keep on with their inquiries. This scene should be played extremely true to life so the audience will feel its reality, almost as if they have mounted the stage themselves.

Li Xiaozhang enters, wearing an old army uniform with a military bag slung over one shoulder. He's blowing smoke rings. He gazes indifferently at the others in the crowd, then throws his cigarette butt down and feels for something in his pocket. *A* promptly comes over.

A: (eagerly) Have you got a ticket?

Li: A ticket?

A: Yeah.

Li: (in a drawn tone) Yes!

A: (overjoyed) That's great!

(When the surrounding crowd hears that Li has a ticket, they immediately surround him, shouting: "Let me have it, give it to me! I want it, I want it!" Unable to hold his own, Li retreats steadily toward the wall.)

A: It should be mine. I was here first!

B: I'll swap you ten movie tickets for it!

C: Let me have it, let me have it. I'll give you three *yuan* for it, how's that?

Li: Be quiet! There's one for everyone. Line up!

(a flap begins as everyone clamors to form a long line in front of Li Xiaozhang)

Li: Don't worry. Don't worry! I have lots of tickets. There's one for everyone, enough for the whole country. I have them all!

A: What?

B: The entire country?

C: What tickets are you talking about?

Li: (bringing out a wallet from which he takes several tickets) Here, food coupons!

A: Huh?

B: What kind of stunt are you pulling?

Li: What? Aren't food coupons tickets too? They're the most important tickets. Without them, you'd go hungry!

C: Damn you!

D: Let's beat this guy up!

Li: (not batting an eye) Dare to come and try? Huh?

B: Forget it, forget it. Let's go.

(They break up unhappily.)

A: Comrade, you shouldn't have deceived them!

Li: It was just a joke! A little joke doesn't hurt anyone. Aren't people deceived by the theatre, too? There are so many real situations in the world that people aren't interested in.

They'd rather come see a false drama in a theatre. Aren't they being cheated here as well?

A: A lot you know! The play being given here today is the world famous *The Inspector General.*

Li: Oh? *The Inspector General?* Any good?

A: It's extremely interesting! It tells about an ordinary civil official of the twelfth rank from St. Petersburg in Russia. He's passing through a city and the mayor of this city thinks he's an inspector general. He fawns on him and toadies to him, showering him with gifts and money. He even wants to give him his daughter in marriage. People laugh until their sides split, watching it.

Li: Oh? Then this inspector general is a fake?

A: He's an imposter!

(Li immediately walks over to the poster and reads it with great interest. After a moment, he takes a look at his watch, looks off into the distance and then continues to read the poster. Presently, Zhou Minghua, carrying a purse, hurries up.)

Zhou: Li Xiaozhang!

Li: Minghua! You're late again!

Zhou: My father wouldn't let me go out.

Li: That old fool.

Zhou: Where do you have any right...

Li: He IS an old fool, I tell you. When I went to your place just a while ago, he wouldn't see me!

Zhou: You can't speak about my father that way! (She takes a bottle of Mao Tai liquor out of her purse.) Here. Daddy told me to give it back to you.

Li: (surprised) Huh? He drank it!

Zhou: He drank what? He didn't drink any of it!

Li: (taking the bottle) Oh...

Zhou: What were you doing buying such good Mao Tai for him?

Li: Flattering my future father-in-law a bit.

Zhou: You're really extravagant buying such an expensive liquor!

Li: It's fake.

Zhou: What? Fake?

Li: Could I afford the real thing? The bottle is genuine, bought in a second-hand stall for two *jiao*. It's filled with cheap liquor.

Zhou: Oh? Weren't you afraid my father would notice?

Li: People only notice what is on the surface. Your father is no different.

Zhou: Why did you do it?

Li: To please your father. For you and me.

Zhou: Then you'd better hurry and get transferred off the farm. Otherwise, no matter what you give him, my father will never consent.

Li: (agitated) What a pain!

Zhou: I'm trying to think of a way out for you too. Actually, you're clever and capable enough yourself. You think of something! Others have been transferred; why can't you be? Haven't a lot of my classmates been transferred recently?

Li: What do their fathers do?

Zhou: One is the secretary of a factory party committee, one is the deputy commanding officer of the fleet, and one girl's father is a bureau chief with theCultural Bureau.

Li: Well of course they get transferred! But what does my father do? (sticks out his thumb and speaks in an ironic tone) He's a member of the leading class—the working class. A selfless worker! Worthless! I should have been transferred the year before last. They're the ones who squeezed me out!

Zhou: Damn. If you had an important father, everything would be O.K.

Li: Next time I'm up for reincarnation, remind me to check and see if my father is a high cadre or not. If not, I'd rather die in the womb!

Zhou: Stop that stupid talk! The best thing to do is to think of a way to be transferred here. You know it can't be put off any longer, don't you?

Li: O.K. O.K. Getting excited won't help. Let's try to come up with two tickets and go in to see the play.

Zhou: I can't; I sneaked out.

Li: Won't you go with me?

Zhou: I'm afraid my father will find out.

Li: It's up to you!

   (She hesitates, but finally leaves. Li wants to follow her but is checked by a car driving up. We see two beams of light from the headlights and hear the sound of its brakes. At the same time, Zhao races out of the theatre dispersing the surrounding crowd. Presently Bureau Chief Sun and his daughter Juanjuan enter. Zhao goes forward promptly to meet them. Li Xiaozhang stares coldly from the sidelines.)

Zhao: (warmly) Aiya! Bureau Chief Sun is here. (shaking hands) How are you?

Sun: Hello.

Zhao: How have you been lately?

Sun: Pretty well.

Zhao: Well, you should still take care! And is this Juanjuan?

Sun: Say hello to Auntie Zhao.

Juanjuan: Auntie Zhao!

Zhao: Aiya! She's so pretty! Were you transferred here from the farm?

Juanjuan: Quite a while ago.

Zhao: And your husband?

Juanjuan: Still in the Northeast.

Zhao: Aiya! A young couple shouldn't be living in two different places!

Juanjuan: Daddy is trying to work on it for me.

Sun: Says who? What nonsense!

Juanjuan: (in a low voice to Zhao) He's the one who's talking nonsense!

Zhao: (smiling) Please come in! (takes out two tickets) Here are the tickets we've saved for you.

   (Another car drives up. Headlights and the sound of brakes again. Zhao and Sun pause, looking at the car.)

Sun: Who's in that car?

Zhao: It looks like Chief Qian of the Organization Department.

Sun: Chief Qian?

Zhao: The wife of Secretary Wu of the Municipal Party Committee.

Sun: Ah...yes, yes!

Zhao: (showing off) We were in the Revolution together. We're very close.

(Section Chief Qian enters.)

Zhao: (immediately goes forward to welcome her) Aiya. Qian, what brings you here?

Qian: Zhao, have you forgotten about me? You didn't invite me to see the play.

Zhao: I thought of asking you several times but was afraid you were too busy. Do you want to see it tonight?

Qian: Are there any tickets?

Zhao: There's always a ticket for you. You may have as many as you want.

Qian: I just need one.

Zhao: Isn't Secretary Wu coming?

Qian: Does he have time to see plays? He's busy all day long. I tell him to take it easy, but he just won't do it. He says he wants to make up for the time lost due to the Gang of Four!

Zhao: Secretary Wu works too hard.

Sun; Please go in, Chief Qian, the play is about to begin.

Qian: And this is...

Sun: I'm with the Cultural Bureau.

Zhao: Bureau Chief Sun. Don't you know each other?

Qian: Oh, yes! Your supervisor! I haven't seen you in ten years. Your hair's gone white!

Zhao: Bureau Chief Sun, you go in with Chief Qian. I'm still waiting for Department Head Ma.

Qian; Which Ma is that?

Zhao: Of the Municipal Propaganda Department.

Qian: Oh, Old Ma, he's going abroad tomorrow on a fact-finding tour. He won't be coming.

Zhao: Oh, well, let's go in then!

Qian: After you!

(Chief Qian and Bureau Chief Sun enter through the main theatre entrance. Troupe Director Zhao is stopped by a call from Li Xiaozhang who has been listening to their conversation throughout.)

Li: Comrade!

Zhao: What is it?

Li: Do you have any extra tickets?

Zhao: No, none!

Li: Isn't that one in your hand?

Zhao: This ticket is reserved for a senior official.

Li: That department head you were just talking about isn't coming, is he?

Zhao: Even if he doesn't show up, I can't sell it.

Li: If it's an extra, why not sell it?

Zhao: I'm keeping it for a senior official.

Li: That young woman who just went in — was she a senior official, too?

Zhao: Her father is. Is yours?

(Troupe Director Zhao goes in.)

Li: Damn her. Even to see a play you've got to have an important
father.

(Li Xiaozhang starts to leave, but stops before the poster and
looks at it, unwilling to go now. He ponders a moment, then
walks over the left side of stage where there's a telephone,
picks up the receiver and dials a number.)

Li: Hello, I'd like to speak to someone backstage. This is Department Head Ma of the Municipal Propaganda Department.
That's right; I'd like to speak to Troupe Director Zhao. O.K.
(waits a moment) Yes, yes it's me. Is that Troupe Director
Zhao? I'm leaving on a fact-finding tour tomorrow, so I can't
come to see your play tonight — Did Secretary Wu's wife
mention it to you? Oh good. I'd like to bother you for a favor
— the son of an old comrade of mine from Beijing is very
eager to see your play. He called me amoment ago to say he
couldn't get a ticket. Could you help him out? No problem?
Good. He only wants one ticket — his name is Zhang, Zhang
Xiaoli — wait for him at the entrance, he's in the neighborhood. I'll tell him to go right over.

Li Xiaozhang hangs up the phone and stands at one side,
leaning against the wall, eyeing the main entrance. Presently
Zhao scurries out carrying a ticket and stands gazing into the
crowd. After a moment she goes up to theatre-goer *D*.)

Zhao: What's your name, comrade?

D: Wu. Why do you want to know?

Zhao: Oh, excuse me!

(She approaches theatre-goer *E*.)

Zhao: What's your name, comrade?

E: It's Ji. Have you got a ticket?

Zhao: No, no...

(Zhao looks at her watch very anxiously. Li walks over to her.)

Li: Comrade, are you Troupe Director Zhao?

Zhao: That's right; and you're...?

Li: I'm Zhang Xiaoli.

Zhao: (startled) Oh, it's you?

Li: That's right. Did Department Head Ma phone you?

Zhao: Yes, yes. Aiya. Why didn't you mention it before? I misunderstood you! Such a small matter, actually you really didn't need to bother Department Head Ma. Next time just come directly to me.

Li: But that's too much trouble for you!

Zhao: Now that Department Head Ma introduced you, it's quite proper; uh, your father and Department Head Ma...

Li: They're old army buddies.

Zhao: Oh. Please, after you!

(Zhao invites Li into the theatre. From now on Li Xiaozhang is Zhang Xiaoli.)

E: Hey, how did that guy get in?

Zhao: His father's a senior official. What about yours?

Curtain

ACT TWO

Evening of the same day, following the play. The VIP lounge. Doors on the right and left, one leading to the seating area, the other backstage. Single and double sofas are arranged along the walls. Photographs from *The Inspector General* hang on a wall. On another, there's a poster advertising the play. As the curtain rises the sounds of enthusiastic applause and of people leaving the theatre can be heard. Presently, Zhao enters from the theatre leading Zhang Xiaoli.

Zhao: (warmly) Come on in. Come in and relax! Sit anywhere you like. Our performance standards are very low compared with Beijing's, aren't they?

(A theatre attendant enters with two glasses of tea, gives them to Zhao and Zhang, and then leaves).

Zhao: Little Zhang, what did you think of the play? Let's have your opinion.

Zhang: (sincerely) Not bad, not bad. I've really never seen such a good play.

Zhao: But do give us your sincere opinion!

Zhang: Really, it was quite good. Ah, I have to go.

Zhao: Stay a while longer.

Zhang: I have to get back.

Zhao: Don't go, don't go! I was just talking to Chief Qian and Bureau Chief Sun. Perhaps they'll come by to meet you.

Zhang: (startled) They want to meet me?

Zhao: They're backstage greeting the actors right now. They'll be here in a moment.

Zhang: No, no, leading cadres are all so busy. I don't want to bother them.

Zhao: Wait a bit. Come, have a bite to eat. (She puts some food in front of Zhang.) Eat, eat. Why don't you have something!

(Zhang can't help but sit down and eat something, though he is a bit uneasy.)

Zhao: How's the weather in Beijing?

Zhang: Bad. Snowing.

Zhao: Does it even snow on hot days?

Zhang: No, no, in the winter. It's the same all over, it snows in the winter.

Zhao: Right, right. Did you come down on official business?

Zhang: No, I hate official business. It's terribly annoying.

Zhao: Then you came to see friends?

Zhang: That's right, to see a friend.

Zhao: And for what else? What other business do you have here?

Zhang: (guardedly) Nothing. I don't have any other purpose. I came looking for you with nothing more in mind than seeing the play.

Zhao: No, what I meant was, other than seeing your friends, what else do you have on your schedule?

Zhang: Nothing. I just want to have fun and see a few plays.

Zhao: See some plays? I have lots of tickets. Oh yes, (brings out some tickets) here are some for restricted movies — American, Japanese, French. They are all for next week. Take them all.

Zhang: (overjoyed) Wonderful! How much?

Zhao: You've come all the way from Beijing, I can't take your money too!

Zhang: Why not?

Zhao: I can afford to treat you to a few movies.

Zhang: (accepting the tickets) How can I accept? (taking the Mao Tai from his pocket) I really didn't bring anything good with me, but I'd like you to have this, Auntie Zhao.

Zhao: Mao Tai?

Zhang: It's nothing.

Zhao: I'm not much of a drinker.

Zhang: Then keep it to give to someone else. Take it. Next time I want to see a play, I'll have to bother you again.

Zhao: (taking the liquor) But I'm embarrassed to take it. Did you buy it in the guest house?

Zhang: No, you can't get it there. This is special. It's for export.

Zhao: Oh? Then it must be superior to most Mao Tai?

Zhang: At the very least the taste is a bit different.

Zhao: Does your father drink this high quality Mao Tai regularly?

Zhang: Yes, at least thirty bottles a month!

Zhao: Oh, your father is...

Zhang: Are you asking about my father?

Zhao: Is it confidential?

Zhang: No, not for you.

Zhao: Then who is he?

Zhang: Take a guess — the name is Zhang.

Zhao: Is it Zhang Jinfu?

(Zhang Xiaoli smiles mysteriously and shakes his head.)

Zhang Qilong?

(Zhang shakes his head.)

Zhang Dingcheng?

(shakes his head)

It's not...Comrade Zhang Tingfa?

(shakes his head)

Oh — Zhang Wentian! No, no he's dead. Zhang...of course, Zhang, Zhang Caiqian!

(shakes his head)

Then who is it?

Zhang: Guess. Anyway, it certainly isn't Zhang Chunqiao.

Zhao: Of course not, of course not, then...which high-level cadre is it?

Zhang: No, he's an ordinary cadre.

Zhao: Impossible, impossible. It has to be a high-level cadre! (suddenly excited) Oh, it has to be...

Zhang: Who?

Zhao: It's...(leans over and whispers in Zhang's ear) Right?

Zhang: What do you think?

Zhao: It has to be. It has to be!

Zhang: (laughing) If you say so!

Zhao: (delighted) Ah! It's really him. Aiyaya, you have such a good father. You're really lucky.

Zhang: Yes, the sad thing is that not everyone has such a good father.

Zhao: Your father's not only Department Head Ma's old chief, he knows our Secretary Wu pretty well too.

Zhang: Secretary Wu?

Zhao: Don't you know him? He is secretary of the Municipal Party Committee.

Zhang: Oh, Secretary Wu of the Municipal Party Committee. I've heard my father speak of him.

Zhao: I've heard Secretary Wu wife's, Qian, say that in the summer of 1953, Secretary Wu went to Beijing for a meeting and went to your house to see your father. You must have still been a baby then? Secretary Wu presented your father with a rare cactus. Your father noticed that Secretary Wu was a heavy smoker and gave him two cartons of *3/5* brand cigarettes. She said Secretary Wu hasn't seen your father in over twenty years. Yes, I'll tell her right away. She'll certainly be pleased to know you're here. You wait.

(Zhao exits through the backstage door.

Zhang Xiaoli shakes his head in the direction of Zhao's exit, then takes a cigarette from the pack on the table and puts it in his shirt pocket, preparing to slip out. He softly opens the door to the theatre and is just about to go out when a look out the door causes him to withdraw promptly into the room again.

Qian and Sun enter.

Zhang Xiaoli goes forward to greet them in an extremely confident manner.)

Zhang: Auntie Qian!

Qian: (taken aback) You...

Zhang: I'm the one Department Head Ma introduced to come and see the play.

Qian: Oh, I've heard. Where's Troup Director Zhao.

Zhang: Auntie Zhao said she was going to find you.

Qian: Sit down, sit down.

Zhang: How's Uncle Wu?

Qian: Fine.

Zhang: Is he still such a heavy smoker?

Qian: (surprised) You little devil, how did you know?

Zhang: My father told me. My father has already given up smoking. He said to tell Uncle Wu to cut down too.

Qian: (perplexed) Your father? Oh. How is he?

Zhang: Fine. He's just too busy, that's all. He doesn't have time for his plants anymore. However, my father has always liked the rare cactus Uncle Wu gave him when he was in Beijing in '53.

Qian: (highly pleased) Ah, then you're...Aiya, why didn't you say so! No wonder you even knew Secretary Wu was a heavy smoker! (Sun turns inquiringly to Qian, who whispers in his ear.)

Sun: (extremely surprised) Oh?

(Sun then sits down off to one side.)

Qian: Wonderful, wonderful! Come, come over here. (pulls Zhang over to sit next to her) Which one are you?

Zhang: In '53, when Uncle Wu came to Beijing, I was still a baby.

Qian: Then you're the fifth!

Zhang: That's right. That's me.

Qian: What is your name, son?

Zhang: It's Zhang Xiaoli — call me whatever you like. Call me Little Zhang, or call me by my first name, Xiaoli.

(Troupe Director Zhao hurries through the backstage door.)

Zhao: Qian...oh, you've already met?

Qian: And why not? Secretary Wu met his father over twenty years ago. Secretary Wu has even been to his home. Do you know whose child he is?

Zhao: Yes, I'm the one who guessed it!

Qian: You don't need to guess. You can tell by looking at him. Doesn't he resemble his father?

Sun: He does, he really does! Why, they look exactly the same!

Qian: Auntie Zhao, he's my guest — mine and Secretary Wu's. You must invite him to see more plays.

Zhang: Auntie Qian, you have things to do; I have to go.

Qian: Don't be in such a hurry!

Zhang: I have to fly back to Beijing first thing tomorrow.

Qian: Stay a little longer!

Zhao: You have several restricted movies to see next week —

Zhang: I'll fly back again then. Auntie Qian, I'll come to see you next time.

Qian: Stay longer. (She pulls him down beside her.) I haven't had a chance to chat with you yet. What brings you here?

Zhao: He came to see friends.

Qian: Male or female?

Zhang: Like me — male.

Zhao: Don't kid us, Little Zhang!

Zhang: I've never teased anyone.

Qian: Where is your friend?

Zhang: He is living at HAidong State Farm.

Qian: Oh, hasn't he been transferred yet?

Zhang: His father is just an ordinary worker. There's no way for him to be transferred. I'm really anxious about him!

Zhao: Well, you can use your father's influence.

Zhang: But my father doesn't know the director of the farm.

Zhao: (remembers suddenly) Bureau Chief Sun, aren't you and the farm director, Old Zheng, old warbuddies?

Sun: Ah...yes, that's right.

Zhao: Then, you ask Bureau Chief Sun to see Zheng, Little Zhang. Ask him to take care of it.

Sun: (a troubled expression on his face) Well...

(Troupe Director Zhao motions to Zhang to explain to Chief Qian.)

Zhang: Auntie Qian, do you think we can bother Uncle Sun with this?

Qian: Old Sun, can't you go to see him?

Sun: (promptly agrees) O.K., O.K., I'll try. Uh, what's his name?

Zhang: It's Li, Li Xiaozhang. He's in Company 57.

Sun: (writing it down) O.K.

Zhang: (extremely pleased, but doesn't show it) Wonderful, if Uncle Sun can really help him with this transfer problem, then I won't go back to Beijing just yet!

Qian: Right, wait here, enjoy yourself a few more days.

Zhang: Uncle Sun, when do you think I'll hear from you?

Sun: Uh — come to my place in a week.

Zhang: O.K., I certainly will.

Qian: Right. Where are you staying, Little Zhang?

Zhang: (without thinking) Nanhu Guest House.

Qian: Which room?

Zhang: 102.

Qian: Since you're not going back to Beijing just yet, why don't you stay at my house?

Zhang: No, no, no, the guest house is fine.

Qian: So is my house.

Zhang: Cancelling the room now would be too much trouble. Let's forget it.

Qian: It's no trouble. (picks up the telephone) I'll talk to them!

Zhang: (quickly takes the receiver) I'll do it, you sit down.

Qian: Do you know the number?

Zhang: Yes!

(He arbitrarily dials a number. A telephone appears at one side of the stage and a middle-aged man answers it.)

Zhang: Hello, Nanhu Guest House?

Man: What? Nanhu Guest House? No, no, this is the funeral parlor.

Zhang: (nods to Qian that he's gotten through) This is Zhang Xiaoli in room 102.

Man: You've got the wrong number. This is the funeral parlor!

Zhang: Oh it's old Guan! No nothing else. I won't be staying there tonight.

Man: (to himself) Huh? Since when is my name Guan? (to the receiver) My name's Li!

Zhang: Oh, you say not to bother about the suitcases?

Man: (unsure whether to laugh or cry) Uh? (to receiver, losing his temper) Did you have too much to drink or what. What are you up to, playing jokes in the middle of the night?

Zhang: A letter? No letters from my father? A telegram then? Oh, no telegram either.

Man: (shouts) You must be crazy!

(the sound of the telephone being hung up is heard.)

Zhang: Don't be polite. Thank you, thank you. (hangs up) The service is really good there!

Zhao: It's a high class place!

Qian: (stands up) Let's go, Little Zhang.

Zhang: O.K. Uncle Sun, I'll expect to hear from you in a week.

Sun: O.K., O.K.

(Zhang pats Bureau Chief Sun on the back excitedly, then, suddenly becoming conscious of his duplicity, he hurriedly withdraws his hand and laughs in embarrassment.)

Curtain

ACT THREE

One morning a week later.

The living room in Bureau Chief Sun's home. There are doors on either side, one leading to the bedroom, the other to the kitchen. A door in the center leads to the hall and the yard. In the living room there is a color TV, a radio, a sofa, rattan chairs, tables, a telephone, etc.

When the curtain rises a barefoot Zhou Minghua, pants rolled up, is on her hands and knees washing the floor. Obviously she has been at it a long time; the sweat is pouring down her face. She feels a sudden urge to vomit, but checks it desperately, rests a moment and then continues to scrub the floor. Sun enters from the hall.

Sun: (dissatisfied) Aiyaya. This is a parquet floor. Why are you using water on it?

(Zhou Minghua is stunned and doesn't know what to do.)

Sun: And I'm having guests for lunch today. Just look. Bah! Leave it now, leave it.

(Minghua picks up the mop and pail and leaves by the door on the right.

Juanjuan enters through another door carrying a book.)

Juanjuan: Daddy, you're back?

Sun: Did you just get up?

Juanjuan: No, I was up at nine, but I've been lying in bed reading a novel.

Sun: You really know how to take it easy. Juanjuan, your mother's not home. Did you hire a servant?

Juanjuan: No.

Sun: Then who was just washing the floor?

Juanjuan: Oh, she's just a classmate of mine.

Sun: A classmate?

Juanjuan: She's really competent. She can do any kind of work, skilled or unskilled. Just look. (points to the skirt she's wearing) This is the skirt she made for me yesterday, and she said she wants to knit me a sweater, too.

Sun: Oh. Why have I never seen her here before?

Juanjuan: The reason she came is that she wants to ask you for help.

Sun: (disgusted) I'm busy enough as it is!

(Minghua enters carrying a large basin of clothes with both hands.

Juanjuan: Minghua, come here, I'll introduce you. This is my father.

Zhou: How do you do, Uncle Sun.

Juanjuan: This is Zhou Minghua. She was transferred from the farm last year and is now assigned to the textile factory as a worker.

Sun: Oh, a moment ago, I thought...(points to the basin of clothes) Put it down, put it down. Let Juanjuan wash them.

Juanjuan: Aiya. How could I wash so much? I've told you to buy a washing machine, but you still haven't done it. Just send them out to the laundry then!

Zhou: (afraid of losing the opportunity to wash the clothes) No, no! I'll do it!

(She is about to leave with the clothes.)

Juanjuan: Wait a minute, Minghua. Daddy!

Sun: What?

Juanjuan: Minghua has a boyfriend on a farm that she has known for a long time. They want to get married, but her father won't agree. He'll only consent if the boy is transferred here from the farm. Daddy, I really feel sorry for her. Can't you help her out?

Sun: She's your classmate. You go point out to her father where his thinking is wrong. Tell him his view is incorrect, that now in our country there aren't any high or low positions. Any job, whether it's on the farm or in the city, has the goal of serving the people. All jobs have a future.

Juanjuan: You make it seem so simple, but who'll listen to that sort of talk anymore?

Sun: Then your friend should wait two years or so. The boy will probably be transferred sooner or later!

Zhou: Uncle Sun, it can't wait any longer...

Sun: You're still young. You should be putting all your energies into work and study!

Juanjuan: Daddy, don't be like this! You know Director Zheng at Haidong Farm, don't you? Have a word with him. You could even call him.

Sun: How can you ask me to do something like this? I'm a government official! How could I do something so unscrupulous!

Zhou: Let it go, Juanjuan. Let's not make things difficult for Uncle Sun.

Juanjuan: He's just putting on airs. All right then! (takes the basin of clothes from Zhou and stuffs it into Bureau Chief Sun's hands) You go wash these clothes! She's done so much for us these last two days! Was it all for nothing?

Sun: You, you! O.K. Let's not talk about it right now. (takes Juanjuan to one side) I'm having guests in a little while. People from Beijing like to eat steamed bread. Go and buy some for me.

Juanjuan: It's too far to go. I won't do it!

Sun: We have the car!

Juanjuan: I want to read!

Zhou: What is it, Juanjuan?

Juanjuan: He wants me to go buy steamed bread!

Zhou: Uncle Sun, there's no need to buy it. I can make it!

Sun: Oh, that's good, that's good. Go into the kitchen and make it then, but it has to be finished by lunchtime.

Zhou: O.K.

Juanjuan: Minghua, you're really great!

(Minghua leaves by the door on the right.)

Juanjuan: And Daddy, you're really terrible. Other people help you, but you won't help them.

Sun: Juanjuan, from now on when you're talking in front of anyone but the family, you have to be careful what kind of impression you're making.

Juanjuan: Everything I said is true!

Sun: You must also consider the situation you're speaking in.

Juanjuan: Even when one speaks the truth? And under what circumstances is it all right to lie then?

Sun: Who tells lies?

Juanjuan: You do. I hear you telling lies everyday!

Sun: You, you're getting more and more impossible! Wait until your mother gets back. She'll discipline you.

Juanjuan: I'm not afraid of Mama. You're the one who's frightened of her!

Sun: Oh you, you! I don't know what to do with you, I really don't! (He shakes his head helplessly and leaves through the door on the left.)

(Juanjuan sits on the sofa, reading.)

Juanjuan: Minghua, what are you doing?

Zhou's voice: Kneading the dough.

Juanjuan: Come out and sit with me.

(Minghua comes out, face covered with flour.)

Juanjuan: Minghua, my mother's not at home, so I'm counting on you for everything!

Zhou: It's nothing. All I ask is for your father to get my boyfriend transferred here, then I'll do anything for you and your family!

Juanjuan: Don't worry, my father is only pseudo-scrupulous. Right now he's busy with my problem. When he's finished with that, I'll speak to him again.

Zhou: What problem do you have? Weren't you transferred a long time ago?

Juanjuan: Yes, but there's still my husband — he's in the Northeast. My mother went there a few days ago, with a letter my father got someone to write. She went to see the leader of my husband's unit to get him transferred back here.

Zhou: Any chance he will be?

Juanjuan: Well, there's always my father's influence.

Zhou: I really envy you!

Juanjuan: Your boyfriend can get trasnferred too, Minghua. I still haven't met him. Is he good-looking?

Zhou: (shyly) Just ordinary.

Juanjuan: Are you madly in love with him?

Zhou: I was at first.

Juanjuan: At first?

Zhou: When he first came to the farm he was wonderful. He had ideals and he was bright, too — he could learn any language quickly. But later the farm became a mess. Everyone who could find a way out left. Last year, according to government policy, he should have been transferred back to the city, but wouldn't you know it, he was squeezed out by someone else. After that he got very dejected, then he began to smoke and drink, he got worse and worse...

Juanjuan: So now you don't love him anymore?

Zhou: No I still do...but he could still change for the better.

(Troupe Director Zhao enters from the hall.)

Zhao: Juanjuan!

Juanjuan: Auntie Zhao!

(Minghua leaves.)

Zhao: Here, I've brought you some tickets.

Juanjuan: Wonderful!

Zhao: (takes out several tickets) They're all for restricted foreign films.

Juanjuan: (takes the tickets) Do you have any more?

Zhao: Greedy, aren't you! There are over three hundred members in our troupe and we receive only ten tickets for each film. We have to draw lots everytime and a fierce argument always breaks out. All the same, I have given you two tickets and you're still not satisfied?

Juanjuan: Thank you, Auntie Zhao!

Zhao: Where is your father?

Juanjuan: Inside. (calls) Daddy, Auntie Zhao is here!

(Juanjuan leaves. Sun enters through the door on the left.)

Sun: (coldly) Huh? What are you doing here today?

Zhao: Didn't you say you'd have an answer for that Little Zhang from Beijing in a week?

Sun: (unhappily) Are you interested in that too?

Zhao: I'd like to do my bit for him too. Everyone knows I'm warmhearted. (takes the Mao Tai liquor from her bag) I asked someone to get this for you.

Sun: (pleased, but affecting severity) What did you do that for?

Zhao: I'm not much of a drinker. What use is it sitting at home? I know you like to drink, so I brought it over.

Sun: I really don't like it when people do this kind of thing.

Zhao: Of course, if it were some other liquor I wouldn't have brought it, but this is no ordinary Mao Tai — this is special, made just for export. There are probably special ingredients in it.

Sun: Oh, special? Not ordinary Mao Tai?

Zhao: How could it be? I asked a lot of people. It wasn't easy to get.

Sun: Then...then keep it! But, if you'll let me pay you, I'll take it.

Zhao: If you give me money I'll take it back.

Sun: (laughing) O.K., O.K., we'll talk about it later!

(He takes the Mao Tai and puts it in a cabinet.)

Zhao: How have you done with Little Zhang's problem?

Sun: We'll talk about it when he comes.

Zhao: (prying) Has Juanjuan's husband been transferred back from the Northeast?

Sun: Don't listen to her nonsense. I have nothing to do with these things.

(Pause)

Zhao: Bureau Chief Sun, about my housing problem...

Sun: Haven't I told you? I can't do anything about it.

Zhao: But you're a bureau chief!

Sun: Your place is perfectly fine. Why do you want a larger one? You're a party cadre; you shouldn't be particular about a little hard work and plain living.

Zhao: But some of those who were in the Revolution with me are already in places measuring over seventy square meters.

Sun: There are always inequities.

Zhao: Bureau Chief Sun...

Sun: Why don't you go to your own organization, the Municipal Party Propaganda Department?

Zhao: (brings out a report) I've written a report, I wanted to ask you to pass it on to Department Head Ma.

Sun: Department Head Ma is abroad.

Zhao: Give it to his secretary first.

Sun: That won't do.If I send it on for you, they'll think I'm recommending it. I think it's better to wait awhile and see what happens.

Zhao: But aren't you doing something for Little Zhang?

Sun: The Municipal Party Committee secretary's wife is taking care of that personally. If this affair of yours had the nod from the higher-ups, then I could handle it for you.

Zhao: But Chief Sun...

(The telephone rings and Sun is about to answerit when Juanjuan runs in through the door on the right.)

Juanjuan: I'll get it Father. (picks up the phone) That's right. Yes. O.K. (excitedly to Sun) Father, it's mama calling long distance from the Northeast.

Sun: Don't make such a racket. (to Zhao) Why don't you go inside and have a seat?

Zhao: O.K., O.K. (takes her time getting up and suddenly deliberately turns her ankle) Aiyo! (takes the opportunity to fall back onto the sofa) Aiyo!

Sun: What is it!

Zhao: I wrenched my ankle.

Sun: Are you alright?

Juanjuan: Is it serious?

Zhao: I need to rub it a bit.

(She rubs her foot obstinately. Sun is burning with impatience.)

Juanjuan: (continues to talk on the phone) Mama, it's me, Juanjuan! What? You say the letter father got him to write played a big part? Wonderful. Wonderful. They agreed to transfer him? (excitedly, to Sun) Father, did you hear? Did you hear that?

Zhao: Chief Sun, Juanjuan asked you if you heard that?

Sun: Hang up...hang up!

Juanjuan: (continues talking) O.K., O.K. (hangs up the phone. Then, to Sun) Mama says that they have agreed to let him go. She wants you to hurry and get the papers on this end settled and to send them off as soon as possible.

Sun: I don't have anything to do with your affairs — with any-one's affairs!

Juanjuan: You don't have anything to do?...hmph!

(She leaves through the right-hand door. Sun is so angry he is about to leave through the left-hand door. Outside, a car's horn is heard.)

Sun: (urgently to Zhao) Is there anything else?

Zhao: (puts on a pained expression) Aiyo! This foot of mine!

(Sun leaves through the door to the hall. Sun and Zhang Xiaoli come in. Zhang carries a basket of fruit.)

Zhang: Auntie Qian asked me to bring you this basket of fruit, Uncle Sun.

Sun: Oh, thank Chief Qian for me when you return.

Zhang: Oh, it's just something small.

Zhao: Little Zhang!

Zhang: Auntie Zhao, you're here too?

Zhao: Come, sit, sit!

(Zhang sits on the sofa.)

Sun: (hands Zhang a cigarette) Have a smoke.

Zhang: No thanks. (takes out a package of a superior brand) Have one of these!

(He hands cigarettes to Sun and Zhao.)

Zhao: You came by car?

Zhang: Yes, Secretary Wu's.

Zhao: Oh? Secretary Wu's?

Zhang: Uncle Wu has gone to Huangshan for a meeting. He left early yesterday morning, so Auntie Qian let me use his car.

Sun: Then you haven't seen Secretary Wu yet?

Zhang: He doesn't know I've come yet.

Zhao: Is Auntie Qian treating you well?

Zhang: She doesn't have any children, so she treats me as if I were her child. Uncle Sun, Auntie Qian told me to ask you how that affair stands.

Sun: (embarrassed) Well, it's no easy task.

Zhang: (attentively) What?

Sun: I went to see Director Zheng at the farm yesterday. He told me that lately there has been too much confusion over those being transferred or replaced. They were criticized by the Municipal Party Committee, so now they're in the midst of rectifying the situation and they've stopped these procedures for the time being.

Zhao: Spoken like a true bureaucrat.

Zhang: Did you tell him that Li Xiaozhang's transfer is a special case and that it's being handled personally by the wife of the secretary of the Municipal Party Committee?

Sun: I told him, but it was no use. Director Zheng said that the door had been closed by a special order from Secretary Wu himself. If that door, front or back, is to be opened again, it must be by a note written by Secretary Wu himself.

Zhang: Only a note written by Secretary Wu will do it?

Sun: He thinks an oral agreement is unreliable. If there were an investigation later, there could be trouble.

Zhang: (angrily) So the word of the wife of the Municipal Party Committee secretary isn't very useful, huh? Okay, I'll ask Auntie Qian to go!

Sun: Wait awhile, Little Zhang —

Zhang: I've waited a week already!

Sun: But without his note, no one will take on the responsibility.

Zhao: I've heard from Auntie Qian that Secretary Wu has very high principles. Aren't you afraid that he won't write the note?

Sun: That's right!

Zhang: Well, Auntie Zhao, how do you think it should be done?

(a silence)

Zhao: (ponders) From the look of it, you must ask your father to show himself.

Zhang: What?

Zhao: You tell Secretary Wu that Li Xiaozhang has a special relationship with your father.

Zhang: What kind of relationship?

Zhao: (An idea strikes.) That he once saved your father's life!

Zhang: Saved his life?

Zhao: Yes! (talking as she thinks, growing more and more excited) You say that in the beginning of the Cultural Revolution, Li Xiaozhang went to Beijing for political activities...uh...Just then he saw your father who was being beaten. Li saved him...hid him...uh...hid him for a number of months. When the policy changed and your father began working again, he never forgot this event and was extremely grateful to Li; therefore, he asked you specially to come down and ask Secretary Wu's help in obtaining Li's transfer. As soon as Secretary Wu hears that it's a request from your father, and that Li Xiaozhang protected your father, he might write the note. (satisfied with herself) How's that?

Zhang: (nods over and over) What do you say, Uncle Sun?

Sun: Uh, can't hurt to give it a try.

Zhang: Good! Auntie Zhao, thanks for thinking up such a good story for me! I'll be sure to get Secretary Wu to write the note.

Sun: Then this thing will be a lot easier to handle.

(The restaurant people enter carrying baskets of food on poles over their shoulders.)

Sun: Put it there.

(They arrange the dishes of food and then leave.)

Sun: It's nothing much; we're just having a bite here, Little Zhang. I'll go see if the steamed buns arready. You sit down.

(He leaves through the right-hand door.)

Zhao: It's too bad my place is so small, otherwise I'd certainly invite you for a meal.

Zhang: How large is your place, Auntie Zhao?

Zhao: Oh, let's not talk about it; it's extremely small, three people living in just over fifty square meters. I've written a report and hope to move to a bigger place, but I'm afraid the leading cadres are busy and won't consider it. Uh, Little Zhang, would you give this report to Department Head Ma for me...oh, no, give it to Secretary Wu, O.K.? Tell him a little about my housing difficulties when you do. Just get him to put in a word for me, that's all.

Zhang: Okay, no problem! Leave it to me!

Zhao: (gives the report to Zhang) I'm really grateful to you.

Zhang: I'm the one who should thank you!

(Sun enters through the right-hand door.)

Sun: The steamed buns will be ready in a minute. Sit, sit!

Zhao: I can't stay, Chief Sun!

Zhang: What? You have to go?

Zhao: My foot doesn't hurt anymore, why stay?

Sun: Then we won't keep you!

Zhao: Goodbye, goodbye!

(She leaves by the door to the hall.

Sun: Little Zhang, did Zhao make a request of you?

Zhang: A trifle. She asked me to pass on a report about her housing problem.

Sun: You're a cadre's son, Little Zhang. You ought to pay attention to the impression you make. If people casually make requests of you rather than going through proper channels, you mustn't agree to them!

Zhang: It doesn't matter. If I can help, I do.

Sun: Oh, really?

Zhang: That's right, Uncle Sun. If I can do anything for you, just ask.

Sun: Well...(begins to speak, then stops) No, no, how can I trouble you with it?

Zhang: Out with it. I'm not a stranger. What are you afraid of?

Sun: Uh...I have a son-in-law in the Northeast, in the countryside. His unit has already agreed to let him come back, but they still want us here to issue a transfer order...

Zhang: It's all right, you write a report and I'll say a few words to

Secretary Wu for you. It'll certainly be all right.

Sun: O.K., O.K., I'll write it now.

(Sun leaves happily by the door to the right. Zhang Xiaoli admires the furnishings in Sun's home. Zhou Minghua enters carrying the steamed buns, puts them on the table and is about to leave when she catches sight of Zhang's back and pauses, trying to decide whether she knows him. Finally she recognizes that it's Li Xiaozhang.)

Zhou: Little Li!

(Zhang Xiaoli is startled.)

Zhou: Little Li!

(He turns slowly.)

Zhou: Little Li, it's you! (greatly surprised, Minghua hurries over to him)

Zhang: What are you doing here?

Zhou: Isn't everything I do for you?

Zhang: For me?

Zhou: I'm a classmate of Chief Sun's daughter.

Zhang: (It dawns on him) Oh...(looks her up and down, all sorts of emotions flooding over him and gratefully shakes her hand.) Minghua, you...

(He takes out his handkerchief and tenderly wipes the perspiration off her forehead.)

Zhou: And what are you doing here?

Zhang: Don't ask now; I'll tell you later!

(Juanjuan rushes in through the door on the left.)

Juanjuan: Minghua!

(Zhang and Minghua promptly separate.)

Zhang: (greets her enthusiastically) You must be Juanjuan!

Juanjuan: That's right, hello. Minghua, you know each other?

Zhou: He's my boyfriend...

Zhang: (promptly interrupts)...her boyfriend's friend, Li Xiaozhang's friend.

Juanjuan: What, you know him too?

Zhou: He...

Zhang: (cuts in again) Of course I know him. We went to Haidong Farm together and are about the same age. We met a long time ago. The reason I came down from Beijing this time was to get him transferred from the farm.

Juanjuan: Oh? That's wonderful. Minghua, his father's a high official — he can do more than my father.

Zhou: Your father's a high official?

Juanjuan: Didn't you know? I heard my father say so just now.

Zhou: Oh?

Zhang: You had no idea?

Zhou: But...

Zhang: I'm doing it for you and Li Xiaozhang!

Juanjuan: That's wonderful. I'll go tell my father a way has been found. (She runs out through the left-hand door.)

Zhou: (indignantly) Little Li, how can you deceive people like this?

Zhang: Minghua, they're deceiving people too. Don't be naive!

Zhou: But this isn't right.

Zhang: Didn't you want me to find a way to get transferred here from the farm?

Zhou: But you can't do it this way!

Zhang: Then what way is there? Didn't you tell me you wanted to get married as soon as possible? Didn't you say we couldn't wait much longer?

Zhou: (softening, to herself) No, we can't wait any longer.

(Sun and Juanjuan enter by the left-hand door.)

Juanjuan: (carries a report which she hands to Zhang Xiaoli). My father has finished it. You're wonderful, helping out with two things at once! No wonder my father asked you to lunch.

Sun: Come, come, please sit down. Sit!

(Sun, Juanjuan and Zhang sit down. Zhou Minghua is about to leave through the door on the right.)

Zhang: Zhou Minghua!

(She stops.)

Juanjuan: Right, there's Minghua. Eat with us.

Sun: Juanjuan...

Zhang: Uncle Sun, she is Li Xiaozhang's friend, and mine.

Sun: Oh, then join us.

Zhang: Move the table over here, Uncle Sun. Juanjuan, you sit here!

(He goes to Minghua and pulls her over to the table.)

Sit here, Little Zhou.

(Zhou Minghua sits down at the table, leaning to one side without moving.)

Zhang: (handing her some steamed bread) Eat it while it's hot!

(She raises her head and stares at Zhang Xiaoli.)

Curtain

ACT FOUR

A week later.

The house of Secretary Wu of the Municipal Party Committee. What, after all, does the house of the Municipal Party Committee's secretary look like? Unfortunately, the authors of this play have never been inside one. If the houses of Municipal Party Committee secretaries weren't so heavily guarded and restricted today, if their doors were open, welcoming the visits of ordinary people, the authors would not have had to expend so much imagination and energy to describe one.

When the curtain rises, Zhang Xiaoli is sitting in the living room reading a book.

(Chief Qian enters.)

Qian: Little Zhang, I see you're up?

Zhang: Good morning, Auntie Qian. Is Uncle Wu awake yet?

Qian: Not yet. His meeting at Huangshan lasted half a month and he is exhausted. He just returned last night, so I'll let him sleep longer than usual today.

Zhang: Did you mention Li Xiaozhang's case to him?

Qian: I did.

Zhang: Well?

Qian: Um, he said they'd temporarily stopped transfers and replacements. It was a decision of the Municipal Party Committee which he can't overturn.

Zhang: Ah? Did you tell him that Li Xiaozhang had protected my father and that he had a special relationship with him?

Qian: I told him that Li had been your father's savior, that he was wounded himself in protecting your father. I made it even more detailed than you told me that day, more vivid. (laughs) Even I believed it!

Zhang: What did Uncle Wu say?

Qian: He said that although your father has a special relationship with Li Xiaozhang, one can't use personal feelings to undermine party policy.

Zhang: He's so strict!

Qian: That's the way the old guy is, scrupulous and methodical, and he brings up party policy in every situation. He's the same with me. When he went to Huangshan for the meeting this time, I asked him to bring me back a monkey, a golden monkey, but he absolutely refused to do so. Furthermore, when the Central Committee wanted to send a large delegation abroad, I asked him to get me a place. Two would have been the best, so we could have gone together, but he wouldn't agree to that either. I think he really has some extreme leftist ideas. He's not at all liberated.

Zhang: Then there's no hope for Li Xiaozhang's case?

Qian: If you had come a month or two earlier, before the Municipal Party Committee had reached this decision, it would have been easy.

Zhang: But how was I to know? Strict one minute and loose the next. Open one minute and closed the next! I've already written to Li Xiaozhang, given him my guarantee, told him there was definitely hope. But to tell me now...(suddenly covers his face and begins to cry).

Qian: Don't worry, don't worry! Auntie will find you another way.

Zhang: What other way is there? I'm afraid my father will be upset when he finds out this hasn't been resolved.

Qian: Don't tell him yet. Transfers and replacements have only been temporarily halted. Wait until this thing blows over. Li Xiaozhang will be the first one I transfer.

(Secretary Wu enters.)

Wu: What?

Qian: Look, you wouldn't agree to write that note and now the child is crying from worry.

Zhang: (wipes his eyes) Uncle Wu!

Wu: You're not convinced, are you? Son, this thing is not easy to do. It doesn't look right, either for that Li at the farm, or for you, or for your father — it's bad for all of you.

Qian: Old Wu, aren't you afraid his father will be upset?

Wu: The phone is out of order. Otherwise, I'd make a call tonight and explain it to his father.

Zhang: (taken aback) You're going to call my father?

Wu: (beginning to pay attention to Zhang) I haven't seen him in over twenty years, but I could call and just ask how he is. (watching Zhang's expression) Do you think it's a good idea?

Zhang: (quickly recovering his aplomb) Of course it would be good. It would keep him from blaming me, but he'd still think I'm no good at handling thesethings. Well, Uncle Wu, let's leave it at that then. You are a busy man.

(He is about to leave.)

Wu: Where are you going, son?

Zhang: I've gone to a play every evening for the past few days; I'm really tired. I'm going to lie down for a little while.

Wu: Stay awhile! Come, come. Do you smoke? (hands him a cigarette) Have a smoke!

Zhang: Thanks, I will.

Wu: You grew up in Beijing, didn'tyou?

Zhang: Yah.

Wu: No wonder your Mandarin is so good. Where is your father from?

Zhang: My father?

Wu: Mmm.

Qian: Hey, you old fool. His father's from Sichuan. Everybody knows that.

Wu: Just asking to make small talk.

Zhang: Auntie Qian's right; he's from Sichuan.

Wu: He joined the Revolution in '34?

Qian: How could it have been '34?

Wu: (cutting her off) You know it all!

Zhang: You've got it wrong, Uncle Wu; it was '24, not '34. He joined the party in June of '25, went to the base at Jinggangshan in '27, was promoted to platoon commander in '28, regimental commander in '29, was wounded in '30, then in '31...

Qian: Hey, why's this old guy asking all this stuff? (picks up the book Zhang has just been reading and hands it to Wu). Here's his father's memoir. The details are all inthere.

Zhang: Is there anything else, Uncle Wu?

Wu: Nothing. Just chatting. I'll call your father and explain things. You go rest.

Zhang: Okay.

(He leaves.)

Qian: Do you really plan to call his father?

Wu: I'm just trying to get things clear. Look at you. You never look into things and try to verify them before you lend out my car. If something happens, it could really look bad.

Qian: What's so precious about your car? In Beijing he rides in a Red Flag limousine. Oh, are you suspicious of him? No wonder you were trying to get right to the bottom of things just now.

Wu: Except that you kept butting in and wouldn't let me get on with my questions.

Qian: I'm telling you, he can't be a fake! If he were, would Department Head Ma have introduced him to come and see the play? Besides, if hewere a fake, how would he have known you had been to his house in '53 and had given his father a cactus?

Wu: But if you'd only investigate things a little more, you'd never make mistakes.

Qian: I can't be mistaken. An imposter wouldn't have the gall to come and stay in our house. As I see it, you ought to help him out with that matter.

Wu: We'll talk about writing the note later.

Qian: I give up. You, you're looking for excuses; you just don't want to do it. It's the same story when I ask you to do something for me. Why didn't you get me that monkey?

Wu: Wouldn't it look ridiculous? A person in my position getting off the plane leading a monkey!

Qian: Then what about getting me into the delegation going abroad?

Wu: There were no seats.

Qian: Couldn't you have asked the Central Committee for two seats?

Wu: As easy as that, is it?

Qian: You just don't think of me. Some people have all the seats they want — you can't even get two!

Wu: You're a chief in the political section of the Municipal Party Organization. What would you be going abroad for?

Qian: To observe and learn — for the Four Modernizations!

Wu: Go to a capitalist country to learn about the political of the party? Don't be absurd!

Qian: If anyone's being absurd, it's you! Other cadres who joined in '38, the same year as you, have all taken their wives abroad. What about you, have you taken me abroad? Well, have you? Let's talk about those ten years of the Cultural Revolution. I've suffered a lot with you. I took a lot of blame. I even came close to losing my life! Now that the Gang of Four has fallen, why can't I accompany you abroad—forget my cares—have a little fun?

(She sits down off to one side, piqued.)

Wu: (comfortingly) O.K., O.K., O.K. We'll talk about it next time the opportunity arises.

Qian: What year will that be? When you retire? When they're holding a memorial service for you?

Wu: Alright. I'll think it over. If there's a chance, you'll go, Little Qian, how's that? (sighs) You!

(He goes out.

Meanwhile, Zhang Xiaoli has frantically ridden his bicycle from the side of the curtain to center stage, where a telephone appears. He picks up the receiver, dials a number and the telephone in Secretary Wu's house rings. Chief Qian answers.)

Qian: Well, who is it?

Zhang: Is this Secretary Wu's residence?

Qian: Yes.

Zhang: This is the garrison command. You have a long-distance

call from Beijing. Wait a moment, please. (puts on a Sichuan-
ese accent) Who's this?

Qian: I'm Secretary Wu's wife. Who is this, please?

Zhang: I'm Zhang Xiaoli's father.

Qian: (startled, but pleased) Ah. It's Mr. Zhang.

Zhang: Your name must be Qian?

Qian: That's right, that's right!

Zhang: Since we've never met, do you think I should call you Old
Qian or Little Qian?

Qian: Little Qian. Of course, call me Little Qian.

Zhang: Well then, Little Qian, my son Xiaoli wrote and told me
he was staying at your place. That's very inconsiderate of
him. You're so busy and then he adds to your troubles. Don't
stand for it, just kick him out.

Qian: No, no, his staying here is fine. I invited him, don't worry.

Zhang: That little boy doesn't know much about anything. He's so
unruly. You discipline him when he needs it; be strict with
him!

Qian: No, no. Little Zhang's very good. Old Wu and I both like
him. Have you been busy lately, Mr. Zhang?

Zhang: Very. There's a large delegation going abroad soon. I'm in
charge of the preparations.

Qian: (extremely happy) Oh? Are there many people in the delegation, Mr. Zhang?

Zhang: Of course. Didn't I say it was a large delegation?

Qian: Have all the places been filled?

Zhang: There are still some open. Are you interested?

Qian: Of course I'm interested. One goes abroad to learn. Old Wu
is interested too.

Zhang: That's good then. I'll put both your names down.

Qian: That's wonderful.

Zhang: Is Old Wu there?

Qian: Yes, wait a moment. (calls to the inner room) Old Wu!

(He enters.)

Qian: (happily) Mr. Zhang is on the phone. He wants to speak to
you.

Wu: (oddly) Oh? (takes the phone) Is that Mr. Zhang?

Zhang: Yes, yes. Is that Old Wu?

Wu: It is.

Zhang: Well, hello!

Wu: Hello.

Zhang: I just told your wife a moment ago — the Central Committee has decided to include you in a delegation going abroad.

Wu: (startled) Oh? (glances at Qian) Did you...?

Qian: It was the Central Committee's decision.

Zhang: How's that?

Wu: I'm just afraid I won't be able to get away.

Qian: (takes the receiver) No, no, he can get away.

Zhang: You can hand the Municipal Party Committee work over to someone else.

Wu: I'm afraid that won't do.

Qian: (moves closer to the receiver) It's O.K. It's all O.K.

(Qian and Wu gesticulate at each other.)

Zhang: After all, this is a decision of the party; you'll just have to put up with a little hardship.

Qian: (moves closer to the receiver) Okay. We're not afraid of a little hardship!

Zhang: That settles it then. How's your health, Old Wu?

Wu: Not bad Mr. Zhang. And yours?

Zhang: O.K., except for my leg.

Wu: What's the matter with it?

Zhang: During the Cultural Revolution someone pushed me off a platform and I broke my leg in the fall. Luckily, there was a young man there who protected me, otherwise I could have lost the leg entirely.

Qian: (moves closer to the receiver again) Was that young man Li Xiaozhang?

Zhang: That's right, yes it was. I'm very fond of him — he's like a son to me. I hear he's still on the farm; he hasn't been transferred yet.

Wu: Uh...

(Qian gestures at Wu for all she's worth, trying to get him to agree.)

Wu: Don't you worry, it'll be taken care of.

Zhang: O.K., I won't worry about it then. How is production going there?

Wu: This year is much better than last. We're in the midst of implementing the Central Committee's Eight Point Policy.

Zhang: And what about discussions on the maxim "Practice is the only criterion of truth?" How are those going there?

Wu: We're still studying it, but it's going pretty well.

Zhang: Good. Well, I'll wish you smooth sailing in your work then. Come and see me when you're free.

Wu: Okay. You're welcome here, too.

Zhang: Maybe I'll be there soon. Who knows?

Wu: That's wonderful, wonderful.

Zhang: Goodbye.

Wu: Goodbye.

(As soon as Zhang Xiaoli hangs up, he remounts his bicycle and peddles off. The telephone disappears as well.)

Qian: How wonderful. I never thought old Mr. Zhang was so concerned about us.

Wu: You're satisfied this time?

Qian: Hmph. Are you going to ruin it for me again?

Wu: Responsible people can't be too careful.

Qian: You won't believe that was Mr. Zhang and a little while ago you thought Little Zhang was a fake.

Wu: I'm just afraid of being made a fool.

Qian: I'll tell you, in my opinion, there can be no mistake. How could he be a fake. If he is, then I'd say the fake is more genuine than the real thing. He couldn't be a fake. Hurry and get Li Xiaozhang transferred. Besides, Mr. Zhang is an old revolutionary fighter — when he makes such a small request, you've got to comply!

Wu: Okay, I'll write the note.

Qian: It's only right that you should. Do it now!

(Sun enters.)

Sun: Chief Qian.

Qian: Oh, Old Sun, Secretary Wu has agreed to that matter. Look, he's writing the note right now.

Sun: That's wonderful. (He takes the bottle of Mao Tai liquor out of a bag.) Chief Qian, I've heard that Secretary Wu is fond of Mao Tai. Here's a bottle—take it.

Qian: He has plenty. You keep it for yourself.

Sun: But he may not have this kind. It's not ordinary Mao Tai. This is made specially for export. It's quite different.

Qian: Where did you get hold of it?

Sun: ...at the Export Company.

Qian: (taking the Mao Tai) Then put it over here. Sit for awhile. I'm going to see Little Zhang.

(Section Chief Qian puts the Mao Tai in the cabinet and leaves. Secretary Wu finishes the note and stands up.)

Sun: Secretary Wu.

Wu: Chief Sun, please take care of Zhang Xiaoli's business.

Sun: (taking the note) O.K....good.

(Qian returns.)

Qian: Eh, that little rascal was fast asleep. I called a long time before I woke him. I told him his father had called and he split his face smiling — he's such a child.

(Zhang Xiaoli runs in, buttoning his clothes on the way.

Zhang: Uncle Wu, my father phoned?

Wu: Mmm. The note has been written and given to Chief Sun.

Zhang: Great.

Qian: Old Sun, give this your full attention.

Sun: Okay, I'll go out to the farm right away. Little Zhang, do you want to go with me and see Li Xiaozhang?

Zhang: Huh? No, I'll go see him tomorrow.

Sun: All right then, I'll be leaving.

Zhang: (goes up to Sun) Uncle Sun, it's really too much trouble for you.

Sun: It's nothing. (in a low voice) Little Zhang, how's that matter of mine coming along?

Zhang: These things take time. Secretary Wu just returned yesterday.

Sun: O.K. I'll be going.

(He leaves.)

Zhang: Uncle Wu, I'd like to use your car for awhile.

Wu: You want to go out?

Zhang: I have some personal business to take care of.

Wu: Okay, tell Auntie Qian to speak to the driver for you.

Zhang: Thank you.

Wu: You little rascal!

(Wu leaves. Zhang Xiaoli begins to jump up and down with happiness.)

Qian: You little rascal — look how happy it's made you.

Zhang: Auntie Qian, as soon as Li Xiaozhang is taken care of, I've got to get back to Beijing.

Qian: Stay a few more days!

Zhang: I've been quite a while as it is!

Qian: You're homesick, aren't you? All right, but next time you come you must stay with me again. Think of this as your own home.

Zhang: No, this is much better than my own home.

Qian: When you go back to Beijing, I'm sending along a present for your father. It's something your Uncle Wu brought back specially from Huangshan. (She takes the Mao Tai out of the cabinet.) It's a special kind.

(Zhang Xiaoli accepts the Mao Tai from her.)

Zhang: Thank you. (He laughs loudly.)

Curtain

ACT FIVE

Afternoon of the same day.

The director's office at Haidong Farm. The place is a fearful mess. Everything seems to be out of place. An ancient flag flutters on a broken wall, nearly touching the ground. A broken broom has been fastened to the pull string of the electric light. Any directives coming out of such an office are most probably ineffectual, perhaps meeting a premature end as soon as they leave the door. Outside a few symbolic weeds make a show of strength; from them the audience can well imagine the scene in the farm fields. When the curtain rises, Director Zheng enters shouldering a spray can of agricultural chemicals. Then he sits down dejectedly at the desk and takes a drink.

(The First Youth runs in.)

1st Youth: Director Zheng.

Zheng: What's up?

1st Youth: (brings out a telegram and pulls a long face) My grandmother is extremely ill and the family's sent a telegram asking me to come home right away!

Zheng: What's the matter with her?

1st Youth: She has cancer.

Zheng: Don't lie to me like that. Okay, if you want time off just ask for it; what are you doing saying your grandmother has cancer?

1st Youth: But she really does!

Zheng: Besides, are you a doctor? Will she be cured as soon as you return? In that case, when I get cancer I won't have to go to the hospital. I'll just have you come to see me everyday and my cancer will disappear.

1st Youth: (from the bottom of his heart) Director Zheng!

Zheng: All right, all right. Did you talk to your company leader about it?

1st Youth: The company leader's father is ill. He went home a few days ago.

Zheng: What about the deputy leader?

1st Youth: The deputy leader's mother is ill; he just left yesterday afternoon.

Zheng: How could they all be ill? Must be an epidemic — they all caught it! Okay. How many days do you want?

1st Youth: That all depends on how soon my grandmother gets well.

Zheng: When someone gets sick in you people's families it's never a short-term thing. It'll be at least a month, a half year at the outside. How many days do you want?

1st Youth: Let's start with a month.

Zheng: All right. Leave the telegram here.

1st Youth: You're a good guy, Director Zheng!

    (The 1st Youth leaves happily and the 2nd Youth enters.)

2nd Youth: Director Zheng!

Zheng: Is your father sick?

2nd Youth: No, no.

Zheng: Then it's your mother?

2nd Youth: No, my older sister's getting married. Here,(takes out a letter) this just came.

Zheng: So you want time off to go home?

2nd Youth: Mmm.

Zheng: If you don't go, you sister won't be willing to marry the guy, is that it?

2nd Youth: No, no. I wanted to be in the ceremony!

Zheng: Did you speak to your company leader?

2nd Youth: The company leader's older brother is getting married. He's gone to take part in the ceremony.

Zheng: And the deputy leader?

2nd Youth: His little sister's getting married, but he hasn't left yet.

Zheng: Okay, then. The epidemic is over; now everyone's started getting married en masse. How many days do you want?

2nd Youth: Not many—a week.

Zheng: Okay. Leave the letter here.

2nd Youth: I'll bring you back some of the wedding sweets, Director Zheng!

    (Zheng waves the 2nd Youth away without raising his head and the youth leaves. He begins humming a tune with great feeling—it's a tune from the Korean War period.

    The sound of a car horn is heard, growing nearer. Zheng leans out the window for a look. The sound of a car's brakes is heard. Presently, Bureau Chief Sun enters.)

Zheng: I've been waiting a long time. I knew you'd come.

Sun: Hmm. You're drinking?

Zheng: How about it? Will you have a drop?

Sun: If you're not afraid of making a bad impression by drinking during office hours, I am!

Zheng: More fake scruples. What office hours? There's no work to do. Take a look out the window at the farm. Who's working in the office? Is there anyone working out there? Come have a drink!

Sun: (drinking as he talks) Even if that is the case you still shouldn't drink. You should be going around to each company and doing ideological work. Immerse yourself in the masses!

Zheng: The masses? They've all been bitten by the city bug and left! Those who could find a replacement did; those who could get transferred have been; those who could get out by the back door already have.

Sun: What are you grumbling about? All this is due to your own inept management!

Zheng: Bad management? Then you take over! You sit in this seat. I'll kowtow to you!

Sun: Enough, enough. (takes out Secretary Wu's note and hands it to Zheng.) Here.

Zheng: (takes it, amazed.) Oh? The secretary of the Municipal Party Committee actually writes notes?

Sun: I stopped at the Labor Bureau before I came so I could bring along the transfer order as well. Hurry and transfer Li Xiaozhang. Secretary Wu said the faster the better.

Zheng: It can't be done. You're just a bit too late.

Sun: What?

Zheng: The Farm Party Committee has come to a decision. Recently the question of transfers has been under review. We must forcefully curtail the use of the back door. Therefore it was decided that there would be a quota of only twenty for those using the back door during the next six months.

Sun: Secretary Wu's association with this matter raises it out of the back door category.

Zheng: Aiya! Sun, my old friend, no need to be embarrassed. (shaking the note at him) This is a perfect example of the back door!

Sun: You dare to say that the Municipal Party Committee secretary opens the back door for people?

Zheng: Not only the Municipal Party Committee secretary; department heads and Central Committee members do it too!

Sun: You're drunk! This isn't using the back door.

Zheng: Yes it is.

Sun: No it isn't!

Zheng: Is!

Sun: Isn't!

Zheng: Is!

Sun: Absolutely not! It's closing that door! (realizes he's gone too far) No! I mean... I've had too much to drink, too. All right, all right. What do you say we should do about this?

Zheng: Well...unless we squeeze out someone else.

Sun: How can you call it squeezing out? It's called showing preference for the key points. Let's have a look at the list.

Zheng: (hands list to Sun) The twenty names are all at the top. Who shall it be?

Sun: (points to the list) How about this one?

Zheng: No good, he's the nephew of Commander Feng.

Sun: Oh? (points to another) This one then?

Zheng: She's the niece of the younger sister of the Vice Minister of Public Health.

Sun: A good guy. (points again) And this one?

Zheng: Grandson of the Vice-premier's cousin's son-in-law.

Sun: The further we go the more important they get! (points) This one's relatives are high officials too?

Zheng: No.

Sun: Oh, wonderful.

Zheng: But that's no good either; she's the girlfriend of our Farm Party Committee Secretary's son.

Sun: (sighs) Aren't there any who are ordinary cadres...

Zheng: (points) There's this one; his father's the eighth vice-director of the Housing Bureau.

Sun: A vice-director, and what's more, the eighth vice-director? That will do; this is the one. Ask him to step aside for Li Xiaozhang and wait until next year. Would that work?

Zheng: (smiles grimly) Of course a bureau's eighth vice-director must step aside for the Municipal Party Committee secretary. The higher the office, the greater the power, and power brings benefits. For some people, this is the truth. Besides it's been proven by experience!

Sun: That's settled then.

Zheng: (Opens a drawer and takes out some papers.) Li Xiaozhang's file, ration card, and residence card are all here. You take them.

Sun: Oh! You already took care of the red tape for his leaving the farm?

Zheng: Higher-ups have far-reaching connections. When they get involved in something, you can smell which way the wind is blowing.

Sun: You, you were deceiving me the whole time!

Zheng: No, I was just waiting for the Municipal Party Committee secretary's note.

Sun: (picks up the file and other papers) Why don't you inform Li Xiaozhang now and tell him to leave as soon as possible.

Zheng: Okay, I'll make the call (picks up the phone). Give me the 57th Company (pause) 57th Company?—CompaLeader Chen? This is Zheng. Is Li Xiaozhang there?—Just got back this afternoon? Don't criticize him; he's going to be leaving us right away—he's being transferred, back to the city, right! What? You don't agree? All right, at least you still have a little revolutionary spirit! You're asking whether he conformed to the procedures? Whether it's a back door case? Wait. (Hands the phone to Sun.) You answer, please!

Sun: (Takes the receiver; slightly drunk.) Hello... Who am I?... If I told you, you'd be surprised. The secretary of the Municipal Party Committee...

Zheng: (amazed) You're the Municipal Party Committee secretary.

Sun: ...sent me!

Zheng: Oh, that really did startle me.

Sun: That's right. You ask if the procedures have been complied with? I can assure you that the procedures were not complied with...

Zheng: Huh.

Sun: No, that would be impossible!

Zheng: Ah!

Sun: If cadres want special privileges, then the use of the back door is legal...

Zheng: What?

Sun: ...according to the Gang of Four.

Zheng: Aiya! Enough, enough. Let me speak (takes the receiver from Sun's hand) Old Chen, the Municipal Party Committee secretary wrote a note requesting that Li Xiaozhang be transferred immediately.—Right, right. Are you thinking of opposing it? Okay, but I'm afraid it won't do any good—tell Li Xiaozhang to come to the office. Yes, tell him to come right away! (hangs up; to Sun) Do you want to wait and have him leave with you?

Sun: No, he still has to get his things together. I'd have to wait too long. I'll go first. Besides I really am a little drunk. No, I'm not, I'm not. Goodbye!

Zheng: Okay, I won't see you out.

(Sun leaves. We hear the sound of a car starting up. Zheng sticks his head out the window and gazes after the car. He shakes his head, then continues with his drinking. Suddenly he takes a piece of paper, lifts his pen and writes furiously. Li Xiaozhang, who has regained his own identity, comes in. He first looks nervously all around, then enters the office. Now his speech and actions reflect his real self.)

Li: (almost shyly) Reporting sir. 57th soldier Li who struggles steadfastly on at the 57th Company of Glorious Haidong Farm, reporting as instructed.

Zheng: You're Li Xiaozhang?

Li: Yes, sir. 1.76 metres tall, weighing 66 kilos, 26 this year, and in 66 days...

Zheng: What?

Li: It will be my eighth anniversary of struggle on Haidong Farm. Let me drink a glass to celebrate.

Zheng: Don't be so naughty. No matter how you grin I know inside you're depressed.

Li: Hallo! Director Zheng is a man of discrimination!

Zheng: The company leader told you that you've been transferred?

Li: I did hear something about that.

Zheng: The formalities have been taken care of for you. Your file and papers have been given to Bureau Chief Sun. You may leave our farm.

Li: Thank heaven!

Zheng: Should I congratulate you or express my regrets?

Li: Regrets? (uncomprehendingly)

Zheng: (bitterly, drunk) Yes, the farm hasn't succeeded. We've wasted the land...and your youth. So...so, as everyone leaves, each one, I...I can't bear it, it seems like I owe you a debt. Yet...what else can I do? Even the Municipal Party Committee secretary...even he trades special privileges, even he opens the back door. No one cares about getting the farm on a solid footing. Whatever revolution we throw ourselves into now, it's no use. Now, not only the young people open the back door to leave...the cadres...the leading cadres of the farm, they too leave by the back door, don't they?

Li: (not unsympathentic) What about you then?

Zheng: I'm depressed. (points to the liquor) I depend on this to dispel my sorrow. The farm...must be well run, it absolutely cannot be run...like this. If...it goes on like this, I...I don't want to...I don't want to stay on. The longer I stay the less I can bear it...

Li: (startled) You want to leave too?

Zheng: (indignantly) I wrote a report requesting to be transferred. Don't you know the son of a high official—a Zhang Xiaoli? You ask him...to help out...to say a word to Secretary Wu for me, and get me transferred to...

Li: (dumfounded) How could I do that?

(The 1st Youth comes in.)

Zheng: Why not? (takes out the note Secretary Wu wrote) You ask him why...why he could write a note to get your transfer, but not one to...to get me transferred? (takes out the transfer request he's just written) This...this is my request for...transfer. The reasons are twofold: The first is, my...my grandmother has cancer; the second is my...my sister is getting married!

(He hands his request to Li Xiaozhang. Li is stunned into immobility. Zheng quickly withdraws his hand, shakes his head sorrowfully and then waves at Li, who leaves. Director Zheng slowly, forcefully, tears up his request.)

Zheng: (loudly) My farm!

(He puts his head in his arms and cries.

Behind him, the 1st Youth tears up his own request for leave.)

Curtain

ACT SIX

An afternoon several days later.

The setting is identical to the one used in Act Four — the home of Municipal Party Secretary Wu. When the curtain rises there is no one on stage for a short time. Then we hear Zhang Xiaoli's voice: "Please come take a look around."

He enters with Zhou Minghua.

Zhang: (standing by the door; very graciously) After you!

(Zhou Minghua silently appraises the room's furnishings.)

Zhang: (like a tour guide) Please note: This is where Municipal Party Committee Secretary Wu greets his guests. There's an upstairs and downstairs, electric lights, telephone, barred windows, closets, carpets and sofas, television, stereo and air conditioning. (pushes open the door to the inner room) The bedroom is in here. Please come in!

Zhou: (stands at the door and stares inside) What!?

Zhang: How else would you be able to enter? Please come in.

Zhou: No, no, no!

Zhang: (opens the cabinet) Have a glass of orange juice. (pours one and gives it to her) Please.

Zhou: The host is not here! How do you dare entertain your guests with other people's things?

Zhang: It doesn't matter. I have this special privilege.

Zhou: No, I've never used other people's things this way.

Zhang: I do it all the time. And the more I do it, the happier they are.

Zhou: You've lived here like this these ten-odd days?

Zhang: Yes, envy me?

Zhou: No.

Zhang: Minghua, all the time I'm enjoying this, I think of you. I keep seeing you at Sun's, barefoot, sweating, washing clothes, scrubbing the floor...

Zhou: You asked me here today to show off, is that it?

Zhang: What I wanted to show you is that when a person has a good father, great changes can take place in his life! There's something else I want to show you too.

Zhou: What?

Zhang: Guess!

Zhou: You're full of tricks. I can't guess.

Zhang: (takes out his work assignment notice) Look at this!

Zhou: (takes it, overjoyed) What! You got it! You!

Zhang: I got everything. Bureau Chief Sun has already taken care of the paperwork for me and tomorrow I go to report for work at a first-rate factory!

Zhou: This...it isn't a dream?

Zhang: No, the dream is over!

Zhou: Wonderful!

Zhang: (mimicking her tone) Wonderful! Didn't you curse me all along for pretending to be a high official's son?

Zhou: It wasn't right.

Zhang: But, without doing that (points to the notice) could I have got my hands on all this? Besides, I should have been transferred last year. Cadres' children squeezed me out. Wasn't that wrong?

Zhou: Anyhow, it was a bit...

Zhang: I'm not a bad person, Minghua. I didn't steal or rob, or kill; I didn't start a fire, or seize power from the praty like the Gang of Four. I didn't plan to start World War III. I did little more than play a joke on those high officials who sit in the seats of power.

Zhou: But I held my breath for you the whole time.

Zhang: Yes, I was scared all the time, too. O.K., starting tomorrow that imposter, the crafty Zhang Xiaoli, will change into the honest and straightforward, law-abiding Li Xiaozhang. I'll never take another risk like this. This was the first and last time!

Zhou: Do you mean that?

Zhang: Yes! You don't like me like this, do you? (with a seriousness he hasn't shown before) It was because I was depressed
and bored. There seemed to be no future for me. I thought I
had nothing left to lose; I hated myself and I thought I'd use
others to...but starting tomorrow...I guarantee the new me
will satisfy you completely.

Zhou: Good, then I'll...I want...I want to tell you some good
news...

Zhang: What news could be better than mine?

Zhou: How is it that you haven't noticed it?

Zhang: Noticed what?

Zhou: (shyly) I'm going to have....

Zhang: Have what?

Zhou: Oh, you...! (She whispers in his ear.)

Zhang: (startled) Ah? Really? Minghua! (He takes her in his arms)
Thank you! Thank you! Why didn't you tell me sooner?

Zhou: I told you a long time ago, didn't I, that we couldn't put it
off any longer?

Zhang: Oh!

Zhou: When do you think we should....

Zhang: Uh, I have to report to work tomorrow; what about next
month....

Zhou: Next month!? No, no, we can't wait that long!

Zhang: Then when do you say?

Zhou: Let's get married tomorrow!

Zhang: (moved) All right, Minghua. Starting tomorrow I'll definitely be the kind of person who'll make you happy!

Zhou: (solemnly) Oh, I hope so! I know you're not satisified with
the way you are now. Well, I'm not satisfied with the way I
am either. And I'm not really happy with what you've done
recently, but I forgive you. Maybe it's because I'm just selfish
and am thinking about my marriage and future child. In that
case, I'm not just forgiving you; I've forgiving myself as well.

Zhang: But why are you telling me all this?

Zhou: Maybe it's because I'd like to recover all the idealism and
enthusiasm we've lost. We really ought to treasure this opportunity, Xiaozhang, and work hard and be good people.

> And promise me—from now on you'll quit smoking!

Zhang: (genuinely) O.K.

Zhou: And no more drinking!

Zhang: Right!

Zhou: And no more deceiving people!

Zhang: For sure!

Zhou: Not just for us, but for our baby's sake!

Zhang: Don't worry. I'll definitely be a good father!

Zhou: I believe you!

Zhang: (moved, takes Zhou's hand) Minghua!

Zhou: Xiaozhang, let's get out of here!

Zhang: No, my little game's not quite over. There's one more act tonight.

Zhou: What're you going to do?

Zhang: I've already told them that I'm flying back to Beijing first thing in the morning. Chief Qian said she'd definitely take me to see another play. I won't be able to bid my final farewell to this place and to the phony Zhang Xiaoli until tomorrow.

Zhou: Then I'll go home now.

Zhang: Aw, come on! Stay awhile!

Zhou: I have to go home and tell my father about your being transferred. And there's tomorrow's arrangements to take care of, too.

Zhang: Do you think your old man...I mean your father, will still oppose our getting married?

Zhou: No, he wouldn't, would he?

Zhang: If your father agrees, you must come back to tell me.

Zhou: There are too many people here, how could I tell you?

Zhang: If he agrees, wear your prettiest dress when you come. You won't need to open your mouth; I'll know just by looking at you.

Zhou: O.K.! (She leaves. Zhang sees her out with eyes brimming with love. Chief Qian runs in excitedly.)

Qian: Little Zhang! I have some good news.

Zhang: More good news? What is it?

Qian: There's someone here to see you!

Zhang: Who?

Qian: Guess!

Zhang: Someone I know?

Qian: Of course.

Zhang: Auntie Zhao?

Qian: Wrong!

Zhang: Chief Sun?

Qian: Wrong.

Zhang: I don't know anyone else here besides Li Xiaozhang. Oh, is it Department Head Ma?

Qian: I'll tell you. It's your father!

Zhang: (taken aback) Father? Which father?

Qian: What? How many fathers can a person have?

Zhang: No, no. I meant which one's father, whose father?

Qian: Yours, of course! He just arrived from Beijing!

Zhang: Oh? (Zhang Xiaoli's legs turn to water. He falls onto the sofa.)

Qian: What's wrong?

Zhang: I'm just...too happy.

Qian: You gave me a start!

Zhang: Where is he now?

Qian: He'll be here right away. (Old Mr. Zhang enters and spots Zhang Xiaoli immediately. Zhang Xiaoli slowly gets up off the sofa. The two of them stand at opposite sides of the room, their eyes meeting. Neither speaks for some time. Zhang Xiaoli is waiting for the storm to break.)

Qian: (chatters on) Huh? Mr. Zhang, please sit, sit down, why don't you sit down? Little Zhang, what's the matter? That's your father, not a tiger! (She glances at the two again.) Look at the two of you—one old, one young—it's fascinating—the way you just stand there, saying nothing. Uh, I get it, it must be like it is in the theater: When meeting again after a long separation, you're so moved you can't find words to speak!

Mr. Zhang: No, I have plenty to say to him!

Qian: (still prating on) Oh, it isn't convenient for you to speak while I'm here? Right, right, I should let father and son have a good private chat. Little Zhang, you keep your father company. We're still going to the play later. Well, I'll be going. You two talk.

(She leaves.)

Mr. Zhang: Don't stand there forever. Sit down. (Zhang Xiaoli sits down. So does Mr. Zhang).

(Silence)

Mr. Zhang: Is your name Zhang too?

Zhang: No, it's Li.

Mr. Zhang: Hmm. This is really a case of "putting Zhang's hat on Li's head"—just like the saying. What is your first name?

Zhang: Xiaozhang.

Mr. Zhang: Oh, so it was you. How old are you?

Zhang: Twenty-six.

Mr. Zhang: You're from Haidong Farm?

Zhang: (nodding in surprise) Yes.

Mr. Zhang: What are you doing impersonating my son?

Zhang: It's a long sad story. I wanted to be transferred.

Mr. Zhang: You didn't do anything else wrong?

Zhang: I could have, but I didn't.

Mr. Zhang: And did you get the transfer?

Zhang: (hastily) It's all finished now that you've come! My hopes are finished, and not just mine, but the hopes of three people.

Mr. Zhang: Three?

Zhang: My girlfriend and I. We planned to be married tomorrow.

Mr. Zhang: And the third?

Zhang: The baby we're going to have.

Mr. Zhang: You're not married but you're having a baby?

Zhang: It happened—partly through love, partly through depression.

Mr. Zhang: Why didn't you get married at the time?

Zhang: It's impossible to receive a transfer after you're married.

(a silence)

Mr. Zhang: But why did you want to impersonate my son and deceive everyone?

Zhang: (emotionally) Am I the only one who's deceiving people? No. Everybody had a part in creating this swindle. Those deceived by me were also deceiving others. They not only furnished me with information and opportunities, they helped me in my deception, and some of those I deceived taught me how to deceive others. I'm not denying I used your name and position to achieve my own goal. But who's to say they weren't using my bogus name and position for their own greater goals?

Mr. Zhang: They? Who are they?

Zhang: (takes some requests, letters and other papers out of his pocket) Look, this belongs to Troupe Director Zhao; she wants larger quarters. This is Bureau Chief Sun's; he wants to get his son-in-law transferred back from the Northeast. This is the request Chief Qian wrote yesterday; she wanted me to hand it to you personally. She wants to use the back door to get places for Secretary Wu and herself in a delegation going abroad. Almost all of them made requests of me, but who could I make requests of? They all curried favor with me, wanting me to solve their problems, but who would solve mine?

(Mr. Zhang looks over the letters and papers, knits his brow and paces in silent thought. He has almost forgotten Zhang Xiaoli's existence.)

Mr. Zhang: (softly but firmly) How filthy! Were you planning to help them?

Zhang: (They're greedy enough as it is! I just kept these things to have some evidence to prove that they're not as "red" as their titles suggest.

Mr. Zhang: You were planning to keep these to lodge an accusation against them?

Zhang: No, to insure they wouldn't inform on me!

Mr. Zhang: You really thought of everything.

Zhang: I have no power or influence. This is the only way I could protect myself.

Mr. Zhang: But are you aware that you're guilty of a crime?

Zhang: Because I impersonated your son?

Mr. Zhang: It's illegal!

Zhang: But why did I impersonate your son? When I became your son, people flattered me, fawned on me and furnished me with every convenience to help me accomplish what I had no way to accomplish as myself. Would they have flocked around me like this if I had impersonated an ordinary worker's or peasant's son? Would they have opened the door of convenience so wide for me? Of course not. Why? Wasn't it because of you and people like you, with names and positions like yours? You all have a kind of unimpeded, boundless power— your special privileges. If you didn't have special privileges, why would I or anyone else impersonate your son!

Mr. Zhang: Is this really a valid reason for such a swindle? Because special privileges exist you use them to your advantage? Because other people cheat, must you do it too? That's the logic of a criminal; it's not the type of thinking an upright youth should have. Sure, our present system does provide some cadres with many unreasonable special privileges. Still, it's not every cadre who takes advantage of these privileges to the point of abusing them.

Zhang: Do you mean to say you're "clean?" Are you an upright honest official? (He laughs sarcastically. Mr. Zhang gives him a stern look which stops his laughter.)

Mr. Zhang: You've impersonated my son, but you don't really understand me. It seems you don't understand the real situation of our party or our cadres either. I wish you'd give me these papers and requests.

Zhang: What for?

Mr. Zhang: It's my responsibility to investigate and deal with these matters.

Zhang: (gives them to Mr. Zhang) All right. You...do you want to arrest me now?

Mr. Zhang: The department involved will take the appropriate action.

Zhang: All right. I'll wait.

(Bureau Chief Sun enters.)

Sun: Little Zhang, we're about to go to the play. I've come to get you.

Zhang: (to Mr. Zhang) See, how friendly they are, they even send a car specially to take me to the play.

Mr. Zhang: Who is he?

Zhang: Bureau Chief Sun of the Cultural Bureau.

Sun: Little Zhang...he...

Zhang: My father!

Sun: (taken aback) Ah? Mr. Zhang!

Zhang: (to his "father") May I go to the play?

Sun: Mr. Zhang, tonight's the final performance. Let him come!

Mr. Zhang: You're responsible for your own actions.

(Secretary Wu and Section Chief Qian enter.)

Qian: Mr. Zhang, here's Old Wu!

Wu: How are you, Mr. Zhang, how are you?

Mr. Zhang: And you, Old Wu?

Wu: Sit down, sit down, I really didn't expect you so soon.

Qian: Old Sun, have you come to take Little Zhang to the play?

Sun: Yes, it's time, we must be going.

Qian: Right. Let's go. Let them chat. Let's go, Little Zhang!

(Qian cordially drags Zhang off and Sun follows.)

Wu: You've come to...Mr. Zhang?

Mr. Zhang: Central sent me to investigate party spirit and discipline.

Wu: Oh?

Mr. Zhang: (takes out a letter) The director of a farm sent me this letter of complaint. It contains a note written by you.

Wu: (taking a look) This...Didn't you know about it?

Mr. Zhang: I knew nothing. You've been had.

Wu: What? (suddenly understands) Oh, Zhang Xiaoli...

Mr. Zhang: He's not my son.

Wu: But he used your name...

Mr. Zhang: Old Wu, I came to see you personally. You should have declined to write the note. (takes out the letters and papers of Chief Qian and the others) Take a look at these too, they're even more preposterous!

Wu: (takes them in great surprise) Troupe Director Zhao, Bureau Chief Sun...Little Qian, too?

Mr. Zhang: (uneasily) It's really distressing. Our party wasn't originally this way—it has a glorious revolutionary tradition! Think about it, Old Wu, how many of your children were lost during the war? It really was for the revolution then. Nothing else mattered! When we took the city we were wearing straw shoes and sleeping in the streets. We shared the people's joys and sorrows. But where have these old traditions gone now? Of course, we don't deny that these are the evil fruits of the Gang of Four. But they've been out of power for over two years now, yet some party members retain these decadent practices. This is the tragedy of our party. Old Wu, we've been in the party a long time, you and I. Isn't all this worth pondering?

Wu: Yes! I'll prepare a letter for Central and draw up a plan to begin education of cadres wihin the party.

Mr. Zhang: It's right to carry out education within the party, but these people are involved in a criminal case as well. The civil courts may bring action against Li Xiaozhang, this imposter, and these cadres connected with the case may all have to appear in court.

Wu: I'm not against it, but I'm a bit worried. If the party's credibility has already been damaged somewhat, if this case is tried publicly, won't it...

Mr. Zhang: That's a problem, but it can't be covered up. The people will find out sooner or later. If we don't tell them face to face, they'll be discussing it behind our backs. Ithe long run there will be an even greater loss of credibility. If we dare to expose the incorrect tendencies and attitudes about special privileges of party members, if we show clearly that our party is open and aboveboard in its dealings, that it can be openly criticized and that it has the power to overcome these evils, then there's a great deal of hope for it!

(Zhou Minghua runs in wearing an extremely pretty dress.)

Mr. Zhang: If they do try Li Xiaozhang publicly, it will be not only for the purpose of educating the cadres, but to educate the youth at the same time—to rescue them, to pull them back from the brink—so we don't have a second or third Zhang Xiaoli/Li Xiaozhang appearing.

(Zhou Minghua turns pale with fright.)

Wu: All right, I'll call the Public Security Department.

(He walks over to the phone and prepares to make a call.)

Zhou: (shouts) You musn't...

(She cries out sharply and falls in a faint. The two men hurry over to her.)

Curtain

EPILOGUE

Unfortunately, I've forgotten who it was that said the stage is a legislative assembly, but this stage of ours really is a court in the midst of a public trial now. As for our beloved and loyal audience, they have become the spectators at the trial. We hope that, having seen the whole case with their own eyes, they'll have their own opinions about the justice of the court's decision.

There is a judge and two jurors. The accused, Li Xiaozhang, sits in the dock; behind him are two guards. In the witness seats are Secretary Wu, Chief Qian, Bureau Chief Sun, Troupe Director Zhao and Director Zheng. Speaking for the defense is Mr. Zhang. The public prosecutor occupies his proper place. As the curtain rises, the public prosecutor is reading the indictment.

Prosecutor. ...As the investigation shows, the evidence is conclusive. Therefore we have particularly brought this matter before the court. The indictment ends here.

Judge: The prosecutor has just read the indictment, explaining the particulars of the crime committed by the accused, Li Xiaozhang. Do you agree with the indictment?

Li: (stands) It's all true.

Judge: Do you think your actions constitute a crime?

Li: I'm not familiar with the law, but I admit I was wrong.

Qian: What? You did wrong? Is it that simple?

Zhao: Where did you go wrong? Speak up.

Judge: Silence!

Li: My wrongdoing was that I was a fake. If I had been the real thing, if I really had been Mr. Zhang's son or the son of some other senior official, then everything I did would have been completely legal!

Zhao: What do you mean by that?

Qian: And so arrogant!

Sun: He should be dealt with severely.

Judge: The witnesses may not speak without the court's permission.

Li: And now I want to express my thanks to the witnesses in the case! The reason I was able to commit a crime and all but succeed in getting myself transferred from the farm was because of the idea given me by Troupe Director Zhao, the road opened up for me by Bureau Chief Sun, the notes written for me by Section Chief Qian and Secretary Wu and the transfer papers given me by Director Zheng. (He bows to the witnesses.) I thank you again for your kindess and for your strong support!

(Troupe Director Zhao is flustered and exasperated. Chief Qian is shamed to anger while Bureau Chief Sun is dumbfounded.)

Zhao: Your honor, may I have permission to speak?

Judge: Granted.

Zhao: What the accused said a moment ago has nothing to do with the case. Would the court please prevent him from speaking.

Zheng: No! Your honor, may I please have permission to speak?

Judge: Granted.

Zheng: In my opinion, what the accused just said is all true and closely related to this case.

Judge: Do the other witnesses have opinions on this?

Wu: (stands up) I agree with Director Zheng. The accused should be permitted to state the facts.

Judge: Li Xiaozhang, is there anything else you want to say?

Li: I'd like to ask why Zhou Minghua hasn't appeared in court?

(The judge and jurors confer in low voices.)

Juror: Zhou Minghua is sick in the hospital and cannot appear in court.

Li: What's wrong with her?

Juror: She's receiving emergency treatment.

Li: (stupefied) Oh?!

Judge: Do you have any other questions?

Li: (weakly) No...none.

(He puts his head in his arms and cries.)

Judge: Now we'll ask the defense counsel to put forward a defense.

Mr. Zhang: (stands) I had no idea that the accused would request me as his defense counsel. Prior to the trial I studied the facts of the case in great detail and spoke many times with the defendant before finally acquiescing to his request. First of all, I feel the defendant did commit a crime. The investigative unit was correct in taking action against him; otherwise public order could not have been preserved and we would have been unable to re-educate and save other misguided youth like him. But I would like to raise two questions for consideration by the judge and his two assistants in making their appraisal: (1) What was the reason, besides his own thinking and character and other subjective reasons, that the accused entered on this wrong and dangerous road? Is there not a profound social-historical reason? It is my opinion that over the ten-odd years that the Gang of Four ran rampant, they wreaked havoc with the policy of sending youth to the countryside and poisoned young people's minds in the process. This was also a major factor in pushing the accused into committing a crime. In this sense, the accused is also a victim. Shouldn't he then be dealt with leniently? Please take this into consideration. (2) The reason the accused's fraudulent actions were able to proceed unimpeded was certainly not due to any specially brilliant ruses he used, but because this society of ours, where there still exists special privileges, where part of the system is unreasonable and inequitable, provides fertile soil for such things. For example, some of the party members involved in this case as victims became active participants in the deception itself, by either providing Li with the information he needed or deceiving others themselves. They did this because they thought they could satisfy their own selfish desires through the accused and because of the force of habit and the power of feudal attitudes toward special privileges. Thus we can see that they were not merely victims of the swindle but accessories to it. They should also bear political responsibility. Shouldn't the court face these facts squarely when weighing its sentence? I hope you will give what I have said your consideration.

Zhao: What? We're accessories?

Sun: We ought to bear political responsibility?

Qian: Mr. Zhang, you've spoken too severely. There's no way I can understand it and I won't accept it! We were all persecuted by the Gang of Four!

Mr. Zhang: And were we the only ones? Our party, our country and our people were persecuted even more! Why do you consider only yourself and not the party, country and people? Ponder this a moment: While we were being persecuted by the Gang of Four, we all hoped for the time when we would be able to hold our heads high again, and what shape did this hope take? We hoped to begin work anew and to do ever-better work for the Revolution, didn't we? At that time the masses' sympathy and enthusiasm for us was boundless. And we waited for the time we would be able to save the country, hoping we could then bring benefit to the people. But you've forgotten all this now! You want the masses to make allowances for the country's difficulties, you want them to work selflessly for the public interest and take the welfare of the whole into account while you're over there working on your housing situation, scheming for personal benefit. You let other people's children work for the Revolution in the country, while you yourselves use any and all methods to get your children transferred back to the city. You want the masses to live simply and work hard, while you yourselves move toward even more luxurious standards of living! How can we expect the masses to dedicate themselves to the Revolution if we can't share their joys and sorrows? I'm really worried about this. Our cadres weren't destroyed by the Gang of Four; but they may destroy themselves if they continue to pursue these unhealthy tendencies. Take warning, comrades! Otherwise, some of you sitting as witnesses in this court may soon find yourselves at the mercy of the Disciplinary Court!

Final Curtain

Five Letters

BAI HUA

(Translated by Janice Wickeri)

The First Letter

Ming:

   Whenever I think about going home, I feel as if I'm in a dream, fluttering my wings, soaring after my desires through sunlight and clouds...

   After three days' travel by bus and train, I was home at last. This is the first letter I've written you. You don't know enough about my family, even though we've been friends for over two years. Our friendship began that day in the autumn of 1976 when I arrived at the oil rig to work as an electrical welder. I met you that first day and you helped me carry in my suitcases. Forgive me, I still only think of us as friends; I can't see our relationship as anything else yet. A lot of our friends regard friendship as a different kind of emotion as soon as they meet someone they think they can love. What a rash mistake this is! And so they constantly change the object and content of their love, which destroys love's basic sanctity. They pick and choose, always looking for something better, while the real emotion in their hearts gradually dies out.

   What kind of family do I come from? You haven't asked and I felt there was no need to tell you. But now I've come home and can't avoid talking about it. What will you think of me when I tell you? I'm sure you won't change your attitude toward me because I'm your friend, not my family. As you know, I began living in a labor collective very early. I'm a girl used to independence. You are my closest friend, surely you know that the scent of my hair and skin comes not from perfume, but from the sunlight. My

323

clothes, to describe them accurately, are workclothes. I'm already twenty-five, but I haven't any feminine clothes. Of course this isn't to say that I don't love beauty. You know that I do. My family is what is commonly called a revolutionary family. Since childhood my older brothers and I have worn army uniforms made over from Daddy's old ones. I called my father "Comrade Daddy" and my mother "Comrade Mamma," just as we called the bodyguard "Comrade Uncle." On Daddy's rare days off our whole family hiked to the country to picnic beside a small river called the Lanxi. There Comrade Daddy, Comrade Mamma, Comrade Uncle and we children fished for shrimp in the little river, using nothing but a straight hook and a piece of string—just like the hero Jiang Ziya. Comrade Uncle caught the most; I caught the least. Besides, I ate as I fished, finally even stealing some from the men's basket. You can see how naughty I was as a child!

My father was a "little red devil" who joined the Red Army during that latter part of the Long March. Before that he had been a cowherd, growing up on a water buffalo's back. He's sixty-two this year. He resumed his position in the deputy headquarters of the military area command after the fall of the Gang of Four. Mamma had some education and was a village school teacher. I have heard that she enjoyed quite a reputation in the Taihang-shan mountain area during the latter part of the Anti-Japanese War because, besides being efficient and capable, she was also beautiful. Perhaps you can see some of this in her daughter (ha!). Now she's over fifty, and because her health isn't good, she hasn't worked in years. My brother Hesheng was an outstanding student at the Military Engineering Academy. He used to work in the Third Line Research Institute, but was recently transferred to the city where my parents are. My sister-in-law, Linyu, is in the same field as my brother and they have a two-year old daughter, Kang-kang. My second brother, who is two years older than I, is a soldier.

Okay, now that you've heard about my family, let me continue. I got off the train and shouldered my pack, and as I went along I met the city people walking with their rather ungainly big strides. I was still dressed as I had been when I jumped onto the communications boat and waved goodbye to you, still in that man's style shirt, the heavy workpants, and the all-purpose plastic sandals. I hadn't been home for a long time, and at the gate of the military compound I hit a snag. The MP didn't recognize me and wouldn't believe that this grubby girl was the daughter of a deputy commander. He had grounds for this, the most important being that no car had been sent to meet me. I asked the officer on duty to telephone my father, but he dallied and even circled around me, looking me up and down as if I were a newly arrived baby elephant from Africa. I really didn't understand it. Did I so little resemble a general's daughter? After half an hour of cross-examination he finally made the call. I spoke to my mother, who shouted:

"Yanan, wait there! Don't move! I'll come to get you..."

The officer suddenly warmed up. He brought over a stool for me, poured me a glass of water, even offered me a cigarette, politely, with both hands. I brought it to my nostrils and sniffed it. Unfortunately I don't smoke and gave it back to him.

Without waiting for Mamma to come, I picked up my pack and went into the compound. Our house has a small courtyard. In order to avoid unnecessary explanations, I took the burglar's route. Fortunately the encircling wall isn't too high, and with the help of a wutong tree I jumped to the top, threw my pack into the courtyard and, leaping into the air, landed on the spongy grass. The elation born of this success was promptly shattered by the wild barking of a police dog. I brandished my heavy pack. As you know, I'm a tomboy and will clench my teeth and never give in. A large crowd of guards and neighbors, including my eldest brother, Hesheng, along with Linyu carrying little Kangkang, was attracted by the warring parties' cries and shouts of false bravado. The dog felt he had the advantage of reinforcements and launched his final attack, barking wildly, spraying saliva all over my face. Only now did Hesheng recognize me. "Yanan!" and then he ran over shouting at the dog, "Kaidi, get away."

Then Mamma arrived. She had certainly put on weight. She ran over clapping her hands and shouting, the words rushing out in one breath:

"Yanan! I told you to wait at the gate, why didn't you listen, I went to meet you in your father's car, but the guard said you'd already come in, so we drove back. When we found that you still hadn't arrived, we drove to the gate a second time. How could you get lost on such a short road? Who would have thought that a big girl like you would be here, fighting with a dog...!"

When she got this far the bystanders broke into uproarious laughter, and at this my family took me home. I had just sat down on the sofa in the living room when Hesheng began to jeer at me: "You're really a typical country hick. You should have telephoned first. Or you could have gone to some army unit and introduced yourself: 'I'm the daughter of Deputy Commander So-and-So of Such-and-Such military post, I'd like to use the phone, may I?' I guarantee the response would have been a respectful one: 'Please do!' Once we knew the time of your arrival, we would of course have driven to the station to meet you...look at you, and you sit there laughing stupidly! Then the first thing you do when you get home is to put on this raucous performance."

Linyu brought Kangkang to me saying, "Tell Auntie: It's so dangerous!"

And Kangkang, mimicking her, said: "Auntie, it's so dangerous!"

I laughed even harder. Only Mamma's bringing me a glass of cold orange juice stopped me. She said, "I know what Yanan is thinking in her narrow-minded way— she's afraid that using the car makes a bad impression. I used to think the same thing. But now there's less and less of that kind of thing. The Cultural Revolution taught me this lesson: One day you hold power, and if you overdo it a bit you're still a good cadre; another day you have no power, and even if you toe the line you're still a capitalist. Now your father has position and power; everything comes easily. People do so many things for us without our asking. In the past we begged everyone for assistance, but no one bothered about us. The year that I was so sick I couldn't get out of bed, your brother had to push me to the hospital on the bicycle. That was suffering...! One month your uncle Jin was relieved of his position as an advisor and the next month the car assigned for his use was taken away. Your Uncle Wang retired, and after that if there were some matter requiring the use of a car, one had to run the gauntlet of those petty secretaries in the administration office."

This speech of my mother's made me stop laughing. I stared at my juice glass in silence. I had to admit that Mamma was sincere. I was moved; there were tears in my eyes. She felt this was a truth that life had taught her.

Then suddenly Daddy came home, his secretary following behind him carrying a large leather case. I hadn't seen him for two years; he looked unexpectedly younger. The depressing life he led two years ago stooped his body and made his complexion sallow. Now he stood upright and his color was much better. I ran over to him as I had as a child and exclaimed, "Daddy!"

He patted me on the head, smiling, and said, "Let's eat!"

At the table Daddy, unusual for him, asked for a glass of Maotai wine and raised it to me many times, smiling. I smiled contentedly in return. The whole family knew that Daddy was happy about my return because he drinks only when he is happy. Then he raised his glass just to me, my own happy face flushed as if I had been drinking too.

After dinner Hesheng and Linyu were determined that I go to their new place for a while.

"What?" I asked them, "Don't you live with Daddy and Mamma anymore?"

Hesheng smiled slyly, "This is where Mamma has really been looking ahead."

"Why?"

"She's considered our future."

"Future?"

"We still want to have a son! Little Kangkang will want a husband! There's a saying: 'He who does not plan for the future will find trouble on his doorstep.' "

"You're really planning ahead!"

We walked for over half an hour to a tall, newly constructed apartment building on a secluded street. Their home is on the third floor in a group of rooms facing south. They have two bedrooms and a living room. Obviously they have made their own painstaking finishing touches—the walls are hung with tasteful fabric, there was a homemade sofa, drawnwork curtains, a hanging glass lamp...Everything gave me a kind of cozy, comfortable feeling.

I asked, "Why did you leave the research institute to come here?"

Hesheng's reply flowed effortlessly out of his mouth: "I govern the home; others rule the nation. Our goal is the same: modernization!" and he proceeded to parade in front of me the progress they had made these past two years: the color TV, the stereo tape recorder, the modern furniture, the clock with the luminous dial —almost all are rare items which I have never seen before. He spoke contentedly: "We couldn't be this well off today without Mamma's help."

Little Kangkang pushed the tape recorder button forcefully with her small hand, and from within the machine came a melody that seemed exceptionally strange to me. At times it seemed to be a woman's voice, then again a man's; sometimes it was sweet, sometimes rough. The melody was strangely fascinating and provocative. Puzzled, I asked: "What is this?"

Hesheng laughed: "It's a pop tune from Hong Kong. Before Liberation they were known as popular songs."

"Popular songs? Why are listening to this garbage?" I said in even greater confusion.

"You really are a boor! What's wrong with it?" Saying this, he acutally began to sing along and Linyu and Kangkang joined him.

Perhaps I *am* hopelessly boorish. Whatever the case, I really couldn't bear this warped music and dubious lyrics, full of dissipated, cheap emotion. It was all the more unbearable since it was *their* tape. I stood up to go, but Hesheng held me back and finally shut off the tape recorder.

All at once, Mamma arrived, panting asthmatically. "Yanan! Come home right away!" Without waiting to explain she pulled me away. In the background I vaguely heard Hesheng's indolent voice remarking to Linyu: "I wouldn't have thought there were still such rare young Bolsheviks around today."

I followed Mamma back. Once in her room, she began to talk in earnest.

"Ai...how I've worried over my children! Thank goodness we did get a transfer so Hesheng's family could be here with me, but this old bird is still nest making for the young ones. Not only do I have to look out for your generation, but Kangkang's as well."

"Yes," I replied, "and there'll be another generation after hers ...and another...and another."

She breathed a long sigh and said, "I've thought of all that. As lone as there's breath left in me, I'll take care of as many as I can! As for your second brother, he's been an enlisted soldier for seven years. Since he hasn't been accepted into the party or been promoted, during demobilization every year I myself have to arrange a deferment. What can you do with someone like him?"

"Well, let him be demobilized then."

"It's not that simple. An enlisted solider of seven years, with no party or youth league membership, good for nothing but eating, drinking and smoking expensive cigarettes...What would he do if he were demobilized? In a few days I'd just have to go out there myself to see him and remind those officers."

"Remind them? Of what?"

"Remind them to take heed. Jiangsheng is the direct heir of a revolutionary! He mustn't be blocked... And as for you, do you really want to drift on the sea all your life? I can't stand the thought of it—it's terrible! A chicken cage of a room, a kerosene stove—foolish little girl—wearing oily pants all year long. You won't find any high official's son out there. Answer me. How will you solve your marriage problem there?"

"Ma! You sound like you think all the young men and women on the oil rig must stay single their whole lives." I stared at her, wide-eyed. "Besides, we oil rig workers aren't really like fish swimming in the sea. And even fish mate."

I knew I had gone too far and couldn't help but laugh.

"Don't laugh!" Mamma held me still and said sternly, "Marriage has always been an important matter. Your brother

Hesheng's was hastily arranged several years ago because at that time your father didn't have his position yet. There's been a lump in my heart every since. I feel I've let him down..."

"But they're fine together, aren't they?!"

"Whenever I see that old Shanghai, I feel terrible."

"Which old Shanghai?"

"Linyu's father, of course!"

"Is he from Shanghai?"

"I'm talking about the old Shanghai model car of his."

"Ah!" With that I finally understood the broader meaning of Mamma's term 'old Shanghai': It referred not only to the man himself and the car he rode in, but his profession, rank, salary...etc. How interesting, Ming! By the same token I ought to call your father, my instructor, Old Yongjiu because he rides an old Yongjiu bicycle. Right?

Mamma continued, "At the time there was no choice! Later I felt more and more that they weren't well matched, but the thing was an accomplished fact. After all, he was an official, a provincial government department head, with exhaust coming out his behind. It could be worse. I explained the situation and people were able to understand. Jiangsheng's first girl was a Russian make, a Zom."

Again I couldn't stop myself from laughing. But Mamma had been really hurt by it all...

"Everyone saw that he would never get into the party, would never be promoted, but no one said anything and the matter was dropped. I wore myself out running around for him. His new girl is a Toyota. The father is a deputy chief of staff in the military. The girl isn't pretty, but then she's an only child and controls the keys of the household." Mamma was silent a moment, then: "However, if Jiangsheng isn't promoted again this year, or accepted into the party; if he just returns a demobilized solider, I'm afraid I can't even guarantee a Toyota."

I tried and tried to hold back but couldn't keep from bursting into laughter.

"And look at you. What is there to laugh at? I really don't understand; you must be crazy or something."

With great difficulty I finally stopped laughing. Mamma wiped my eyes with a handkerchief and continued:

"Yanan! In the course of these two years many people have asked about you. Auntie Sun—you know—the Red Flag—she says their Dongping is especially fond of you..."

I knew the people Mamma spoke of—a deputy political commissar's family in the military area. Dongping is just a big dope.

He likes to show off all the time. Once, in front of a lot of people, he bragged about how magnificient the pyramids of the American West were—just as if he had seen them himself. When someone pointed out that the pyramids were in Egypt, not the U.S., he even claimed that that person didn't know and they nearly came to blows. Because of this he acquired an impressive nickname— "American Pyramid." Everytime I think of that nickname I have to laugh. Mamma looked at me in surprise, but couldn't seem to figure out why I was laughing. She went on:

"Your Auntie Li—Mercedes 250—is also very fond of you. Her Shenshen has a girlfriend, but her family owns merely a Flying Pigeon bicycle, and their home isn't as big as Shenshen's family pigeon coop. Auntie Li is thinking of breaking it off; it's not a good match at all... 'Give me a call as soon as Yanan gets back,' your Auntie Li said, 'I'll bring Shenshen to see her!' " Mamma looked me up and down as she spoke.

I remembered Shenshen. He wore glasses as a child and was very obtuse in dealing with people and things. He spoke very little, but when he did, every sentence surprised you, every sentence showed he'd read a lot. His memory was excellent. Clearly, he had thought deeply about many things.

In the winter of 1969 Lin Biao thought he was in a position to proclaim himself emperor whenever he wished. At that time, we young revolutionary fighters had nothing much to do and frequently got together to talk about anything and everything. Once, great actors of the world came up. Our generation is really pitiful on this subject. We saw some films and plays as children, but the ones we were most familiar with were the Soviet actors. We hadn't even seen Chaplin. Fortunately some of us had taken advantage of the campaign to Eliminate the Four Ancients, to grab some books from the library on the subject, so we were able to know about America's Garbo, Charles Laughton, Joan Fontaine and Lawrence Olivier—those stars that had never shone in the night skies of our youth—through the written word. We knew the names of some Peking opera masters too—Yang Xiaolou, Gai Jiaotian, Mei Lanfang, Cheng Yanqiu...We would each take up the argument on behalf of our favorite, arguing groundlessly, of course, but with all the air of old fans, as if we had enjoyed their performances any number of times, spouting words until we were red in the face. Only Shenshen said nothing, just kept pushing his glasses up on his nose. Finally everyone was pressing him, but he still wouldn't open his mouth. Some of the boys already had their fists out, hitting him till his shoulders shook. I couldn't stand it and dashed over and shielded him behind me: "Let him speak!" I turned to Shenshen and asked in a friendly way, "Who do you say is the best actor in the world?"

Shenshen pushed at his glasses once more, and then in a soft voice that caused everyone there to let out an icy breath: "Lin Biao."

I felt my hands go numb. For some time everyone stood as if rooted to the spot, each one in a daze. Then one boy breathed a soft sigh of heartfelt admiration: "Wow!"

Because of those two words—Lin Biao—Shenshen could be courting death. Everyone there was clear about that.

I said firmly, "I didn't hear anything!"

The murmurs of the others rose and fell, "I didn't hear a thing..."

But Shenshen continued. I jabbed him with my elbow and pulled him away. After Lin's death in 1971, whenever the kids saw Shenshen, they gave him the "thumbs up" sign and said, "Wow!"

But this didn't make Shenshen any happier and he would say, "I never said anything."

To tell the truth, after I heard this I even loved him a bit. Pay attention! I said "a bit." And notice the tense—it means finished; over...

As I sat there remembering, Mamma continued with a Volga and a Warsaw and a Xun Feng, but I was too tired, my eyes grew heavier and heavier. I have no idea what was mentioned after that. She was getting a little angry and shook me, saying, "How can you fall asleep! Go take a bath and go to bed."

Rubbing my eyes, I climbed off the bed and left.

When I got to Daddy's open door I stopped. There was a mountain of papers on his desk and he was in the midst of writing something. He was the same as he had been during the war years —in the command post, his mind filled with the units' fighting strength, arms, provisions, the order of battle, the line of march...the confidential phone on the table in front of him for keeping in touch with the tens of thousands of troops in the field. I couldn't help thinking: How much did he and this family have in common? Hesheng and his wife found their pleasure in the pop tune style of modernization; Mamma in the different makes of cars—because to her the make of car indicated the person's worth —while Daddy still devoted himself to the goals he had chosen in his youth.

For a long while I watched his thin back and I felt a moment of inexpressible melancholy. I really can't name it, at least not yet...

When I returned to the small room that had been prepared for me, I completely lost interest in sleeping. This was Daddy's study. There was nothing on the bookshelves but cloth-bound classics of Marxism-Leninism and works on military science. There was not one volume dealing directly with feelings or thought in our times, nor was there even one volume of ancient or modern literature. Such extreme one-sidedness! The majority of Daddy's generation are this way; they know so much, yet are so ignorant. I surprise myself as I write this. To think that I could be so bold as to make such a reckless comment about the brilliant military achievements of the older generation!

Three days ago at this time we were sitting silently on the pier, listening attentively to the waves; the sea breeze blew my hair across your face, getting you excited. The breeze was pleasantly cool, bringing with it the salty smell of the sea. It seemed as if that breeze were urging us to fly away. It was late at night but I hardly felt sleepy, even after a hard day's work. Now, suddenly, I'm homesick for that place where both you and the sea are—I realize that I've grown used to that air, that sunlight, those clouds, the smell of crude oil, the intense heat of the electric arc, our talks about the future, the excitement, the anxiety, the restlessness. Although it's only been three days, it's as though I've traveled from an especially familiar and beloved planet to an alien and distant one. Isn't it odd that the home I was always flying to in dreams should produce this strange reaction. I've never had any trouble sleeping before, but tonight I was tossing and turning. I've heard people say that counting things brings on sleep; I counted to 1,542 and still found no trace of it. Then I stared out the window at the stars and my eyes gradually closed. But I immediately felt another kind of agitation. My imagination was filled with automobile headlights, growing stronger and stronger. A number of cars circled around me, sounding their horns: Red Flag, Zom, Mercedes 250, Warsaw, Toyota, Shang-hai...I felt like an acrobat taking a curtain call with the spotlights focused on me. Suddenly one car made a quick turn and came roaring straight at me. I couldn't dodge it in time, screamed once loudly and woke up, my whole body wet with perspiration. Then I decided to take another bath. I walked stealthily out and looked at Daddy. He still hadn't gone to bed and was at his desk writing something. I don't think he moved even once.

So I'm using what's left of the night to write you this letter. The stars have already faded; dawn is approaching.

It comes from the sea, from where you are...

Yanan
October 6, 1978

The Second Letter

Ming:

This is the second letter I've written you since returning home. Let me tell you about Daddy! My father is like so many generals who experienced the long revolutionary war. They came through one victory after another and now they are confident that they can't fail. They even carry this conviction into their family lives. He takes it for granted that the values of each family member are similar to his own; he doesn't even bother to ask. I once heard an old bodyguard of his say that in action he usually stood in the front line; when the force of a blast blew off his helmet, he didn't even flinch. His men had only to see him standing there heedless of the danger and the troops surged forward like a wave. There was no need to sound the charge. Even now Daddy still thinks of himself as the family's absolute authority and mode. He thinks this...but what are the facts?

Daddy always gets up promptly at daybreak. After doing some *taiji* exercises in the yard, he sits at the table and drinks a cup of green tea while listening to the half-hour news broadcast from the People's Central Broadcasting Network. A simple breakfast follows. Then Secretary Liu quietly brings him the most urgent of the military communiques.

On this particular day the Red Flag limousine had been driven out of the garage. The engine was humming quietly; only the whirring of the fan was audible. Daddy and I finished breakfast in silence. When he got up he took my hand and we walked out the door together. He didn't say anything, just stroked my hand. Secretary Liu hastened forward to open the car door. Just as Daddy was about to get in, Mamma called:

"Jungfeng!"

Daddy, with his hand still on the door, turned.

"I was just thinking of our younger son," Mama continued. Yanan was thinking of her brother Jiangsheng too..."

All I could do was nod my head to confirm what Mamma had said. Actually I really hadn't given him much thought. Daddy looked at me and said with a smile, "Then go see him."

This made Mamma very happy and she laughed and said with the coyness of her younger days, "But we must go today!"

Daddy nodded and got into the car.

"Secretary Liu." Mamma winked at Secretary Liu, meaning, "Did you hear that?"

Secretary Liu nodded repeatedly, smiling. This meant, "I

heard. Everything will be taken care of. Don't worry!"

An hour later the train tickets were bought. Mamma went out in the car to buy Jiangsheng's favorite foods. These must meet certain requirements: They must not call attention to themselves and they must be things which could be enjoyed by Jiangsheng alone. After they were purchased care was taken to repackage them. The liquor-filled chocolates were put into a box that once held medicine capsules; a "not for internal use" medicine label was pasted onto a bottle of condensed milk, the superior China brand cigarette package was exchanged for those of an inferior brand; the best Wuliangye liquor was poured into a military canteen and resealed. I really admired Mamma's patience, the lengths she went to. She did it all under the rubric of motherly love. As she worked her expression was serious and very moving. She murmured continually, "Poor Jiangsheng. He really has it hard. Poor, poor Jiangsheng...."

When everything was ready Secretary Liu returned. Carrying her various packages and dragging me along, Mamma got into the car. We were at the railroad station a short time and the car stopped at the door of the VIP lounge. The attendant hastened to open the door of our impressive Red Flag and ushered us into the air-conditioned lounge. We had just finished a cup of tea when the train pulled into the station.

Towards evening we got off the train at a small station near Jiangsheng's regiment. The regiment's political commissar and the officer in charge of general affairs met us on the platform. A Peking cross-country vehicle took us to a room specially prepared for us by the regiment. It was just like a village bridal chamber, decorated in bright reds and greens, everything looking brand-new. There was even a round, fringed mirror, inscribed with the character for conjugal happiness, hung on the wall. First the orderlies bustled about, bringing a thermos of hot water for tea, pouring water for us to wash our hands; next were visits by the head of the regiment and the political commissar. Mamma said glibly, over and over, "I'm so grateful for your help to Jiangsheng," but I sensed that the two of them were acting very awkwardly and the atmosphere was somewhat tense.

While we were having dinner with the political commissar, Mamma suddenly came out with a strange request; she wanted to see the political instructor of Jiangsheng's company before seeing Jiangsheng himself. The officer agreed and went immediately to make a phone call.

That evening, Mamma had just taken the food she brought for Jiangsheng out of the traveling bag when we heard a light knock at the door. She hastily stuffed the food back into the bag before I opened the door. A short, dark-skinned young soldier stood there. He smiled, but very briefly, then became serious again and saluted us. "Sixth Company, Second Battalion political instructor Lian Yunbi reporting."

"Please come in; sit down."

I didn't quite believe this was the battalion political instructor. He looked so young!. Could he possibly command respect among a combat collective of over a hundred men?

Lian Yunbi sat down. I discovered that he was weighing Mamma and me with an unusual glint in his eye. Mamma poured him a cup of tea.

"Please have some tea."

"No thank you, I don't drink it," he said carefully.

I just laughed at his blunt reply. Mamma tore open a pack of cigarettes.

"Smoke?"

"I don't smoke."

What a stupid answer!

"You're so young!" Mamma didn't look too happy.

"Comrade," Lian Yunbi stammered, "why did you ask me here?"

"Oh, that..." Mamma was not a bit embarrassed herself. "Well, I thought..."

"Comrade!," Lian Yunbi said, "if you have something to say, say it!"

"Good!," Mamma said, relieved, "Then I'll come straight to the point! I want to ask the political instructor about Jiangsheng; I'm talking about deputy commander Zhang's son, also my son, her brother..."

"I know you're Jiangsheng's mother."

"What I want to know is why Jiangsheng hasn't been accepted into the party by now?"

Lian Yunbi smiled. From his manner it seemed he had known Mamma would bring this up, and he seemed slightly less forthright as he said, "This problem...well, you shouldn't ask me...."

I felt a chill come over me and began to realize that this young political instructor was not so simple after all.

"Who should I ask then?"

"Ask your son."

"Him?"

"Yes. Ask him...ask him why he still isn't qualified to be a Communist Party member." Lian Yunbi expressed this uncompromising stand in a very gentle voice.

Mamma was somewhat ruffled, but she kept control of herself and pressed on, smiling. "Where are you from?"

"From Fenglai, Shandong province. My parents are machine workers."

"Well, isn't that marvelous!" Mamma seemed to have found an opening. "Since you're the son of workers, you naturally have a deep class feeling toward the offspring of a revolutionary. You should help him join the vanguard of the proletariat as quickly as possible."

"Right! Since he's been a solider, Zhang Jiangsheng has changed companies three times. Like us, the party branch people in the first two tried their best, but unfortunately, without success..." Lian Yunbi's eyes gleamed with sincere dejection.

"What's wrong with him anyway?"

"For example, he has never once returned to the unit on time from leave."

"And is that so serious?" Mamma smiled grimly.

"Comrade! I can't think of anything more serious in the army than violating discipline..."

"You make such a big deal about trifles. What good does it do the party when you deliberately make things difficult for him?" Mamma spoke persuasively. "His purpose in entering the party is to carry on the work of the older revolutionaries in his family for the sake of communism. How do you have the heart to keep an idealistic, vigorous heir of the revolution outside the party's door?"

Mamma's words took me by surprise. Her voice trembled as she was saying these proud words.

Lian Yunbi looked somewhat surprised too. Then he lowered his head, watching us from under his brows. He said in a near-whisper: "Zhang Jiangsheng never put it like that; he said openly that the only way to be promoted is to get hold of a party ticket; once you're promoted you can shed this soldier's jacket, then you can get into the civil service and come by an official title; only party officials have position and power, their family needs are taken care of...you have to give him credit for being honest..."

At that moment I really felt embarrassed for Mamma. I felt my own face burning, but she was unyielding: "My son, the deputy commander's son, would never have spoken such impolitic nonsense!"

"He in fact said it," said Lian Yunbi, scrupulously honest. "The party branch discussed Comrade Zhang Jiangsheng's case recently. It was felt that his active service period has been extended much too long. For his own good and that of the army, it was decided to demobilize him immediately."

"Demobilize him?" Mamma simply couldn't believe her own ears.

"It's already been reported to the battalion party committee..."

"The battalion party committee wouldn't dare do that! I can tell you a thing or two."

The tone of Mamma's voice turned my whole body cold.

"If we were to want a battalion officer demobilized or promoted, we wouldn't have to put it into words. A glance would suffice...do you believe me? Comrade political instructor?!"

"Yes..." Lian Yunbi's expression turned suddenly melancholy, then he shook his head, "and yet I don't believe it...."

"Then wait and see. First of all, not only will my son *not* be demobilized, but he *will* join the party, he *will* be promoted! If this regiment won't do, we'll change to another; if this division won't do, we'll put him in another! As his mother, I'm determined to defend the revolutionary honor of our family!"

I raised my head and looked at Lian Yunbi. He stood up, slowly put on his cap and said in a voice so soft it was hardly audible, "For the good of the Revolution, I...as a soldier...will also defend...the party...."

The word "party" seemed to give him courage. He suddenly straightened up, saluted, did a regulation about-face, and then, swinging his arms as if he were in the midst of an advancing army, marched out.

Mamma suddenly sank down on the side of the bed, tears flowing from her eyes. I had planned to tell her some of my own opinions, but seeing her so hurt, I didn't know what to say.

We stayed that way a full three minutes, and then I really couldn't stand the suffocating atmosphere anymore. Taking advantage of Mamma's inattention, I went out quietly.

In the distance I could still see Lian Yunbi striding along the avenue in the deepening dusk, while the tall white poplars lining the street rustled like waves in the wind. I gazed at the back of this soldier, who seemed particularly short beneath the tall trees, until he had faded completely into the night. Then I wandered around the athletic field for awhile. When I walked back into the room, Mamma was stuffing the packages of cigarettes and food into a military satchel with Jiangsheng's help. He was even taller than he had been, now fully one point eight meters, and his beautiful eyes flashed greedily. Mamma said, as though coaxing a three-year-old child: "Don't let it weigh you down, Jiangsheng, don't worry. Mamma and Daddy will take care of you."

Ming! You can't imagine how awful it was, how bad I felt.

Luckily they hadn't seen me and I hurried out again.

It was time for the evening roll call—the sound of whistles and commands all blended together. Listening to the soliders counting off, I could imagine their innocent faces and youthful vigor, and this gradually calmed me down.

Jiangsheng and I hadn't seen each other for a number of years. How could I avoid him now? I had to walk into the room again, calling, "Jiangsheng, brother!"

"Ah." Jiangsheng jumped up and grasped a lock of my hair as he used to do when we were small, saying, "Little Rabbit, how are you?"

"Fine." I don't know why, but I couldn't act at all enthusiastic; I just couldn't cover up my inner frustration.

He let go of my hand and looked at me in surprise. I looked at him too, this familiar stranger—the uniform he was wearing fit so poorly it seemed to have been borrowed.

He asked.

"What is it? Has this camp with its stupid soldiers left you speechless? Are we so scary? Huh?" He pinched my nose, trying to make me smile.

"On the contrary, I think it's terrific—full of vitality."

"Vitality? Now that proves you're lying. Vitality! It's not vitality, it's insanity! It suffocates a person. Do you think I enjoy wearing this two-pocket, two-and-a-half-footer enlisted man's jacket? I'd say I'm at the end of my rope. I've been a stupid soldier for seven years and haven't got a party ticket yet. If I could just get a party ticket and throw on an officer's four pockets...excuse me! Bye-bye! I'd be off to the civil service. Mamma already has it all set up for me: a position, a wife, a house...everything is just waiting for me! Our Mamma is really a good mother—she looks ahead and knows how to get things done."

As the political instructor had said, he was very frank.

Jiangsheng lowered his voice, "I'll tell you the truth. Mamma's the real commander, not Daddy."

"Jiangsheng." Mamma was trying to look stern. "Don't talk nonsense!"

"Right. I can't say it. But I can think it. My problem is that I'm stuck in this company. These stupid soldiers are just making things difficult for me. Anyway, nothing I do is right. Why does the party membership process have to move bottom to top? Now if it could work the other way round, Mamma would have fixed everything for me long ago! Damn!"

Suddenly he glanced at his watch and was shaken out of his complacency: "Mamma, I'm not going to make it back to the unit on time again."

"Never mind. Just say I kept you."

"But you don't know; this gang of petty officers is extremely mechanical. I have to go, Mamma, Yanan!" Saying this he picked up his satchel and went, still muttering to himself...

Ming! You know me and you can imagine how troubled my sleep was that night. Mamma couldn't sleep either and we both tossed and turned.

"Yanan, you can't sleep either?"

"Uuh..." I said hoarsely.

"Because of your brother Jiangsheng?"

"uuh...yes, you could say it's because of him..."

"It really worries me," Mamma said. "I have never run into anything so difficult to deal with as his situation."

I didn't answer. I stared at the sky, hoping for daybreak. Mamma didn't speak again. I did my utmost to recall what Jiangsheng looked like; no matter, it was all fuzzy. But when I thought of that little politcial instructor Lian Yunbi, everything was extraordinarily distinct: his salute, his regulation about-face, the way he marched away...one foot after the other. Ming! It was really a mistake to think of him as a coward.

Mamma and I are leaving the company at noon. It's early morning now and Mamma has gone to take leave of the regiment head. I am alone by the window, peacefully writing to you.

Ming! On the sea, it's already a magnificent morning. When I think of that vast ocean, I tremble with delight. About now you should be speeding along in the little communications boat on your way to the drilling platform. The sea wind is tossing that disheveled hair of yours as the salt water splashes on your hands that rest of the side of the boat. I really envy the sea, the wind and the waves for being closer to you than I am. I'm even a little jealous of them...just a little...

Yanan
October 8, 1978

The Third Letter

Ming:

In the small hours after returning from Jiangsheng's unit, Kaidi and I walked into Daddy's office. (Kaidi, as you probably recall, is the police dog that I had the big battle with.) Now he knows me, and because he senses that the master who dotes on him dotes on

me even more, he really likes me. Daddy, seeing my unusual expression and bloodshot eyes, grasped my hand and asked:
"What's wrong? The whole world is waiting for oil, our oil
maiden! What are you worrying about...It is a personal problem?
Go and talk to Mamma, go on! I don't have time. I'm utterly ignorant of life and I know my limitations. No one ever asks me these
questions."

"I'm asking you, Daddy! I have to talk to you, no matter how
busy you are..."

"Ah—is it so serious?"

"I'm not sure..."

"How long will it take?"

"You ought to listen no matter how long it takes."

"O.K." Saying this, he pulled up a chair for me and made me
sit down facing him.

Then I told him what I had seen and heard since coming home
and my reactions to it, as frankly and in as much detail as in the
first two letters I wrote to you. He didn't interrupt me while I
talked. He was holding a glass in his hands—he doesn't smoke,
drinking tea is his only habit. He bent his head and looked at the
floor, making it impossible for me to see his expression. I felt like
an actor giving an especially intense performance, unable to hear
any reaction from the audience. When I finished we sat as if absorbed in mutual meditation. It was so quiet I could hear the tick-
ing of the desk clock.

At last Daddy raised his head. He asked softly, "Are you finished?"

"Yes."

"Go to bed, Yanan," he said very nicely.

I stood up and went out the door. I had just got into my own
room and sat down when I heard glass shattering, then everything plunged into silence once more...

Next morning I was the first one out of bed. I went into Daddy's office and carefully picked up the fragments of the broken
glass from the floor.

At the breakfast table no one spoke. Only Kaidi, by Daddy's
side, was as affectionate as ever. Mamma's eyes were swollen,
pear-like, evidence that Daddy and Mamma had had a very fierce
and very secret argument. When Daddy finished eating he threw
his chopsticks onto the table and left. The sound of the car door
closing was especially loud and even Kaidi was startled. He hesitated, then bolted out to chase the car.

Mamma began to cry bitterly and ran upstairs to her own
room. The whole house was filled with the sound of her crying.

The servants and the old cook withdrew into the kitchen, not daring to come out. I cleared away the dishes and went back into my own room, where I sat with my head in my hands, listening to the sound of Mamma's crying. The door to her room must have been left open, for the sound of her crying was very loud. She changed gradually from loud weeping to a very musical half-crying, half-complaining, which suddenly made me think of those women of the Tang dynasty who made weeping their profession. How mean of me to have such an association! Mamma began to complain in a sing-song voice: "I have no interest in doing this for myself, it's for my children! All this suffering and I get nothing but complaints!...From now on it's none of my concern whether they live or die...."

See how stupid I am! The saying goes, "Don't wash your dirty linen in public" and I write you letters about this! But I think you should know, you should know everything about me....

Just as Mamma was crying with gusto, melodiously, the telephone rang. Her crying ceased immediately. She picked up the receiver, and when she began to talk, she was a different person:

"Yes, it's me. How are you? What? The old man is looking into Jiangsheng's records? And the report from the company officer recommending demobilization? Yes, I know," Mamma said indifferently. "Anyway, a father is still a father and a son is still a son. I've never heard of a father deliberately blocking his son's path. One says anything in anger. Don't pay any attention to him...the child's affairs are still mainly dependent upon you uncles looking out for him. The chief (I knew this referred to Daddy) always praises you as his loyal subordinate...and why not! Right now the most important thing is to create some new criteria for the child, change his status, change his environment...you good uncles must request this for him, let him progress more quickly. If he can get into the party in two months, and be promoted in six, would that seem too fast...?" Mamma laughed. "Doesn't it just depend on a word from you as division head? Good!" and Mamma added in the resolute tone of a commanding officer, "Then it's settled." Having said that she hung up the phone.

For what was left of the day I shut myself up in my room. I lay on the bed. I couldn't read since I kept hearing Mamma's voice, now cajoling, now threatening as she continued her telephoning. I couldn't hear very clearly and I didn't really feel like listening. Her bedroom was a command post in the midst of a fierce battle.

Near dusk I heard a sound outside my window and got up to take a look. It was Kaidi. He was standing up like a human, with his chin on the window ledge, holding a note in his mouth. I went over to get it, patting his head through the iron grating, and he looked at me with gratitude. The note, of course, was from Daddy. It contained only fourteen words: "Yanan, Daddy is on duty tonight at headquarters. Don't wait for me at supper."

He didn't call, and had told me, not Mamma. Obviously his heart was heavy and he was confused.

I felt a sense of loss all evening without Daddy there. Mamma's calls were even more numerous and they continued till after midnight....

Yanan
October 9, 1978

The Fourth Letter

Ming:

I've received all your letters. You're really terrible. When I'm especially homesick for the sea, you have to describe it so beautifully: that dragon-like pipeline, the electric arc at evening brighter than the stars, the oily faces of the workers singing in the sampans, the lights on the beach used to attract the little crabs. If I close my eyes I can see all those little crabs in a row. As soon as they spot any people they dive for dear life into the holes they have dug. To pull them out you have to put your whole arm in, and if you aren't careful they'll pinch your hand.

I hope you don't think my letters are just reports of a lot of depressing, petty family affairs. This one will be different. I've had an opportunity worth bragging about. You'll never guess what it is. I've had the good luck to observe large-scale maneuvers—war games—involving the army and air force.

At the scene of battle, dust flew, tanks roared, planes thundered and under cover of heavy gun and missile fire, infantry officers launched an all out attack, just as in actual warfare. Daddy got me an observer's pass so I could see what a 'real war' was like. I was crowded into a command car with some newsmen. I had never expected Daddy to do this; it was so unlike his usual strict ways. It was probably because he is so fond of me and felt I badly needed a course in war! But in this war I saw an entirely unfamiliar Daddy.

Once there was a break in the fighting, but the troops from Danqiao couldn't get to the Huai River crossing on time. A vanguard infantry regiment was crowded helplessly on the river bank, which caused the regiment following them to get bogged down. My father sped to the scene in the command car. The regiment leader was very young and vigorous. You could see that he was a 'dove' who had never been in a war before (this is a term the old officers use to refer to the young officers, meaning 'green.') He spoke confidently, methodically reporting to Daddy all the difficulties they had encountered. Daddy's brows arched, his eyes widened, he pounded on the command car and shouted, "Shut up! Will the enemy bombs listen to your stinking long report? Are you going to endanger the safety of the whole regiment here? Can't you cross the river without the Danqiao troops? In half an hour I want the whole infantry to be constructing fortifications on the opposite river bank."

"Yes, sir!" The young officer was suddenly not so vigorous. He saluted in a disorderly fashion, turned on his heel and sped away.

Daddy's face was an iron mask as he noted the watch on his wrist. I felt very uncomfortable. Why was Daddy being so brutal? How could he dress down a subordinate so severely? And a regiment leader at that.

It hadn't yet been twenty-eight minutes when the whole regiment, except for supplies and heavy ammunition, had forded the Huai and begun construction of fortifications. The Danqiao troops finally arrived and quickly joined in the work. The remaining troops crossed quickly. I was uncomfortable again.

During the following three days of rapid march, Daddy chanced to see my brother Jiangsheng in an ambulance. He was astounded and immediately ordered a staff officer to fetch Jiangsheng's battalion political instructor. This little man, whom I had already met, came to the command car dog-tired, shouldering three rifles, and saluted, squinting up at Daddy, who asked him, "Hasn't Zhang Jiangsheng been demobilized?"

"We haven't received any instructions from above."

Daddy wrinkled his brows, but one could see he was in control of himself. "What's wrong with him today?"

"Reporting to the deputy commander: He said his stomach ached."

"*He* said...? Tell him to come over here!"

A moment passed. Then Lian Yunbi returned with Jiangsheng. Jiangsheng took one look at Daddy and became exuberant, even more so when he saw me, and he sprang over to shake my hand.

Daddy beckoned to him. Jiangsheng went over and greeted him softly, "Daddy."

"I hear you've come down with stomach trouble?" Daddy's voice trembled slightly. Maybe Jiangsheng thought it was due to Daddy's affection for him. He spoke close to Daddy's ear: "No, you know how tiring this rapid marching is. I used that excuse to get a ride in the ambulance. I don't mind doing a thousand *li* a day in that! Daddy, have you got any sausage on you?"

Daddy's face turned ashen. He pursed his lips. After a long pause he said to Lian Yunbi:

"Instructor! Private Zhang Jiangsheng has feigned illness on the eve of battle. What is the punishment?"

Jiangsheng said, laughing, "Oh come on, Daddy."

Lian Yunbi did not respond for a long time.

"Comrade Instructor?"

Lian Yunbi searched my Daddy's face and replied: "Reporting, deputy commander! He should undergo criticism and education. If he does not respond, the punishment can be increased."

Jiangsheng, secure in the knowledge that he had strong backing, said to Lian Yunbi, "Comrade Instructor, maybe you're not aware that this is my father!"

Lian Yunbi said softly, "If he acts like this, the punishment should be increased!"

Daddy said severely, "This is a warning! Order him to fall in!"

Lian Yunbi immediately plucked up his spirits and replied loudly, "Yes, sir! Warning! Ordered to fall in!"

"Daddy!" Jiangsheng said in amazement.

Daddy looked wrathfully at Lian Yunbi and shouted: "March!"

Lian Yunbi said softly, but very firmly, "Zhang Jiangsheng, get going!"

Jiangsheng cast an enraged look at Lian Yunbi, turned and left. This punishment caused the occupancy of the ambulance to be reduced by one-half.

During the whole of the maneuvers, the superior qualities forged in Daddy during the long war period showed themselves in abundance. He was old but vigorous, firm and courageous, charging at the head of his men. No matter where a problem emerged, he could always find the means to deal with it. He did it all for victory, for progress. After several days of effort, his cheeks were sunken, his throat raw, his eyes red and his lips parched, but the maneuvers were a total success.

On the evening of the day the maneuvers ended, all units were camped on the steep banks of the river. The battlefield, which had been smoke- and dust-filled, was once again a carefree, peaceful field. Birds came back to the trees. The village dogs, which had been too scared to venture outdoors for many days, came in a pack to vist the green tents. They looked like a congratulatory committee, but the real reason they came was to circle round the large steaming pots of food.

Daddy and I were walking along the river bank with the guard following some distance behind. We walked silently for half an hour, shoulder to shoulder, before Daddy finally stopped. He asked suddenly, "Yanan, can you do me a favor?"

"What?" I was taken aback and looked at Daddy's reflection in the water. He was serious. What problem could a general who commanded thousands of men and their equipment have that required the aid of his insignificant worker daughter?

"Can you tell me, all these...problems. How can they be resolved?" He gestured with his hands but I really couldn't make out what problems he was talking about. I asked, "What do you mean...?"

"I mean all those problems we talked about that night. And also...a deputy commander like me can command an army in a war game, but...when I give an order to demobilize a soldier who isn't up to scratch, every level of the military affairs department finds a thousand and one delays...What's at the bottom of it all...?" Daddy wrinkled his brows in great distress.

I said nothing.

Daddy sighed and walked slowly as he spoke: "Ai! The family owes its existence to me, but I don't understand this family at all. All these set ideas about family and society are harder to destroy than a solid enemy line. No matter how high your position is, how much wisdom you have, your moral virtue and example all seem to be too weak. I have only just realized it. I fell into all kinds of pitfalls long ago...thirty years of socialism! Thirty years! Yanan! These ideas—the burden this history has left upon our people. Isn't this what we've started so many large revolutionary movements to shake off? For this we've bled rivers of blood, piled up hills of corpses! But now we have to take up this burden again! It's not enough to change its color...Whose mistake was this? We old folks? No! Such a sweeping statement is unfair. So very unfair...!"

How could Daddy bring up philosophy and sociology with me? His eyes were particularly bright in the dusk and a bit remorseful. He asked hoarsely: "Yanan! What do you think?"

I don't know why, but under Daddy's questioning look my whole body became drenched with perspiration. I felt chilled. I answered cautiously, word by word: "Let me think, Daddy, let me think...I'm afraid one can't look for reasons and solutions just on the basis of society. I'm afraid the problem is deeper than that...let me think, Daddy! But for now at least I can say, you...and your generation of revolutionaries did outstanding service in the historical progress of our people...Daddy! Why are you asking me these things?"

"Why? Because you're young."

"Daddy! This is a difficult problem!"

"If it wasn't, would I ask you? Yanan, the future isn't ours, it's yours."

Ming, you're young, too! Can you help me think? We'll think together...This age has given our generation too many problems to ponder. But I really don't feel discouraged. Just the opposite. I have a feeling of true responsibility!

The future is ours!

Yanan
October 25, 1978

The Fifth Letter

Ming:

When I tell you this I'm afraid you won't believe it. I've lost my freedom. I'm writing this from prison. Why? It's a long story. When Daddy returned from the maneuvers he went straight to headquarters to write a report on them. I went home alone. Mamma was very affectionate toward me. She brought out the three dresses and five nylon scarves she had recently bought for me. She pointed out that these things weren't easy to come by; they had been bought at a store where only foreigners and a few high officials are allowed to shop—and they weren't cheap. She went over each one in detail, describing its quality and up-to-date design. She told me to try them on to show her how they looked and she made much of each one, calling it fine, beautiful! She hugged and kissed me. I said I hadn't the least use for these things, but she pinched my nose and teased me for being a stupid girl. When I told her that my holiday was already over, that to-morrow I had to leave to go back to the oil rig, her expression changed. She pursed her mouth and asked: "There's some guy named Ming waiting for you there, isn't there?"

I realized immediately that she had intercepted your letters to me. What was in them to make her consider the relationship between us so awful? She forced me to give her a thorough account of your family and class background, political behavior (actually only whether or not you were a party member), educational history, financial history, your family's financial circumstances, means of livelihood (including savings, property)...of course my account couldn't satisfy her. I know your class background, political behavior, educational history and means of livelihood, but not the rest of the ledger. As Mamma listened, the sound of her asthmatic breathing grew louder. Finally, she burst out with a completely vulgar comment: "In other words, he's just another petty bourgeois."

Mamma has no idea of the definition of petty bourgeois. Like so many members of high officials' families, she calls everyone except high officials and peasants petty bourgeois. She shouted: "You don't know your own value!"

I was completely in the dark. Mamma had never spoken to me like this. What had I done? What law had I broken?

"You can't even tell the difference between superior and inferior."

What! When had I become privileged? Mamma saw that I still didn't understand and stamped her foot, saying, "The blood in your veins is a general's blood."

This was the first I had heard of it; in the same way the blood in my father's veins was that of a poor peasant. What did this have to do with superior and inferior? Aren't we materialists? In materialists' eyes blood can be distinguished scientifically by type. When did it ever reveal class distinctions? Of course my view of the problem is very elementary, very simple, so it made Mamma extremely angry. She said, like a foreign affairs official announcing the final ultimatum: "Tomorrow Auntie Sun is coming in their Red Flag; she's bringing Dongping...to take a look at you."

This struck me as really comical and a ghost of a smile might have crossed my face. Mamma mistakenly thought I liked the idea. Her voice warmed, she said: "You're always such a mess. Fix yourself up."

"Mamma!" I said seriously, "I have to leave early tomorrow morning."

She cut me off, "Your mother's word is law." And with that she went out.

Well, wait and see! I can leave if I want to! I mean what I say too! I packed a few things and lay down on the bed, indifferent. Because I'd been so tired the last few days, I fell asleep the moment I lay down, and when I woke it was already broad daylight. I first discovered that I was "in jail" when I tried to open the door after washing up. To begin with I wasn't at all alarmed. I thought it exceptionally funny. Here I was, a twentieth century Yingtai.* The more I thought about it, the more I felt like laughing —one

*The Chinese Juliet

person alone in a room, laughing out loud. The windows downstairs were barred with iron grills. There was no possibility of escaping. On my window sill there was a glass of warm milk, a plate of pickled vegetables and two small steamed buns. I ate everything up in one gulp and felt a little better, but I wasn't in the mood for laughter anymore. As time wore on the pain of having lost my freedom grew. I began to shout for Mamma. No one answered. Next I shouted for the servants and no one answered. Then I shouted for the old cook, but still no one answered. Obviously Mamma had given strict orders. I did my utmost to calm down and sort out what was happening, but no matter how I tried I couldn't do it. If I wore an embroidered silk dress with the traditional long sleeves instead of a man's shirt, if my hair were full of jade and silver ornaments instead of being naturally disheveled; if I were a delicate beauty so weak the wind would blow her away instead of an awkward worker, if these were the case, my circumstances would be completely understandable; then I would consider it all predestined. I'd just wait for the sound of the horn to accompany me to the bridal sedan chair, learn to suppress my tears and die young.

But what does it matter now? Daddy is a general in the Chinese People's Liberation Army, a Communist Party member. Although Mamma hasn't worked in a long time, she is, after all, an old comrade from the War of Resistance, a longtime party member. When she was young she was a progressive, she taught school and led the regional women's welfare association. After liberation, she was secretary of the general party branch in the Academy of Science for many years. Though very young, I tagged along behind my older brothers and have been a Red Guard, chanting quotations, eliminating the Four Ancients...What organic link was there between all this and the immediate situation? It's more sad than funny; so, so sad. I began to cry! Ming! I've always been a tough person. As young as I was, I went down to work in the country. Through all the fatigue, the pain and the scoldings I never shed one tear, but I'm crying now. Do you think I'm crying over my own individual destiny? No! I'm the master of my own fate. To put it in terms of the theatre, Mamma didn't lock me up to excite the audience's sympathy. No one will worry about me, but I'm not going to attempt suicide either.

I had long ago forgotten what the American Pyramid who was coming to size me up, looked like. Now the American Pyramid of my imagination most resembled Gao Yanei and Ma Wencai of the Peking opera; a streak of white powder on the bridge of his nose, waving a folding fan, walking with measured steps...Thinking of him, I was again seized with a sudden impulse to break from tears into laughter. Crying and laughing; history's turning topsy-turvy had turned me topsy-turvy as well.

Suddenly Kaidi appeared! This clever beast had stealthily stretched his front claws up to the window sill. I went to the window and rubbed the satiny fur on the top of his head through the grill. He gazed at me innocently as if wanting to ask, "What's with you? Can I help?" That reminded me. I immediately wrote a note to Daddy:

> Daddy! Come back right away and rescue me!
> Yours,
> Yanan

I drew three chicken feathers on the note to express urgency, folded it into a tiny triangle and gave it to Kaidi. He didn't waste a moment, but took it in his mouth, turned and raced off with the air of a warrior going off to battle. My once mortal enemy had become my faithful and dependable courier. I regretted that the note had been overly brief. What would Daddy think when he got it? Wouldn't it be funny if he brought an entire battalion of guards to surround the place? Ming, I would never have thought that my rescue would require a veteran general, but I was secretly satisfied. Especially so when I thought that after I had been rescued by Daddy, when Mamma and Auntie Sun discovered that I had already flown, there would be a note on the table:

> Join the two Red Flag limousines! They're a perfect match!

Mamma and Auntie Sun's faces would be quite a sight. And the American Pyramid's even better!

A horn sounded! Yes! It was the horn on Daddy's car! Daddy was here! There was the sound of the car door opening and closing, the sound of Daddy's footsteps coming gradually closer. I put my ear to the door to listen....

Whenever I think about going home, I feel as if I'm in a dream, fluttering my wings, soaring after my desires through space....

Isn't it strange, the same homesick feeling as before! Why? Only now did it suddenly dawn on me—this was never my home!

Yanan
October 26, 1978